Defining Public Administration

Defining Public Administration

Selections from the
International Encyclopedia of Public Policy and Administration

Jay M. Shafritz
Editor in Chief

RAWAT PUBLICATIONS
Jaipur • New Delhi • Bangalore • Mumbai • Hyderabad • Guwahati

ISBN 81-316-0142-0

Indian Reprint, 2007

Published in 2000 in the United States of America by Westview Press, 5500 Central Avenue, Boulder, Colorado 80301-2877, and in the United Kingdom by Westview Press, 12 Hid's Copse Road, Cumnor Hill, Oxford OX2 9JJ

Published by
Prem Rawat for **Rawat Publications**
Satyam Apts., Sector 3, Jawahar Nagar, Jaipur - 302 004 (India)
Phone: 0141 265 1748 / 7006 Fax: 0141 265 1748
E-mail : info@rawatbooks.com
Website: rawatbooks.com

New Delhi Office
4858/24, Ansari Road, Daryaganj, New Delhi 110 002
Phone: 011-23263290

Also at Bangalore, Mumbai, Hyderabad and Guwahati

Printed at Chaman Enterprises, New Delhi.

Contents

PREFACE

Public administration is the totality of the working day activities of all of the world's bureaucrats, all of the people who work for governments—whether their activities are legal or illegal, competent or incompetent, decent or despicable. It is very much like the cosmos once described by the British scientist J. B. S. Haldane: "The universe is not only queerer than we suppose, but queerer than we can suppose." Things are much the same with public administration. It is not only far vaster in scope than most citizens suppose, it is so extensive and pervasive in modern life that not even the most imaginative of us can imagine it all. Yet, we must try because the administration of the public's business is too important to ignore, too much a part of our everyday lives, and too potentially dangerous to what Thomas Jefferson famously called our "life, liberty, and pursuit of happiness."

This book, appropriately entitled *Defining Public Administration*, is thus designed to stir the imaginations of readers. The articles collected herein are all reprinted from the *International Encyclopedia of Public Policy and Administration* (Boulder, CO: Westview, 1998). This collection of articles from the *Encyclopedia* was created to offer a sampling of the riches to be found within the larger work. The articles have been organized so that they can be easily used as a supplement to a core text in an introductory public administration course at either the undergraduate or graduate level. The articles selected are among the most readable and most interesting to be found in the larger work. Indeed, one goal in creating this collection was to encourage students to delve into the rest of the *Encyclopedia*.

The four-volume *Encyclopedia* has 900 articles written by 462 contributors from 23 countries and 42 of the 50 U.S. states. It was designed so that its contents—a combination of historical and descriptive articles, procedural presentations, and interpretive essays—would be of interest to the general reader as well as the specialist. Contained therein are definitions of the vocabulary of public policy and administration as it is used throughout the world from the smallest towns to the largest national bureaucracies. And when we say definitions we mean just that; all articles start by defining their topic. So if all the reader is seeking is a quick explanation of the meaning of a concept or practice, they need read no further than the first paragraph. The rest of the article will still be there if and when the reader needs more detailed information. It is this definitional format that inspired the title of the book you are holding.

It is very important that public administration be defined in the most expansive manner possible. How else to examine its richness and subtlety? How else to become aware of its historical significance, universal application, and current developments? Public administration is both direct and indirect. It is direct when government employees provide services to the public as varied as local bus service, mortgage insurance, mail delivery, water, and electricity. It is indirect when government pays private contractors to provide goods or services for citizens. For example, while NASA operates the space shuttle, the shuttle itself was built by the employees of private corporations. The security guards and cleaning staffs of many government buildings are employees of private companies. Does this put any of them outside the realm of public administration? Not at all. Remember that a government agency must hire, evaluate, and hold them accountable for the quality of their performance—whether these companies see to the cleaning of toilets or the building of spaceships.

Throughout the world, government employees do things that affect the daily lives of their fellow citizens. These things range from the heroic (such as a firefighter rescuing a child from a burning building) to the mundane (such as cleaning the streets). Usually these efforts are beneficial. Sometimes they are not. Most of the time in most countries public administrators tend to the public's business; for example, they build schools and highways, collect trash, put out fires, plow snow where it is cold, kill mosquitoes where it is hot, and provide essential social services for the middle class as well as the poor. Unfortunately in some lands public employees may be engaged to torture the innocent and murder children. Amnesty International is the Nobel Prize–winning organization that seeks to gain the release of political and religious prisoners by publicizing their plight. Each year it publishes a report on the states that brutalize and violate the civil rights of their citizens. Now who do you think does all this brutalizing and violating? None other than their local public administrators! As a profession, public administration has developed values and ethical standards. But as an activity, it has no values. It merely reflects the cultural norms, beliefs, and power realities of its society. It is simply government doing whatever government does—in whatever political and cultural context it happens to exist.

The *Encyclopedia* is a major effort toward the international integration of the literature on public policy and administration—which are two sides of the same coin (policy being the decisionmaking side while administration is the implementation side). We called the *Encyclopedia* "international" because it contains extensive coverage of public policy and administration concepts and practices from throughout the world. Indeed, public administration is increasingly an international discipline. While the administrative systems of nation-states were once largely self-contained, today cross-fertilization is the norm. The national marketplace of ideas wherein policies and techniques once competed has been replaced by an international marketplace. Thus the *Encyclopedia* contains articles on reinventing government in the United States, Thatcherism in the United Kingdom, and the New Zealand model. The reforms discussed in these articles (further elaborated upon by conceptual articles on devolution, managerialism, and market testing, among others) have been widely influential. Different political cultures, let alone differing administrative machinery, require different administrative solutions. Nevertheless the compelling reason for students of public administration to be fully aware of the wealth of new management ideas and administrative experiments happening in other states is not so much to be able to imitate as to adapt.

In order to provide a sense of the cultural differentiation of the world's administrative regimes, many articles focus on the administrative traditions of a society—for example, the American administrative tradition, the German administrative tradition, and the Islamic administrative tradition. Other articles focus on unique administrative institutions within a state—for example, the Ecole Nationale d'Administration in France, the Federal Reserve System in the United States, and the Prime Minister's Office in Canada. Extensive coverage is also given to the practices and institutions of the European Community; for example directive, pillarization, and subsidiarity.

Finally because so much of the public's administration is conducted outside of traditional government bureaucracies, extensive coverage has been given to nongovernmental and nonprofit organization management. Thus, there are major articles on foundations, voluntary action, and the independent sector, among others. A complete list of all of the articles in the *Encyclopedia* is included in an appendix to this book. It is an enticing menu. Use it to decide which articles you may want to read in addition to those reprinted here.

While Jay M. Shafritz of the University of Pittsburgh, the editor in chief, initiated the *Encyclopedia*, it was from the beginning very much a team effort. First he consulted extensively with David H. Rosenbloom of the American University in Washington D.C. and E. W. Russell of Victoria University in Australia. Thus, they became the "consulting" editors. These three developed the overall design and dimensions of the *Encyclopedia*. Then they invited thirteen other public policy and administration scholars at major universities to join the team as associate editors. All the editors then sought out the 462 contributors. Each editor was eventually responsible for a few dozen to more than a hundred articles. Most editors also wrote articles themselves.

Many of you would not be reading this book if you were not engaged in or contemplating public service activities. What follows is not so much a comprehensive survey—the field is too vast to be encompassed in one or even a dozen readers—but a reconnaissance. Herein is the lay of the land that you will encounter in the environment of public administration. Learn how to tinker with the machinery of government, see how employees adapt to life in public organizations, discover the ancient secrets of modern strategic management, review the arcane rules of public personnel administration, buy into the politics of the budgetary process, and finally, examine how ethical it all is. Public administration is not only a play that has a cast of millions, it is also a show that's been going on for more than 5,000 years. The modest goal of this collection is to make your journey into the sometimes untamed frontier of the public sector more successful by providing the necessary definitional, historical, and conceptual perspectives on this strange world. And how strange is it? As Haldane said: stranger than we can imagine. Nevertheless, if you read on, you will stretch your imagination and develop a fuller appreciation for the importance and diversity of public administration.

Jay M. Shafritz

Part One

Overviews of Public Administration

1

PUBLIC ADMINISTRATION

Frank Marini,
University of Akron (emeritus)

1. The occupational sector, enterprises, and activities having to do with the formulation and implementation of policy of governmental and other public programs and the management of organizations and activities involved. 2. The academic field concerned with the study of, improvement of, and training for the activities mentioned in 1.

Public administration refers to two distinguishable but closely related activities: (1) a professional practice (vocation, occupation, field of activity), and (2) an academic field which seeks to understand, develop, criticize, and improve that professional practice as well as to train individuals for that practice. The simple meaning of the term is quite direct: it refers on the one hand to the administration or management of matters which have principally to do with the society, polity, and its subparts which are not essentially private, familial, commercial, or individualistic, and on the other hand to the disciplined study of such matters. In this simplest meaning, public administration has to do with managing the realm of governmental and other public activities. This simple definition conveys the essence of public administration and probably covers the vast majority of activities and concerns of contemporary public administration.

Such a simple view, though, needs modification to account for at least two important considerations: First, it must be recognized that professional management of the public's affairs involves not only management in the narrowest sense (keeping the books, handling personnel decisions, implementing decisions which have been made elsewhere in the politico-socio-economic systems, etc.), but also significantly involves the planning, formulating, modifying, and urging of goals and purposes of much of public affairs. Second, it must be recognized that some matters of public administration are handled in ways which are not purely private but are also not precisely governmental.

The first consideration—that public administration is involved in the substance of policy as well as in the implementation of policy decisions—is frequently alluded to with terms such as the demise of the politics-administration dichotomy, the impossibility of value-free public administration, and the need for proactivity by public administrators. These terms reflect the widespread, though not universal, belief or allegation that it is no longer, if ever it was, defensible to interpret public administration as solely involved in technically objective solutions or in the neutral implementation of decisions made by nonadministrative parts of the political system (e.g., partisan leadership; electoral processes; party processes; partisan bargaining; and parliamentary, legislative, and judicial institutions). This belief and related understandings have led to significant public administration attention to policy and policy process. Some have felt a need for a rubric which emphasizes such a policy focus and which might also encompass or indicate receptivity to areas of studies which are closely related (e.g., planning, urban affairs, economic analysis, public policy analysis), and terms such as public affairs are sometimes used for this purpose. In general, though, public administration still functions as the umbrella term throughout the world, though it must be realized that the term implies a broader range of concerns and activities than the narrow meaning of management or administration may convey.

The second consideration—that not all public administration occurs in and through governmental organizations—also has led to a broadening of the meaning of public administration. At various times in the past of public administration it has seemed that its essence and activities could be identified by referring to nonmarket approaches to social purposes, but this perspective has been mitigated by the recognition that public programs and benefits could be developed through and provided with some market characteristics. Thus there have been developments such as governmental or quasi-governmental activities which compete with private sector activities or provide benefits through use of a price mechanism; sometimes water, utilities, sewers, health care, education, and other benefits are provided in this way. There are also devices such as public corporations, quasi-public corporations, public-private cooperative enterprises, and government contractual arrangements with nongovernmental organizations to provide certain benefits or perform certain functions. Indeed, even for large parts of the world where the private-public distinction has not been as prevalent or obvious as other places (for example, where the economy is essentially directed or nonmarket), the movement toward market or marketlike mechanisms for the provision of public goods is increasingly a matter or rhetoric, planning, or action.

When these considerations are taken into account, public administration is probably best defined as the practice and study of the professional formulation and influence of public policy and the implementation of such policy on a regular and organized basis on behalf of the public interest of a society, its civic subparts, and its citizenry.

Development of the Field

As first defined above, public administration has existed virtually since human beings first cooperated on behalf of their society for common purposes. Clear and explicit discussion both of the task of formulating decisions and of carrying out the details of those decisions may be found among the most ancient documents of various civilizations. Attention to the proper education and training of individuals for the various tasks involved is also clear and explicit in many such documents. The systematic study and codification of the technical aspects of such endeavors in a style reflecting the contemporary field of public administration may be variously dated.

It is usual, for example, to date the contemporary social scientific awareness of bureaucracy (a term which can include both private, or "business," administration and public administration) with the work of the German social scientist Max Weber (1864–1920). Such dating, though, is more a matter of convenience or recognition of important scholarly influence than of historical accuracy. For example, the German and French writer Baron de Grimm (1723–1807), the German philosopher Georg W. F. Hegel (1770–1831), and other philosophers and social commentators explicitly discussed bureaucracy; and the English economist and social philosopher John Stuart Mill (1806–1873)—especially in his 1861 *Considerations on Representative Government*—offered profound insights into public bureaucracy and its possible relationship to representative government. Similarly, in many European countries—especially those which see public administration as essentially a subfocus of public law—understandings of systematic modern public administration may be traced to ancient Roman law and its heritage, to the eighteenth-century German and Austrian Cameralists and Prussian government, to the nineteenth-century Napoleonic Code and its influences, and to the general heritage of positive law.

In the United States, it is usual to credit the reformism of the Populist and Progressive era of politics (about 1880–1920) and especially Woodrow Wilson's academic article "The Study of Administration" (in the *Political Science Quarterly* in 1887) for the systematic and self-conscious development of the field of public administration. It is usual also to identify the early years of U.S. public administration with scientific management, a school of thought largely attributed to Frederick Winslow Taylor (1856–1915) which emphasized a task analysis and efficiency approach to management; and with the subsequent human relations movement, which emphasized the human and social aspects of work environments and motivations somewhat in contradistinction to the scientific management movement. Both of these latter movements had their orgins in industrial and business management, but were very influential on public administration in the United States and around the world. The period of U.S. history between the Great Depression and World War II (about 1929–1945) is commonly held to represent U.S. public administration in a self-confident—though some also say naive—phase; this period is frequently referred to in the United States and elsewhere as the period of classical public administration or orthodox public administration. The period between the end of World War II and the 1960s is usually interpreted as a period of the growth of a behavioral, empirical approach to the social sciences and to public administration and its concerns. Not only in the United States, but in the industrialized and industrializing world generally, this period has been characterized as bringing scientific and technological advances to public administration. The dynamics of the Cold War competition between the United States and Western allies and the USSR and its allies, and the manifestation of this competition in various forms of technical assistance, aid in economic development, and administrative assistance had an impact upon public administration. In the 1960s and 1970s, much of the world of science and technology came under attack. In the United States, these decades and their challenges have come to be interpreted against the backdrop of the civil rights movement (and related movements such as feminism), Vietnam War activism, the "new left," anti-institutionalism, and particular manifestations of youth rebellion. Other parts of the world also experienced similar movements, frequently exacerbated by issues of neocolonialism, nationalism, anti-institutionalism, environmentalism, anti-technologism, and general critiques of scientific and technological perspectives and, indeed, the entirety of "modernity." All of these matters had effects upon politics, the social sciences, and public administration. In the United States and elsewhere, many of these developments were accompanied by significant critiques of public administration. One manifestation of this was a dialogue about the need for fundamental rethinking in public administration (and, for some, the need for a "new public administration"). In the last couple of decades, this had been augmented by tremendous technological developments (e.g., in computer applications and in communications developments) on the one hand, and ever more sophisticated philosophical and methodological interpretations asserting that we are transcending "modernity" in ways which call much of our contemporary understanding and technological approaches into question on the other hand. At the present time, public administration worldwide is in creative tension and undergoing rapid change and attempts at reconceptualization. What the effects of all this will be over time, or what the next developmental stage will be, is unclear but generally appears to have an energizing effect upon the field.

Configuration of the Field

Public administration is sometimes treated as though it is one of the social sciences, a discipline in some sense. As the number of programs offering doctoral degrees in the field has increased, this interpretation has gained strength. In some countries, public administration is a formal, degree-granting field at both the baccalaureate and postbaccalaureate levels. In some countries, public administration is not a degree-granting field, and education for the public administration academic and practitioner is pursued through undergraduate and graduate degree programs in economics, political science, law, and other such fields. In some other countries, public administration is a degree program at the post-baccalaureate but nondoctoral level (i.e., degrees or certificates exist at the master's level, but undergraduate study and doctoral study are pursued under the disciplinary auspices of other disciplines such as law, economics, history, sociology, political science, etc.). In some countries, those who aspire to public administration careers at the highest levels of the professional civil service compete for admission to special academies and schools which serve this specific purpose. And, of course, some of these types of educational programs exist in mixed forms in many places.

In the United States, it is relatively unusual for public administration to be a free-standing degree program at the baccalaureate level (though there are some well-established and prestigious programs of this sort—especially in schools of public affairs, schools of management, or schools of public administration—and this approach may be on the increase). The more traditional and still usual pattern is for baccalaureate education in public administration to be a major or minor specialization within a political science degree program. Master-level degrees are increasingly emphasized as desirable or expected credentials for full commitment to professional careers in many fields (e.g., not only in business administration and public administration, but also in fields such as education, social work, nursing, and education where the appropriate degree for professional entry was once the baccalaureate), and the master's degree—usually, but not always, the master of public administration (MPA)—is becoming the recognized degree for those who aspire to careers in public administration. It should be remembered, though, that public organizations and activities cover virtually the whole spectrum of contemporary specialties and that the educational background and specialties of public administrators therefore reflect this diversity. Many individuals who spend their working lives in public administration (as well as business administration) organizations and enterprises will have come from educational backgrounds such as police, justice, firefighting, engineering, health services, liberal arts and sciences education, and technical training of a broad range. Increasingly, though, the expectation is for postbaccalaureate (degree or nondegree, and frequently "in-service" or "on the job") education for those who spend a career in the public service regardless of what the preservice education or training may have been.

Education for the academic part of the field of public administration—especially at the doctoral level—continues to rely heavily upon the social science disciplines. Even when doctoral degree education is in public administration (or public affairs, public policy, urban affairs, or other labels), the program of studies is interdisciplinary with heavy reliance upon the social science disciplines. Doctoral education for public administration—as for business administration and the social science disciplines—also involves significant attention to statistics, information systems, computer-assisted modeling, and other technical areas.

As modern and contemporary public administration evolved, it tended to develop a more or less regular set of subfields, approaches, and topical interests. These generally have to do either with the functional and technical specializations of public administration, with specific methods and approaches, or with the phenomena of specific locales and issue areas of public administration.

Thus, public administration has some subfields which deal with concerns which, in one form or another, have been part of the field since its earliest days. Budget and finance (how to provide, handle, and account for material resources), personnel (the policies and management of human resources), planning, operations management, organizational design and management, communications and communications systems, record-keeping, accounting of various kinds, reporting of various kinds and for a variety of purposes and clientele, internal and external public relations, and a host of similar concerns constitute some of the technical and functional foci of the field. In addition to these, there are various concerns dealing with the environment and context of administration: the constitutional and legal context; the context of the political, economic, and societal structure, requirements, and processes; the values, history, traditions, and habits of the society and its components; the values, history, requirements, and processes of the organizations, programs, and components of specific relevance at any given time; and many other such factors (as well as their interrelationships).

Specific approaches, methods, or procedural preferences sometimes also have aspects of subfield about them. Specializations such as program and organizational evaluation, organizational development, operations research, quantitative aids to management, and the like are partly defined by methodological affinity or choice, but tend also to become subfields of research, education, and training. Similarly, participative management, participative policy processes, focus group approaches, some approaches to leadership, some aspects of strategic planning, and the like are partly defined by conclusions about organizational and administrative dynamics; partly by epistemological and methodological preferences; and partly by political or civic values and theories—and they, too, tend to become something like subfields in research, education, and training. The general dialogue in the social sciences and humanities—and even in some aspects of the physical and life sciences—concerning methodologies and epistemologies which are sometimes referred to with terms such as positivism and postpositivism, while not manifesting itself as subfield concentrations or subfields, manifests itself as something of a watershed in public administration as it has in other fields.

There are also specializations and foci having to do with the specific form and level at which administration occurs: international administration; national administration; federal/confederal administration, state/province administration, district/department/sector administration; city, county, and local administration; intergovernmental and interorganizational administration; "not for profit" administration; and so forth. Issue areas present other topics and specializations: police, fire, schools, military, medical, environmental, technology and technology transfer, science and scientific applications, government-business-industry cooperation, and a host of other specific issue concerns spawn specializations of knowledge, application, training, and experience.

When one realizes that all these (and many more) can be viewed as components of a huge matrix where any one (or more) can be related to any other one (or more), the complexity and variety of the field of public administration is suggested. A good sense of the present configuration of the field can be gained by consulting the considerable set of general public administration textbooks in use around the world. Perusal of these will give a good sense of the functional, topical, methodological, and curricular definition of the field. Comparison of current textbooks with earlier ones can provide a good sense of the changes and development of the field, and comparison of textbooks from one country to another can provide a sense of how approaches may vary internationally. There are also many professional and academic journals of the field worldwide; these journals can provide a good sense of the current state and interests of the field, as well as some sense of the different emphases from one setting to another.

Public Administration as a Cultural and Social Phenomenon

The phenomena of public administration are also objects of study for purposes other than the development of public administration. That is, public administration can be the focus of study of other disciplines or concerns, much as religion can be a topic of investigation for a sociologist who is not religious and has no interest in improving religious experience for the godly. Thus, complex organizations, bureaucracy, and a variety of organizational, administrative, and policy phenomena constitute topics of interest to scholars from a variety of disciplines, fields, and perspectives. Economists, sociologists, political scientists, philosophers, historians, students of literature and of communications and rhetoric, and a host of other academic specialists find public administration and its phenomena worthwhile objects of investigation. The field of public administration, for its part, contributes to, profits from, and incorporates such studies.

Concern for Identity and Legitimacy

A characteristic of public administration in recent decades has been a concern for the identity or legitimacy of the field. This may, in fact, be several separable concerns, which are frequently subsumed under the idea of "identity crisis." There are at least six aspects of this concern: (1) questioning and clarification which is typical of the formation of disciplines and fields; (2) concern over whether public administration is, properly speaking, a profession; (3) unease about theoretical unification; (4) puzzling effects of the applied nature of the field or the fact that the field has a professional or occupational concern as well as a scholarly or academic concern; (5) ambivalence about bureaucracy, hierarchy, and instrumental relationships; and (6) concern about the political legitimacy of public administration.

A concern for disciplinary identity is a typical concern in the general configuration and reconfiguration of disciplined understanding of the world. As public administration worries about its own identity, and especially as it does so against the backdrop of the social sciences and related fields of practice, it sometimes does so without clear memory or full appreciation of the recency of the present configuration and identities of disciplinary identities. Political science and sociology—to take two examples close to public administration dialogue—have only within the last century and a half invented themselves in their present identity. The history of such fields has been one of dialogue, tension, and uncertainty about epistemology, methodology, identity, and even chief phenomena of study. Indeed, this state of affairs is characteristic not only of the history but also of the present state of such fields. Thus, it is not surprising that identity questioning and insecurity has been characteristic of public administration from the inception of its self-conscious awareness as a field. The Wilson essay frequently cited as an example of the birth of a self-aware field of public administration in the United States was concerned precisely and explicitly with the question of the identity of a field of study and practice. The development of the field as a focus for study and training, concerning as it did an emphasis upon a new field or an interdisciplinary field, obviously had to focus on the continual definition of itself and on the distinguishing of itself from other foci and fields; this would seem true of all such developments, though it is sometimes not remembered in discussions of the development of fields which have been long established.

Though questions about the autonomy of the field may be less seriously raised than they have been in the past, they are still encountered from time to time and from several directions. For example, while a generic approach (i.e., the idea that administration or management is essentially the same field regardless of whether it is applied to business, education, health institutions, social work or social services, and so on) may not be as strongly asserted as it once was, the basic idea is still encountered in various forms. Sometimes institutions of higher education organize in ways which reflect this notion (e.g., a public administration department in a college or school of business or management), though there are many reasons other than the epistemological, intellectual, professional, or pedagogical why an institution might choose a particular organizational arrangement. There are professional and academic conferences, associations, and journals which project public administration as a subunit in a somewhat generic field of management.

On the other hand, countervailing interpretations are indicated by professional and organizational conferences, associations, and journals which project public administration as a subfield in the discipline of political science. As indicated earlier, such dynamics seem to be a normal part of configuration and reconfiguration of intellectual enterprises generally. It is likely that public administration has as much integrity and clarity about its enterprise as most other fields have at a comparable stage of development; it seems unlikely that worry over precise disciplinary status should be more of a hindrance to public administration than it has been or is to other fields.

Sometimes worry over the issue of professional status is part of the perceived identity crisis. Thus, it is sometimes asked whether public administration is or can aspire to be a profession, and frequently this is framed with specific reference to traditional professions. Though such a question may have interesting implications, there seems to be a developing consensus that it is important to articulate appropriate professional standards, expectations, and ethics without worrying unduly about whether the field is a profession in all the senses of the traditional professions (e.g., law, medicine, and religious ministry). Still, questions about professional status have contributed to the sense some have of identity crisis.

A related aspect of this identity insecurity is concern over unifying theory: it is frequently said that public administration lacks a unifying theory such as some other fields or disciplines are alleged to have. It is true that public administration may tend to draw from a more multidisciplinary pool of knowledge than some fields, though even this is more often than not exaggerated (as reflection upon the developing edges of even hard sciences would suggest). It may be true that the practitioner connection gives public administration a somewhat more eclectic appearance than some fields; but, again, this eclecticism and its related complexities and nuances may be more usual in the development of fields than is sometimes recognized (as reflection upon the diversity of investigations and applications in most of the social or human sciences may suggest). As to theoretical unity or clear dominant paradigms, it is likely that the presence of such in many fields, as well as its absence in public administration, may be regularly overstated.

The fact that the field of public administration is both an academic endeavor and a professional field is sometimes thought to limit the field's disciplinary possibilities. Thus some suggest that public administration should be thought of as an applied field of practice and training, while basic research and education should be recognized as taking place in other fields which are thought to be more clearly disciplines or sciences. Sometimes the suggestion is made—most notably identified with Dwight Waldo—that public administration may be a field, discipline, or science in the way that medicine is; and that like medicine, it may be both a scientific and practitioner concern which draws on such other fields of learning as it finds fruitful to its own purposes and activities. The roles of basic research and applied purpose are likely to be the focus of dialogue in public administration (as well as in many other fields) for the foreseeable future. Public administration is likely to continue to have research, education, training, and practice concerns for the foreseeable future also. In this regard, the field may resemble established fields such as medicine or engineering and new fields such as genetic science, polymer science, or cognitive science; and it is as unlikely that the field of public administration will be limited by practical and applied concerns as it is that these other fields will.

An interesting aspect of public administration as a field of academic study and as a field of training for professional practice is its seeming ambivalence about itself. For example, a few years ago, Aaron Wildavsky, a friendly critic, wondered in print why, since public administration seemed so essentially involved with hierarchy and bureaucracy, public administration scholars seemed so unwilling to embrace or defend these characteristics. Thus it may seem from some perspectives that scholars of public administration seem to deplore so much of which seems characteristic of, indeed definitional of, their field. Even within the field itself there have been arguments and dialogue which seem to interpret large parts of the academic field of public administration as essentially opposed to public administration. From a somewhat different perspective, though, the "critics from within" frequently feel they are not attacking the essence of public administration, but rather arguing that some characteristics which have seemed essential to others are in fact not essential but could be changed, eroded, reduced, or removed to the improvement of the field. From this perspective, then, characteristics such as bureaucracy and hierarchy may not be unavoidable and definitional characteristics of public administration, but rather may be unfortunate aspects which an improved public administration would mitigate or avoid.

Perhaps the most important aspect of the concern about legitimacy and identity of the field has to do explicitly with the question of political legitimacy. Long ago, most debate about whether a specific government was legitimate or not would have rested upon questions of the line of succession or mystical or religious indication of the identity of the legitimate ruler. For much of the present-day world—and certainly most of the world in which public administration would have conscious identity—the question of governmental legitimacy turns on the public good (in many cases expressed in terms of the interest of the citizenry or even the will of the people). Under this understanding of legitimacy, questions of the legitimacy of public administration (essentially nonelected skill-based participants in rule) are difficult. A traditional answer to the problem posed has been that the public administrators bring their skills, training, and job experience to serve the purposes and directions indicated by the people's representatives (who frequently, and especially within representative governments, have been selected through some devices, such as elections, in which the citizens have had a voice). This is sometimes referred to as administrative neutrality: the idea that civil servants will bring their knowledge and skills to the service of whichever party or set of individuals is chosen to govern from time to time. This answer is still the largely unquestioned theory of public administration legitimacy in many parts of the world. Where public administration has been interpreted more frequently as having large aspects of discretion, policy formulation responsibilities, and relatively autonomous leadership roles, though, the possibility or appropriateness of neutrality has been increasingly called into question. This has left the field of public administration with the need to understand and explicate precisely how public administrators are or can be legitimate with reference to the citizenry and duly established political orders. Working out the important ramifications of such questions leads to dialogue and debate about the foundations of public administration legitimacy, and this leads some to articulate a sense that the field is in search of its role, identity, and purpose.

When these and other aspects—the mix, priority, and relative weight of specific aspects varies from context to context and polity to polity—of public administration identity are given serious and continuous deliberation and debate, it is understandable that fundamental questions about the status of public administration take on critical importance. The issues and the dialogue are not presently at rest, and they are not likely to be in the foreseeable future.

Future of the Field

Though the field of public administration is perennially concerned about the identity and security of the field, the future and identity seem secure even if the exact intellectual configuration cannot be precisely predicted.

The "practice" of public administration is affected everywhere by political and resource changes. Visible aspects of such changes at the present time are concerns over the resources devoted to governmental and public activities (taxes, the portion of the economy devoted to governmental or public sector activities, etc.); increased interest in many places in introducing greater aspects of market factors into heretofore nonmarket public sector activities; continued interest in countering hierarchical and impersonal ("red tape," etc.) aspects; and continued concern about responsibility and accountability to the citizenry and its interests. The practice of public administration also experiences today, as it always has, the challenges of technological developments. Such concerns and interests bespeak possible changes in public administration, but they probably do not threaten the existence or identity of the practice, occupations, or vocations of public administration.

The "academic" part of public administration has continually undergone change, and in recent history it has continually interpreted such change as fundamental or as a matter of identity and essence. Intellectual history and the sociology of knowledge would suggest that we should expect the study of public administration to be buffeted by the winds of intellectual change, growth, and challenge (as all active fields of thought will be). Thus, public administration will participate in, and be influenced by, developments in virtually all areas of human thought. Presently, the field is visibly influenced not only by incremental developments of preexisting themes and directions, but also by the host of intellectual, philosophical, methodological, epistemological, and esthetic developments which are loosely grouped under labels such as postmodernism. The field has always been influenced by, and participated in, the intellectual climate and dialogue of its times. It will continue to do so. And this will be a sign, not particularly of crises of identity or future, but rather of vitality and engagement.

Bibliography

Gladden, E. N., 1972. *A History of Public Administration*. 2 vols. London and Portland, OR: Frank Cass and Co., Ltd.

Lynn, Naomi B. and Aaron Wildavksy, eds., 1990. *Public Administration: The State of the Discipline*. Chatham, NJ: Chatham House.

Mill, John Stuart, (1861) 1991. *Considerations on Representative Government*. Buffalo, NY: Prometheus Books.

Mosher, Frederick C., ed., 1975. *American Public Administration: Past, Present, Future*. Tuscaloosa, AL: University of Alabama Press.

Perry, James L., ed., 1989. *Handbook of Public Administration*. 2nd ed. 1996 San Francisco: Jossey-Bass, Inc.

Shafritz, Jay M. and Albert C. Hyde, eds., 1992. *Classics of Public Administration*. 3d ed. Pacific Grove, CA: Brooks/Cole.

Wilson, Woodrow, 1887. "The Study of Administration." *Political Science Quarterly*, vol. 2 (June).

2

American Administrative Tradition

Nicholas Henry,
Georgia Southern University

The administrative cultures and management practices of governments within the United States.

The tradition of public administration in the United States is the griffin in the globe's menagerie of national managerial traditions: mythical and improbable, but fierce in demeanor and capable of occasional flight. To phrase it more prosaically, the core of the American public administrative tradition may be reduced to a single word: constraint.

A tradition is not, we should note, the same thing as a profession, that is, a largely self-regulating practice and self-aware field of study. "Tradition" is, to borrow a definition from *Webster's*, "Belief, habit, practice, principle, handed down verbally from one generation to another, or acquired by each successive generation from the example preceding it" (p. 1574). Compared to a profession, a tradition is more visceral than intellectual, more cultural than practical, more grassroots than grand, more encompassing than specializing.

As the title of this encyclopedia indicates, we shall focus on the American administrative tradition as it is found in the public sector, not in the private sector. Whereas "constraint" is the watchword in explaining the American tradition of public administration, it is not a term that comes readily to mind in describing the national tradition of business administration; in the private sector, "aggression" is perhaps the appropriate moniker of the American administrative tradition. It is difficult, after all, to conceive of the shrewd, daring, and rapacious "robber barons"—the flamboyant tycoons of the nineteenth century who founded the American corporate state—as being associated with any administrative tradition of constraint. The tradition of administering governments differs dramatically from the tradition of administering businesses in the United States.

All national traditions are shaped by strong and deep undercurrents peculiar to the national culture. When cultural currents are recognized and articulated by intellectuals, a society's brawn and brain unite in powerful forms. Traditions are born. Nowhere is this combination more evident than in the American tradition of public administration. We shall consider, first, those cultural characteristics that seem unique to the United States, and, second, the intellectualization of those characteristics by the nation's early political thinkers.

Origins: Cultural Underpinnings of the American Tradition of Public Administration

There seems to be an unshakable faith among scholars that the characteristics of a people stem from the thoughts of their great thinkers, and a corresponding skepticism towards the notion that the great thoughts of these thinkers derive from the characteristics of the people in whose midst they think. We tilt toward the latter bias.

In the eighteenth century when the republic was being founded, Americans were, by and large, revolutionary yet rational, enlightened but often uneducated, anti-authoritarian but cautious—and (despite the genius of the U.S. Constitution) occasionally fumbling in establishing democratic institutions. These cultural characteristics have since evolved into new forms, but forms that would still be quite recognizable as basic American traits to a citizen of the United States living 200 years ago.

Understanding one's own culture, as Alexis de Tocqueville taught Americans, is best done with help from observers who are not of the culture which they observe. We shall rely on just such observers, and, more to the point, concentrate on those analysts who focus on the hub of any culture's administrative tradition: the administrative organizations in which that tradition manifests itself.

One such observer is, like de Tocqueville, French. Michel Crozier identified what he believed to be the core characteristics of the American administrative organization that derived directly from the American national culture: division of labor and due process of law.

American organizations are dominated by their specialized and splintering divisions of labor and their obsequiousness in observing due process of law, and these twin cultural factors produce organizational pathologies unique to American bureaucracies. Functional specialization results in an abnormally high number of jurisdictional disputes among and within American organizations, while Americans' passion for due process of law produces a plethora of impersonal bureaucratic rules that are designed to protect the individual from injustices, but which also are obstacles to organized action. Both cultural traits tend to magnify the role of lawyers, or any official who is in a position to interpret organizational rules, jurisdictions, and prerogatives, and this aspect often impedes change in American organizations.

In Crozier's view, American organizations, on the whole, tend to protect the rights of individuals more effectively, are better attuned to reality, are characterized by more cooperation, and are generally more open than are those of other nations. But the existence of many centers of authority in American organizations, and the difficulties that must be surmounted in coordinating them, pose problems of change for American organizations. Although American organizations are likely more open to innovation than are others, "Willful individuals can block the intentions of whole communities for a long time; numerous routines develop around local positions of influence; the feeble are not protected so well against the strong; and generally, a large number of vicious circles will protect and reinforce local conservatism" (p. 236).

A Hollander, Geert Hofstede, places the organizational pathologies unique to the American administrative tradition in comparative and systematic perspective. By analyzing the common cultural manifestations of managers in the offices of an American-based multinational corporation in over 40 nations, Hofstede identified five fundamental dimensions of national culture: power distance, uncertainty avoidance, individualism-collectivism, masculinity-femininity, and long-term/short-term orientation. Specific national cultures can be any combination of these. Without indulging in an extended description of each of these dimensions, we shall attempt to synopsize how they pertain to the American administrative tradition.

The United States is a small power distance country (that is, its citizens value equality); a weak uncertainty avoidance nation (in fact, it is well below average, indicating high risk-taking propensities and tolerance for dissent, among other characteristics); exceptionally individualistic as a society; well above average as a masculine culture; and has a short-term orientation.

Relying on these characteristics, Hofstede describes the United States (and the other English-speaking nations) as an "achievement motivation culture," which relates to a hierarchy of human needs that places personal achievement near the top and security near the bottom. But other cultures have different motivations. Some cultures, for example, may be masculine (like the United States) but also have strong needs to avoid uncertainty (such as Italy, Japan, and Mexico). These nations are "security-motivated cultures," or cultures which turn the pecking order of values found in the United States upside down; security-motivated cultures place security near the top of the pyramid of human needs, and personal achievement near the bottom.

Other nations may, like the United States, have weak uncertainty avoidance qualities, but are feminine cultures (a combination found in all the Scandinavian nations), and still others may be polar opposites of the United States, being feminine societies that have strong uncertainty avoidance needs (a combination found in Israel and Thailand). These are "social motivation cultures," or cultures that place a high premium on the quality of social life. In the case of the Scandinavian countries, a propensity to take risks is combined with a commitment to society's well-being; in Israel and Thailand, a need for security is combined with a commitment to social health.

Individualism, masculinity, a sense of fairness, a preference for equality, and low needs for security number prominently among those national traits that distinguish American culture from others, and which have had a particular salience in the formation of the American administrative tradition. But it is in the public sector where these cultural characteristics have had their greatest impact on that tradition.

Articulations: Early and Influential Expressions of the American Tradition of Public Administration

At least three early and highly influential articulations of these uniquely American cultural characteristics placed them squarely in the tradition of American public administration that was beginning to gel in the eighteenth century: the Articles of Confederation, the first state constitutions, and the debates and writings of the nation's founders, especially Alexander Hamilton and Thomas Jefferson.

The Articles of Confederation—which, from 1791 to 1789, provided the first framework for the new nation—were as emblematic of the early Americans' fondness for managerial mish-mash as they were evidentiary of Americans' insistence on administrative constraint. The relatively scant attention paid in the Articles to such notions as matching accountability with authority and specialized divisions of public labor (notably in the Articles' disinclination to distinguish legislative responsibilities from executive responsibilities in the government's structure) no doubt was the product not only of a grassroots revulsion with princely prerogatives, but equally of the nation's early political thinkers wrestling with the dilemma of how to organize something truly new: big democracy. Because the nation's first charter had to account for a vast territory and a large population, it somehow needed to be devised so that it could transcend the only governmental form that democracy had ever used before, the town meeting. Unfortunately, the Articles of Confederation did not meet this historic challenge.

The state governments reigned supreme under the Articles. Congress was really a convention of ambassadors from the states, rather than an assembly of legislators. The Articles of Confederation did set up a rudimentary national civil service, but it was a bizarre bureaucratic beast that had no authority to act on its own or enforce much of anything. The national civil service, consisting of the Departments of Foreign Affairs, War, and Treasury, and an existing Post Office Department, reported directly to committees of the Continental Congress. There was no national chief executive; in fact, the first draft of the Articles of Confederation, written in 1776, was rejected by the Second Continental Congress on the specific grounds that it had proposed an overly empowered executive.

When Daniel Shays ignited his ill-conceived rebellion in 1786, the new nation's political leaders discovered that no arm of "American government," such as it was, had been authorized or organized to put down the disturbance, and eventually that chore fell to the Massachusetts state militia. At least one petulant English observer foresaw the impossibility, as demonstrated by Shays's Rebellion, of his former colonies ever founding a government worthy of the name, and he attributed this failure to Americans' fixation on a weak executive: "As to the future grandeur of America, and its being a rising empire under one head, whether Republican or Monarchial, it is one of the idlest and most visionary notions that was ever conceived even by writers of romance" (Josiah Tucker, as quoted in Smith, 1980, p. 82).

At about the same time that the Articles of Confederation were being written, the states were busily drafting their own constitutions. Eleven of the 13 states adopted constitutions between 1776 and 1780. Connecticut and Rhode Island did not write their constitutions until well into the next century, and instead retained their charters, which had been granted to them by England in the 1600s. This was because these charters actually created genuine republics within those states, including reasonably authoritative chief executives and legislators who were elected by the people, and the only emendation that was required was the elimination of references in the charters to the king.

The eleven states that adopted constitutions were notably aggressive in limiting the powers of the chief executive. Only New York's constitution (with Massachusetts's running a distant second) provided a reasonably strong executive, and this comparatively exceptional power vested in New York's governor seems to have been attributable to the unique combination of John Jay, Robert Livingston, and Gouverneur Morris—New Yorkers who had a heavy hand in drafting their state's constitution, and all of whom were unusually able men who believed in the utility of a relatively central authority.

The remaining constitutions stipulated that the chief executive was to be appointed by the legislature or the courts, and all of them, in turn, severely restricted their chief executives' appointment powers. With only two exceptions, Massachusetts and New York, the governors in all of the 11 states amounted to little more than a military commander, and all executive and most judicial powers—as well as legislative authority—were placed firmly within the legislatures. With the exceptions of New York and arguably Massachusetts, states determinedly ignored the notion that their governments and people might benefit from the presence of an empowered executive. In fact, 10 of the 13 original states had gubernatorial terms of only a single year.

Perhaps even more ominous from the viewpoint of both effective and democratic government was the fact that the drafters of state constitutions in most of the states simply did not conceive that there were distinctions between branches and even functions of government. Making laws and making them work were one and the same, and this blurring of basic governmental responsibilities, which appear so separate and distinct to us today, may have been at least a partial product of the tradition established by the English shire. The shires were largely the creation of the masterful medieval manager, King Edgar the Peaceful (959–975), some 800 years before the American Revolution. They served as subunits of his majesty's government, and were based on the premise that the king's delegate, the shire-reeve (now called the sheriff), could make, manage, and have a loud voice in the adjudication of the laws within the bounds of his (that is, the sheriffs) shire. That all of the states were influenced by King Edgar's administrative creativity during the Dark Ages of Europe is indisputable; each of the 13 states had adopted England's use of shires in the form of counties well before the Revolution.

This confusion of governmental function and governmental branch, as evidenced in most of the states' first constitutions (or, more accurately, this innocent ignorance about the benefits of matching function with structure), still continues in the United States in its most vivid form in the nation's 3,043 county governments. American counties and their citizens always have displayed a structural and attitudinal ambivalence as to whether they were freestanding local governments or administrative arms of state governments. One standard dictionary of American history notes that American counties "have been maintained here through three centuries with surprisingly little modification" (Anderson, 1962, p. 237).

It might appear to some that the absence of authority granted by the Articles of Confederation to the national government, and the virtual absence of authority provided by the great majority of the original state constitutions to elected or appointed state administrators, were Rousseauan testaments to true, populist, and "natural" democracy. Hardly. Passing few people (about 6 percent) were allowed to vote on anything or anyone in any of the states, and only three states (Massachusetts, New Hampshire, and New York) permitted their chief executives to even be elected independently by those few people who were qualified to vote. In only one state, Massachusetts, were the people permitted to ratify their own state's constitution by popular vote. Democracy was not only new—it was distrusted.

Layering and striating all of this early American activity in drafting confederations and constitutions was the massive brilliance of the early American political elite, but particularly that of Hamilton and Jefferson.

Hamilton displayed throughout his writings on government a strong interest in the administrative apparatus of the state. A friend of Hamilton's reported that Hamilton was contemplating a "full investigation of the history and science of civil government and how practical results of various modifications of it upon the freedom and happiness of mankind . . . and to engage the assistance of others in the enterprise" (Kent, 1898, pp. 327–328).

Interestingly, in light of the later thinking of early twentieth century contributors to a theory of public administration, Hamilton never bought in to the idea that there were "principles of administration." Consider a sample of this view provided by the illustrious Leonard D. White, who wrote in 1936 (at the height of the "principles of administration" movement) that a principle of administration "is as useful a guide to action in the public administration of Russia as of Great Britain, of Irak as of the United States" (p. 25). Hamilton would have quickly dismissed such bombast, noting that efficient public administration "must be fitted to a nation, as much as a coat to the individual; and consequently, that what may be good to Philadelphia may be bad to Paris, and ridiculous at Petersburg" (Syrett and Cooke, 1961–1979, vol. 22, p. 404).

As these differing perspectives imply, Hamilton's approach to public administration was above all practical. Hamilton therefore extolled a strong chief executive in the public sector, equating a strong executive with the "energy" needed to make a government function: "A feeble executive [by contrast] implies a feeble execution of the government. A feeble execution is but another phrase for a bad execution; and a government ill executed . . . must be, in practice, a bad government" (1961, "No. 70," p. 423). Things, in sum, had to get done.

But, even more than a strong chief executive, Hamilton advocated a very strong bureaucracy. Hamilton urged that department heads be paid exceptionally well, that they possess substantial powers, and that their tenure in office should extend beyond that of the chief executive who appointed them. In fact, Hamilton felt that a brief tenure of bureaucrats in high office would "occasion a disgraceful and ruinous mutability in the administration of the government" (1961, "No. 72," p. 436). Compare Hamilton's views with what has happened in the United States today, in which the average tenure of an undersecretary or assistant secretary in the federal government averages 22 months (Heclo, 1977, p. 103), and in which fully one-third of the political appointees in the federal Senior Executive Service change jobs or leave government every year (Ingraham, 1987, p. 429).

One logically would infer from such realities of the federal condition that Hamilton's views did not have a lasting impact on the early formulation of the American administrative tradition, and one would be right. Hamilton's notions on how public administration ought to work were in direct contradiction to the ideas and ideals of Jefferson, whose influence on the American administrative tradition was far more pervasive than was Hamilton's.

In stark contrast to Hamilton, who embraced a dynamic government, Jefferson disdained the very idea of it. Jefferson wrote to James Madison, "I am not a friend to a very energetic government. It is always oppressive. It places the government more at their ease, at the expense of the people" (Bowen, 1966, p. 105). As president (1801–1809), Jefferson practiced what he preached—he remains the only president who never vetoed an act of Congress.

Jefferson celebrated and, to be blunt, romanticized, the ideals of localist, yeoman democracy as the core of the American political experiment. Lynton Keith Caldwell suggests that, because of Jefferson's abiding belief in the perfectibility of the common man and woman, it followed that the best government was the most participatory government, and the most participatory government was "no friend to bureaucracy, to professionalism in public administration . . . or to the administrative state as a shaper and director of national development" (1990, p. 482). Jefferson's "profound distrust of bureaucracy" (p. 483) is in part responsible for the "presidential tendency" to be "proactive in relation to foreign affairs and reactive in relation to domestic issues where power must be shared with Congress. Thus, America today has a powerful, costly, and energetic executive who intervenes abroad on numerous occasions but who often seems politically incapable of rational, informed forecasting or planning for the nation's future" (p. 484).

Of Hamilton, Paul Van Riper has written, "If anyone deserves a title as *the* founder of the American administrative state . . . it is not Wilson, Easton, or Ely but Alexander Hamilton" (1983, p. 480). Perhaps. But Hamilton, brilliant thought he was, nonetheless rejected as intellectually tenuous and administratively debilitating many of the basic cultural values of his new nation as they pertained to the conduct of public administration. Van Riper may well be correct in his identification of Hamilton as the founder of the profession of public administration in the United States. But it is to Jefferson that credit must be given as the founder of the tradition of American public administration. It was Jefferson who, by his eloquent articulation of what he believed to be the transcendent goodness of the average American, gave intellectual credence to those currents in the American political culture that have resulted in the lasting American tradition of constrained public management. It is a tradition against which Hamilton's professional and academic progeny still war.

By the end of the eighteenth century, as a result of the nation's founders putting into words (whether as civic charters or as philosophic ramblings) what they saw as their fledgling nation's deepest character—and the reality of that character itself—the American social contract was given recognizable form.

A social contract is an agreement, often more understood than expressed, between the citizens and the state that defines and limits the duties and responsibilities of each. For example, although there is a richer variety of apparent social contracts in Africa than in most continents, Aidan W. Southall describes early African governmental structures as "half enlarged household, half embryonic state" (1953, p. 195), emphasizing the familial nature of the African social contract. In Asia, a foundation of Confucian philosophy has supported a social contract which, in many nations, legitimates the head of both government and society as a highly authoritative, compassionate, and wise father figure. And in Europe, the contract is a covenant, subject to adjustment, in which those who govern and those who are governed are seen as equal partners. Not so in the United States, where the social contract is a consequence of revolution; all power is held by the people, and is delegated by them (if they wish) to their government. Government is very much a "servant" of the citizenry in every sense of the word, and this uniquely American social contract is partly responsible for the constraint that permeates the American tradition of public administration.

Attenuations: The Legacy of Limited Public Administration in the United States

A tradition of administrative constraint—some would say of governmental gridlock—is especially evident at the federal level. That gridlock is, undeniably, at least partly the result of different parties controlling different branches of the federal government throughout much of the twentieth century, as well as a conservative strain in the American polity which passionately holds that gridlock is good because government is not—a conservatism that obtains some of its nourishment from Jefferson's belief in human perfectibility. But gridlock also is a consequence of the inevitable undermining of administrative action that accompanies such cultural dimensions as a people's deep commitment to a person's right to due process of law (an arduous and time-consuming effort), functional specialization (with its unavoidable battles over jurisdictional turf), and highly individualistic and masculine values (guaranteeing *mano a mano* confrontations among agencies, branches, and levels of government, when more collective and feminine values likely would achieve more concrete results in a public context).

Nearly a generation ago, the distinguished and politically sophisticated Washington insider Lloyd Cutler, in his capacity as then-counsel to the president, bemoaned his government's seeming inability to act: "Under the U.S. Constitution, it is not now feasible to 'form a government.' The separation of powers . . . whatever its merits in 1973, has become a structure that almost guarantees stalemate today" (1980, p. 127), and argued for a new constitutional convention that would amount to a wholesale rewriting of the Constitution along parliamentary lines. (Shades of Hamilton!) Cutler described the problem, but mistakenly ascribed its cause to what is really a symptom; the American tendency to govern by gridlock is less a consequence of an outdated Constitution, and more the product of a still-vigorous political culture which wrote it. Scrapping the Constitution, as Cutler advocates, will not change the reality of an administrative and political tradition in which frustration is the only constant.

The subnational governments display their own tradition of constrained public administration. They are less reflective of governmental gridlock (although the states and localities have their share, too), and more expressive of the dilemmas endemic to the uniquely American administrative tradition of the feeble public executive. The intellectual and practical connections between the first spindly structures of American public administration erected in the eighteenth century, and the contemporary executive role in American subnational governments, but especially local governments, are unusually clear and direct.

More than 67 percent of American municipalities and over 23 percent of counties (Renner and De Santis, 1993, pp. xiv, 67) hire city managers or chief administrative officers who typically have large powers, and who usually report not to the elected chief executives of these governments, but to their legislative bodies, such as city councils or county commissions, which have the sole authority to hire and fire them. As a result of the growing popularity of this long-dominant practice among local governments, the majority of elected local chief executives have few powers.

Only 26 percent of American mayors have the sole authority to appoint municipal department heads (Renner and De Santis, 1993, p. 67), and mayors have "input" in the dismissal of department heads in less than 28 percent of cities and towns. Only nine out of a hundred mayors in the United States are responsible for preparing the agenda for the city council (Anderson, 1989, p. 28).

In more than half (52 percent) of all American cities and towns with populations of 2,500 or more, well over 90 percent of the mayors cannot veto legislation passed by the council or commission; astonishingly, over four-fifths of the mayors in the 41 percent of municipalities that use the mayor-council plan, which ostensibly is the "strong executive" form of American local government, have no veto power (Adrian, 1988, p. 10).

Counties have even weaker chief executives. Only 8 percent of chief executive officers in American counties have a veto power. Fifty-eight percent of these executives have terms of only a single year, and only 22 percent are elected directly by county voters—a much lower proportion than in municipalities, where the overwhelming majority of mayors are elected directly by the people (De Santis, 1989, pp. 60–61). It is in county governments where the original American administrative values, as reflected in those first state constitutions, still flourish most verdantly.

The American tradition of public administration is orthodox in that it reflects the dimensions of the culture in which it is embedded. But it is unique in that it is a tradition in which administrative constraint, symbolized by gridlock and executive limitations, is the overriding feature.

The emblem of the American tradition of public administration is not the same as that of the nation—the eagle. The emblem of American public administration is the improbable griffin.

Bibliography

Adrian, Charles R., 1988. "Forms of City Government in American History." In *The Municipal Year Book, 1988*. Washington, D.C.: International City Management Association, pp. 3–11.

Anderson, Eric, 1989. "Two Major Forms of Government: Two Types of Professional Management." In *The Municipal Year Book, 1989*, Washington, D.C.: International City Management Association, pp. 26–32.

Anderson, Wayne, ed., 1962. "County Government." In *Concise Dictionary of American History*. New York: Charles Scribner's Sons.

Bowen, Catherine Drinker, 1966. *Miracle at Philadelphia*. Boston: Little, Brown.

Caldwell, Lynton K., 1990. "The Administrative Republic: The Contrasting Legacies of Hamilton and Jefferson." *Public Administration Quarterly*, vol. 13 (Winter) 470–493.

Crozier, Michel, 1964. *The Bureaucratic Phenomenon*. Chicago: University of Chicago Press.

Cutler, Lloyd N., 1980. "To Form a Government." *Foreign Affairs*, vol. 59 (Fall) 126–143.

De Santis, Victor S., 1989. "County Government: A Centry of Change." In *The Municipal Year Book, 1989*. Washington, D.C.: International City Management Association, pp. 55–84.

Hamilton, Alexander, 1961. "No. 70" and "No. 72." In Clinton Rossiter, ed., *The Federalist Papers*. New York: New American Library, pp. 423–431 and pp. 435–440.

Heclo, Hugh, 1977. *A Government of Strangers: Executive Politics in Washington*. Washington, D.C.: Brookings Institution.

Hosftede, Geert, 1980. *Culture's Consequences: International Differences in Work-Related Values*. Beverly Hills, CA: Sage.

Ingraham, Patricia W., 1987. "Building Bridges or Burning Them? The President, the Appointees, and the Bureaucracy." *Public Administration Review*, vol. 47 (September / October) 425–435.

"Introduction," 1993. In *The Municipal Year Book, 1993*. Washington, D.C.: International City Management Association, pp. ix–xv.

Kent, William, 1898. *Memoirs and Letters of James Kent*. Boston: Little, Brown.

Renner, Tari and Victor S. De Santis, 1993. "Contemporary Patterns and Trends in Municipal Government Structures." In *The Municipal Year Book, 1993*. Washington, D.C.: International City Management Association, pp. 57–69.

Smith, Page, 1980. *The Constitution: A Documentary and Narrative History*. New York: Morrow Quill Paperbacks.

Southall, Aidan W., 1953. *Alur Society: A Study in Processes and Types of Domination*. Cambridge: Cambridge University Press.

Syrett, Harold and Jacob E. Cooke, eds., 1961–1979. *The Papers of Alexander Hamilton*. 26 vols. New York: Columbia University Press.

Van Riper, Paul P., 1983. "The American Administrative State: Wilson and the Founders—An Unorthodox View." *Public Administration Review*, vol. 43 (November / December). 477–490.

White, Leonard D., 1936. "The Meaning of Principles of Public Administration." In John M. Gaus, Leonard D. White and Marshall E. Dimock, eds., *The Frontiers of Public Administration*. Chicago: University of Chicago Press, pp. 13–25.

3

Feminist Theory of Public Administration

Camilla Stivers,
Cleveland State University

The theory that interprets or explains public administration or its various aspects from a feminist perspective. Although feminism includes a wide range of viewpoints, most, if not all, feminists maintain a critical perspective on women's current economic and social status and prospects, employ gender as a central element in social analysis, and are committed to the idea that men and women should share equally "in the work, in the privileges, in the defining and the dreaming of the world" (Lerner 1984, p. 33). Feminist theories of public administration, then, use gender as a lens through which to analyze critically women's current status and role in public agencies, bring to light ways in which gender bias inhabits ideas and practices in the field, and formulate new theoretical approaches.

Two types of feminist theory can be observed in the literature of public administration. Descriptive theory, based on empirical study, reports on how gender influences current practice in public agencies, especially its effect on women's access to and status in public agency employment, and sometimes attempts to account for observed differences between men's and women's employment experiences. Conceptual theory aims to use gender to rethink the existing philosophy of public administration, focusing on such issues as the politics-administration dichotomy, public bureaucratic structure and practice, the bases for defending the legitimacy of the administrative state, professionalism, leadership, and citizenship in public administration. Initial feminist theorizing in public administration was largely descriptive; more recent literature includes both descriptive and conceptual theories.

Descriptive Theories

In comparison to closely related fields such as political science and business management, public administration was relatively slow to develop feminist perspectives, but beginning in the mid-1970s work began to appear that documented federal, state, and local government discrimination against women in public employment. This early work notably included a 1976 symposium in *Public Administration Review* edited by Nesta M. Gallas on "Women in Public Administration." Gallas was serving at the time as the first female president of the American Society for Public Administration (ASPA). In addition to two articles assessing the status of women in ASPA itself, the symposium included analyses of why so few women had by that time managed to land top jobs in federal agencies; the role of affirmative action in overcoming employment discrimination against women; strategies to help women administrators perform effectively; and the idea of women's rights as a basis for public policy.

Other examples of early feminist critiques of the status of women in public employment include Lorraine D. Eyde (1973), "The Status of Women in State and Local Government," in which she critically examined the segregation of women in low-level jobs, and Judith Mohr (1973), "Why Not More Women City Managers?" in which she found only seven women out of more than 2,300 city managers.

Debra Stewart (1990) reviewed a number of quantitative analyses of the proportions of women found at various grade levels in public agencies and found that in the 1980s there was a shift in quantitative analysis from a straightforward description of public executives' roles to an investigation and understanding of the important differences between male and female executives' attitudes about their work and how they achieve advancement; thus understanding the forces that drive them, in order to better predict alternative strategies for change.

An example of the type of comparative analysis referred to by Stewart is Mary E. Guy's edited collection (1992), which presents results of several studies finding consistent differences between the status of men and women managers in the governments of six states with widely varying political cultures, thus suggesting the persistence of factors that work against the equality of women in public employment. The articles in the collection, reflecting the focus on differences between men's and women's status characteristic of descriptive feminist theory, cover career patterns, personal characteristics, the impact of domestic responsibilities on individuals' ability to cope with work demands, mentoring, sexual harassment, and management style preferences and behaviors. Guy has concluded: "Only through a process of significant change and reform can we expect to see a more equitable balance between the numbers of female and male managers in state agencies" (p. 211). Her recommended strategies include job enrichment for women managers, mentoring, eliminating sexual harassment, job restructuring to facilitate family obligations, and promoting child care and family leave policies.

Conceptual Theories

Descriptive theories take for granted existing modes of thought in public administration and examine the extent to which women have gained access to the world of practice, but conceptual theories call into question the frameworks within which public administration is typically understood. The basic premise of conceptual feminist theories is that existing perspectives, for all their apparent objectivity, contain hidden gender biases. Taking gender into account, therefore, involves more than simply adding women to public agencies; instead it entails rethinking fundamental theoretical assumptions, approaches, and concepts.

An early example of this approach to the theory of public administration is that of Robert B. Denhardt and Jan Perkins (1976), who argued that mainstream organizational analysis works from within a paradigm in which the reigning means-ends model of rationality, though purportedly universal-neutral, is in actuality culturally masculine. Denhardt and Perkins suggested that feminist theory provides an alternative paradigm in which process replaces task as the primary orientation, and hierarchy is challenged by an egalitarian framework. They noted that simply adding women to public organizations will not be enough to dislodge the "administrative man" paradigm; instead, a change of consciousness is necessary, one that replaces traditional ideas of professional expertise with the feminist notion of the authority of personal experience as the ethical basis of administrative practice.

Kathy Ferguson (1984) expanded the idea that liberal reforms, such as increasing the number of women in management positions, is not enough to end gender bias in public administration; real change entails a new approach grounded in the historical-cultural experiences of women. Ferguson argued that to encounter bureaucracy on its own terms, such as by integrating women into public organizations, precludes a decisive attack on typical bureaucratic patterns of hierarchy. Only women's "marginal" perspective, which has emerged as a result of their historical exclusion from the public realm, offers the hope of real transformation, redefining notions of power, rationality, and leadership. As Ferguson has noted, "To challenge bureaucracy in the name of the values and goals of feminist discourse is to undermine the chain of command, equalize the participants, subvert the monopoly of information and secrecy of decision-making, and essentially seek to democratize the organization" (pp. 208–209).

Suzanne Franzway, Dianne Court, and R. W. Connell (1989) brought feminist theory to bear on the idea of the bureaucratic state, viewing it as an agent in sexual politics, maintaining and perpetuating through its policies gender bias in society at large and, in turn, being shaped by this bias. The bureaucratic state, in other words, is not "outside" society but enmeshed in it, including its patterns of gender relations. The authors maintained that no theory of the state can avoid issues of sex and gender; they are present, if not always visible, as grounding assumptions or limitations to argument. The bureaucratic state supports the interests of men over those of women not only directly through policies but also ideologically, through characterizing what are actually gender-biased state processes as being simply impersonal and neutral.

Camilla Stivers (1993) presented a feminist reading of the literature on the legitimacy of the administrative state, a central theme of current public administration scholarship. She argued that ideas of expertise, leadership, and virtue that mark defenses of administrative power have culturally masculine features that privilege masculinity over femininity. This characteristic masculinity of public administration, though ignored by most theorists, contributes to and is sustained by gender bias in society at large. In Stivers' (1993) view, "As long as we go on viewing the enterprise of administration as genderless, women will continue to face their present Hobson's choice, which is either to adopt a masculine administrative identity or accept marginalization in the bureaucratic hierarchy" (p. 10).

Even though scholars of public administration tend to praise its differences from private business, Stivers argued, the publicness of public administration is problematic because of the historical and theoretical exclusion of women from the public sphere, which has barred issues such as the division of household labor from policy debate. The administrative state can only function as it does because women bear a lopsided share of the burden of domestic work, without which society would grind to a halt; thus public administrative structures and practices depend for their coherence and their effectiveness on the oppression of women.

Conceptual theorists agree that simply adding women to the bureaucracy will not be enough to end enduring patterns of gender bias; instead, new modes of thought are required, ones that call into question the neutrality of such central ideas as professionalism, leadership, and the public interest. The extent to which administrative agency policies and practices can change will also depend partly on such larger social transformations as the sexual division of labor in the household, a sphere that shapes and is shaped by the administrative state.

Future feminist theorizing in public administration is likely to continue to proceed on both descriptive and conceptual fronts; and indeed, careful empirical study of existing practices in government agencies and conceptual deconstruction and reconstruction reinforce one another. Empirical data on the status of women in public administration have the potential to reshape understanding of issues and justify the need for conceptual transformation, and new, gender-conscious modes of thought can revamp field research approaches in fruitful ways, opening researchers' eyes to new questions and new forms of evidence. Empirical and conceptual work in this area to date strongly suggests not only that gender is a cutting edge issue in public administration but also that there is a great deal of work still to be done.

Bibliography

Denhardt, Robert B., and Jan Perkins, 1976. "The Coming Death of Administrative Man." *Public Administrative Review*, vol. 36, no. 4 (July-August): 379–384.

Eyde, Lorraine, D., 1973. "The Status of Women in State and Local Government." *Public Personnel Management* (May-June): 205–211.

Ferguson, Kathy E., 1984. *The Feminist Case Against Bureaucracy*. Philadelphia: Temple University Press.

Franzway, Suzanne, Dianne Court, and R. W. Connell, eds., 1989. *Staking a Claim: Feminism, Bureaucracy, and the State*. Sydney, Australia: Allen and Unwin.

Gallas, Nesta M., ed., 1976. "A Symposium: Women in Public Administration." *Public Administration Review*, vol. 36, no. 4 (July-August): 347–389.

Guy, Mary E., ed., 1992. *Women and Men of the States: Public Administrators at the State Level*. Armonk, NY: M. E. Sharpe.

Hall, Mary M., and Rita Mae Kelly, eds., 1989. *Gender, Bureaucracy, and Democracy: Careers and Equal Opportunity in the Public Sector*. Westport, CT: Greenwood Press.

Lerner, Gerda, 1984. "The Rise of Feminist Consciousness." In E. M. Bender, B. Burk, and N. Walker, eds., *All of Us Are Present*. Columbia, MO: James Madison Wood Research Institute, Stephens College.

Mohr, Judith, 1973. "Why Not More Women City Managers?" *Public Management* (February-March): 2–5.

Stewart, Debra, 1990. "Women in Public Administration." In Naomi B. Lynn, and Aaron B. Wildavsky, eds., *Public Administration: The State of the Discipline*. Chatham, NJ: Chatham House.

Stivers, Camilla, 1993. *Gender Images in Public Administration: Legitimacy and the Administrative State*. Newbury Park, CA: Sage.

Part Two

Policy Making

4 — Policy

William H. Park,
United Kingdom Joint Services Command and Staff College

A decision or, more usually, a set of interrelated decisions concerning the selection of goals and the means of achieving them. The identification of policy as a set or web of decisions is useful in that it underlines the notion that policy is best seen as a course of action—or inaction—rather than a single, discrete decision or action.

It is tempting, and common, to regard policy and the policy process as somehow ordered and rational. According to rational assumptions, the policy process consists of the identification of a problem demanding a solution or a goal worth achieving, assessment of the alternative means of achieving the desired outcome, the making of a choice between these alternatives, the implementation of the preferred option, and the solution of the problem or the attainment of the objective. However, such a process would imply the involvement of a small number of decisionmakers, a high degree of consensus concerning what constitutes a policy problem or a desirable objective, an ability to calculate and compare the likely consequences of each alternative, smooth implementation of the chosen option, and the absence of obstacles to the achievement of policy goals. It also implies that the process is terminated by the making and implementation of a decision. In the real world, however, policy processes are likely to be less well structured. Multiple decisionmakers, little consensus, incalculable probabilities, imperfect implementation, and unknown or unknowable outcomes might be encountered, and policy can appear messier, less coherent, and less able to achieve the desired outcome than rational models suggest. Policies are in any case distinct from single decisions and incorporate continuity and dynamism.

Sometimes, policy is understood and indeed presented at such a level of generality that notions of implementation or even of decision are barely factors at all. For politicians, policy may on occasion simply reflect a stance or orientation. Policy may be exclusively or primarily declaratory—"to contribute to the creation of a more peaceful world," or "to strive towards a more equal society." Of course it is possible to envisage a kind of hierarchy of policies, whereby subordinate policies—diplomatic support for a specific peace proposal, or progressive taxation—serve to concretize these more abstract aspirations. Such an approach would shift attention away from a focus on policy content and towards a concern with the presence or lack of systematic and ordered attempts at implementation. We would want to know how interrelated and coordinated is the set of decisions which make up the policy as a whole. In other words, an exclusive or excessive emphasis on policy content is unsatisfying. We want to know about the policy process, policy implementation, and policy success.

The policy process is sometimes characterized as a "black box" which converts inputs into outputs. As with the rational approach, this too tends to assume that policymaking only begins after the policy agenda has been set, and that it ends once a decision or set of decisions emerges from the black box. However, it might be useful to regard the policy process as incorporating the determination of what constitutes a policy issue in the first place, and as continuing during the implementation stage. The conceptualization of policy as a set of decisions serves to raise questions relating to which decisions are part of the problem or goal identification stage, which part of the selection of options stage, and which part of the implementation of the policy.

Take implementation. Empirical studies of policies in the real world sometimes cast doubt on the idea that policy can usefully be understood solely as plan or design, and instead draw attention to policy as practice. Decisions which contribute to an overall policy might be made at the implementation stage. Policy is not only what is intended, but also what is done. This suggests a muddier reality in which policy can appear reactive, pragmatic, or adaptive, as well as or instead of proactive, coherent, and purposive. The agents whose formal task it is to implement policy might receive imprecise or ambiguous directives that require them to exercise judgment or discretion. Furthermore, experts in the implementing bureaucracy might not only take the opportunity but be expected to interpret policy and how it should be applied in practice. The presence of complexity will encourage this tendency. In this way, policy might evolve or develop incrementally. In resembling a learning process, policy can become dynamic over time.

What happens inside the black box might also have a bearing on policy. "Policy" has the same linguistic root as "politics"—indeed, in some languages the same word is used—and the notion of politics conjures up the prospect of conflict, power struggles, and clashes of ideas and interests. Given that most policymaking involves large numbers of individuals, groups, and agencies, then we should not be surprised that politics take place. As a result, policy decisions might reflect compromises resulting from debates and bargaining between the various contributors. Compromises such as these might fully satisfy few of the contributors, and might be incoherent or ambiguous in content. Indeed, they might not even address the policy problem at all in any very rational or structured way, and might best be seen as driven by the internal dynamics of the policy process. The definition and determination of the policy problem might itself reflect the interests and power relationships of the various parties engaged in the policy process, and their relative capacity to force a perceived problem or desired objective onto the policy formulation agenda.

We have noted the role agencies as well as individuals might play in policy formulation. The growth of bureaucracy has been a major feature of modern government, and although bureaucracies are formally instruments of government it is a fact that they often play a role in policymaking itself. There are a number of explanations for this phenomenon. Bureaucrats are often experts whose opinions are sought and who expect to be consulted. Furthermore, bureaucracies often have interests of their own to pursue—in maintaining or expanding budgets or missions, for example. They might also develop broad policy goals, preferences, or perspectives of their own—that higher education is good for the economy, that surface navies enhance national security, and so on. Thus bureaucrats might operate both as political participants in the setting of policy as well as incremental decisionmakers in its application.

A policy process can produce an output—for example, a set of decisions resulting in a given allocation of resources—but this does not necessarily mean that the overall objectives of the policy will be achieved. The impact of policy actions might not be what was desired. Unintended consequences and unanticipated effects may stem from the ambiguity or contradictions of policy, from imperfections in implementation, from ill-appreciated complexities in the environment within which a policy is to operate, or from the decision of insufficient or maldistributed resources. Thus economic growth might not correlate very well with, say, reduced taxation or increased expenditure on education. Social inequality might not be greatly affected by the establishment of a social security system. Policies often tacitly incorporate causal theories linking policy actions with policy impacts, but faith in such theories might be misplaced.

Thus, although on first consideration the notion of policy might appear to be a simple and straightforward one, further analysis indicates a much greater complexity. The discipline of policy analysis has grown up around this complexity, containing competing schools of thought and offering differing definitions. A policy must be distinguished from a decision. Policies can be purposive and far-reaching or adaptive and incremental—or even static. Scrutiny of the whole process, from the emergence of a policy issue through to evaluation of a policy outcome, might be necessary if a policy is to be fully comprehended. The policy formulation process might be so intensely political as to render the prospect of coherence improbable. Policies might fail to achieve their objectives, or even have results opposite to those intended. Yet policies are unavoidable, for they are the means by which societies and other social organizations regulate, control, and at least endeavor to advance themselves.

Bibliography

Braybrooke, D. and C. E. Lindblom, 1963. *A Strategy of Decision*. New York: The Free Press.

Hill, Michael, ed., 1993. *The Policy Process: A Reader*. New York and London: Harvester Wheatsheaf.

Hogwood, B. W. and L. A. Gunn, 1984. *Policy Analysis for the Real World*. Oxford: Oxford University Press.

Jenkins, W. I., 1978. *Policy Analysis*. London: Martin Robertson.

Lasswell, H. D., 1958. "The Policy Orientation." In D. Lerner and H. D. Lasswell, eds., *The Policy Sciences*. Stanford, CA: Stanford University Press.

Wildavsky, A., 1979. *Speaking Truth to Power: The Art and Craft of Policy Analysis*. Boston: Little Brown.

5

Policy Leadership

Jeffrey S. Luke,
University of Oregon

The act of stimulating the formulation and implementation of public policy among multiple, diverse stakeholders and constituencies. Policy leadership is different from the more common notions of organizational leadership; policy leadership mobilizes attention to problematic conditions, and then forges agreement on appropriate policy responses among diverse, often competing groups and constituencies.

Background

Definition of Public Policy

There exists no universally accepted definitions that clearly distinguish policies from non-policies; as a result, there is considerable ambiguity about what constitutes a policy (Polsby 1984). A public policy is generally characterized as a combination of decisions, commitments, and actions directed toward achieving a particular outcome or result which is deemed in the public interest. Public policies can be further distinguished from public programs and projects; a public program is a set of concrete actions and implementation steps directed toward the attainment of a public policy, while a project is typically a single segment or operating activity within a program. A second distinguishing characteristic is that public policies are different from organizational policies; organizational policies are directed at influencing the behavior of employees to achieve an agency's goal or objective.

Public Problems, Policy Discourse, and Policy Leadership

Public policies are developed and implemented as a collective response to address problematic conditions. In pluralist societies, however, public policies are formulated in an environment typically characterized by disbursed authority and shared power among multiple agencies and institutions, and by conflicting goals and values among multiple constituencies and interest groups (Bryson and Crosby 1992). In addition, the social, economic, and environmental problems that public policies increasingly address are most often boundaryless and intertwined with other public problems. As a result, the context of policy leadership is complex and interconnected, and effective policy responses are seldom clear-cut or obvious. No longer is crime "just a police problem," or education "just a school problem," or economic development "just a problem of attracting new industries." Each has multiple interrelated causes, creates ripple effects that spread out over historically separate institutions and jurisdictions, and generates competing and conflicting perspectives on what should be done to improve the situation. One result is that there is seldom a natural consensus on how to approach critical public problems. Policy leadership thus requires a communication and decisionmaking process—a policy discourse—that engages many diverse interests and perspectives in addressing public problems. Effective policy discourse involves individuals, interest groups, stakeholders, and institutions moving through four unique but interrelated phases: converting a problematic situation to a policy problem, setting policy agendas, making decisions, and taking actions.

Policy leadership occurs when an individual or group focuses attention on an issue or problem and raises it to the public agenda; stimulates collaborative and concerted action among diverse stakeholders to address the issue; and ensures sustained action during implementation. A policy leader in an interconnected public policy context is one who can stimulate collective action toward a particular outcome when no one agency or jurisdiction has enough power—resources, influence, or authority—to dictate solutions unilaterally. Policy leadership is essentially interorganizational or transorganizational in nature, and thus follows different steps and requires different skills than contemporary definitions of organizational leadership and small group leadership.

Leadership in Organizational Contexts

Contemporary theories of leadership, however, focus on organizational and intraorganizational contexts and settings. Historically, leadership research has focused on leadership of groups or teams in organizations by people in positions of organizational authority. During World War II, for example, submarine crews and bomber teams were intensively studied to improve their effectiveness, with group leadership identified as a significant variable in group productivity and morale. Following World War II, the growing interest in productivity in business and industry sparked continued and expanded research on morale, employee motivation, and small group dynamics. Supervisory or managerial leadership was thus initially defined as a process of influence by one individual who steers or motivates other individuals or group members toward a predetermined goal, typically on matters of organizational relevance.

In the mid-1980s, these earlier small group leadership theories gave way to theories on leading a whole organization. These approaches prescribed a set of skills or steps for effective leadership within U.S. organizations, and aimed to help corporate executives to pursue excellence (Peters and Waterman 1982; Peters and Austin 1985), to take charge (Bennis and Nanus 1985), to stimulate extraordinary performance by employees (Kouzes and Posner 1987), or to change an organizational culture by being transformational (Tichy and Devanna 1990). A clear break with past research and writings on small group leadership, the essence was a focus on leadership of an organization, rather than small group leadership within an organization—a process of influencing the organization as a whole, changing and adapting organizations to better fit and perform in the complex, global environment in which corporations exist. Three of the more common theories of organizational leadership are transformational leadership, visionary leadership, and charismatic leadership.

Transformational Leadership

A wide-ranging and historical analysis of political and social leadership by Burns (1978) identifies two different forms of leadership in society throughout history: transformational and transactional. Transactional leadership involves some form of exchange between the leader and follower, such as wages, gifts, votes, prestige, advancement, or other valued things, in exchange for the individual following the leader's wishes or meeting the leader's objectives. The exchange can be economic, political, or even psychological. Other than exchanging things of value, the bargainers have no enduring purpose to hold them together. Transformational leadership, on the other hand, involves a leader drawing followers out of a narrow, parochial interest into a "higher" purpose. Rather than exchanging one thing for another in a process of bargaining, a transformational leader engages followers by tapping their existing and potential motives and aspirations, and then through inspiration, teaching, and modeling transforms them into higher order needs and visions for the purpose of achieving intended change.

It is transforming in that the leader transforms or elevates the followers' interests from self-oriented ends to mission-oriented ends. As a result, leaders and followers experience a shared sense of fates and interdependence of interests, where the higher aspirations of both the leader and follower congeal into one. In an organizational setting, two different descriptions of transformational leadership have emerged, both building on the historical analysis by Burns. The first focuses on leadership that transforms employee performance from the expected to performance beyond expectations, using transformational leadership strategies that engender high performance levels within organizations (Bass 1990). Although there are different transformational leadership styles, they each include four common characteristics that transform followers in this fashion: charisma, inspiration, individualized consideration, and intellectual stimulation. The other transformational approach to leadership highlights strategies to transform organizations in response to the complex and rapidly changing environments that organizations face. Tichy and Devanna (1990) identified three strategies that successful corporate leaders utilize in transforming their organizations to respond to new markets and vastly increase competitiveness: recognize the need for revitalization, create a motivating vision, and create a new organizational architecture that institutionalizes change.

Visionary Leadership

The emphasis on having a compelling vision is a central theme in transformational leadership. Other leadership approaches similarly highlight the importance of visionary leadership, beginning with Berlew (1974), who noted that leadership that "excited" organizational members was one that offered a vision for the organization and which expressed a set of common values and goals. Focus on visionary leadership increased in the mid-1980s and highlighted the need for a compelling, persuasive vision in order to mobilize organizational members to move from where they are to where they have never been but need to go according to the leader's assessment of the situation. Although vision is defined in several different, but related, ways, the central ingredient of visionary leadership is the articulation of a compelling vision that attracts, excites, and animates followers in pursuit of an organizational common goal (Bennis and Nanus 1985).

Charismatic Leadership

The notion of charisma, Greek for "divine gift," captures a third general theory of organizational leadership. Traditionally, a charismatic leader was an individual who had considerable emotional power over followers, particularly in times of crisis that required strong direction. The followers' bond was highly emotional, and the leader relied on this power to influence followers' actions. More recently, charismatic leadership is characterized by a leader-follower bond where the leader grips followers with a specific vision for action or by other means than merely emotional appeals to survive a crisis. A charismatic leader is one who has a strong vision or mission, who produces high levels of personal loyalty and commitment to his or her vision or mission, who is perceived as exceptional and extraordinary, and who therefore enjoys the personal devotion of a large portion of the organizational membership (Bryman 1992).

Common Themes in Contemporary Definitions of Organizational Leadership

Leadership is one of the most studied concepts in the world today. With only a few exceptions, however, the focus is almost entirely on leadership performed by individuals within formal organizations. These three general theories—transformational, visionary, and charismatic—are the most recent perspectives used to analyze and illuminate the types of leadership required for improving organizational performance in a turbulent, unpredictable, and global economy. The three approaches interrelate and overlap, but with only minor differences and emphases: each recognizes that a leader is an instrument of organizational change and prescribes a common set of skills or actions necessary to successfully renew, revitalize, or enliven organizations:

- Having a strong and compelling vision that challenges the status quo, and takes an organization to a new place it has never been;
- Infusing the vision in a way that inspires and motivates employees throughout the organization, dramatically influencing followers to perform in goal-directed ways;
- Empowering others and enlisting followers in the vision to stimulate extra effort to achieve it;
- Developing mutual trust and personal loyalty between the leader and followers.

Leadership in Public Policy Contexts

Leadership outside organizational contexts—policy leadership that targets solving complex, boundaryless public problems in highly interconnected policy arenas—is less well understood and much less researched. Leadership for public policy occurs outside of organizational boundaries—is intergovernmental and intersectoral in nature—and therefore faces constraints and challenges substantially different than those facing contemporary organizational leadership. Richard Neustadt, a noted presidential scholar, pessimistically noted that the constraints and challenges for contemporary presidential leadership are much different than ever before in history and are characterized by at least three interconnected restraints (1991): telecommunications media, particularly television, that encourage leaders to strike poses rather than address real issues; the declining power of political parties and increasing interest group pressure to pursue more narrow agendas; and hardening institutional boundaries between the White House and Congress. Histories and analyses of U.S. presidential and congressional leadership have provided some insights into political leadership at the national level, but are less clear on the steps or tasks needed today for policy leadership.

External Constraints in Providing Policy Leadership

Government executives tend to be driven by the constraints imposed from outside the organization, rather than the unique mission and tasks of the agency (Wilson 1989). First, public problems cross jurisdictional, organizational, and functional boundaries, and are interconnected with other problems. Most public problems are so complex and interconnected, and power to solve the problem is so shared and disbursed (Bryson and Crosby 1992), that no single person, agency, or jurisdiction has sufficient power or authority to develop and implement policy solutions unilaterally.

Second, public policies on any particular issue can affect an increasingly larger number of agencies and constituencies, and perceived adverse effects can evoke widespread resistance. In many Western countries, people's trust and confidence in the ability of government, and of leaders, to solve problems effectively has declined to perhaps the lowest it has ever been. As a result, there is an increasing number and diversity of impassioned activists, special interests, and legitimate agencies and institutions who seek involvement in the development and formulation of public policy, and who can apply considerable resistance to policy change.

Policy leadership is thus provided within a unique interorganizational web of political, economic, environmental, social, and technological concerns; and addressing public problems in such an interconnected policy arena requires many individuals and groups to be involved, decreasing the ability of any one individual, agency, or institution to mobilize a sufficient number of individuals behind any particular policy agenda.

Four Essential Tasks in Policy Leadership

Policy leadership, therefore, is a form of leadership that works in political and interorganizational contexts where authority is shared and power is disbursed in a community, region, and country. In such contexts, policy leadership involves four specific, but interrelated, tasks for developing policy responses aimed at pressing public problems:

1. Raise the issue on the public and policy agendas by focusing attention on the issue or problematic condition;
2. Convene the set of individuals, agencies and interests—stakeholders and knowledgeholders—needed to address the issue;
3. Forge agreements on policy alternatives and viable options for action;

4. Sustain action and maintain momentum during implementation.

Each of these four essential tasks summarizes, in shorthand, a more complex set or pattern of activities and processes commonly found in successful policy leadership efforts. However, it must be emphasized that the policy leadership process is not sequential, nor a formal linear model.

Raise the Issue to the Public and Policy Agendas

Effective policy leaders intervene into the policy arena by first directing attention toward an undesirable condition or problem, defining and framing the issue in ways that can mobilize others around the search for responses. The initial step in policy leadership is to act as a "catalyst" focusing the attention of the public, government officials, and members and leaders of many separate organizations and agencies, as well as the broader community of interests. They promote a new issue to higher prominence, or get people to see an old problem in new ways. Because the full list of potential problems requiring public attention is vast, and resources to address each problem are limited, policy leaders fix attention on a particular problem, making the issue more salient, important, and urgent than other issues that may be competing for attention and resources.

Policy Agenda Setting. There exists two types of policy agendas, each encompassing a smaller set of issues (Cobb and Elder 1983). The systemic or public agenda is the larger set of problems or societal concerns that the general public is paying some serious attention to at any given time. There is a smaller, more formal governmental or policy agenda that includes issues being paid serious attention by people in and around government. (A smaller subset of the policy agenda, the decision agenda, includes an even narrower set of issues, alternatives, and policy choices being actively discussed and considered.) Agenda setting is a prelude to policy action. Policy leaders raise an issue in a way that commands increasing attention and increases the likelihood that key stakeholders will either be recruited or attracted to address the issue.

Agenda Setting Is Unpredictable. Policy ideas typically reach a stage of "common currency" and then fade into the background, following a general pattern of appreciation, articulation, debate, adoption, institutionalization, and decay (Schon 1971). However, there is no one single factor which places an issue or problem high on the public, policy, or decision agendas.

Analysis of U.S. federal policy development reveals that agenda setting does not go through a rational, problem-solving process that proceeds neatly in stages, steps, or phases (Kingdon 1984). Rather, there are separate, independent streams of problems, proposed solutions, and politics occurring simultaneously but separately on specific problems, and at some critical point, or succession of points, a catalytic effect occurs, pushing one problem higher on the agenda, and displacing other issues from prominence.

Life Cycle of Issues. Yankelovich (1992) further clarified this life cycle of issues; analyzing the cycle of public opinion and attitudes (expressed in national opinion polls) of two specific issues—AIDS and the "greenhouse effect"—he found that issues reached the public agenda, or what he called the "public consciousness," in widely variable times, from minutes to decades. Although he found that there was a vast variability in the amount of time required for each issue to reach the public agenda, he found some common features: an event that forcefully dramatizes an issue and serves to focus attention, perceived applicability to one's self, the concreteness and clarity to the general public of the issue, the credibility of the sources of information the public receives, and the quantity of publicity the issue generates.

These analyses reveal that issues go through three phases to reach a prominent point on the policy agenda: starting as a condition or latent concern, it rises to the public's attention as a problem when there is sufficient dissatisfaction with the condition. Finally, it becomes an issue that is seen as urgent and pressing, generating political attention and displacing other issues from the policy agenda.

Often, issues move forward on the policy agenda due to the opening of policy windows which are taken advantage of by policy leaders. There are three types of policy windows: those opened by the sudden publicity and emergence of a pressing public problem, those opened by significant political shifts, and windows opened as a result of key decision points being reached (Bryson and Crosby 1992). After the issue has reached the policy agenda, however, attention does not remain sharply focused for a long period of time. It will eventually fade from public attention, even if largely unresolved, and will be replaced by another pressing and urgent issue (Bryson and Crosby 1992; Downs 1972).

Salience, Urgency, and the Use of Stories. Policy leaders focus attention on a condition or problem in such a way that others embrace the issue as a priority. Data is often used to highlight "troubling comparisons"—differing employment rates between regions or states, for example—or to show "worsening trends"—for example, dramatic increases in juvenile crime over the last several years. Data may convince some that an issue is urgent; however, data does not necessarily make a condition or problem salient or tangible. Information is more salient and vivid when it conjures up images, is easy to imagine, is easy to explain or elaborate, and is more likely to be recalled. Vivid information such as stories and anecdotes are thus given greater weight than mere data because it captures one's attention and remains in one's thoughts for longer periods of time—for example when one hears about a neighbor being a victim of juvenile crime—and is particularly salient if the story depicts causal relationships (Nutt 1989)—for example, when a personal story also includes very tangible reasons why juvenile crime is increasing significantly in one's particular neighborhood.

Convening Stakeholders to Address the Issue

Once this issue is on the policy agenda, the second task of policy leadership is to convene the diverse set of people and interests—stakeholders, knowledgeholders, and decisionmakers—needed to stimulate collective action to address the issue. Policy leaders bring people together, different factions with often different perspectives and different sensitivities, to address an undesirable condition, problem area, or urgent issue.

There is a wide variety of ways that collective efforts are successfully mobilized, including, for example, advocacy coalitions, collaborative alliances, issue-oriented networks, political action committees, and stakeholder groups. Some are more formal and permanent, while many are temporary and ad hoc; each, however, attempts to convene major stakeholders, knowledgeholders, and decisionmakers to address an issue they consider problematic in some way. Successful efforts are tailored to the unique local circumstances of that issue (Bryson et al. 1990) as well as to the broader environment and national context in which the particular issue is embedded (Gray and Hay 1986).

There are two distinct approaches to convening critical stakeholders around policy issues: one approach is to organize around the problem. Here, policy leaders do not promote solutions; they promote problems. Rather than convening around specific policy alternatives, they mobilize a group around doing something about a problem in a certain direction. This is a policy issue approach where individuals are mobilized around an issue, rather than mobilizing around a particular solution, and they have a passionate stake in getting an issue addressed, but do not necessarily have a strong stake in any particular way to solve the problem (Luke 1997). The second approach is to convene around particular solutions, and is followed by policy entrepreneurs who champion a particular policy response, and mobilize interest and develop coalitions around a particular proposed policy already deemed feasible for addressing the problem (Kingdon 1984; Roberts and King 1989). Mobilizing and coalition-building are common strategies that are used—in addition to political bargaining, trade-offs, and other sorts of compromise strategies—to win support for one's position or preferred solution.

Mobilizing Participation. Whether following the issue approach or the solution approach, policy leaders use their knowledge of the issue domain, their knowledge of stakeholders' interests and interrelationships, personal contacts in related networks, personal charm, and available authority to convince key stakeholders that participation in the effort is worthy of their involvement. One's willingness to respond to the recruitment efforts, and join in a policy development effort, is typically explained in terms of whether stakeholders and knowledgeholders feel they (a) have something to gain by participating, or (b) something to lose if they do not participate. Closer analysis, however, reveals that willingness to participate is more detailed and linked to

- perceptions of positive benefits relative to personal or organizational interests;
- perceptions of interdependence with other stakeholders or groups in dealing with the issue—it can't be accomplished independently;
- perceptions of convenors' legitimacy and credibility;
- perceptions of other stakeholders' legitimacy, power, and resources.

There are also common reasons for unwillingness or inability to join including potential loss of power, and ideological or cultural differences that create uncompromising conflict in core values.

Convenor Legitimacy. The critical factor in mobilizing participation is convenor legitimacy (Gray and Hay 1986). Without adequate legitimacy by the policy leader, the participation and commitment of stakeholders and knowledgeholders is unlikely to materialize. A convenor can be an individual, an existing group, or agency, and does not necessarily have to be a stakeholder in the particular issue domain; but as a convenor, the policy leader must be perceived as legitimate, having sufficient credibility to elicit the participation of key stakeholders and knowledgeholders. Legitimacy comes from several sources: a perceived expertise and knowledge in the issue area; an ability to be evenhanded, characterized by a willingness to consider diverse points of view, but not necessarily unbiased; competence in group facilitation and group processes; a formal or informal position of authority and influence that is recognized by potential participants; and a reputation, history, or track record of successful collaborative efforts that were not merely a vehicle for private gain.

Forge Agreements on Policy Options and Alternatives

Policy leaders convene stakeholders and knowledgeholders and then help convert and transform their concerns for the issue into viable policy responses. This is a critical dimension of policy leadership, and is best characterized as multiparty problem solving among diverse interests that results in the development of multiple strategies to achieve agreed-upon outcomes. The substantial amount of research on collaboration and multiparty problem-solving, however, clearly shows that there is no one theoretical perspective nor single model that guides this direction-setting process among diverse stakeholders.

Forging agreement on policy options and strategies among diverse stakeholders does not follow the textbook notion of a comprehensively rational process—for example, beginning with problem definition to clarify the issue one is trying to change, followed by the generation of a wide variety and comprehensive array of possible strategies for resolving this issue. Finally, following the rational model, an optimal course of action is selected, based on well-defined criterion of preference, from the set of alternatives already identified.

The specific process followed by successful groups is unique and tailored to each situation. The process for generating and selecting appropriate policy responses to public problems seldom, if ever, follows an undisturbed progression through a series of rational, concrete steps which kick in sequentially one after another. Research clearly indicates that there is no single model of policy formulation, no exact order of decisionmaking steps, nor a common set of sequential stages that are followed in designing and selecting strategies for addressing public problems (Wood and Gray 1991; Gersick 1988; Mintzberg et al. 1976). Rather, it is more like a stream of individual subdecisions and multiple iterations between information gathering and processing, generating and exploring options, narrowing down, and selecting options.

Essential Routines in the Policy Development Process

Although the process does not progress through a universal sequence of stages or common set of steps, the policy development process is amenable to some conceptual structuring, and revolves around essentially three common or core routines. Communication dominates each of these distinct tasks, yet the core decisionmaking routines are interdependent and occur in a reiterative fashion, and include direction setting, option generating, and analyzing and selecting policy options.

Direction Setting. Direction setting involves two related tasks: defining and clarifying the issue, and identifying the outcomes or results desired from a policy response. The hardest part of forging agreement on policy options is agreeing on what the problem is; people are unlikely to find or agree on solutions in the absence of an agreed-upon understanding of the problem (Bryson and Crosby 1992). The original issue or problematic condition that mobilized stakeholders is often too ill-defined initially by the group to generate immediate agreement on policy responses. Further, individuals see the problem differently based on their experience, circumstances, and interests. Particularly with complex, interconnected problems—where responsibilities for and causes of problems are indefinite—individuals within a particular "policy system" typically define the problem in a fashion that is optimal to them or their agency (Milward 1982), that ensures one particular solution is considered while obscuring or eliminating other potential solutions, protects an agency's turf, or reflects the way in which a particular agency or stakeholder group collects and analyzes its information (Fischoff 1985).

Disagreements about the definition of the problem are central elements of intense policy debates because different definitions of a problem suggest different strategies for resolving it (Fischoff 1983). In fact, if there is strong conflict around the definition of the problem, with multiple competing definitions, no action will likely be taken (Cobb and Elder 1983). Or, they may turn to the least controversial way to define the problem, which is most likely not the best problem statement for generating innovative and effective alternative strategies (Volkema 1983). Policy leadership thus requires careful defining and framing of the problem in ways that motivate action and mobilize a coalition of stakeholders large enough to secure adoption and implementation of preferred solutions (Bryson and Crosby 1992).

Option Generation. A major barrier to effective option development is inadequate consideration of alternatives. For example, most groups generate only one alternative which receives serious consideration; full and open searches for options are often avoided because of the potential to expand conflict and delay agreement (Nutt 1989). The task of policy leadership is to encourage and stimulate a broader, more systematic search and analysis process that generates multiple options for consideration. Options are generated in two ways: first, by searching for existing ideas, proposals, programs, and strategies that can readily, or with modification, be applied; and second by inventing or designing new strategies, custom-made in order to reach the desired outcome.

Searching. In many cases, policy alternatives already exist in the "policy primeval soup" where solutions to public problems float around, bumping into one another, forming combinations and recombinations (Kingdon 1984). Policy development targeting critical public problems more often resembles this process of "recombination," the coupling and blending of already familiar elements (Kingdon 1984).

Designing and Crafting Policies. Another method for generating potential options is the design of a custom-made policy option. In policy development, this custom-design approach is less frequently used than the recombination approach (Kingdon 1984) due to its time-consuming, and sometimes expensive, nature. In custom design, workgroup members begin with a general notion of a comprehensive strategy to achieve the outcome, engage in a sequence of reiterative design and search cycles, and build a strategy brick by brick, with the workgroup not really knowing what the strategy will look like until it is nearly completed (Mintzberg et al. 1976). This option generation method typically produces only one fully developed strategy because most workgroups are unable to spend enough resources to generate more than one alternative.

Selecting Policy Options. The process of selecting one policy response over other options is not purely rational or analytical; selecting strategies always contains elements of personality, emotions, bargaining, and power. It is essentially a social and political process as well as an intellectual task, which reflects consideration of multiple constituencies, competing values and interests, and specific criteria. Using structured approaches based on problem solving and resolving conflict are more effective in stimulating committed and sustained action than are approaches using coercion or compromise (Bryson et al. 1990). The political process in policy development revolves around the persuasion of preferred courses for action; the use of specific criteria in selecting a preferred policy response can reduce dependence on political solutions and can facilitate wider agreement on policy options.

Criteria. Decisionmakers only use a few evaluation criteria to judge and select strategies (Nutt 1989), and typically use four interdependent categories. Conflicting criteria do not necessarily have to be reconciled for agreement, and neither must key stakeholders be equally enthusiastic for each criteria; however, the extent to which all four are discussed and considered enhances the selection process.

Impact criteria seek to assess whether a policy option strategically targets causes rather than symptoms, and impacts change over the long run. Although there are multiple linkages, and multiple causes, not all are equal in influencing the particular public issue. Systemically, there are a few causes that are more impactful and influential in addressing the problem; and some policy responses will more effectively achieve the outcome over the long run because of a more direct causal linkage.

Interest-based criteria seek policy responses based on common or similar interests that will generate sufficient commitment to ensure implementation. Even when interests are not common or similar, they may be complementary and noncompeting. When interests are truly in conflict, there are also strategies where stakeholders can "trade" or bargain things that are valued differently, trading less important items for more important ones (Susskind and Cruikshank 1987).

Resource criteria are used to judge whether there are sufficient resources that can be generated and leveraged to implement the policy. Financial resources are always a primary criterion; seldom is there sufficient funding available to fully fund all potentially effective policy options. The resources necessary to take action, however, are more broadly defined as information, expertise, funding, and competencies.

Policies to address public problems generate varying levels of public acceptance and political support. Public acceptance and *political criteria* therefore evaluate whether the policy option will be acceptable politically and publicly. Public acceptance requires both intellectual and emotional acceptance (Yankelovich 1992), while acceptance by elected officials is facilitated when the policy response satisfies their key constituents, enhances reelection prospects, and appears to be "good public policy" without being too controversial (Kingdon 1984).

Authorization and Adoption. Once sufficient agreement is forged to commit to one policy option, or a set of policy options—a "strategic portfolio"—attention turns to discussions of outsiders' expectations and to the preparing, editing, and packaging of written materials (Gersick 1988). The workgroup must seek and secure authorization in either general or specific terms if individual members do not have the authority to commit critical actors and agencies to the courses of action. Seeking permission or authorization is critical to success and involves such mobilizing strategies as developing sponsors and champions, building networks and coalitions, and gaining access to the formal agenda of the necessary decisionmaking arenas (Bryson and Crosby 1992).

Policy Implementation: Sustaining Action and Maintaining Momentum

Policy adoption is followed by implementation of the policy—either all at once or in stages—and evaluation of the policy changes. Finally, the policies are reviewed by leaders and subsequently maintained, modified, or terminated (Bryson and Crosby 1992). Policy implementation, however, is more complex and difficult than historically assumed, and in most cases, the real task of policy leadership is not in policy adoption or approval but in ensuring its implementation. Solving policy problems requires sustained attention and effort by numerous and diverse policy actors and agencies, most of whom are independent of each other; it is thus easy for the momentum required for successful implementation to fade and for sustained action to fail. The rate of failure of many policies is high—from major policy reform in developing countries and ambitious social welfare mandates in the U.S. to more local efforts of improving community livability

Unfortunately, the research on implementation focuses predominantly on program and project implementation, rather than policy implementation; nevertheless, general tasks have been derived for the successful implementation of public policy. For example, policy leadership stimulates implementation and sustains action by

- gaining support and legitimation for the policy;
- building constituents to ensure that supportive coalitions will advocate and champion continued implementation (Sabatier 1988);
- establishing appropriate implementation structures or "action vehicles" (Kanter 1983) to institutionalize the policy;
- accumulating and mobilizing resources;
- managing the interorganizational relationships through rapid information sharing and feedback, producing visible successes and small wins (Weick 1984); and
- maintaining a policy learning approach or adaptive learning posture to monitoring implementation.

Policy Legitimation. Policy implementation will not go forward without policy legitimation. Unless the policy is viewed as legitimate by key decisionmakers, significant movement will not occur. Policy leadership requires an individual or agency to assume the role of policy champion, asserting and persuading that the policy is necessary, vital, and workable. An excellent example is the transition in Eastern European countries from socialist or state-driven economies to more market-oriented economies that occurred in the 1990s. Respected and credible policy leaders with substantial political capital were necessary to initiate the changeover, and policy legitimation confronted a vast array of entrenched interests with much to lose in the economic reform (Crosby 1993). Regardless of the popular sentiments within the countries toward a market economy, without such policy legitimation by credible policy leaders, the reform would not have gone forward.

Building Constituent Support and Advocacy Coalitions. Action cannot be sustained solely on the shoulders of the policy champion. Successful implementation requires that an adequate constituency be developed to support and sustain the policy, and that strong advocacy coalitions be created and maintained. Constituents are typically those who benefit by the new policy; for example, they are the principle clients affected by the policy, or individuals who will have their status or position enhanced by the policy changes, or groups who can bring some sort of resource to its implementation (Crosby 1993). Coalitions are organized around common interests, and can provide a valuable source of energy for implementation. Constituent groups and advocacy coalitions are positive stakeholders which lend force to policy champions, and amplify the legitimation process. Yet their purpose is not merely to gain support and acceptance from the wider environment; rather it is to operationalize the policy through the creation of new beneficiaries and advocates who can sustain the new policy (Crosby 1993).

Implementation Structures. Public policies must be institutionalized if new ways of doing things are to be practiced and expected to become the norm. Mechanisms to institutionalize the new policy are required and become the "action vehicles" (Kanter 1983) to implement and sustain momentum. Ongoing institutional commitment is critical to sustain implementation, and a wide variety of mechanisms are used, from informal networks, partnership agreements (such as joint powers agreements and memoranda of understanding), and formal interorganizational networks to strategic alliances. Solving policy problems requires sustained attention and efforts, often by multiple and independent agencies which transcend a single organizational authority structure, and the more complex policies can further require systemic changes based on shared interests and new levels of interaction. Some sort of institutional structure is thus needed to orchestrate and sustain the ongoing involvement of the multiple agencies, to institutionalize new procedures and communication channels, and to provide new incentives and rewards.

Resource Accumulation and Mobilization. There is always competition for scarce resources in public policy, and successful implementation can easily fail if sufficient human, technical, and financial resources are not allocated or reallocated. The challenge goes beyond securing initial funding, but also requires that the policy has a legitimate and sustained place in agencies' resource allocation process. Even when sufficient resources are accumulated, they must be mobilized in appropriate directions and moved into the right places to implement the policy. Resource mobilization and reallocation often causes the most resistance (Crosby 1993), and may include the elimination of existing programs or functions; realignment of human and material resources to fit the new policy; or the modification or creation of entirely new incentive mechanisms to facilitate action within the new policy framework.

Rapid Information Sharing and Feedback. Successful implementation fundamentally requires information and feedback to assess whether the policy is being implemented as expected, and whether the results produced by the policy are the ones intended. Such information collection is problematic since there is always some time delay between when the change begins and when results can be noticed. Clear milestones for monitoring and reviewing progress, however, must be developed, based on the regular collection and analysis of outcome information, not just activity information. Multiple measures are necessary because no single indicator can provide an accurate picture, and because appropriate measures vary from agency to agency and jurisdiction to jurisdiction. The rapid sharing and feedback of the information is also critical; momentum will not be sustained if real accomplishments are not revealed through data collection. Visible successes and small wins (Weick 1984) maintain focus on the desired outcomes, build confidence, draw attention to new directions resulting from the new policy, and build support and momentum.

Maintaining a Policy Learning Approach. Successful implementation requires not only active guidance to assure and monitor performance, but also adaptation, adjustments, and ongoing learning. In addition, policies should be viewed as experimental attempts to resolve public problems, not the final solution. Effective policy leadership exhibits a "policy-oriented learning" perspective during implementation; as events unfold, and as unanticipated "policy windows" open, policy leaders adapt earlier decisions and actions to the new information generated and take advantage of opportunities that emerge. A policy learning approach to implementation enhances the potential for comparing the results of alternate policy strategies, and learning which policies have bigger impacts on reaching the desired results.

Policy Leadership Skills Are Different

Leadership for pursuing organizational goals is different than leadership in policy arenas that transcend individual organizations—where public problems are defined, addressed, and solved by a multiplicity of diverse and often conflicting stakeholders. In such settings, interorganizational or policy leadership is necessary for bringing an issue or problem to the public agenda, stimulating collaborative and concerted action among diverse stakeholders to address the issue, and ensuring sustained action during implementation. It is a type of leadership that can move diverse, often competing groups toward workable consensus on complex, interconnected problems.

Policy leadership emphasizes stimulating action by diverse groups and interests toward agreed-upon outcomes, and is thus different from organizational leadership, which focuses on influencing organizational members (followers) to achieve organizational improvements. Policy leadership is interorganizational in nature, and at a minimum requires an ability to think strategically about how public issues can be raised to the policy agenda; an ability to foster dialogue and agreement by multiple agencies on appropriate policy responses; and an ability to sustain policy action over time.

Bibliography

Bass, Bernard M., 1990. *Bass and Stogdill's Handbook of Leadership: Theory Research, and Managerial Applications*. 3d ed. New York: Free Press.

Berlew, D. E., 1974. "Leadership and Organizational Excitement." *California Management Review*, 17:21–30.

Bennis, Warren and Burt Nanus, 1985. *Leaders: The Strategies for Taking Charge*. New York: Harper and Row.

Bryman, Alan, 1992. *Charisma and Leadership in Organizations*. Newbury, CA: Sage Publications.

Bryson, John, P. Bromiley and Y. S. Jung, 1990. "Influences of Context and Process on Project Planning Success." *Journal of Planning Education and Research*, 9(3): 183–195.

Bryson, John and Barbara Crosby, 1992. *Leadership for the Common Good*. San Francisco: Jossey Bass.

Burns, James McGregor, 1978. *Leadership*. New York: Harper and Row.

Cobb, R. and C. Elder, 1983. *Participation in American Politics: The Dynamics of Agenda Building*. Baltimore: Johns Hopkins University Press.

Crosby, Benjamin, 1993. "Policy Implementation and Strategic Management: The Challenge of Implementing Policy Change." Washington, D.C.: Implementing Policy Change Project.

Downs, Anthony, 1972. "Up and Down with Ecology—The Issue Attention Cycle." *Public Interest*, vol. 12: 38–50.

Fischoff, Baruch, 1983. "Strategic Policy Preferences: A Behavioral Decision Theory Perspective." *Journal of Social Issues*, vol. 39, no. 1: 133–160.

______, 1985. "Managing Risk Perception." *Issues in Science and Technology*, vol. 2: 83–96.

Gersick, Connie, 1988. "Time and Transition in Work Teams: Toward a New Model of Group Development." *Academy of Management Journal*, 31(1): 9–41.

______, 1989. "Marking Time: Predictable Transitions in Task Groups." *Academy of Management Journal*, 32(2): 274–309.

Gray, B. and T. M. Hay, 1986. "Political Limits to Interorganizational Consensus and Change." *Journal of Applied Behavioral Science*, vol. 22: 95–112.

Kanter, Rosabeth Moss, 1983. *The Change Masters*. New York: Simon & Schuster.

Kingdon, J., 1984. *Agendas, Alternatives and Public Policy*. Boston: Little, Brown.

Kouzes, J.M. and B.Z. Posner, 1987. *The Leadership Challenge*. San Francisco: Jossey-Bass.

Luke, Jeffrey, 1997. *Catalytic Leadership: Strategies for an Interconnected World*. San Francisco: Jossey-Bass

Milward, H. B., 1982. "Interorganizational Policy Systems and Research on Public Organizations." *Administration and Society*, 13(4): 457–478.

Mintzberg, H., D. Raisnghani and A. Theoret, 1976. "The Structure of 'Unstructured' Decision Processes." *Administrative Science Quarterly* vol. 21 (June) 246–275.

Neustadt, R. E., 1991. *Presidential Power and Modern Presidents*. New York: Free Press.

Nutt, Paul, 1989. *Making Tough Decisions*. San Francisco: Jossey Bass.

Pasquero, Jean, 1991. "Superorganizational Collaboration: The Canadian Environmental Experiment." *Journal of Applied Behavioral Science*, vol. 27, no. 2 (June) 38–64.

Peters, Thomas J. and R.H. Waterman, Jr., 1982. *In Search of Excellence*. New York: Harper & Row.

Peters, Thomas J. and Nancy Austin, 1985. "A Passion for Excellence." *Fortune* (May 13) 20–32.

Polsby, N. W., 1984. *Political Innovation in America: The Politics of Policy Initiation*. New Haven, CT: Yale University Press.

Roberts, Nancy and R. T. Bradley, 1991. "Stakeholder Collaboration and Innovation: A Study of Public Policy Initiation at the State Level." *Journal of Applied Behavioral Science*, vol. 27, no. 2 (June) 209–227.

Roberts, N. and P. King, 1989. "Stakeholder Audit Goes Public." *Organizational Dynamics* (Winter) 63–79.

Sabatier, P. A., 1988. "An Advocacy Coalition Framework of Policy Change and the Role of Policy-Oriented Learning Therein." *Policy Sciences*, vol. 21: 129–168.

Schon, Donald, 1971. *Beyond the Stable State*. New York: Norton.

Susskind, L. and J. Cruikshank, 1987. *Breaking the Impasse*. New York: Basic Books.

Tichy, Noel M. and Mary Anne Devanna, 1990. *The Transformational Leader*. New York: John Wiley & Sons.

U.S. Advisory Commission on Intergovernmental Relations, 1992. *Changing Public Attitudes on Governments and Taxes: 1989–1992*. Washington, D.C.: U.S. Government Printing Office.

Volkema, Roger, 1983. "Problem Formulation in Planning and Design." *Management Science* 29(6): 639–652.

Weick, K. E., 1984. "Small Wins: Redefining the Scale of Social Problems." *American Psychologist*, vol. 39, no. 1 (January) 40–49.

Wilson, James Q., 1989. *Bureaucracy: What Government Agencies Do and Why They Do It*. New York: Basic Books.

Wood, Donna and Barbara Gray, 1991. "Toward a Comprehensive Theory of Collaboration." *Journal of Applied Behavioral Science*, vol. 27, no. 2 (June) 139–162.

Yankelovich, D., 1992. "How Public Opinion Really Works." *Fortune* (October 5).

6

Policy Network

Charles J. Fox,
Texas Tech University

Hugh T. Miller,
Florida Atlantic University

An assortment of inter-related policy actors interested—for civic, professional, intellectual, or selfish reasons—in pursuing a matter of public policy. The concept policy networks evolved from related notions such as policy subsystems, issue networks, cozy triangles, and iron triangles. All of these phrases depict policymaking processes that reside outside the formal categories of the representative government model. From the vantage point of public administration they are significant because they imply the presence of political administration as opposed to neutral, scientific administration.

Iron Triangles and Economic Interests

Though policy networks are conceptually more sophisticated than notions of iron triangles, it is useful to rehearse the lineage because much of the conceptualization behind iron triangles remains relevant to the meaning of policy networks. Political scientists noted the presence of informal relationships among governmental and nongovernmental agents, an awareness that followed on the heels of an increased awareness of the roles of lobbyists and special interest groups in the governing process. The attempts of journalists writing in newspaper columns to popularize awareness of this pattern of informal relationships led to metaphorical terms such as iron triangles or cozy triangles. Iron triangles referred to not quite legitimate policy processes wherein (1) lobbyists representing special interest groups, (2) staff from a government agency, and (3) members/staff of congressional committees and subcommittees collaborate in ways mutually beneficial to them, but not to the citizenry as a whole. At each point in the triangle, actors are presumed to be motivated by material self-interest or by the economic interests of the organizations they represent. Specifically, congressional representatives are presumed to seek campaign contributions, agency representatives seek budgetary approvals, and interest groups seek favorable legislation leading to government outlays or agreeable regulations. These triangles are sometimes termed cozy because in the process of mutual influence, services are performed, information is exchanged, and relationships are built. They were iron triangles because the relationships were perceived to be so strong and durable that legitimate policymaking processes—whereby legislators are beholden only to voters and to the public interest—are effectively preempted. These images of cozy, iron triangles connote the presence of fragmented yet dominant elite groups who manipulate public policy on behalf of private interests.

All players are presumed to be utility maximizers (that is, rational and self-interested). The governmental agency—along with the legislature and lobbyists—is also conceptualized as a utility-maximizing, self-interested player seeking aggrandizement and expansion of turf in the cozy/iron triangle framework.

Looking at the informal interactions through the lens of issue networks, the above connotations are not self-evident. Again, the underlying assumption of iron triangles is that policy actors wish to maximize self-interest. Iron triangles are arenas for economic exchange. This sort of exchange theory differs markedly from an alternative conception of issue networks as places where intellect, emotion, and values are engaged. By describing these informal interactions as an issue network rather than an iron triangle, Hugh Heclo, in his classic 1978 essay "Issue Networks and the Executive Establishment," introduced a less pejorative view of them. By focusing on a few powerful iron triangles, observers had, according to Heclo, overlooked the multitudinous webs of influence that animate public action and modify the exercise of power. Issue networks are comprised of a large number of participants with varying levels of commitment to the group project and varying degrees of dependence on others in the network. Further, participation is not necessarily based on narrow economic interests. Issue networks have vague boundaries, which for researchers makes them a difficult subject of inquiry. But in practice the ill-defined boundaries make entry into these networks of policy discourse accessible. Participants come and go and may not have coalesced around any particular ideological predisposition. And compared to more structured social systems such as bureaus or corporations, networks appear out of anyone's control. Whether or not any coalition dominates the processes and content of the network is something to be investigated rather than deduced from some arguable theory of human nature. It may be that the glue that holds the network together is a combination of intellectual fascination, emotional commitment, and engagement of one's value system.

Nonetheless, the notion that agencies seek to expand their power and domain represents a feasible hypothesis in explaining agency participation in networks. This assumption—that agencies will maximize self-interests—may be applied when investigating the motives of other participants in the networks as well. Some corporations may rely on governmental agencies and legislative bodies for ensuring a deliberate, paced process free of erratic regulatory demands. The attraction of the policy network may be stable procedure or it may be the possibility of economic gains. For others, the attraction may be the passage of some policy that will enhance their profits or interests. The motivator may be prevention of policy that will detract from their profits or interests. Legislators participate in networks because (from the exchange theory point of view) they need the help of friendly groups who will commit campaign contributions necessary for funding the next electoral campaign. Obviously then, whether the influence of these informal policy subsystems is benign or malignant is a matter of intense debate. The malignant view is usually arrived at by thinking of policy networks as a system of economic exchange. Political scientists were able to offer explanations for why policy turned out the way it did (and why there often was lack of action on proposed legislation) by assuming that all actors were motivated by self-interest to achieve particular ends.

Whether benign or malignant, this network policy process was not the one citizens of the U.S. were brought up to expect: Voters, armed with policy preferences and votes, exercised sovereignty by selecting political candidates who then represented these preferences in the formal legislative arena where policy was formulated and enacted into law. Civil servants were then hired to implement the law. These same civil servants were organized into hierarchical organizations controlled by elected officials, who were in turn controlled by voters. Hence, public administrators were accountable to elected legislators, who were themselves accountable to the voters. The role of public administrators in this democratic accountability model was to implement the legislature's policy pronouncements in a neutrally competent manner. But in policy networks one finds political administration, not neutral administration.

The extent to which issue networks accurately describe the process of policy making is indicative of the extent to which the politics-administration dichotomy lacks viability. To understand policy networks is to uncover a distinctly political relation between democratic-pluralistic politics and the executive establishment. All these network/triangle models challenge traditional notions of how representative government is supposed to work. The strength of these models is that, to some extent at least, they do offer an explanatory description of public policy outcomes and process.

Improved understanding of policy processes may be useful, but many observers have lamented the way political decisionmaking has moved into these informal arenas. The implications of policy networks for democratic theory are weighty.

Theft of Sovereignty

Whether they are called policy issue networks, iron networks, iron triangles, or cozy triangles, their troubling feature is that they presuppose politics, and are therefore regarded by some as a theft from the people of their sovereignty. Theodore Lowi in his influential book *The End of Liberalism* (1969) lamented the interest group liberalism that was the result of the positive government that grew out of the economic hard times of the 1930s, a government whose sphere seemed to be expanding. What had once been liberal programs designed to restore and maintain, say, the economic vitality of farmers whose livelihoods were at risk, had over the years become a series of mechanisms useful only for maintaining the status quo, a conservative function. Farm price supports remain in place thanks to the iron triangle of agricultural agencies, agribusiness lobbies, and legislators from rural farming districts. Rather than continuing to abide informal policy subsystems, Lowi urged that respect for formal institutions of representative democracy be restored. Informal bargaining weakens democracy, according to this view, and gives rise to cynicism and distrust of government. Spreading access to government by informal means was not, for Lowi, an acceptable democratic alternative. Democratic accountability would be problematic under informal government as exemplified by policy networks.

But not everyone saw it that way. There were certain integrative functions that only these loosely organized networks of policy activists could perform.

Policy Networks as Coherent Political-Administrative Process

Informal issue networks have continued to propagate, despite the protestations of governmental formalists, and one explanation for this is that they perform integrative functions necessary to policy formulation and successful implementation. The yearning for a return to the days of formal democracy seemed nostalgic in the face of an ever-increasing presence of organized groups seeking some say-so in public policy debates. The ubiquity of private lobbying organizations as well as a growing intergovernmental web of associations was an increasingly apparent actuality of the public policy process. Throughout the policymaking apparatus of government there were collections of issue-conscious groups influencing events in a complex system of interrelationships. Participants did not necessarily represent monied interests or economic interests, but often brought technical, specialist understanding to questions of policy. Meanwhile, the demand by groups for a place in the policy process did not subside.

Policy networks came to be perceived as more than triumvirates of lobbyists, legislative committees, and executive agencies; more than a raid on the public treasury by privileged networks of venal policy actors. Observers detected crucial integration tasks being performed in policy networks. Policy networks operated as functional subsystems linking program professionals through all levels of government. The presumed autonomy of iron triangles was not in evidence in the functional subsystem conception of policy networks; to the contrary, they were pragmatically indispensable for the coordinative and communicative tasks performed there. Policy networks may be simply a necessary outgrowth of a fragmented polity. Without them policy implementation would be more snarled and jumbled than it is.

The functional utility of policy networks is both political and administrative. They are political in the sense that funds, or regulations, or other policy collateral are extracted from the larger political system. They are administrative in that managerial functions such as coordination, communication, and integration are provided through them. Interorganizational networks link policy actors located at different levels of government, not in a hierarchical way but by virtue of interest, be it economic, professional, or intellectual. The network metaphor directs attention to the relationships between and among political administrators and reconceptualizes the simplistic and reductionist iron triangle metaphor.

Proactive Public Administrators in Political Arenas

Amid the complex of interrelationships, the neat boundaries once presumed to exist between administration and politics break down. The image of public administrators as neutrally competent and possessing a passion for anonymity is difficult to sustain if the policy network model has any credibility. Public administrators who participate in policy networks may be conversant in various networks and knowledgeable about substantive issues, even if they are not conspicuously identifiable with one political position or another.

> The price of buying into one or another issue network is watching, reading, talking about, and trying to act on particular policy problems. Powerful interest groups can be found represented in networks but so too can individuals in or out of government who have a reputation for being knowledgeable. Particular professions may be prominent, but the true experts in the networks are those who are issue-skilled (that is, well-informed about the ins and outs of a particular policy debate) regardless of formal professional training. More than mere technical experts, network people are policy activists who know each other through the issues (Heclo 1978, pp. 102–103).

Though not the sole source of knowledge and ability in a policy network, public administrators are, from the policy network perspective, political administrators. They are activists in their own right. Some writers argue explicitly for an activist posture, as when Michael M. Harmon in 1981 extolled the proactive administrator. Some have urged activism on behalf of social justice, as the new public administration movement did; others have argued for an "entrepreneurial government." Charles J. Fox and Hugh T. Miller (1995) proposed that public administrators be actively involved in policy networks, but conditioned their proposal by offering standards of authentic discourse against which actual policy discourse may be judged democratic or not. Still others contemplate a public conversation involving direct interaction of citizens with agency officials.

Thus public administrators are engaged in "what to do" questions, not only "how" questions. They mobilize key actors and help make policy an actuality. With knowledge as their key asset, uncertainty over the "what to do" question leads others to value their expertise and comprehension of the important dimensions of the problem. Knowledgeable people, along with those who need answers, interact in policy networks. It is here where issues become articulated, evidence debated, and alternative approaches explored.

The network model makes it clear that political interaction is endemic to the craft of public administration. Political administrators frequently find themselves interacting among members of the public, struggling to sort out meanings and values, trying to establish or adjust institutional arrangements, working to route public resources in desired directions. The mutual understandings that stem from the conflict inherent in such undertakings shape subsequent action.

Policy Networks as a Form of Social Organization

Some observers contend that the network form is a third type of social structure, distinct from either markets or hierarchies, two forms of social structure that, rightly or wrongly, dominate theoretical formulations among students of public policy and administration. The nature of the interaction between people is presumed in markets to be driven by rational self-interest. In hierarchies, relations are premised on superior-subordinate obedience. But in networks, the interaction is indeterminate. This indeterminacy possesses some coherence, however. Fox and Miller used the term energy field to allude to a situation which has captivated the intentionalities of policy actors. These policy actors are drawn to some robust, substantive event, and engage in social interaction for the purpose of sense-making and, possibly, policy action. The meaning that persons in the network ascribe to their relationships and activities is not known in advance, but is worked out in situ. Decisions, actions, group conflict, and policy change take place as a consequence of network interactions. As they interact, network participants socially construct meaning and thereby reinforce one another's sense of the importance of the set of issues at hand. Participants may eventually articulate their political demands in ways that can be acted upon. Or, the network may lose its attraction as events and issues lose their salience. With loose boundaries, people can leave. If they stay, there must be some attraction. The policy network model directs attention to the meaning-making taking place among participants, and is less focused than iron triangles on the idealized form of interaction known as rational self-interest.

Bibliography

Fox, Charles J. and Hugh T. Miller, 1995. *Postmodern Public Administration: Toward Discourse*. Thousand Oaks, CA: Sage Publications.

Harmon, Michael M., 1981. *Action Theory for Public Administration*. New York: Longman.

Heclo, Hugh, 1978. "Issue Networks and the Executive Establishment." In Anthony King, ed., *The American Political System*. Washington, D.C.: American Enterprise Institute for Public Policy Research, Ch. 3, pp. 87–124.

Kaufmann, Franz-Xaver, 1991. "The Relationship Between Guidance, Control, and Evaluation." In Franz-Xaver Kaufmann, ed., *The Public Sector: Challenge for Coordination and Learning*. Berlin: Walter de Gruyter.

Lowi, Theodore, 1969. *The End of Liberalism*. New York: Norton.

Miller, Hugh T., 1994. "Post-Progressive Public Administration: Lessons from Policy Networks." *Public Administration Review*, 54(4).

Milward, H. Brinton, and Gary L. Wamsley, 1984. "Policy Subsystems, Networks and the Tools of Public Management." In Robert Eyestone, ed., *Public Policy Formation*. Greenwich, CT: JAI Press, pp. 3–25.

Powell, Walter W., 1990. "Neither Market nor Hierarchy: Network Forms of Organization." *Research in Organizational Behavior*. Greenwich, CT: JAI Press, pp. 295–336.

Smith, Martin J., 1991. "From Policy Communication to Issue Networks: Salmonella in Eggs and the New Politics of Food." *Public Administration*, 69 (Summer) 234–55.

7 — RULE

Cornelius M. Kerwin,
The American University

A binding statement of law or policy issued by an agency of government that establishes future rights, obligations, or procedures.

Rules profoundly influence the conduct and success of public administration in the United States. A good case can be made that rules are the most important products of government agencies. Rules give specific form and meaning to statutory provisions that are often broad, imprecise, and incomplete. In performing this function, rules establish both the benefits one can expect from government and the obligations one bears. Rules, by providing the content of many public programs, also structure their subsequent implementation and administration. In so doing, they channel the expenditure of enormous resources, human and otherwise, in both the public and private sectors. In this way rules are the form of law and public policy that have the most direct, immediate, and profound effect on the performance of public programs, and, ultimately, the quality of life in the United States. Despite concerted efforts over the past two decades to reduce their prominence and impact, rules remain a dominant force in all aspects of U.S. society.

A Definition of Rule

Defining the term "rule" is not a trivial exercise in semantics. On the contrary, when it is determined that an action of the public sector is or will be a rule, the government bears heavy legal obligations to proceed with that action, using certain prescribed techniques. It is important to be quite clear about how one defines what is arguably the most important product of government agencies.

The best starting point in any consideration of the meaning of "rule" is with the authoritative definition of the term found in the Administrative Procedure Act (APA) of 1946 (60 stat. 237; as amended). Its Section 551 (4) states that "rule means the whole or part of an agency statement of general or particular applicability and future effect designed to implement, interpret, or prescribe law or policy." This definition is worthy of careful deconstruction because it, in fact, does contain reference to the most important dimensions of rules.

Agencies as the Sources of Rules

The definition makes it clear that rules are not the products of the major institutions created by the framers in the Constitution. Rules are not written in Congress, by the President, or the courts. Rules are the responsibility of public bureaucracies. Because their authorities and powers are derivative, one generally considers these varied agencies and departments inferior to Congress, the President, and courts. The power to issue rules is, however, a great equalizer. The constitutional branches have recognized the enormous power that agencies can exert through the instrumentality of the rule. These branches struggle mightily with agencies, and with each other, for influence over the content of rules.

Law and Policy as the Proper Subjects of Rules

It is important to note that the Administrative Procedure Act's substantive limits on the contents of rules could not have been written more broadly. This section of the definition confers no independent authority on agencies; all rules must be at least authorized, if not mandated, by congressional legislation. Nevertheless, Congress assumes by the APA that agencies are fully competent to fashion rules in any area of law or policy in which a valid statute exists. A perusal of the *Code of Federal Regulations*, the official compilation of all rules currently in effect, confirms that their substantive range is simply vast.

Implementation, Interpretation, and Prescription: The Functions of Rules

The Administrative Procedure Act established a robust role for rules in the larger political system. Each of these functions is important in its own right, but, taken together, they establish for rules the fullest scope of influence over law and policy. The least influence is felt when rules "implement." This function suggests that rules need add little if any substance to existing law and policy. In this instance, they may provide procedural guidance or minor elaboration on already well-defined terms. When rules "interpret," the role is more substantial. Law and policy may already be well developed and understood, but an effort is required to adapt them to new or unanticipated circumstances. Alternatively, statutory terms may be subject to variable interpretations, and effort is needed to give them a more precise, and authoritative, meaning.

The most dramatic power is in evidence when rules "prescribe." In this instance, congressional statutes establish goals and objectives using obscure, vague, or incomplete language. Rules are then needed to give meaning to terms, such as "healthy" or "safe," that would otherwise be subject to widely divergent interpretations. Rules also provide specific requirements that establish how the defined goals are to be achieved. Political scientist Theodore Lowi (1987) has commented extensively, and critically, of the tendency in landmark regulatory status, such as the Clean Air Act and the Occupational Safety and Health Act, to adopt such language and thus greatly increase the importance of rules. It is when rules prescribe that agencies assume the legislative function most fully. Such uses of delegated authority are destined to be controversial.

General and Particular Applicability: Circumstances Affected by Rules

This element of the APA definition parallels that devoted to subject matter, in that it addresses the range of affected parties and circumstances that rules may affect. Similarly, the APA adopts a comprehensive view of applicability by allowing rules to apply to parties and circumstances ranging from individuals to very large groups. The notion of constructing legislative instruments, be they laws or rules, to benefit or harm individual persons, firms, groups, institutions, or units of government is highly suspect. Such acts that confer benefits may bespeak special privilege or corruption; those bringing harm must confront the constitutional prohibition on bills of attainder.

There is no evidence that the APA intended to promote such questionable practices in rules. Instead, the effect of this element of the definition is to avoid confining rules to those circumstances in which broad categories of parties or circumstances are affected. In this sense, the APA definition anticipated the enormous expansion of governmental activity that occurred in subsequent decades. American society and its economy are now swept broadly and penetrated deeply by contemporary law and public policy. Rules must deal with small segments of the population or sectors of the economy in order to fully interpret, implement, or prescribe law and policy.

Future Effect: Rules and the Legislative Function

Legislation attempts to structure the future, to create conditions that improve the quality of life for citizens. The future orientation of legislation is emphasized in the Constitution, most directly in its prohibition of the enactment of ex post facto legislation. With the phrase "future effect" Congress reinforces the legislative origins, nature, and purposes of rules.

Types of Rules

It should be evident from the foregoing that any attempt to establish a complete and coherent categorization of rules will face daunting obstacles. Nevertheless, there are a variety of approaches that provide some insights, and, taken together, they at least convey the tremendous variety, and volume, of rules.

There are two notable official means of classifying rules. The *Code of Federal Regulations* is organized by titles, each containing a distinct policy area and/or agency of origin and responsibility. The *Code* has 50 such titles and fills hundreds of volumes and thousands of pages. The rules that apply to protection of the environment, for example, can be found in Title 40, while those governing banks and banking are contained in Title 12. Another schema is the three-part categorization of rules found in the Administrative Procedure Act (60 stat. 237; 1946, as amended). The APA, sec. 551, 553, refers to "legislative," "interpretive," and "procedural" rules. These categories correspond roughly to the functions of rules outlined previously. "Legislative" rules are those that prescribe law and policy. The APA adopts this term in recognition that, in these types of rules, agencies are acting clearly as surrogates for Congress. "Interpretive" rules do what the title suggests. "Procedural" rules correspond to one important dimension of the implementation function. These rules establish the internal organization and process of the agency and thus inform the public how the agency intends to manage and administer its statutory obligations.

Although they draw useful distinctions, the APA categories do not capture the rich variety of rules. The categories of the *Code* are very useful in summarizing the substantive range of the content of rules, but are not very helpful in identifying the next level of general functions of rules that flow from their role in interpreting, implementing, and prescribing law. Nor do they suggest the general types of activities and parties that rules affect. To better understand these features it will be helpful to think about three types of rules—those affecting private behavior, rules for those who approach the government, and rules for government itself.

Rules affect private behavior in a number of ways. On occasion, a rule will contain an outright prohibition on certain types of activities. Bans of cyclamates, cigarette and hard liquor advertising on television, and drinking alcohol by airline pilots in the 24 hours prior to takeoff are good examples of this type of rule. More common are rules that set standards or establish limits for a substance, product, or activity. These rules are very common and include such standards as limits on occupational exposures to dangerous chemicals and standards to ensure safety of consumer products and levels of purity expected in drinking water. There is an obvious relationship between these types of rules and those that prohibit acts. Behavior of a private party that does not fall within prescribed limits or meet established standards is, in effect, prohibited. Finally, there are many rules that require private parties to collect, maintain, and report information about their activities. These rules are usually adjuncts to others that prohibit or set limits and standards, and they are a primary means by which the government monitors private sector compliance with legal obligations.

Persons, organizations, and firms approach the government to secure benefits to which they are entitled, to sell goods and services, to obtain licenses or other forms of permission to engage in certain types of businesses or activities, or simply to complain about actions of others or the government itself. Rules establish channels for these approaches and set criteria to inform the private parties what they can expect when the government responds. Many of these rules could be classified as the "procedural" rules referred to in the APA. Others that specify eligibility criteria for benefits or licenses are more likely to be "interpretive" or "legislative" rules.

Finally, all the rules for government could be considered variants on the "procedural" category. But, it would be a serious mistake to consider them bureaucratic minutiae. They include agency policies for compliance with landmark laws, such as the National Environmental Policy Act, the Freedom of Information Act, the Privacy Act, sunshine statutes, and many, many others.

Effects of Rules

Rules pervade American life. Any effort to calculate the value of the benefits they produce and the costs they impose confronts major methodological obstacles. More effort has been devoted to measuring and reporting costs than to valuing benefits. Here, the numbers are simply staggering. Recent estimates of the total economic burden of rules related only to regulation have ranged from US $100 billion to $500 billion, according to the Center for the Study of American Business at Washington University (Warren, 1992, p. 2). The effects on particular sectors vary considerably. The Federal Financial Institutions Examination Council estimates that compliance with federal regulation alone constitutes 6 percent to 14 percent of noninterest costs to depository institutions. A 1992 study sponsored by the Air Transport Association estimated the removal of one group of rules affecting major carriers would, over a five-year period, result in over $17 billion in savings and create 127,000 jobs (WEFA Group, 1992, p. 4). Even if one were to control for the normal tendency in affected persons to overestimate the effects, the impact of rules on the United States is enormous. Any effort to reduce significantly their role in society will have to be equally massive and sustained.

Conclusion

Colin Diver (1989), dean of the University of Pennsylvania Law School, in a paraphrase of Oliver Wendell Holmes, has written that a rule is "the skin of a living policy. . . . It hardens an inchoate normative judgement into the frozen form of words. . . . Its issuance marks the transformation of policy from the private wish to public expectation. . . . The framing of a rule is the climatic act of public policy" (p. 199). The significance of rules as instruments of governance has never been captured better than in these words. They also underscore the profound importance of the process by which rules come into being.

Bibliography

Diver, Colin, 1989. "Regulatory Precision." In *Making Regulatory Policy*, eds., Keith Hawkins and John Thomas. Pittsburg: University of Pittsburgh Press.

Kerwin, Cornelius M., 1994. *Rulemaking: How Government Agencies Write Law and Make Policy*. Washington, D.C.: Congressional Quarterly, Inc.

Lowi, Theodore, 1987. "Two Roads to Serfdom." *American University Law Review*, vol. 36: pp. 295–322.

Warren, Mclinda, 1992. *Government Regulation and American Business*. St. Louis: Center for the Study of American Business.

WEFA Group, 1992. *The Potential Impact of Selected Airline Tax and Regulatory Changes in the U.S. Economy*. Bala Cynwyd, Pa: WEFA Group.

Bibliography

Part Three

Intergovernmental Relations

8

INTERGOVERNMENTAL RELATIONS

Dale Krane,
University of Nebraska, Omaha

Deil S. Wright,
University of North Carolina, Chapel Hill

The various combinations of interdependencies and influences among public officials—elected and administrative—in all types and levels of governmental units, with particular emphasis on financial, policy, and political issues.

Intergovernmental relations (IGR) as a term originated in the United States of America in the 1930s. It was a new way of describing significant changes in relationships among levels of government and among the officials who held important policymaking posts. Many of these changes and interactions resulted from efforts to ameliorate the effects of the Great Depression, but some even antedated that major economic and social upheaval. The United States national government inaugurated many new activities and programs that altered the relatively separated spheres of national and state government functions, commonly referred to as "dual federalism" (see **federalism**). These progressive adaptations, consisting mainly of national policy initiatives, created new and complex working arrangements that could not be easily described using the constitutional-legal language typical of federalism issues. Because of its origins, IGR is viewed as a dynamic concept, which "pictures the intergovernmental relationship as one of constant change in response to social and economic forces as well as to changes in such significant political factors as the party and electoral systems" (Reagan, 1972, p. 3).

Origin and Historical Development

William Anderson (1960), who is often credited with originating the term, defined IGR as

> an important body of activities or interactions occurring between [or among] governmental units of all types and levels within the US federal system. . . . Underlying the concept . . . is the fact that the nation as a whole, each one of the [fifty] states, and every county, town, city, school district and other special district or local unit is a territorial and corporate or quasi-corporate entity that has a legal existence, rights, functions, powers, and duties within its territory [that are] distinct from those of every other such unit (p. 3).

Notice that this approach to the relationships among and between all manner of public units and jurisdictions "goes far beyond such formal matters as structure and legal powers" and pragmatically emphasizes that "few if any basic problems of local, state, or national government can be successfully resolved without reference to their intergovernmental aspects or implications" (Casella, 1995, p. 43).

For some scholars, IGR transcends the traditional denotations of federalism. For example, Gordon (1992) observes that "IGR involves virtually all governments and public officials, though, largely out of public view; it is highly informal and very dependent on human interactions; and it involves the private sector" (p. 111). Denhardt (1991) explains that a "key to understanding intergovernmental relations . . . is understanding the changing patterns used to fund public programs. Although intergovernmental relations involves more than money, financial questions are inevitably at the core of the process" (p. 69). Glendening and Reeves (1977) expand the meaning of IGR to include "all public officials—administrators as well as elected executive, legislative, and judicial officers—and it encompasses political, economic, and administrative interactions as well as legal ones" (p. 9). Glendening and Reeves include not only the behavior of officials but also their attitudes and perceptions. This shift toward behavioral and attitudinal features as distinctive aspects of IGR moves the concept further away from formal, legal, and structural characteristics. In this sense, there are no relationships among governments; rather, there are arrays of complex cooperative and conflictual relationships among officials who govern.

Some scholars have gone so far as to declare "Federalism—old style—is dead. Yet, federalism—new style—is alive and well and living in the United States. Its name is *inter-governmental relations*" (Reagan 1972, p. 3). Other scholars are not yet willing to entomb federalism as a dead concept. Elazar (1987) distinguishes IGR from federalism by saying, "Federalism is the generic term for what may be referred to as a self-rule/shared-rule relationships; 'intergovernmental relations' has to do with particular ways and means of operationalizing a system of government" (p. 16). He goes on to point out that IGR, because of its American origins, is a highly "culture-bound" term that does not easily comport with the European theories of the state. Hamilton and Wells (1990, pp. 9–12) reject IGR because it is a term limited by its "how-to-control" perspective, and they prefer federalism because, for them, federalism includes ideas about political economy that more correctly reflect the reality of interactions among governmental units. Subsuming IGR under federalism, Zimmerman (1992, p. 201) recently called for a general theory of [American] federalism that combined elements of classic federalism with more contemporary matters such as regulatory controls, the political maneuvering of subnational jurisdictions, and efforts to coordinate changes in national-stage relations.

Because Zimmerman's prescription is a large order, most scholars differentiate between the two terms. Cochran et al. (1993) succinctly note:

> The term *intergovernmental relations* is sometimes used interchangeably with federalism, but the two do not really mean the same thing. Federalism refers to the formal, legal structure of the political system, whereas intergovernmental relations refers to all the interactions of governmental units within the political system. Therefore, although not provided for specifically in the formal document establishing the political system, some intergovernmental activities occur anyway (p. 138).

Because IGR activities happen with or without formal constitutional status, the term has been accepted in comparative studies of unitary governments as well as of federal governments (for example, Rhodes 1980; Muramatsu 1982; Samuels 1983). Thus, despite the lack of agreement among scholars, the term IGR increasingly serves as the conceptual basis for the analysis of interactions among units of governments and officials, even in nations without the formal features of federalism.

Conceptual Approaches

Descriptive analyses of the features and practices of intergovernmental relations in a given country represent one prominent approach to this topic. Wright (1988, pp. 14–26) sets out a list of items that is commonly used to guide studies of IGR. Five distinctive features are identified: (1) number and types of governmental units, their legal status, and changes over time; (2) the number and types of public officials by jurisdiction and unit, their backgrounds and training, the attitudes and perceptions of their roles and responsibilities, and the actions they normally pursue; (3) the patterns of interaction among and between officials representing various jurisdictions and governmental units; (4) the range of involvement by all public officials—elected and appointed, national and local, executive, legislative, and judicial—especially in the formulation of policies and programs that have impact on more than one unit; and (5) the policies and programs implemented through intergovernmental arrangements, with particular concerns about administrative discretion by official and by unit, control over and flow of fiscal resources, and differential effects of policies and programs delivered via different intergovernmental routes. Typically, descriptive studies of IGR focus on one or more of the above features.

In contrast to the focus on structure common to descriptive studies of IGR, a second analytic strategy, which in the United States of America is one of the most characteristic styles of analyzing IGR, classifies changes and trends in the relations among governments by historical eras or phases. Analysis proceeds by describing the main problems, the most commonly used mechanisms of public action, and the attitudinal and behavioral shifts that typify a given time period. Some analysts use presidential terms (e.g., Nixon's New Federalism, Reagan's New-New Federalism) to demarcate changes in IGR (Conlan 1988). Other analysts utilize metaphors to portray the distinctive features of a given phase; for example, one finds references to "layer-cakes" and "marble-cakes," even "fruit-cakes" as well as references to "picket-fences," "whiplashes," and "fending-for-yourself" (Grodzins 1966; Stewart 1984). While highly informative about the details of change from one time period to the next, this historical or metaphorical approach to IGR is atheoretical and offers no framework for theory-building.

European scholars have adopted a focus on decentralization issues as an analytic approach to IGR within the context of a unitary government

(Smith 1985). This approach moves away from the historical-legal tradition in political research to one that measures changes in the degree of decentralization, the extent of devolution, and the creation of autonomous jurisdiction. A somewhat similar approach to IGR found on both sides of the Atlantic is an emphasis on political power, especially as exercised by local government officials. Who makes which decisions and to what extent local decisionmakers may act without constraint by the central government are common questions in this "community power" approach to IGR.

Several attempts to transcend the atheoretical nature of IGR analyses grounded in structural relationships have been made in the last decade (Krane 1993a, pp. 188–189). The first of these nonhierarchical approaches derives from the recognition that the policy process is intertwined with the basic features of a country's IGR. Thus, the focus shifts to policy arenas and issue types, policy professionals and implementation networks, agenda-setting and coalition-building (Treadway 1985; Peterson, Rabe, and Wong 1986; Anton 1989; Robertson and Judd 1989). The advantage of this policy strategy approach to IGR is to facilitate a linkage between the behavior of IGR players (e.g., elected officials, interest groups, program administrators) and the impacts (benefits and costs) of policy choices on citizens.

Fiscal federalism and public choice theory constitute a second significant effort to go beyond simple descriptive studies of IGR. Using the theory of markets, fiscal federalism and public choice analyses strive (1) to model IGR by formal or quantitative means and (2) to prescribe an optimal division of functions among levels of government. Much of the impetus for this market-based analysis comes from an argument that competition among jurisdictions is widespread, desirable, and yields efficient results (Ostrom, Tiebout, and Warren 1961; Peterson 1981; Schneider 1989; Dye 1990; Kenyon and Kincaid 1991).

A third attempt to develop a theory of IGR relies on concepts commonly used in the analysis of interorganizational relations. In the 1970s, European scholars applied organizational sociology and the emerging public policy models to the study of center-local relationships and argued that complex dependencies within matrixlike networks typified intergovernmental policy implementation (Hanf and Scharpf 1978; Rhodes 1980; Smith, 1985). Similar developments in the USA produced a growing body of studies based on the problems of IGR implementation, network management, and interjurisdictional and interorganizational coordination (Pressman 1975; Van Horn and Van Meter 1976; Hjern and Porter 1981; Mandell and Gage 1988; Goggin et al. 1990; Jennings and Krane 1994). Interorganizational concepts permit the development of IGR models that capture the complexities and dependencies that determine the courses of action that are possible among and between governmental jurisdictions.

Over 20 years have passed since Edner (1976) declared that a "virtual wasteland" in the development of a theory of IGR existed. Recent efforts to model IGR have not yet produced consistent results, but these proposed conceptual frameworks do hold the promise of ameliorating the long-standing "conceptual crisis" in IGR studies (Lovell 1979).

Current Practices

In today's modern governments, public officials utilize numerous types of public authorities and jurisdictions to satisfy citizen demand for a wide array of public goods and services. Administrative, programmatic, and territorial differentiation produces complex and diverse patterns of activity among units that vary by authority, resources, and tasks. This organizational complexity and functional fragmentation across tiers of government result in intricately intertwined relationships that do not form a coherent system. At the same time, these fragmented and pluralistic politico-administrative units must be integrated, at least partially, in order to deliver public services with reasonable efficiency and effectiveness. Not all of this policy activity can be directed by a central government or by a single government. Some aspects of public service(s) provision emerge from choices made autonomously by, or at the discretion of, subnational units. Consequently, IGR is generally characterized by reciprocal activity and interdependent choices among multiple governmental units and political interests.

The various combinations of interdependencies, even in one country, can be bewildering. For example, in the United States one finds, in addition to the national government and the 50 states, nearly 83,000 units of local government. Each of these jurisdictions is represented by one or more elected officials who exercise varying degrees of authority over the policies, finances, and administration of the governmental unit. Similarly, many of the major administrative organizations of the national government (e.g., the 14 cabinet rank departments and several independent executive agencies) are replicated at the state and local government level (so-called counterpart organizations). Policy, financial, and political networks link the national government through state governments to local governments and create differing structures of program implementation. It is within these networks that public officials engage in the intergovernmental pursuits of their preferences. The behavior of public officials and the features of the linkages among and between governmental units shape the particular character of IGR in each country.

Because there are so many possible combinations of action and influence, it is impossible to catalogue them all in a brief discussion. The following subsections offer some selective illustrations of the principal forms of IGR in the United States and in other nations.

Financial Issues

One of the principal dynamics in IGR is the struggle over the allocation and distribution of funds by jurisdiction and by function. Mismatches between the needs or problems found in local communities and their ability to raise revenues and to develop sufficient capacity to solve local problems drive many local officials to seek additional resources from superior levels of government. In particular, a "vertical fiscal imbalance" or "fiscal mismatch" exists because (1) it is relatively easier to raise revenues at higher levels of government, which can tap the resources of a wider geoeconomic area, (2) most problems affecting the quality of life require action by local authorities, and (3) variations in the wealth of local communities can lead to inequities in service accessibility and quality (Break 1980, pp. 76–87; Reagan 1972, pp. 31–36). The result of this "fiscal mismatch" is that local governments in almost all nations exhibit a higher degree of fiscal dependence on the central or national government than in the past (Bahl and Linn 1994, p. 6).

Different countries devise different mechanisms for distributing funds to subnational units. One can simplify these intergovernmental fiscal transfers into three basic forms: (1) shared revenues, (2) grants-in-aid, and (3) loans. Shared revenues are funds collected by a higher level of government, some proportion of which is returned to subordinate (receiving) governments. The amount returned can be a guaranteed (constitutional or statutory) percentage of the monies collected or may be the amount collected less an administrative fee. Typically, the receiving governments have no direct control over the determination of the rate, base, and proportion of revenues distributed. To alter the amount "shared" usually requires political action at the higher level of government (Bahl and Linn 1992). Taxes levied on motor vehicle fuels is one of the most common shared taxes. The 50 American state governments impose a tax on the sale of gasoline, and these monies are divided by formula for state highways, county roads, and municipal streets. The national government also levies a motor fuel tax, which pays for the federal highway system. Similar arrangements for sharing motor fuel taxes are found in countries around the world. In some countries as much as 90 percent of local government expenditures have their source in fiscal transfers from the national government (Bahl and Linn 1994).

Grants-in-aid, which are monies raised by a higher level of government and distributed to lower levels of government, come in different forms—the three most common are (1) formula grants, (2) reimbursements, and (3) discretionary grants. Formula grants are funds distributed to lower tiers of government according to a formula composed of demographic, economic, political, and/or social factors. Formulas may be fixed (in a constitution or statute) or may change annually; whatever the case, the factors included in the formula become the focus for political maneuvering by various interests seeking to write the formula to their benefit. Once the formula is set, the administrative agency responsible for allocations can calculate the monies to be received by each jurisdiction or recipient.

Reimbursement grants are payments by a higher government for all or a portion of the costs incurred by a local government for some specified purpose (e.g., education or police). Reimbursements differ from formula grants in that reimbursements normally take into account the actual costs of the approved activity. Formula grants may fall short of actual costs. The key features of a reimbursement are the items eligible for cost recovery and the percentage of the item's cost to be reimbursed.

Discretionary grants are fiscal transfers completely controlled by the donor government. That is, the amount of money appropriated, the criteria by which funds are to be awarded, the conditions and obligations imposed on the recipients, and the selection of the recipients are all at the discretion or choice of the donor government. Unlike formula and reimbursement grants, a system of discretionary grants typically does not guarantee or provide funds to every lower level jurisdiction or even very eligible recipient. Rather, the funds available in any one budget cycle are distributed by the officials in the national (or provincial) agency to local governments. Sometimes a competition is established among the eligible jurisdictions, who must submit an application for the funds (Break 1980, pp. 123–186; Bahl and Linn 1992, pp. 432–450).

Loans of money from superior governments to lower units form a third type of intergovernmental fiscal transfer. Critical to any loan are the terms of the contract—the amount of the principal, the interest due, the time allowed to repay the principal and interest, and the purpose(s) of the loan. In addition to loans, higher level governments may act to guarantee (to the lender) loans taken by lower units of government (Kettl 1988, pp. 97–119; Lund 1989, pp. 125–166).

Each form of intergovernmental fiscal transfer embodies one or more choices about its features that structure the way in which the specific transfer mechanism can be used to attain policy goals. Examples of the choices officials make in designing a mechanism for transferring money between governments include amount, duration, eligibility, function or purpose, intended impacts and outcomes, recipient discretion and obligations, and targeting to places or to people. These design choices are also intensely political and open to innumerable "games" of strategy for increasing one's share of the transferred funds (see Wright 1988, Appendix B).

It is important to remember that IGR encompasses horizontal as well as vertical movements of authority and money. Consequently, interactions among jurisdictions located on the same plane of government constitute an important source of IGR. Three of the most common horizontal mechanisms are (1) contracts and agreements, (2) the transfer of functions, and (3) the use of interjurisdictional agencies (Berman 1993). A common motive for interjurisdictional cooperation is cost savings. Two or more jurisdictions may purchase or support a service (e.g., an emergency response system) that would be too costly for each jurisdiction to buy individually. Other reasons for interjurisdictional collaboration include more effective action (e.g., law enforcement), complementary planning (e.g., roadways), and reducing negative externalities (e.g., pollution control). The horizontal dimensions of IGR add to the complexity of possible arrangements and greatly increase the points of access by which public officials and citizens may influence policy choices.

Policy Issues

Questions about intergovernmental fiscal transfers invariably provoke important policy issues. Decisions about where to allocate funds (from central to local government) and how to transfer funds (shared taxes, grants, or loans) are joined to decisions about the goals and objectives to be achieved and which officials will be in control of monies for given parts of a specific program. The growth in United States national government aid to state and local governments from 1960 to the early 1980s was so expansive and rapid (Walker 1995, p. 206) that many officials and many observers of IGR developed a "fiscal fixation," which led them to see IGR as mostly moving money among jurisdictions. In addition to fiscal transfer decisions, intergovernmental policy choices include the imposition of legal penalties, the use of regulatory authority, and the nature of implementation structures. Intergovernmental policy issues go beyond the fiscal instruments of public action to encompass choices that affect the outcomes in all types of policy areas—distributive, regulatory, redistributive, and boundary-spanning.

From a policy perspective, IGR involves the effort by one or more public officials to impose some degree of control over their interaction with officials in another public jurisdiction or unit. Put another way, there is much more to IGR than moving money. Higher level governments may "donate" or transfer money and authority to lower level governments in order to achieve specific national (or provincial) purposes. At the same time, officials in recipient governments seek to obtain additional resources, but they also strive to retain autonomy and discretion in the use of the transferred resources. Officials in donor governments, to achieve their ends, must obtain the compliance of local officials. The trade-offs that result from the interaction among officials of national and local levels directly determine the character of the policy or program established (Pressman 1975). How the particular program is designed (e.g., the grant formula) and how it is to be administered (e.g., by local governments) go a long way in determining the distribution of benefits and costs among the intended as well as actual targets (jurisdictions and/or citizens) of the public program.

Intergovernmental regulatory issues can conveniently illustrate the policy aspects of IGR. Donor governments usually impose some rules on the use of transferred funds, even if only to prohibit the misappropriation of funds. The number and variety of conditions and rules that may be attached to intergovernmental fiscal transfers is extensive and nearly defies enumeration. In the United States, for example, state and local government officials who accept grants-in-aid from the national government must comply with regulations on (1) general administrative and procedural standards, (2) access to government information and decision processes, (3) standards for public employees, (4) health, safety, and welfare, (5) labor and procurement standards, (6) nondiscrimination, (7) protection of the environment, (8) advancement of the economy, (9) the utilization of nonprofit organizations, and (10) state and local government-related administrative and fiscal requirements (Walker 1981, pp. 180–183).

The policy issues embodied in rulewriting vary from mundane operational matters about which there is little disagreement to fundamental and politically charged questions about the balance of authority between national and subnational governments (ACIR 1984; ACIR 1993). For example, few would disagree that donor governments should impose rules that make local officials liable for the embezzlement or theft of grant monies or that require local officials to create drug-free workplaces. By contrast, rules attached to grants from the national government that require local officials to use crumb rubber from recycled tires in future street projects or that require local officials to house juvenile offenders outside of the local jail provoke intense opposition from local officials who see their authority and autonomy severely reduced, if not eliminated. Recently, this battle over intergovernmental regulatory policy in the United States has been exacerbated by the national government's decision to impose unfunded mandates—that is, new rules governing the actions of state and local officials without any new money for the implementation of the rule. American state governments, it must be noted, have long imposed unfunded mandates on their respective local governments.

Although the examples of regulatory IGR have been drawn from the United States national experience, these same types of policy issues can be found in the relationships between the levels of government in other countries. As pointed out above, donor governments want to achieve their objectives, so they seek to control the actions of recipient governments through regulation. However, provincial and local officials want more discretion to pursue their own preferences. Because both parties need each other to achieve their own ends, continuous political jockeying characterizes IGR.

Political Issues

The constitutions of federal countries, by giving significant autonomy to officials of regional and local governments, create a framework of multiple structures and interests, which cannot be easily controlled by national government officials. In the United States of America, national government officials rely substantially on state governments to implement national government programs; at the same time, state government officials depend on the national government for additional resources. Furthermore, the United States constitution, like other federal constitutions, gives state and local areas direct input into the making of national policy. Although there is an asymmetry of authority and resources, state and local officials possess sufficient autonomy and freedom to force national officials to bargain over the formulation and implementation of public policy. As a consequence, national, state, and local officials adopt various strategies by which to influence each other's actions (Pressman 1975, pp. 10–16; Krane and Shaffer 1992, pp. 250–251). It should be noted that even in unitary nations, with their formal "top-down" legal relationships, many of these same intergovernmental dynamics prevail (Graham 1982).

Studies of IGR often analyze these political battles by classifying them according to the type of government officials involved. It is commonplace to find descriptions of national-state, national-local, or interstate and interlocal conflicts. Officials from one tier of government (e.g., municipalities) often advocate for the interest of their tier to officials representing other, usually superior, tiers of government. Using levels of government as the unit of analysis may have the merit of simplicity. It can, however, divert attention from more important underlying dynamics, such as the policy or program area in which the official is seeking advantage, the constituency base of the official, the official's professional background and training, or the organizations in which the official participates. Asymmetry of influence based in the formal, legal structures may be altered by other informal networks of association and organization.

If there is any statement bordering on a generalization about the politics of IGR, it is this last idea—that informal networks emerge within the formal legal structures of government and make it possible for officials representing different interests to exercise varying degrees of influence over policy. One of the most venerable metaphors of American IGR—"picket-fence" federalism—illustrates this informal exercise of influence across levels of government. Because the administration of most national programs depends on the "shared responsibility" (see **intergovernmental management**) of national, state, and often local governments, the vertical implementation network creates a program-based access for the program managers and beneficiaries at all levels of government (e.g., child development, mental health). These "vertical functional autocracies" enhance the influence of the program specialists vis-à-vis the elected, generalist officials (e.g., governors or mayors). Second, the vertical network also creates "an alliance of like-minded program specialists or professionals, regardless of the level of government in which they serve" (Wright 1988, p. 83). Program specialists at all levels become allies in defending and enlarging their particular program, whether or not this course is desired by the elected, generalist officials of a given level. Program administrators have even constructed national associations, for instance, the National Community Development Association, for the purpose of lobbying elected officials. Consequently, political tension between generalist and specialist officials prevails.

Generalist officials at the state and local level are not without their own resources in the politics of IGR. First, governors and mayors, by the nature of their office, possess advantages in the articulation of local citizen preferences to national officials (Krane 1993b). Second, governors and mayors, because of national rules, also possess significant leverage (via the "sign-off" authority) with specialist officials over the use of grants-in-aid within their jurisdiction. Third, these generalist officials have organized their own national associations for the purpose of representing to the United States president and to Congress their collective policy positions. The "Big Seven" public interest groups, termed by Beer (1977) the "intergovernmental lobby," include (1) the National Governors' Association (NGA), (2) the National Conference of State Legislatures (NCSL), (3) the National League of Cities (NLC), (4) the U.S. Conference of Mayors (USCM), (5) the National Association of Counties (NaCO), (6) the Council of State Governments (CSG), and (7) the International City/County Management Association (ICMA) (Wright 1988, pp. 281–283).

The presence of overtly political alliances and associations of public officials—elected and administrative—within the matrix of the United States federal arrangements contributes to several important features of American IGR. First, the political actions of these officials are important variables influencing outcomes. Second, the degree of influences exercised by a given type of official or organization varies significantly; that is, some officials and organizations are more influential than others. Third, proposals for "program shifts and policy redirections [will] take substantial amounts of time to take effect and to be observable throughout the IGR system" (Wright 1988, pp. 283–284). And fourth, while a tendency toward equilibrium exists, because all parties are organized and active, no output is final (Leach 1970, p. 64). The politics of IGR result in a never-ending struggle to influence the shape of public policy at each and every level of government. It is this continuous dynamic action that distinguishes IGR from federalism, in which some structural features must remain relatively permanent.

Future Issues and Trends

The open-ended nature of IGR makes any discussion of the future problematic, but it is worthwhile to convey some sense of what we and others believe to be important issues and trends. Robert W. Gage (1990), after surveying a group of persons knowledgeable about IGR and a group of state and local officials, identified three key intergovernmental issues that the respondents suggested will affect the future course of IGR in the United States: first, and it comes as no surprise, that the budget difficulties of the United States national government are perceived to be a powerful force driving actions and outcomes in the intergovernmental system; second, the rising role of state governments, with their enhanced executive and administrative capabilities, has resulted in an impressive array of innovations since 1980 and shows no signs of stopping (e.g., reforms of education finance, health care, and public welfare); third, the continuing expansion of funded and unfunded mandates imposed by the national government on states and localities heightens the political conflict between national and subnational officials. We concur with Gage's issues assessment, and we have no reason to doubt the importance of these three issues for the future of American IGR.

We also believe that several distinct trends driven by specific political controversies will dominate the IGR agenda in the decade ahead. Pressure to hold the line on taxes with little or no reduction in the demand for public services will continue to strain public budgets at all levels of government. The ongoing structural realignments in national economies will exacerbate both the resistance to enhanced public revenues and the demand for public services. Thus, fiscal-economic trends suggest that the intergovernmental burden sharing and cooperation of the recent past may well be replaced by burden shifting and interjurisdictional competition.

A related trend derives from the effort to economize by using improved public management techniques. Emerging as an important concern in the 1970s and gaining momentum in the 1980s and 1990s, the various efforts to redesign, reengineer, reform, and reinvent the institutions and procedures of government put a premium on the management dimensions of IGR (Cigler 1995, pp. 1–2). In a time of tight agency budgets, overcoming turf wars and fostering joint action toward program goals become critical to policy success and to cost control (Stone 1992). The co-ordination and orchestration of the many different organizations (public, nonprofit, and for-profit) necessary to the implementation of public programs has now become the primary task of public managers (see **intergovernmental management**).

Ideological battles over social issues are forcing government officials to confront choices that are not easily reduced to fiscal problems. The effort by various jurisdictions or levels of government to shift the fiscal burden for particular services has been joined by efforts to completely pass the buck for the responsibility. This avoidance of service provision and payment is most likely to occur in the social services area. Rather than relying on economic evidence (there are not enough funds available), the push to avoid program responsibility is justified on moral grounds; that is, the recipients of the services are not "worthy" or do not "merit" aid.

Underlying the growing appeal to ideological or moral reasoning are social trends influencing the shape of IGR. Few nations are homogeneous and most are becoming more heterogenous in ethnic, racial, and religious groupings. This increasing sociodemographic diversity coupled with the longstanding movement to expand civil and political rights to all persons fuel conflicts among various social groups. The movement to the suburbs in the United States, for example, has resulted in a new and the fastest growing form of government, the residential community association (ACIR 1989). "A major reason people move out to suburbs is simply to be able to buy their own government. These people resent it when politicians take their money and use it to solve other people's problems." (Schneider 1992, p. 37). With income disparity related directly to demographic diversity in many places, the resulting polarization reinforces the fiscal-economic and political-ideological trends to reduce spending for services (provided to other persons) and to leave problems to the mercy of the marketplace.

The quickening pace of global economic competition impels subnational governments to act as entrepreneurs for their region's population. Not only are nation-states engaged in economic trade, so also are cities, metropolitan areas, provinces, and states (Fry 1990; Rose 1991). International activity by local and regional governments heightens the effort on their part to be granted more autonomy and to exercise more discretion. At the same time, the global involvement of subnational governments can easily run counter to central government plans (Brown and Fry 1993; Hobbs 1994).

Another important IGR trend is the emergence of intermestic issues (Manning 1977). These are issues that result from the increased interconnection(s) between international and domestic problems—hence, intermestic. These issues are noteworthy for their novelty, intensity of conflict, and the degree to which the issue "comes as a surprise" to individuals and jurisdictions. Examples include the taxation of foreign corporations by subnational governments, the promotion of direct foreign investment, the enforcement of international treaties protecting the environment and wildlife, and actions in support of United Nations sponsored agreement (e.g., on the rights of children). Intermestic issues constitute a new source of likely IGR tension because the catalyst causing the conflict can be any one or a combination of different planes of government—international, national, state, local—often located in another country. Global agreements, for example, to reduce the use of toxic chemicals, can create an unexpected source of mandates or regulations that local authorities must enforce, whether or not the local industries or populace wishes it.

The decade ahead will see these several trends work to intensify the fundamental conflicts associated with IGR in all nations. The problems of fiscal mismatch and interjurisdictional disparities are not likely to be resolved in this era of constrained resources. Similarly, the tensions caused by the struggle of local governments to gain more autonomy will grow as economic and social problems force local officials to maintain their local political support. Whether these twin tensions—finances and authority—result in more centralization or decentralization will depend on the political alignments within given countries. What can be said for sure is that the basic struggle among public officials at all levels of government to pursue their own and their jurisdiction's preferences will drive the politics of IGR.

Bibliography

Advisory Commission on Intergovernmental Relations (ACIR), February 1984. *Regulatory Federalism: Policy, Process, Impact, and Reform*. Washington, DC: A-95.

______, 1989. *Residential Community Associations: Private Governments in the Intergovernmental System?* Washington, DC: A-112.

______, 1993. *Federal Regulation of State and Local Governments: The Mixed Record of the 1980s*. Washington, DC: A-126.

Anderson, William, 1960. *Intergovernmental Relations in Review*. Minneapolis: University of Minnesota Press.

Anton, Thomas J., 1989. *American Federalism and Public Policy: How the System Works*. New York: Random House.

Bahl, Roy, and Johannes Linn, 1992. *Urban Public Finance in Developing Countries*. London: Oxford University Press, published for the World Bank.

______, 1994. "Fiscal Decentralization and Intergovernmental Transfers in Less Developed Countries" *Publius: The Journal of Federalism*, vol. 24, no. 1: 1–19.

Beer, Samuel H., 1977. "Political Overload and Federalism." *Polity*, vol. 10 (Fall): 5–17.

Berman, David R., 1993. "Relating to Other Governments." Chapter 7 in Charldean Newell, ed., *The Effective Local Government Manager*, 2nd ed. Washington, DC: International City/County Management Association.

Break, George, 1980. *Financing Government in a Federal System*. Washington DC: Brookings Institution.

Brown, Douglas M., and Earl H. Fry, eds., 1993. *States and Provinces in the International Economy*. Berkeley: Institute of Governmental Studies Press, University of California.

Casella, Jr., William N., 1995. "The National Civic League and Intergovernmental Relations." *National Civic Review*, (Winter) 42–47.

Cigler, Beverly, 1995. "Governance in the Re—Ing Decade of the 1990s." *SIAM Intergovernmental News*, vol. 18, no. 2 (Spring). Section on intergovernmental administration and management, the American Society for Public Administration.

Cochran, Clark E. et. al., 1993. *American Public Policy: An Introduction*, 4th ed. New York: St. Martin's.

Conlan, Timothy, 1988. *New Federalism: Intergovernmental Reform from Nixon to Reagan*. Washington, DC: Brookings Institution.

Denhardt, Robert B., 1991. *Public Administration: An Action Orientation*. Pacific Grove, CA: Brooks/Cole.

Dye, Thomas R., 1990. *American Federalism: Competition Among Governments*. Lexington, MA: D. C. Heath.

Edner, Sheldon, 1976. "Intergovernmental Policy Development: The Importance of Problem Definition." In Charles O. Jones and Robert D. Thomas, eds., *Public Policy Making in a Federal System*. Beverly Hills, CA: Sage.

Elazar, Daniel J., 1987. *Exploring Federalism*. Tuscaloosa: University of Alabama Press.

Fry, Earl H., 1990. "State and Local Governments in the International Arena." *The Annals of the American Academy of Political and Social Science*, vol. 509 (May) 118–127.

Gage, Robert W., 1990. "Key Intergovernmental Issues and Strategies: An Assessment and Prognosis." In Robert W. Gage and Myrna P. Mandell, eds., *Strategies for Managing Intergovernmental Policies and Networks*. New York: Praeger.

Glendening, Parris N., and Mavis Mann Reeves, 1977. *Pragmatic Federalism: An Intergovernmental View of American Government*. Pacific Palisades, CA: Palisades.

Goggin, Malcolm et al., 1990. *Implementation Theory and Practice: Toward a Third Generation*. New York: HarperCollins.

Gordon, George J., 1992. *Public Administration in America*. 4th ed. New York: St. Martin's.

Graham, Lawrence S., 1982. "Intergovernmental Relations in Comparative Perspective: Results from a Five-Country Study." Paper delivered at the annual meeting of the American Society of Public Administration, Honolulu, Hawaii.

Grodzins, Morton, 1966. *The American System: A New View of Government in the United States*. Chicago: Rand McNally.

Hamilton, Christopher, and Donald T. Wells, 1990. *Federalism, Power, and Political Economy: A New Theory of Federalism's Impact on American Life*. Englewood Cliffs, NJ: Prentice-Hall.

Hanf, Kenneth, and Fritz W. Scharpf, eds., 1978. *Interorganizational Policy Making: Limits to Coordination and Central Control*. London: Sage.

Hjern, B., and David O. Porter, 1981. "Implementation Structures: A New Unit of Administrative Analysis." *Organization Studies*, vol. 2, no. 3: 211–227.

Hobbs, Heidi H., 1994. *City Hall Goes Abroad: The Foreign Policy of Local Politics*. Thousand Oaks, CA: Sage.

Jennings, Jr., Edward T., and Dale Krane, 1994. "Coordination and Welfare Reform: The Quest for the Philosopher's Stone." *Public Administration Review*, vol. 54, no. 4: 341–348.

Kenyon, Daphne, and John Kincaid, eds., 1991. *Competition Among States and Local Government: Efficiency and Equity in American Federalism*. Washington, DC: Urban Institute Press.

Kettl, Donald F., 1988. *Government by Proxy: (Mis?)Managing Federal Programs*. Washington, DC: CQ Press.

Krane, Dale, 1993a. "American Federalism, State Governments, and Public Policy: Weaving Together Loose Theoretical Threads." *PS: Political Science & Politics*, vol. 26, no. 2 (June) 186–190.

———, 1993b. "State Efforts to Influence Federal Policy." In Edward T. Jennings, Jr. and Neal S. Zank, eds., *Welfare System Reform: Coordinating Federal, State, and Local Public Assistance Programs*. Westport, CT: Greenwood.

Krane, Dale, and Stephen D. Shaffer, 1992. *Mississippi Government and Politics: Modernizers Versus Traditionalists*. Lincoln: University of Nebraska Press.

Leach, Richard H., 1970. *American Federalism*. New York: W. W. Norton.

Lovell, Catherine, 1979. "Where We Are in Intergovernmental Relations and Some of the Implications." *Southern Review of Public Administration*, vol. 3: 6–20.

Lund, Michael, 1989. "Between Welfare and the Market: Loan Guarantees as a Policy Tool." In Lester M. Salamon, ed., *Beyond Privatization: The Tools of Government Action*. Washington, DC: Urban Institute Press.

Mandell, Myrna P. and Robert W. Gage, eds., 1988. "Management in the Intergovernmental System: Networks and Strategies." *International Journal of Public Administration*, vol. 11, no. 4 (Special Symposium).

Manning, Bayard, 1977. "The Congress, the Executive, and Intermestic Affairs." *Foreign Affairs*, vol. 55: 306–324.

Muramatsu, Michio, 1982. *A Lateral Competition Model for Japanese Central-Local Relations*. Kyoto, Japan: Kyoto University.

Ostrom, Vincent, Charles Tiebout, and Robert Warren, 1961. "The Organization of Government in Metropolitan Areas: A Theoretical Inquiry." *American Political Science Review*, vol. 55, no. 4 (December) 831–842.

Peterson, Paul E., 1981. *City Limits*. Chicago: University of Chicago Press.

Peterson, Paul E., Barry G. Rabe, and Kenneth K. Wong, 1986. *When Federalism Works*. Washington, DC: Brookings Institution.

Pressman, Jeffrey L., 1975. *Federal Programs and City Politics: The Dynamics of the Aid Process in Oakland*. Berkeley: University of California Press.

Reagan, Michael, 1972. *The New Federalism*. New York: Oxford University.

Rhodes, R. A. W., 1980. "Analysing Intergovernmental Relations." *European Journal of Political Research*, vol. 8: 289–322.

Robertson, David B., and Dennis R. Judd, 1989. *The Development of American Public Policy: The Structure of Policy Restraint*. Glenview, IL: Scott, Foresman.

Rose, John Eck, 1991. "Foreign Relations at the State Level." *Journal of State Government*, vol. 64, no. 4 (October/December) 1–8.

Samuels, Richard J., 1983. *The Politics of Regional Policy in Japan: Localities Incorporated?* Princeton, NJ: Princeton University Press.

Schneider, Mark, 1989. *The Competitive City: The Political Economy of Suburbia*. Pittsburgh, PA: University of Pittsburgh Press.

Schneider, William, 1992. "The Suburban Century Begins." *The Atlantic Monthly* (July) 33–44.

Smith, B. C., 1985. *Decentralization: The Territorial Dimension of the State*. London: George Allen & Unwin.

Stewart, William H., 1984. *Concepts of Federalism*. Lanham, MD: University Press of America.

Stone, Donald C., 1992. *Improving Local Services Through Intergovernmental and Intersectoral Cooperation*. Pittsburgh, PA: Carnegie Mellon University, Coalition to Improve Management in State and Local Government.

Treadway, Jack M., 1985. *Public Policy-Making in the American States*. New York: Praeger.

Van Horn, Carl E., and Donald S. Van Meter, 1976. "The Implementation of Intergovernmental Policy." In Charles O. Jones and Robert D. Thomas, eds., *Public Policy Making in a Federal System*. Beverly Hills, CA: Sage.

Walker, David B., 1981. *Toward a Functioning Federalism*. Cambridge, MA: Winthrop.

______, 1995. *The Rebirth of Federalism: Slouching Toward Washington*. Chatham, NJ: Chatham House.

Wright, Deil S., 1988. *Understanding Intergovernmental Relations*, 3d ed. Pacific Grove, CA: Brooks/Cole.

Zimmerman, Joseph F., 1992. *Contemporary American Federalism: The Growth of National Power*. New York: Praeger.

9

MANDATES

Jeffrey D. Straussman,
Syracuse University

Impositions by higher-level governments on lower-level governments that require the lower-level governments to do something or refrain from doing something under the threat of criminal or civil sanction and/or the removal of funds. They take the form of procedures, responsibilities, and activities that must be carried out by the lower-level government. The sources of the mandates are the federal and state constitutions, statutes, administrative rules and procedures, and court orders. Mandates may be "direct orders" or they may be "conditions of aid" (Catherine Lovell and Charles Tobin 1981).

Mandates are the subject of much political, legal, and fiscal debate in the United States because of their number, penetration, and cost throughout the intergovernmental system. To understand mandates, it is first necessary to have a comprehensive classification of the different types that exist. Catherine Lovell and Charles Tobin (1981) have provided the following useful classification of the myriad mandates that exist in the U.S. intergovernmental system. The following draws heavily from their work.

The first way to think about mandates is to consider the requirements that mandates impose, the method that is used to impose them, and the application of the mandates.

Requirements

Requirements may be either programmatic or procedural. Programmatic mandates specify the content of what should be done. They may identify the quality or the quantity of the content. For example, a federally funded school lunch program that is implemented at the local level may specify nutritional standards that must be met by the school districts that receive the federal funds. Programmatic quantity mandates require specific amounts of a government service that is financed, in part or in whole, by a higher-level government. An example is the Davis Bacon Act, which requires that local contractors pay union wages when federal funds are involved in construction projects.

Programmatic mandates may also be procedural. An example here would be personnel requirements such as equal opportunity and affirmative action steps that must be taken to fill public personnel vacancies. Personnel requirements may also pertain to the skills and education of employees hired with funds from a higher-level government. An example would be the requirement that bilingual teachers be hired with federal funds. State government education departments routinely regulate local school district teacher hiring through mandated educational specifications and licensing requirements.

Constraints

Mandates impose constraints on governments. Mandate constraints are particularly noticeable in the areas of taxing and spending. State finance laws, for instance, specify the kinds of property that are exempt from local property taxation. This means that some local governments find that more than half of the real property in their jurisdiction—government buildings, religious institutions, and nonprofit organizations—are not subject to property taxation. Such property tax restrictions act as a revenue base constraint since they limit the aggregate value of taxable property in the jurisdiction. Similarly, state governments also set limits on revenue rates for various types of taxes. One example is a state limit on the rate that a local government may set on a gross utility tax, which is a tax on the consumption of energy. State referenda that have established tax and/or expenditure limitations apply not only to the fiscal environment of the state but to local governments as well. These limitations may try to limit the growth of property taxation at the local level, restrict the annual growth of state government expenditures, and/or limit the growth of state revenues by tying revenues to changes in personal income.

How Mandates Are Imposed

Mandates are imposed as "direct orders" or "conditions of aid." A direct order comes from either a regulation imposed by an administrative agency or a statute. When direct orders are imposed by the federal government on state and local governments, the failure to comply with them carries the threat of criminal and/or civil penalties. One illustration is the Equal Opportunity Act of 1972. This statute prohibits state and local governments from discriminating on the basis of sex, race, color, religion, or national origin. In addition to public employment, direct orders prohibiting certain types of actions are commonly found in the area of environmental protection. Wastewater treatment standards defined by the Clean Water Act are a case in point. When the federal government sets minimum standards in various environmental programs, this is also known as "partial preemption." For example, the federal government's Clean Air Act establishes emission levels and requires that the state governments administer and enforce the statute.

Some mandates are "crosscutting." Mandates that are attached to all federally funded programs would have this characteristic. An example is a mandate that prohibits discrimination in hiring. Similarly, some mandates apply "crossover sanctions" to federal funding sources when the statute allows the federal government to withdraw funds from the states for noncompliance. A good example is federal highway funds. Here, the federal government has threatened state governments with the loss of funds if they do not enforce federal government speed limits, the regulation of the legal drinking age, billboard regulations, and the implementation of the Clean Air Act.

Mandates may also be attached to programs as conditions of aid. This means that when lower-level governments accept funding from a higher-level government, the lower-level government must agree to implement specific requirements that accompany the funds. For instance, a local government that accepts mass transit funds from the federal government must ensure that a given percentage of the buses are accessible to the physically handicapped. The distinction, however, between conditions of aid and direct orders is not so straightforward in practice. Consider the following situation. The federal government may offer grant funds for subsidized housing. If a local government receives the grant funds, it is required to implement mandates such as nondiscrimination provisions.

Suppose a local government objects to what it interprets as excessive federal government interference with local preferences. Logically, the local government can simply forego the grant funds and thereby avoid the mandates. However, in such a case the federal government may initiate litigation against the recalcitrant local government for circumventing a crosscutting mandate (a nondiscrimination requirement in this example).

Why Mandates Are So Controversial

Edward Koch, a former mayor of the City of New York wrote a now famous article in 1980 in which he complained that "a maze of complex statutory and administrative directives has come to threaten both the initiative and the financial health of local governments throughout the country" (p. 42). Koch's criticism has been echoed by local government officials who have continually complained about the intrusiveness, inflexibility, and burden of state and local government mandates. The first complaint is one of classic federalism; higher-level governments are said to intrude into activities that are better left to the discretion of lower-level governments. Critics of mandates often point out that the high governmental level of intrusion via the imposition of mandates is coercive and out of character with "grassroots" democracy. The burden, measured simply as the number of federal mandates on state and local governments, is significant. As of 1992, it was estimated that there were 172 separate pieces of federal legislation that imposed mandates on state and local governments (*National Performance Review*, "Strengthening the Partnership in Intergovernmental Service Delivery, September 1993, p. 13). The myriad number of mandates is also criticized for inflexibility. State and local governments have complained that some federal mandates fail to take account of the unique conditions of some jurisdictions and therefore require action that is unproductive.

Furthermore, mandates are criticized for being vague. Consider the Americans with Disabilities Act (ADA), which, among other things, requires state and local governments to make new facilities and renovated facilities accessible to the disabled. However, the federal courts are filled with cases that are contesting what it means to be a renovated facility and what it means to make a facility accessible. A good example comes from Philadelphia, where the federal courts held that street resurfacing qualified as a renovation, which therefore required the city to improve accessibility. All street resurfacing projects had to add curb cuts to comply with ADA, obviously increasing the cost of the projects.

The most consistent criticism of mandates focuses on their budgetary burden. Although the charge is uniformly shared by local governments, estimates of the budgetary burden of mandates are difficult to make and suspect to conceptual and empirical challenges. For example, in a 1970s study of mandate costs, researchers from the Urban Institute in Washington, DC, estimated the cost impact of six federal government mandates on seven local governments (Fix and Fix 1990, pp. 35–37). Costs ranged from US $6 per capita to US $51.50, with an average per capita cost of US $25. The study, however, did not standardize different compensation costs, and the costs did not include overhead expenses. Some budgetary burdens may be due to local fiscal conditions rather than direct mandate costs. Finally, no attempt was made to estimate the benefits of mandate compliance.

A more recent survey of 314 cities was conducted by Price Waterhouse in 1993 for the U.S. Conference of Mayors. The survey examined the financial impact of ten federal government mandates: Underground Storage Tanks, Clean Water Act, Clean Air Act, Resource Conservation and Recovery Act, Safe Drinking Water Act, Asbestos Abatement, Lead Paint Abatement, Endangered Species Act, Americans with Disabilities Act, and Fair Labor Standards Act. The survey found that 1993 cost estimates for the ten mandates totaled US $5.6 billion for the 314 cities. The study provided a five-year total (1994 to 1998) of US $54 billion. Environmental mandates (Clean Water Act, Solid Waste Disposal, and Safe Drinking Water Act) were the most costly (Hearing, United States Senate, Committee on Governmental Affairs, 1993, pp. 125–126).

A study by the Advisory Commission on Intergovernmental Relations (ACIR) assessed the impact of federal mandates on state and local governments. Several conceptual and methodological issues hamper precise estimates of mandate burdens. First, some mandates are clearly unfunded (where the entire cost is borne by the local government), whereas others are embedded in grant conditions. In the latter case, mandate costs should be separated from the grant so that one could estimate the net budgetary increment of federal funding. Some mandate costs may be passed along to users of services in the form of fees; others are covered by local taxes. Both should be included in any estimate of per capita mandate costs; however, only the latter would be included in an estimate of fiscal or budgetary burden. Similarly, some mandates are known to have future local budget costs (based on start-up dates) but may not have current costs. Public officials need to clarify what is counted and when mandates are included in local cost estimates (Dearborn 1994, p. 22).

Conceptual and methodological issues concerning mandate cost estimating were examined by the ACIR. Consider the following illustration. In 1995, 20 states taxed food sales. However, purchases of food with food stamps are exempt from state sales taxes. Therefore, the mandate, which in this case is a prohibition, clearly has a cost implication for those 20 states in the form of uncollected sales tax revenues (Dearborn 1994, p. 24). Multiyear capital costs are particularly difficult to estimate. The ACIR study offered the Americans with Disabilities Act as an example. To comply with the act, some governments must implement substantial physical improvements that are multiyear and frequently require local governments to incur debt from the issuance of municipal bonds. Since capital spending is not linear, estimating year-to-year costs of this type of mandate is difficult.

The budgetary impact of mandates varies greatly depending on whether one looks at actual budgeted costs or estimates based on full compliance. The ACIR illustrated this point with reference to the city of Lewiston, Maine. In 1992, Lewiston budgeted US $414,000 to comply with safe drinking water, clean water, and occupational safety federal mandates. This represented 0.8 percent of a US $53 million budget in 1992. Full compliance with (then) existing mandates was estimated at US $1.6 million, or 3.1 percent of the budget. A third estimate was the amount needed to comply with proposed federal mandates. This was estimated at US $7.7 million, or 14.5 percent of the budget. If all of the proposed mandates were enacted by the federal government, it would mean that the city would be spending 18.4 percent of the budget on federal mandates (Dearborn 1994, pp. 24–25).

Despite obvious conceptual and methodological problems in estimating the fiscal impact of mandates, there is little disagreement that the federal government imposes budgetary burdens on lower-level governments. Often cited figures from the Congressional Budget Office compared total mandate costs in 1986 of US $225 million with US $2.8 billion in 1991. Aggregate estimates like this mask the real criticism of mandates from local government officials—that mandates distort local government spending priorities. Testimony by Gregory S. Lashutka, Mayor of Columbus, Ohio, before the Senate Committee on Governmental Affairs on November 3, 1993, is telling:

> [T]he U.S. EPA requires removal of many of our city's underground fuel tanks. Incidentally, we are going to do this well above what we believe will be further regulations coming about that won't tell us whether we are doing it correctly above the ground. Our Columbus fire division will have to spend over $800,000 to move those tanks. That means to us we could have hired 24 new firefighters or buy two new engines and ladder trucks for that amount. I didn't get to make that decision. It was forced on us by the Environmental Protection Agency (Hearing, United States Senate, Committee on Governmental Affairs, 1993, p. 27).

The previous reference to the curb cuts in Philadelphia required under ADA regulatory guidelines is also instructive of the budgetary pressures faced by local officials. During Senate testimony, Philadelphia Mayor Edward Rendell complained that the implementation of the curb cuts requirement would cost US $140 million over a two-year period when the total annual capital budget (in 1993) was US $95 million (Hearing, United States Senate, Committee of Governmental Affairs, 1993, pp. 30–31).

Advantages of Mandates: Are There Any?

There are few defenders of mandates when they are said to impose regulatory and budgetary burdens on lower level governments. The strongest defense of some federal mandates is that they promote laudable national objectives. Civil rights, certain health care regulations, environmental mandates that are designed to monitor pollution, and constitutional guarantees for the incarcerated all require national enforcement. Advocates of vigorous federal action would claim that, in the absence of mandates, state and local governments would be lax in the enforcement of many national objectives. The continuing debate, therefore, is over three broad features of mandates: (1) the amount of flexibility that will be given to lower-level governments in their administration and enforcement, (2) a careful accounting of the benefits of mandates compared with their costs, and (3) the appropriate sharing of the burden in the intergovernmental system of the United States.

Bibliography

Advisory Commission on Intergovernmental Relations, 1994. *Regulatory Federalism: Policy, Process, Impact, and Reform*. Washington, D.C.

Dearborn, Philip M., 1994. *Local Government Responsibilities in Health Care.* Washington, DC: U.S. Advisory Commission on Intergovernmental Relations.

Fix, Michael, and Daphne Fix, eds., 1990. *Coping with Mandates.* Washington, DC: Urban Institute Press.

Koch, Edward, 1980. "The Mandate Millstone." *The Public Interest*, no. 61 (Fall): 42.

Lovell, Catherine, and Charles Tobin, 1981. "The Mandate Issue," *Public Administration Reviews*, vol. 41, (May/June): 318–331.

United States House of Representatives, Committee on Science, Space, and Technology, 1994. *Unfunded Federal Mandates: Who Should Pick Up the Tab?* Hearing, March 22.

United States Senate, Committee on Governmental Affairs, 1993. *Federal Mandates on State and Local Governments.* Hearing, November 3.

Wright, Deil, 1988. *Understanding Intergovernmental Relations*, 3d ed. Pacific Grove, CA: Brooks/Cole.

10 GOVERNMENT CORPORATION

Jerry Mitchell,
Baruch College, City University of New York

An organization owned by the government, but independently managed and financed like a private business. Most government corporations are governed by a board of directors, administered by a professional executive, and financed through the issuance of tax-exempt bonds and the marketing of a service.

Government corporations exist at every level of U.S. government, but are perhaps most prominent at the federal and state levels. Other names for such organizations include public authority, public corporation, special purpose government, public enterprise, and public benefit corporation.

History

Quasi-public organizations have long been a part of U.S. government. In the 1800s and early 1900s, most corporations were considered to be performing functions of a public character. Consider, for example, the Erie Canal Commission, established in 1816 to manage New York's canal system; the Panama Railroad Company, purchased by Congress in 1903 to assist in building the Panama Canal; and the Emergency Fleet Corporation, formed in 1917 to supply vehicles during World War I. These early government corporations were designed to be free of the uniform guidelines applied to other traditional government departments so that they could act efficiently in building public works or in financing projects.

They were not exactly what is thought of as a government corporation today because each was largely funded by legislative appropriations.

The Port Authority of New York and New Jersey was the first modern-day government corporation. Created in 1921 to reflect the Progressive Era values of businesslike efficiency and public interest representation, the Port Authority was to coordinate port activities in the New York and New Jersey region. Under the clause in the Constitution permitting compacts between states, the authority's jurisdiction was called the "Port District," a 17-county bistate region within a 25-mile radius of the Statue of Liberty. The Port Authority's mandate was, and continues to be, to promote and protect the commerce of the bistate port and to undertake port and regional improvements not likely to be invested in by private enterprise nor to be attempted by either state alone. Governed by an appointed board of commissioners, the Port Authority does not use tax revenues to fund itself, but it is allowed to charge for the use of terminals and other facilities, and most important, to borrow money and secure the same by bonds.

The Port Authority's first major project was the construction of the George Washington Bridge over the Hudson River. The bridge, completed in 1931, was noteworthy because it symbolized the ability of a government corporation to transcend state and local political interests, to build a public conveyance ahead of schedule and under budget, and to do all this without the use of public funds. And most important, the bridge was built while Franklin D. Roosevelt was governor of New York. Through the bridge, Roosevelt came to see in the Port Authority a model for public administration, something to be replicated in New York, in the federal government, and throughout the nation.

When Roosevelt became president in 1933, he created several new agencies in his administration's first 100 days, including dozens of government corporations, such as the Federal Deposit Insurance Corporation (FDIC), the Commodity Credit Corporation (CCC), and the Federal Housing Administration (FHA).

The most prominent corporation established during the New Deal period was the Tennessee Valley Authority (TVA). Patterned after New York's government corporations, Roosevelt described the TVA in his State of the Union message of 1933 as "clothed with the power of government but possessed of the flexibility and initiative of private enterprise." Its mission was to improve regional conditions along the Tennessee River by developing river navigation, controlling frequent flooding, and producing electricity. Soon after it was formed, the TVA designed and built high-voltage lines that carried the first electricity to homes, schools, and factories in the region. The prominent leader of the TVA during its formative years was David Lilienthal.

In 1934, the federal government distributed to the 48 states a sample of model legislation for the creation of what was termed "municipal improvement authorities" and "nonprofit public benefit corporations." Roosevelt followed this with a personal letter to the governors of each state, encouraging them to endorse this legislation and to modify their debt laws. By the time of Roosevelt's death in 1945, government corporations were operating throughout the federal government and within most states and localities.

After World War II, government corporations were created to develop housing, roads, bridges, airports, and parks. At the time, President Dwight D. Eisenhower was not especially in favor of government corporations; he referred to them as "creeping socialism." Nonetheless, many public officials were more than willing to use such agencies. Two notable individuals in this regard were Robert Moses and Austin Tobin.

Moses contributed to the overall development of government corporations in several ways. First, through his management of the New York State Triborough Bridge and Tunnel Authority (TBTA), New York Power Authority, and other state-level government corporations, he showed that it was possible to enlarge the mission of such agencies from single purposes to multipurposes. He transformed the TBTA, for instance, from an agency that built bridges to one that designed entire roadway systems. Second, Moses demonstrated that private investors could be drawn to government corporation projects by pledging that the revenues of existing projects would be used to pay off the bonds of new ones. And third, he gave government corporations a distinct identity, one that clearly distinguished them from traditional government agencies. The TBTA, for example, had its own logo, police force, and distinctive license plates.

Another person who transformed government corporations was Austin Tobin, the executive director of the Port Authority of New York and New Jersey from 1942 to 1971. With private financing and the use of proceeds from one project to finance another, Tobin greatly expanded the mission of the Port Authority. During his tenure, the Port Authority built two tunnels under the Hudson River; took control of LaGuardia, Idlewild (now Kennedy), and Newark airports; constructed a large bus terminal in Manhattan, began operating truck terminals in New Jersey and New York; and built the World Trade Center in lower Manhattan. Tobin's strategy, like Moses', was to develop strong relationships with the investment community, to enhance the Port Authority's independence through consolidated bonds, and to emphasize credit and bond marketability as the dominant criteria for evaluating the Port Authority's performance.

Beginning in the 1960s and extending into the 1990s, several additional uses were found for government corporations. Consider the following examples. In 1964, the Texas Legislature sought to ensure that hazardous wastes were disposed of safely and efficiently and so it established the self-financing Gulf Coast Waste Disposal Authority. In 1965, the North Carolina Education Assistance Authority was created to provide financial aid to postsecondary educational institutions. In 1968, the state of New York created the Urban Development Corporation to finance the construction of housing in blighted areas. In 1971, Congress formed a quasi-autonomous enterprise to deliver the mail—the U.S. Postal Service. In 1975, the Delaware General Assembly created the Delaware Solid Waste Authority to manage and control the disposal of solid waste in the state. In 1981, the New Hampshire Housing Finance Authority was authorized to provide low-interest mortgages for the purchasing of new homes by eligible residents. And, in 1985, the Maryland Stadium Authority was formed to construct a baseball stadium in Baltimore.

Theoretical Framework

The invention of government corporations has been the responsibility of chief executives (the president, governors, and mayors) and legislators (members of Congress, state representatives, and county or city commissioners). Public officials have used government corporations not only to resolve pressing public problems but also to further their own personal careers.

Information about the mission, governance, management, and financing of a government corporation can be found in its authorizing statute. There is no such thing as a model statute, so there is much variation among government corporations with regard to such things as the size of governing boards and the terms of office of board members. For example, the size of a board may range anywhere from three to 49 members and terms of office may extend from two to nine years.

In the political process, four public arguments have been made for government corporations. First, it is asserted that government corporations have a superior governance and management structure. Ideally, each is governed by a board of "average" citizens who serve part-time and without compensation. As a policymaking body concerned with the overall public interest, a board's job is to oversee matters broadly and to select a highly educated, experienced individual to actually manage the organization. The corporate manager, relieved of the rigid requirements that typically constrain traditional government agencies (civil service rules, pay scales, etc.), is supposed to carry out existing tasks with competence, but also with an entrepreneurial eye toward new strategies and new projects that will add to the organization's overall strength—in financial terms and in relation to broad social needs. The end result is an organization that maintains its linkage to the public interest through board governance and achieves its goals through professional management.

Second, government corporations are believed to have unique financial advantages. Government corporations are expected to generate from their own initiatives all, or almost all, of the moneys they require for development and operation. They are not subject to constitutional or statutory debt limitations, and as government entities, they can raise needed funds in the tax-exempt bond market. Government corporations are usually monopolies, so they do not have to be concerned with either private competition or making a profit. This, in turn, allows them to provide services at a lower cost than private firms. If government corporations do get in financial trouble, their parent governments can always provide them with subsidies.

Third, it is argued that government corporations are independent and nonpolitical. They are designed to be free of the politics surrounding the appointment of department heads, the claims of organized interest groups, and the pressures of elections. Governing boards, for instance, are appointed for fixed, overlapping terms so newly elected chief executives can not sweep out old boards and bring in new people, except over a period of several years. Many government corporations are even removed from jurisdictional politics because they are designed to deliver services or finance projects that cross city and county lines, state borders, or international boundaries. It is assumed that the employees of government corporations, distanced from politics, can dispassionately focus on the efficient achievement of public purposes.

Fourth, it is thought that government corporations get things done. It is easy to find bridges, highways, baseball stadiums, power plants, housing projects, canals, parks, and a host of other public works developed by government corporations. The facilities of government corporations usually appear well maintained. Government corporations appear to act as traditional public agencies vacillate and when private companies hesitate to risk their own capital.

Current Issues

The exact number of government corporations in the United States is difficult to determine because of differences in how they are defined. There are at least 47 government corporations operating at the national level. Examples include the Bonneville Power Administration, Saint Lawrence Seaway Development Corporation, and the Resolution Trust Corporation. Government-sponsored enterprises, such as the Student Loan Marketing Association, are not included because they are privately owned.

There are approximately 3,000 government corporations at the state level. This includes many state-level government corporations that operate with localities, such as New York's Metropolitan Transportation Authority in New York City and the Southeastern Pennsylvania Transportation Authority in Philadelphia. Subsidiaries of government corporations are counted separately, such as the Chicago Transit Authority, which is part of the Northeastern Illinois Regional Transportation Authority. Special districts are excluded because they have elected governing boards and the power to impose taxes or special assessments.

The central issue for government corporations is whether they are living up to expectations. Although most officials of government corporations see themselves as doing a good job, many Americans think otherwise. Government corporations are thought to be poorly managed, increasingly dependent on tax subsidies, politically biased toward economic elites, and generally unable to deal with pressing and complex problems of housing, education, health, economic development, transportation, and the environment. Anecdotal evidence of the problems with government corporations include such things as

- The Port Authority of New York and New Jersey built a luggage tunnel at Kennedy Airport for US$21 million in 1990 even though the airlines said they would not use it.

- Of 17 nuclear power plants built by the Tennessee Valley Authority since the mid-1970s, 8 were canceled after $4 billion had been spent, one closed after a fire, and 4 others had their operations suspended for safety reasons.
- Between 1954 and 1973, the Delaware River Port Authority's board chairman benefited as the owner or principal in several construction companies that received $3 million in authority construction contracts.
- The Louisiana Public Facilities Authority issued $41 million in tax-exempt bonds in 1984 and then retired them in 1987, for a housing project that was never developed.
- The secretary-treasurer of the Kentucky Infrastructure Authority and his father made over $7,000 by buying bonds they knew could be resold to the authority at higher prices.

There is also evidence that indicates that government corporations are not controlling their debt issuance. In Illinois, for example, the state's per capita off-budget debt nearly doubled in a decade, from $5.1 billion in 1981 to $9.9 billion in 1990. Similarly, in New York, the debt of state corporations has risen three times faster than direct obligations of the state. The outstanding debt of New York's Energy Research and Development Authority, for instance, rose almost tenfold from 1982 to 1990, from $327 million to $3.7 billion.

Even though it is difficult to generalize from specific cases, the perception and reality of problems has led to various reform initiatives. One approach has been to give elected officials greater control over the operations of government corporations. Beginning in the late 1980s, New York state required its corporations to adopt and publish comprehensive guidelines covering the whole spectrum of personal service contracts, such as how subcontractors were selected and the methods used to measure vendor performance. Similarly, at the federal level, the 1954 Government Corporations Act was strengthened in 1990 to require standardized financial record-keeping among government corporations. Chief executives (the president and governors) have also been given the power to install their department heads as ex officio members of governing boards. For example, New Jersey's Commissioner of Transportation—a cabinet-level official—is now a member of the governing boards of several state transportation corporations.

A second approach has been to advocate the privatization of some or all of the functions of government corporations. To those who support privatization, it does not matter whether it is the Department of Education or the TVA, the public sector is necessarily inefficient, unresponsive to citizen needs, and a drain on taxpayers. For these reasons, arguments have been made to turn over New Jersey's Sports and Exposition Authority to a private company, to contract-out most of the functions of the Massachusetts Turnpike Authority, to transfer the facilities of the Tennessee Valley Authority to private utilities, and to sell-off the airports run by the Port Authority of New York and New Jersey. Although such proposals have received much attention, no major privatization has yet occurred, primarily because of the difficulty in transferring the tax-exempt debt of government corporations to private firms.

Comparisons to Other Nations

U.S. government corporations are strikingly similar to so-called public enterprises in other nations. Public enterprises also have boards of directors, professional managers, political independence, and separate systems of financing. In fact, the Port of London Authority was the model used for the creation of the Port Authority of New York and New Jersey.

One difference between the United States and other countries is that many public enterprises—such as those found in Europe, Africa, and Asia—are nationalized industries financed largely with tax receipts. Another distinction is that there is often a cabinet-level department responsible for the oversight of government corporations in parliamentary systems, but not in the United States.

Since the 1980s, there has been a committed effort to privatize nationalized industries in several nations, including Great Britain, Ireland, India, and much of Eastern Europe. Interestingly enough, even as the United States has been quick to champion the cause of private competition throughout the world, it has been slow to privatize its own government corporations. There appears to be an unwillingness among Americans to equate their government corporations with the public enterprises found in other nations, even though there are as many similarities as differences.

Bibliography

Axelrod, Donald, 1992. *Shadow Government: The Hidden World of Public Authorities—And How They Control over $1 Trillion of Your Money*. New York: John Wiley.

Caro, Robert, 1974. *The Power Broker: Robert Moses and the Fall of New York*. New York: Vintage Books.

Cohen, Julius Henry, 1946. *They Builded Better Than They Knew*. New York: Julian Messner.

Dimock, Marshall E., 1934. *Government-Operated Enterprises in the Panama Canal Zone*. Chicago: University of Chicago Press.

Doig, Jameson W., 1983. "'If I See A Murderous Fellow Sharpening a Knife Cleverly' . . . The Wilson Dichotomy and the Public Authority Tradition." *Public Administration Review* 43 (July/August): 292–304.

Henriques, Diana, 1986. *The Machinery of Greed: Public Authority Abuse and What to Do About It*. Lexington, MA: Lexington Books.

Mitchell, Jerry, 1993. "Accountability and the Management of Public Authorities in the United States," *International Review of Administrative Sciences* 59 (September): 477–492.

______, ed., 1992. *Public Authorities and Public Policy: The Business of Government*. New York: Greenwood Press.

National Academy of Public Administration, (NAPC) 1981. *Report on Government Corporations*. Washington, DC: NAPC.

Seidman, Harold, 1954. "The Government Corporation: Organization and Controls." *Public Administration Review* 14 (Summer): 183–192.

Selznick, Philip, 1966. *TVA and the Grassroots: A Study in the Sociology of Formal Organizations*. New York: Harper & Row.

Thurston, John, 1937. *Government Proprietary Corporations in the English-Speaking Countries*. Cambridge, MA: Harvard University Press.

Van Dorn, Harold A., 1926. *Government Owned Corporations*. New York: Knopf.

Walsh, Annmarie Hauck, 1978. *The Public's Business: The Politics and Practices of Government Corporations*. Cambridge, MA: MIT Press.

Wettenhall, Roger, 1978. "Public Enterprise in Eight Countries: A Comparative Survey." *Australian Journal of Public Administration* 37 (December): 398–403.

Part Four
Bureaucracy

11

BUREAUCRACY

Ralph P. Hummel,
University of Akron

From "bureau" and "kratos": the power of the office. The bureaucracy is the administrative apparatus of the modern state; but also any organization or part of an organization with specifically modern characteristics. In business administration, the rationalized parts of the firm are bureaucratic.

Next to "charisma," "bureaucracy" is probably one of the most popularly used terms derived from sociology, specifically the sociology of Max Weber, and perhaps the most misused and misunderstood by layman and professional alike.

The popular use of "bureaucracy" refers to what a large part of clients in the late industrial welfare states perceive as the negative characteristics of the administrative apparatus: impersonality, slowness, oppressiveness, and rigidity. Closer examination shows these are the obverse side of neutrality, deliberateness, capacity to mobilize for projects of unprecedented magnitude, and predictability. These may be considered positive values of a civilization claiming legitimacy of its authority based on the rule of law and reason. In short, the negative side of the coin is not composed of deviations from an ideal bureaucracy but of necessary latent functions. (But, see Merton, 1936, and Selznick, 1949, who see unanticipated negative functions; and Goodsell, 1994, who minimizes them.)

The professional misuse of "bureaucracy" stems from the isolation of inner structural characteristics from external functions, as these were developed within the Weberian theory of knowledge that gave birth to the sociological concept. Especially nation builders, organizational consultants, and analysts tend to treat "bureaucracy" within the tradition of post-Platonic idealism, encouraged by Weber's use of the term "ideal type." Idealism suggests that once the component parts of a structure are perfected and connected, a bureaucratic structure will result. Weber's concept of the ideal type refers to something more earthy and quite different: an observer forms ideal types as pure mental constructs based on an empirically observed set of social orientations by which social actors typically orient themselves and their actions toward each other. Once an ideal type is constructed it is then possible for the analyst to operate with clear ideas that can be brought into logical relationships with each other (see **Max Weber**). Bureaucracy as an ideal type is not ideal in the sense of *desideratum*. It is a construct with admitted internal characteristics but whose outer meaning is determined by the context within which it was formed. In the case of Weber's concept, this context was the millenia-long development of the specific form of legal-rationalist culture, society, and institutions that characterized Western Europe in the nineteenth and early twentieth centuries and which conquered much of the world.

Bureaucracy, then, cannot be allowed to be defined only by its inner characteristics but must be defined within the context of the growth of a civilization. To do otherwise has the result of setting up formal structures that imitate bureaucratic traits but whose actual operations are deflected from the legal-rational path by the prevailing indigenous culture, for example, those of Bangladesh or Oklahoma (for the latter, Elazar, 1972).

The inability to distinguish between popular, idealizing, and ideal-typical uses of the term is responsible for great confusion about what is being advocated or defended in the public administration literature. This is remedied by placing bureaucracy in its economic, cultural, and general civilizational context.

Bureaucracy in Its Context

Bureaucracy is the administrative apparatus of modern civilization, whether in the private or public sector. In the study of both business and public administration, this form of organization, however, has been caricaturized. In the typical textbook presentation, bureaucracy as modern organization is alleged to be present wherever six characteristics are present in an organization, stenographically: division of labor, hierarchy, written documents, staff of trained experts, full working capacity of the official, and the presence of general rules under which it operates. Attempts to modernize so-called underdeveloped or developing countries, however, show that instituting these characteristics does not produce modern business, modern government, or modern civilization in general. That such effects are expected shows that bureaucracy is still quietly conceived in the Western mind as not merely an administrative apparatus but as an engine of development as, indeed, it was by its first investigator.

Within modern Western civilization as a whole, bureaucracy is the means to assure the application of the authority of law conceived as a coherent system of rules for which rational grounds can be given. Legal-rationalism requires not only a rational legislative procedure but also an administrative procedure that follows and nurtures faith in the rule of reason: law must be transparent as to its justifications and apply to all alike. From the sociological point of view, all alike must be able to direct their behavior according to the expectation that the monopoly of force to which the state ultimately lays claim will be applied in a predictable manner.

Culturally, bureaucracy becomes an educator and enforcer of general, predictable, calculable values of living life.

Whatever the position given to economics in the generation of the modern state, culture, and society—whether as a substructure that carries the rest as superstructure (Karl Marx) or as a sector separate from politics (Adam Smith and the liberal economists)—the function of bureaucracy in the development and maintenance of modern economics becomes crucial as the context for understanding the meaning of bureaucracy. Weber subscribes both to a materialist and to an idea-oriented explanation for the generation and function of bureaucracy. This is crucial also for understanding the type of individual who can qualify to inhabit its structures and the kind of individual who can qualify to be served and ruled by them (Hummel, 1977).

Economically, bureaucracy is a response to modes of production that separate ownership and management of industry and business from the personal household. This, however, is achieved in Western civilization only once personal short-term interests are subordinated to a higher, long-term value resulting in an economic system of self-denial: "otherworldly asceticism" (Weber, 1930 [1904–1905]). This orientation makes it worthwhile for investors to reinvest the profits produced by an enterprise (Weber: reinvestment capitalism) because wealth is an indicator of future salvation.

Weber saw modern capitalism's material conditions and the spirit that legitimated it as originating in separate developments of "elective affinity": the scientific and technical developments that made the modern mode of production possible and the rise of the "Protestant ethic," whose spirit legitimated the new economic attitudes and behaviors. Both the material procedures and the spirit, however, required conditions of the larger environment that could make them viable. Not only did Weber see bureaucracy as the governmental structure that evened the playing field for the rising industrial and merchant classes but he took it for granted that only a bureaucratic spirit compatible with the economy's entrepreneurial spirit could produce officials dedicated to applying law evenhandedly and predictably on the field of economic activity. A duty ethic would correspond to the entrepreneurial reinvestment ethic: the one originating with Luther, the other with Calvin (cf. also Bendix, 1962, pp. 312–313, fn. 13).

If this interpretation of the development of modern civilization is not taken into account, as it generally has not been in the narrow precincts of public administration, the spirit of officialdom needed in a truly modern bureaucracy cannot be understood. In short, the structures of bureaucracy also require the presence of people who will feel bound to the ultimate functional values of bureaucracy within the context of reinvestment-capitalist economic development. These values stem from a now-faded religious sense of God's way in the world (theodicy).

The entire symptomatology of complaints about latter-day bureaucratic dysfunctions is already contained in Max Weber's depiction of its founding functions. Say, for example, officials lack the duty ethic. This ethic requires that they consciously subordinate themselves to the economic spirit that requires stable markets and other legal constraints (such as the guaranteed enforcement of contracts and collection of debts). In the absence of the ethic, bureaucracy gets in the way of economic development. This applies to already established modern countries or countries still hoping to become modern. Alternatives originating in organizational structures of the past then threaten to be resurrected in the present and future. Without a neutral and reliable bureaucracy, for example, the present Russia and mainland China cannot produce the stable and predictable playing field that will encourage original capital investment, much less reinvestment. The six characteristics of bureaucracy plus one—the duty ethic is subordinate to something resembling the Protestant ethic (see Bellah, 1957)—must therefore be carefully read in the context of alternative history of future culture.

The Meaning of Bureaucracy's Inner Structures

Once the external functions of bureaucracy are held clearly in mind, the meaning of the structures of bureaucracy can be grasped by contrasting them against their most recent alternatives (although this does not exclude logical speculation about the constellation of future alternatives). We do so by following Weber (1968, pp. 956–958).

Division of Labor

In government, this refers to fixed official jurisdictional areas. These are contrasted against the vague, unsteady, and unsystematic splitting of tasks under previous patriarchal and patrimonial systems, clear obstacles against rational economic development.

Hierarchy

The principle of office hierarchy, levels of graded authority, a firmly ordered system of super- and subordination provides orderliness fostering internal control that can produce outward predictability. Where jurisdiction produces clear division between tasks at any given level, hierarchy produces a vertical division of levels concerned with matters of different scope and importance. Hierarchy is also the control mechanism that holds the division of labor together resulting in a unified policy and program structure. In contrast, with premodern organizations it is not reliably possible for clients to tell who is in charge of what, that is, whose commands are responsible or authoritative in relation to another's. Technically, hierarchical structure allows the creation of a massive administrative structure within which the higher-ups can at least claim abstract knowledge of what is going on below, even if millions are involved.

Written Documentation

Written documentation produces a third referent between disagreeing parties to a dispute, contrasting against word of mouth in which one party's claim is directed without further evidence against another. In contrast to the oral history of patriarchal or patrimonial authority, documentation provides bureaucracy with a memory independent of the minds and mouths of officials, enabling both internal controls and external controls by the political authorities. Documentation makes the actions of bureaucrats traceable and at least in principle inspectable by authoritative outsiders. This paper trail seen from the negative side is red tape.

Staff of Trained Experts

The separation of action from purely personal qualifications and the subordination of such qualifications to impersonal and general standards, is further advanced by the requirement for expert training of officials. This produces a culture and psychology amenable to standardized administrative rules and procedures. In contrast, earlier forms of administration tended to be personalistic and dependent on the luck of the draw in the assignment of a judge or official (rule by amateurs in the original sense of the word).

Full Working Capacity of the Official

This term is not understandable, or understandable only in ergonomic terms, except for a previous comprehension that the official is driven by a duty ethic that draws on the generalized work ethic of the modern civilization. Under this ethic, fulfillment of one's duties is naturally assumed to be of the highest priority before any personal needs, preferences, or wants. The duty ethic guarantees all clients probable fulfillment of their expectation that their legitimate needs will be taken care of with all possible human effort.

General Rules

In contrast to the prior publication and continuous imposition of general rules, premodern organization works under arbitrary, often unpublished ex post facto rules, the very opposite of predictable administration that the economy and law of a modern civilization require.

Bibliography

Bellah, Robert N., 1957. *Tokugawa Religion: The Values of Pre-Industrial Japan*. Glencoe, IL.: Free Press.

Bendix, Reinhard, 1962. *Max Weber—An Intellectual Portrait*. Garden City, N.Y.: Doubleday.

Elazar, Daniel J., 1972. *American Federalism: A View from the States*, 2nd ed. New York: Crowell.

Goodsell, Charles, 1994. *The Case for Bureaucracy: A Public Administration Polemic*, 3rd ed. Chatham, N.J.: Chatham House.

Hummel, Ralph P., 1977. *The Bureaucratic Experience*. New York: St. Martin's.

Merton, Robert K., 1936. "The Unanticipated Consequences of Purposive Social Action." *American Sociological Review*, vol. 1: 894–904.

Selznick, Philip, 1949. *TVA and the Grass Roots*. Berkeley, CA: University of California Press.

Weber, Max, 1930 [originally, 1904–1905; collected in 1920]. *The Protestant Ethic and The Spirit of Capitalism*. Tr. Talcott Parsons. New York: Scribner's. [*Die protestantische Ethik und der "Geist" des Kapitalismus*, 1904–1905; collected in *Gesammelte Aufsaetze zur Religionssoziologie*, vol. 1. Tuebingen: J. C. B. Mohr]

______, 1968. *Economy and Society: An Outline of Interpretive Sociology*. Eds. Guenther Roth and Claus Wittich; trs. Ephraim Fischoff et al. New York: Bedminster Press.

12

BUREAUCRAT BASHING

Charles T. Goodsell,

Virginia Polytechnic Institute and State University

A slang term meaning unjustified attack on government employees, used primarily in the United States and often in reference to career civil servants of the federal government.

While the word "bureaucrat" has a technical meaning in the sociology of large organizations, in lay parlance it is a pejorative term referring to any long-term government employee or civil servant. The bureaucrat in this sense is regarded as personifying the allegedly negative features of "bureaucracy," that is, being lazy, rule-minded, rigid, wasteful, and eager to retain power.

The verb "to bash" has had a number of slang meanings in the English-speaking world over the past two centuries. In this context, it means to strike with a crushing or smashing blow or to flog. Some etymologists believe the term is echoic, that is, an example of onomatopoeia, a word whose pronunciation imitates the sound of its referent. Other historians of language think the term may be a blend of the verbs "bang" and "smash" or, alternatively, a thickening of "pash."

"Bureaucrat bashing" probably entered the American political vocabulary in the 1970s. The expression has since spread to some other English-speaking countries, but seems not to be as popular there as in the United States. The term, on its face, would appear to be useful to those who are disgusted with government. Yet, those most likely to use it tend to have the opposite view, that condemnation of government employees is often unjustified and should itself be condemned. To them, "bureaucrat bashing" means an undesirable or unneeded flogging of public employees.

It is possible that the term was used this way for the first time during the 1976 presidential campaign of Jimmy Carter. Some observers, particularly journalists and academicians empathetic with federal civil servants or the existing political establishment, were dismayed by Carter's attacks on "the bureaucrats" as entrenched defenders of the Washington status quo. During his presidency, Carter continued this line of rhetoric from time to time, accompanied by small acts considered insulting by federal employees, such as levying parking charges and turning off the hot water in government bathrooms. Critics said he was "bashing" federal bureaucrats.

The term's use was reaffirmed in the following decade in the aftermath of the 1980 presidential campaign of Ronald Reagan. He attacked bureaucracy with renewed vigor, connecting the theme to his ideological conservativism. The federal bureaucrats, particularly those holding key positions in Washington, were depicted as contemptible loafers, incompetents, meddlers, and—above all—spenders. Once in office, he continued, like Carter, to sound the theme in speeches, giving the impression that a smaller and less interfering government would be possible only if the permanent bureaucracy could be beaten back. Also, as under Carter, a number of workplace practices further infuriated federal workers, such as monitoring phone calls, reducing office size, seeking antileak pledges, and sampling urine for drugs. The Administration's Private Sector Survey on Cost Control, otherwise known as the Grace Commission, heightened tensions further by conducting a campaign to save billions of dollars by investigating the supposedly wasteful practices of government with a view to replacing them with efficient business methods.

The administration of Bill Clinton, coming to power in 1993, did not "bash" bureaucrats overtly but did take the position that the federal government was "broken" and needed drastic overhaul. Its program, known as "reinventing government," was led by Vice President Gore and institutionalized by means of an organization and process called the National Performance Review (NPR). The problem with government, according to the NPR, was bad systems rather than bad people, yet many federal civil servants felt that the underlying objective was to lower federal expenditures and numbers of employees in preparation for Clinton's 1996 reelection campaign.

Since the mid-1980s, those disturbed by bureaucrat bashing have taken a number of steps to counter the practice. Paul A. Volcker, former chairman of the Federal Reserve, contended that a "quiet crisis" of lowered morale and recruitment attractiveness had emerged in the federal service. He hence organized the National Commission on the Public Service, or Volcker Commission, to promote respect and enhancement of the federal career service. The American Society for Public Administration launched a National Campaign for the Public Service and the Public Employees Roundtable, a coalition of pro–civil-service associations, sponsored an annual Public Service Recognition Week. Recognizing that all of these activities were directed at the national government, a National Commission on the State and Local Public Service, known as the Winter Commission, was formed to promote study, reforms, and renewed appreciation of government service at the state and local levels.

Yet, bureaucrat bashing will not come to a halt in the face of such bureaucrat boosting. Indeed, its further intensification can probably be expected in the years and decades ahead. The reason is not an objective inferiority on the part of America's public servants; they are among the most efficient, honest, and responsive in the world. The explanation lies, rather, in the simple fact that bureaucrats make a handy scapegoat for disenchantment with government. Elected officeholders can point to the bureaucrats to explain why their policies did not work as promised. Campaigning politicians can say that inefficient bureaucrats are a source of budgetary fat that can be cut in order to reduce taxes even while increasing programs.

Condemnation of government employees occurs in every country of the world, of course. In authoritarian regimes it is often deserved because of arbitrary and unfair conduct by officials. In developing countries it may be justified by corrupt behavior or inadequate levels of service quality or quantity caused by lack of funds. But in some nations, such as Western European states and the industrialized polities of the Pacific Rim, the public service has a dignified history and is sufficiently professionalized to enjoy substantial respect. The United States, with its individualistic culture and market-oriented economy, together with a tradition of limited and checked government power, does not possess the historical legacy or contemporary context required to support such a view. Hence bureaucrat bashing will continue to be a feature of its political landscape.

Bibliography

Goodsell, Charles T., 1994. *The Case for Bureaucracy*, 3rd ed. Chatham, NJ: Chatham House.

Lane, Larry M. and James F. Wolf, 1990. *The Human Resource Crisis in the Public Sector*. New York: Quorum.
Wamsley, Gary L. et al., 1990. *Refounding Public Administration*. Beverly Hills: Sage.
Wickwar, Hardy, 1991. *Power and Service*. Westport, CT: Greenwood Press.
Wilson, James Q., 1989. *Bureaucracy*. New York: Basic Books.

13

BUREAUPATHOLOGY

Ruth Hoogland DeHoog,
University of North Carolina at Greensboro

A sickness found in governmental organizations that reduces their effectiveness in meeting policy and program goals in an efficient, yet responsive manner.

Modern bureaucracy has been viewed by many observers as an efficient method of structuring large organizations that perform routine and complex tasks. The Weberian model of legal-rational authority as found in bureaucracy is believed to be an ideal that in practice may take varied forms. Nonetheless, certain features are considered most common: hierarchy, division of labor, adherence to written rules, record-keeping, objective and impartial decisionmaking, and full-time, expert career professionals. Bureaucracy as an efficient machine is a metaphor for its ability to perform tasks consistently, impartially, and economically.

However, modern bureaucracy has its critics in organization theory, as well as among the general public. Their criticisms range from the witty to the sophisticated. Several simple "laws" of bureaucracy draw attention to "dysfunctional," even "pathological," administrative behaviors, that is, behaviors that are considered pathological because they do not enable the organization to accomplish its goals. For example, Parkinson's Law is "work expands so as to fill the time available for its completion," and the Peter Principle states, "Employees tend to be promoted to their level of incompetence." These light-hearted jabs at bureaucracy point to the perceived inefficiency and incompetence of bureaucrats.

More serious criticisms of bureaucracy were written in the mid-to-late twentieth century by organization theorists who believed that seemingly desirable characteristics of bureaucracy can become dysfunctional or pathological for the organization. This can occur due to individual needs or because of the bureaucracy's structure and reward system.

An early critic, Robert Merton (1940), argued that strict adherence to rules can become an end in itself, resulting in "goal displacement," that is, where the organization's goals are replaced by conformity to rules. Often promoted by the bureaucratic training and reward system, this process in turn produces bureaucratic rigidity, red tape, and resistance to change.

Another pathology focuses primarily on the interpersonal behavior of bureaucrats, both in client and subordinate relationships. Victor Thompson (1961) defines "bureaupathology" as the behavior pattern of insecure people using their authority to dominate and control others. Personal anxiety and insecurity may be produced by certain personality traits but can also be encouraged by the bureaucracy's elaborate system of rules, oversight, and punishments. With employees, managers may develop a host of procedures, policies, and standards that govern even the most trivial decisions of subordinates. In trying to follow the rules to the letter to avoid reprimands, officials may make little accommodation for the exceptional case. As bureaucracies stress impartiality and impersonality in public contacts, bureaucrats may also adopt an arrogant, harsh, and domineering attitude toward those they serve.

A fascinating study of dysfunctional bureaucratic behavior in two French public bureaucracies was written by sociologist Michel Crozier (1964). He observed these characteristics: impersonal rules, centralization of decisions, ineffective communication between hierarchical levels, peer group pressures on the individual, and the development of internal power relationships. These resulted in an organization's inability to correct its behavior by learning from its mistakes. Crozier also argues that some observed behaviors may be exacerbated by society's culture, especially in his cases, the French reliance on formal (rather than informal) relationships, the isolation of the individual, and the lack of collective, cooperative norms.

Scholars in the 1970s and 1980s drew attention to the debilitating effects on individuals from a lifetime career in bureaucracy. Drawing on Max Weber and German philosopher Jurgen Habermas, Ralph Hummel (1982) describes the bureaucrat as a "truncated" personality who is able to understand life only in the structured terms of hierarchy and technical competence. As a result, humanistic values are absent in one's personal and professional life, as well as in the organization. Technocratic and bureaucratic values are thus dominant within public organizations that should be held accountable by outside political and constituent forces but often are not.

More recent critics of bureaucracy have suggested that public agencies are inherently inefficient because they tend to maximize their own self-interest in a fashion that may be rational for managers and the agency, but pathological for the government and for the public interest. Bureaucrats are thought to seek budget growth, to expand the number of subordinates, and to control information flows in order to improve individual and organizational power and prestige. These behaviors are encouraged not only by the traditional characteristics of bureaucracy, but also by key economic factors—that is, the lack of market competition for public services and the nature of public goods that are usually supplied by government.

Bibliography

Crozier, Michel, 1964. *The Bureaucratic Phenomenon*. Chicago: University of Chicago Press.

Hummel, Ralph, 1982. *The Bureaucratic Experience*, 2nd ed. New York: St. Martin's.

Merton, Robert K., 1940. "Bureaucratic Structure and Personality." *Social Forces*, vol. 17: 560–568.

Parkinson, C. Northcote, 1975. *Parkinson's Law*. New York: Ballantine.

Peter, Laurence J. and Raymond Hull, 1969. *The Peter Principle*. New York: William Morrow.

Thompson, Victor A., 1961. Modern Organization. New York: Alfred A. Knopf.

Part Five

Organization Behavior

14

ORGANIZATIONAL CULTURE

Dvora Yanow,
California State University, Hayward
Guy B. Adams,
University of Missouri, Columbia

A concept in or an approach to the study of organizations focusing on elements thought to be overlooked by the more prevalent functional and rational approaches such as organizational design, human relations, systems, and organizational politics. The study may focus on organizational artifacts, such as stories, symbols, ceremonies, rituals, myths, sagas, tales, heroes, taboos, jargon, slang, metaphors, gestures, signs, humor, gossip, rumor, and proverbs, and/or on the values, beliefs, and feelings that are seen as underlying such artifacts; and/or on the context-specific meanings made by members of the organization and other organizationally relevant publics, as well as researchers' interpretations of those meanings. Which of these is seen as defining organizational culture depends on the way "culture" is understood. Organizational culture studies developed largely in the 1980s, although there are earlier works that can be included under this heading. Simultaneous developments in Europe and the U.S. largely followed distinct themes.

Origins, Definitions, and Early History

Culture as a concept has historically been the concern of anthropologists, who, however, have developed no consensus on its definition. Various schools of thought and methodologies within anthropology have influenced definitions and treatments of organizational culture. For example, anthropologists Kroeber and Kluckhohn (1952) developed a functionalist perspective, while Levi-Strauss (1964) pursued a structural approach. Their influences and others from anthropology can be seen in the five perspectives on organizational culture presented in Smircich (1983). Two of the perspectives she discusses construe culture as a variable: one examines differences between organizations across national cultures (with culture as an independent variable), while the other looks at culture as a dependent variable within particular organizations (the corporate culture approach). The remaining three approaches treat "culture" metaphorically, as a way of seeing organizations. These include a symbolic approach; a clinical, psychodynamic approach; and a cognitive approach. This early framework still accurately describes the range of current approaches to organizational cultures.

The notion of culture in an organizational context goes back at least as far as a 1951 study by Elliott Jaques. The English sociologist Barry A. Turner made the first extensive use of the concept of culture in studying organizations in 1971. Within public administration, some of the early work of the institutionalist school has much in common with later work in organizational culture. Selznick (1949) and Kaufman (1960) are two examples.

The Recent Development of Organizational Culture

Current work in organizational culture developed rapidly at the end of the 1970s and early 1980s. In the later 1970s, the Organizational Symbolism Network, a group of primarily U.S. academics, was formed. In the early 1980s in Europe, the Standing Conference on Organizational Symbolism (SCOS) was started (a part of EGOS, the European Group on Organization Studies, the counterpart of the U.S. Academy of Management). A 1979 conference at the University of Illinois led to the publication of a collection of essays, edited by Louis A. Pondy and others (1983). Beginning in 1981, several iterations of a summer conference on "Interpretive Approaches to the Study of Organizations" were held through the auspices of the Communications Department at the University of Utah. In 1983, Michael Owen Jones and others organized a conference entitled "Myth, Symbols and Folklore: Expanding the Analysis of Organizations" at the University of California–Los Angeles. This was followed by another conference in 1984, "Organizational Culture and the Meaning of Life in the Workplace." Held at the University of British Columbia in Canada, it was the first institutional naming of the field as organizational culture (the essays are collected in Frost et al. 1985). Two other conferences were also held in 1984: "Corporate Culture: From the Native's Point of View," in California, and "Managing Corporate Cultures" at the University of Pittsburgh. Others followed. Five influential academic journals devoted entire issues to the topic of organizational culture. The first was the *Administrative Science Quarterly* in Fall 1983. It was followed by the *Journal of Management* and *Organizational Dynamics* in Spring and Fall 1984, respectively, and the *Journal of Management Studies* and *Organization Studies*, two European journals, in 1986.

This early outpouring of work developed into two fairly distinct schools of thought. One evolved out of comparisons between increasingly more successful Japanese firms and lagging U.S. productivity at the time. Largely developed in the U.S., it came to be known as the "corporate culture" school. Today, its scholars are often searching for quantitative measures of culture, and many European and other non-U.S. scholars are active in this stream.

The second school of thought evolved out of a more diffuse dissatisfaction with traditional theories of organization and management, on the one hand by those taking qualitative, field-based methodological approaches to studying organizations, on the other hand by those with concerns rooted in the philosophy of science (including social science), which were receiving increasing attention in a wide variety of disciplines (including cultural anthropology, social history, literary criticism, qualitative sociology). This latter approach, in particular, has been more extensively developed by European scholars and professional associations. Largely under the influence of their work, it has come to be known as the "organizational symbolism" school.

Between them has emerged a third camp, the more general "organizational culture" school, that seeks to develop generalizable typologies of cultures informed by context-specific data. These three streams will be examined in turn.

Corporate Culture

Much of the attention, both popular and academic, to organizational culture studies dates to the publication of several popular books in the early

1980s. Two books concerning Japanese management styles are often included in this historical reckoning: Ouchi's *Theory Z* (1981) and Peters and Waterman's *In Search of Excellence* (1982). But it was Deal and Kennedy's *Corporate Cultures* (1982) that gave the field one of its names and established a framework for debate. The authors identified various rituals, symbols, and heroes of contemporary corporate American life and prescribed their adoption by other companies wishing to be "successful." This book and other work in the same vein seem to treat culture almost as if it were a souvenir for corporate tourists: collections of departmental celebrations, retirement mementos, office costumes, phrase book terminologies, and the like, which were claimed to be unique to the culture in which they were found. These authors argued that organizational leaders and managers could develop successful companies and agencies by creating, deploying, and managing these cultural artifacts.

Among other things, the discovery that identical stories appeared in different organizations led to a broadening of this view of culture. It led, for example, to a new line of inquiry exploring whether "industries" could be said to have unique cultures. An interesting variant of this research seeks to determine whether a geographic region further distinguishes among organizations within a single industry: for example, are Silicon Valley (California) electronics firms different culturally from Route 128 (Massachusetts) electronics firms (Weiss and Delbecq 1987)?

The question of regional influence has its parallel in studies that seek to determine the intersections of national cultural effects and organizational cultural effects, of which Geert Hofstede, the Dutch organizational scholar, has been the central figure. His research in multinational corporations (MNCs) claims that even within a single MNC, employees in different national offices reflect national culture more than corporate culture (e.g., Hofstede 1984). Others, however, have been unable to replicate Hofstede's research, suggesting that he was also finding the effects of a particular profession's culture (in this case, engineers).

Organizational Culture

Edgar H. Schein, the MIT organizational psychologist, has produced the best known writing within this stream. The ideas that first appeared in a number of working papers and journal articles are developed in *Organizational Culture and Leadership*, first published in 1985 and expanded and revised in a second edition in 1992. Schein's analysis was then, and the second edition still is, the most thorough conceptual treatment of the subject, albeit from the standpoint of a social psychologist interested in client-driven research (what he calls a "clinical" perspective), as distinct from research driven by the researcher's interests. His treatment reflects the functionalist approach to culture developed by Kluckhohn alongside Schein's own open systems approach, developed in his earlier work in organizational psychology. The 1992 edition retains the chapter entitled "Ethical Problems in Studying Organizational Cultures" (chapter 10), still the best (and perhaps only) discussion of what it means from the client's point of view to have a consultant/researcher make public that which is organizationally private (if not tacit) knowledge.

Schein begins by defining organizational culture, giving an archeology of levels of culture from the more visible "artifacts" to the "espoused values" that underlie them (the strategies, goals, philosophies) to the more deeply buried "basic underlying assumptions," the "unconscious, taken-for-granted beliefs, perceptions, thoughts, and feelings" that are the "ultimate source of values and action" (1992, p. 17). When it first appeared, Schein's theoretical argument raised several of the issues that still mark debate in the field today. As his title indicates, he considers organizational leaders to be the active creators of organizational cultures, a position logical—as he himself has remarked—in the context of his own access as a consultant to top organizational levels.

This leader-focused approach was adopted by many scholars. It raised a key conceptual question: are organizational cultures established *only* by leaders at the top of the organization? A second conceptual issue derives from this top-down view: whether there is a one-to-one relationship between organizational boundaries and culture—one organization, one unitary culture. There is no room in this view for subcultures or countercultures. Both of these assumptions, shared by the corporate culture school, have been challenged by other researchers who have studied culture on the shop floor, among employees and midlevel managers, and in occupational and professional subcultures. Most organizational culture theorists (e.g., Sackmann 1991; Trice and Beyer 1993) now accept that any organization may contain multiple cultures or subcultures, not all of them created by organizational leaders or managers.

These later studies move closer to a phenomenological point of view, seeing artifacts as the expressions of less visible values, beliefs, feelings, meanings. Yet the approach is still a positivist view that sees the reality of culture *in* the organization, rather than in the researcher's *view* of the organization. It is an approach that seeks to discover universally applicable rules.

Organizational Symbolism and Cultural Studies of Organizations

Some organizational culture scholars have followed the "interpretive turn" made by many in reaction against the perceived limitations of positivist science. This represents an ontological shift to a view that organizational cultures are perceived, not factual, realities. More recently, others have made a "narrative turn" to focus on language and rhetorical issues (see, e.g., Czarniawska-Joerges 1997; Golden-Biddle and Locke 1993; Hatch 1996; O'Connor 1995; Smircich 1995; Van Maanen 1995; White 1992; Yanow 1995). This includes attention to forms of (re)presentation of field work, parallel to developments in anthropology that explore how the writing up of field notes can, itself, create (a view of) culture.

Those following these paths make a radical departure from earlier treatments of the concept of culture. Here, integral questions of reality, knowledge, and methodology are being worked out. If culture is understood to be "real," then it can be studied and known through objective fact-gathering means such as those specified by positivism and the scientific method, and researchers can generate "laws" or principles about organizational culture that are generalizable across organizations. But an interpretive position argues that this is not the case: that culture, rather than being "real," is a way of seeing organizations that entails methodological implications as well. Cultural analyses of organizations generate situation-specific knowledge that reflects organizational actors' understandings of their situations and researchers' interpretations of those understandings as well as of their own experiences. Both the subject of study and the researcher are understood to be situated in specific contexts. Generalizable typologies are not possible, in this view.

Initial arguments about the distinctions between positivist and interpretive theories cast them as differences between quantitative and qualitative methods. But that is a misleading distinction: researchers who conduct open-ended interviews or who act as participant observers also quantify when it is necessary. Neither quantitative nor qualitative methods inherently require the researcher to turn away from the ontological and epistemological assumptions of positivist science.

The interpretive turn in organizational culture has rested, in part, on the question of unitary versus multiple cultures. Seeing organizations from the perspective of agency executives implied that there was only one legitimate view of each organization's culture—and that culture was singular. When researchers looked at the organization from other positions—from the shop floor, for example, or from inside various departments—cultural singularity disappeared in the face of the meanings made of organizational actions by employees in the situation. The interpretive turn places the problem of *meaning* at the center of research: meanings made by organizational actors, as well as meanings made by researchers who interpret actors' meanings.

Seeing organizational cultures from different vantage points introduced a world of multiple realities. Organizational reality was no longer seen to exist external to the person perceiving that reality, whether that person is an employee or a researcher. Knowledge came to be seen as a creation by subjects in a situation; it is subjective knowledge (in the sense that it pertains to the subject), not objective (externally derived) knowledge. Following on or recreating the thinking of European philosophers (Schutz and phenomenology, Ricoeur and hermeneutics) and their U.S. counterparts (Garfinkel and ethnomethodology, Goffman and Mead and symbolic interactionism), theorists working from this view see a representational relationship between cultural beliefs, values, and feelings and the artifacts that express them. This view has led them to focus on symbolic objects, language, and acts as representations or embodiments of meanings. This school of thought is often referred to as "organizational symbolism."

Much of this work has been done by European and other non-U.S. researchers, particularly within the Standing Conference on Organisational Symbolism (SCOS) formed over a decade ago. Two edited collections of SCOS conference papers, Gagliardi (1990) and Turner (1990), are noteworthy both in their symbolic-interpretive approach to the subject and in their inclusion of public agencies as subjects of study (the Danish Ministry of Domestic Affairs, NASA's Space Shuttle, the Luneberg, Germany, municipal saltworks, the Washington State Ferry System, an English prison, and so forth).

In the U.S. most of the work from a symbolic perspective has appeared in academic journals. One exception is Ott (1989), who places symbolism at the heart of what culture is all about, while building on Schein's three-part cultural structure. Another is the work of Ingersoll and Adams

(1992), an ethnography of the takeover of the Washington State Ferry System by the state's Department of Transportation (DOT). Theirs is a view of culture as cognition, including its tacit aspects, taking a cultural approach to the study of the ferry system—one that focuses on meanings made by actors in the situation—rather than seeing the organization's culture as a set of objects or rituals. In a related vein, Yanow (1996) explores ways in which the organizational metaphors, buildings, and acts of a public agency, the Israel Corporation of Community Centers, were symbolic representations of policy and organizational meanings, thereby communicating those meanings, even as tacit knowledge, to multiple audiences or "readers." Kunda's (1992) may also be considered a cultural approach. Finding that managerial uses of corporate culture concepts have produced feelings of alienation among middle- and lower-level employees, without necessarily enabling greater control over them, Kunda addresses the moral responsibility of culture researchers providing managers with tools to alter workers' realities. The question of meanings made by the actors in the organizational situation is central to these analyses.

Turning to culture as an approach, rather than a variable to be studied, situates methodological concerns within their related questions of knowledge and reality. This links cultural studies of organizations to other recent theoretical developments: feminist, critical, literary, and postmodern theoretical approaches. Feminist and critical theorists (e.g., Minow 1990) have called attention to the fact that much of what is presented as neutral and universal knowledge is actually based on an assumed norm. (For feminist theorists, that norm has been seen typically as male; for critical theorists, the norm is seen to embody a power-based status, resting typically on class and/or race and/or, lately, gender.) These critiques call attention to the context of the researcher producing knowledge, as well as to the subject of knowledge. In narrative, rhetorical, and literary critical theories, this point appears in analyses of writing that argue that the text is as much a representation of the author as a reflection of the subject (see, e.g., Golden-Biddle and Locke 1993; Van Maanen 1988). In anthropology, for example, the language used by ethnographers convinces (or fails to convince) the reader that the ethnographer was truly present in and conversant with the place that is being presented. Such analyses invoke methods of literary criticism to analyze representations of culture as narratives that use rhetorical tools to persuade the reader of the veracity of the account. By extension, organizational practices may also be "read" as "texts" intended to convince multiple audiences ("readers"), who may read those texts quite differently. To judge from recent scholarly work in economics, policy analysis, and other fields, this is an important new direction that cultural analyses of organizational theories and practices are now taking.

Bibliography

Czarniawska-Joerges, Barbara, 1997. *Narrating the Organization*. Chicago: University of Chicago Press.

Deal, Terrence E. and Allen A. Kennedy, 1982. *Corporate Cultures*. Reading, MA: Addison-Wesley.

Frost, Peter J., Larry F. Moore, Meryl Reis Louis, Craig C. Lundberg, and Joanne Martin, 1985. *Organizational Culture*. Newbury Park, CA: Sage.

Gagliardi, Pasquale, ed., 1990. *Symbols and Artifacts*. New York: Walter de Gruyter.

Golden-Biddle, Karen and Karen Locke, 1993. "Appealing Work: An Investigation in How Ethnographic Texts Convince." *Organization Science* 4:4 (November).

Hatch, Mary Jo, 1996. "The Role of the Researcher: An Analysis of Narrative Position in Organizational Theory." *Journal of Management Inquiry* vol. 5, no. 4: 359–374.

Hofstede, Geert, 1984. *Culture's Consequences*. Abridged edition. London: Sage.

Ingersoll, Virginia Hill and Guy B. Adams, 1992. *The Tacit Organization*. Greenwich, CT: JAI Press.

Jaques, Elliott, 1951. *The Changing Culture of a Factory*. London: Tavistock.

Kaufman, Herbert, 1960. *The Forest Ranger*. Baltimore: Johns Hopkins Press.

Kroeber, Clyde and Theodore Kluckhohn, 1952. *Culture: A Critical Review of Concepts and Definitions*. Cambridge, MA: Harvard University Press.

Kunda, Gideon, 1992. *Engineering Culture*. Philadelphia: Temple University Press.

Levi-Strauss, Claude, 1964. *Structural Anthropology*. New York: Basic Books.

Minow, Martha, 1990. *Making All the Difference*. Ithaca, NY: Cornell University Press.

O'Connor, Ellen, 1995. "Paradoxes of Participation: A Literary Analysis of Case Studies on Employee Involvement." *Organization Studies* 15:2.

O'Connor, Ellen, with Mary Jo Hatch, Hayden White, and Mayer Zald, 1995. "Undisciplining Organizational Studies: A Conversation Across Domains, Methods, and Beliefs." *Journal of Management Inquiry* 4:2, 119–136.

Ott, J. Steven, 1989. *The Organizational Culture Perspective*. Pacific Grove, CA: Brooks/Cole.

Ouchi, William, 1981. *Theory Z*. Reading, MA: Addison-Wesley.

Peters, Thomas J. and Robert H. Waterman, 1982. *In Search of Excellence*. New York: Harper and Row.

Pondy, Louis A., Peter N. Frost, Gareth Morgan, and Thomas C. Dandridge eds., 1983. *Organizational Symbolism*. Greenwich, CT: JAI Press.

Sackmann, Sonja A., 1991. *Cultural Knowledge in Organizations: Exploring the Collective Mind*. Newbury Park, CA: Sage.

Schein, Edgar H., 1985. *Organizational Culture and Leadership*. San Francisco: Jossey-Bass.

______, 1992. *Organizational Culture and Leadership*, 2d ed. San Francisco: Jossey-Bass.

Selznick, Philip, 1949. *TVA and the Grass Roots*. New York: Harper and Row.

Smircich, Linda, 1983. "Concepts of Culture and Organizational Analysis." *Administrative Science Quarterly* 28:3, 339–358.

______, 1995. "Writing Organizational Tales: Reflections on Three Books on Organizational Culture." *Organization Science* 6:2, 232–237.

Trice, Harrison M. and Janice M. Beyer, 1993. *The Cultures of Work Organizations*. Englewood Cliffs, NJ: Prentice-Hall.

Turner, Barry A., 1971. *Exploring the Industrial Subculture*. London: Herder and Herder.

______, ed., 1990. *Organizational Symbolism*. New York: Walter de Gruyter.

Van Maanen, John, 1988. *Tales of the Field*. Chicago: University of Chicago Press.

______, 1995. "Style as Theory." *Organization Science* 6:1.

Weiss, Joseph and Andre Delbecq, 1987. "High-technology Cultures and Management." *Group and Organization Studies* 12, 39–54.

White, Jay D., 1992. "Taking Language Seriously: Toward a Narrative Theory of Knowledge for Administrative Research." *American Review of Public Administration* 22:2 (June).

Yanow, Dvora, 1995. "Writing Organizational Tales: Four Authors and Their Stories About Culture." *Organization Science* 6:2, 225–226.

______, 1996. *How Does a Policy Mean? Interpreting Policy and Organizational Actions*. Washington, D.C.: Georgetown University Press.

15

GROUPTHINK

Robert T. Golembiewski,
University of Georgia

The psychological drive for consensus, which tends to suppress both dissent and the appraisal of alternatives in small decisionmaking groups. Groupthink tends to occur when individuals value membership in the group and identify strongly with their colleagues. It may also occur because the group leader does not encourage dissent or because of stressful situations that make the group more cohesive. The essence of it though, is that the members suppress doubts and criticisms about proposed courses of action, with the result that the group chooses riskier and more ill-advised policies than would otherwise have been the case. Groupthink, because it refers to a deterioration of mental efficiency and moral judgment due to in-group pressures, has an invidious connotation. The term derives from Irvin L. Janis, *Victims of Groupthink: A Psychological Study of Foreign-Policy Decisions and Fiascoes* (1972).

Social commentary in Western settings has long been full of references to the negative features of groups or other human collectivities. The autonomous individual has reigned in many circles as the ideal, and human aggregates often have been portrayed as a major cause of the fast fall from inherent grace of people when they are part of some human aggregate. Thus many early commentators were impressed by the power of people in collectivities, and this basic perception often got translated as a fear of "the mob" or the "the group mind" that could arouse normally docile and God-fearing folk to do things they otherwise would not even contemplate (e.g., Golembiewski 1962, esp. pp. 8–26).

Freud's theoretical interpretation is as elegant as anyone's, and as extreme. He proposed directly that "In a group an individual is brought under conditions which allow him [or her] to throw off the repressions of . . . unconscious instincts." That constituted a fateful unshackling for Freud, no doubt about that. For the "unconscious" is nothing less than the mental databank "in which *all that is evil* in the human mind is contained as a predisposition" (quoted in Strachey 1955, p. 74, emphasis added).

Put a person in a group context, then, and (at least for Freud) a troubling array of "apparently new characteristics" will appear. Those characteristics are not really new, however, but activations of potentialities for evil already in the person, and suddenly released by a "group condition."

Among the latest variants in this tradition about human collectivities as generally troublesome, if not absolutely evil, is the concept of "groupthink" elaborated so brilliantly by Janis (1972). In turn, the two sections below detail Janis's views, and then emphasize several elaborations of his basic model.

Janis on "Groupthink"

There is not much doubt about where Janis came down concerning the consequences of "groupthink." That evaluation is clearly implied in the subtitle of his seminal book: *A Psychological Study of Foreign-Policy Decisions and Fiascoes*. Janis grounded his analysis in a number of case studies chosen to illustrate why and how decisions became fiascoes, given common features of groups. The cases include the abortive and aborted invasion of Cuba at the Bay of Pigs; the United States war with North Korea; and a revisit to the tragedy of Pearl Harbor, among other detailed illustrations-in-action.

What is "groupthink," then? Janis detailed eight generalizations about the symptoms of the "groupthink syndrome," as well as three hypotheses concerning the probability that the condition will develop (1972, pp. 197–198). Here, consider only a thumbnail summary. The key for Janis is *high cohesiveness*, by which he means a high degree of "amiability and esprit de corps among the members." As cohesiveness grows, so increases the insulation from "outsiders," or individuals or groups that might challenge the decisions or processes of the insiders. In part, this insulation reflects the optimism among group members, and even their sense of invulnerability, which are reasonably associated with high cohesiveness.

Relatedly, the insulation also can result from the group members' happy sense of self, which can encourage the undervaluing of outsiders, when they are not seen as overt enemies of the in-group. The tendencies toward groupthink get a big push when the group's leader promotes his or her own point of view.

Now, nowhere has Janis said that all groups generate "groupthink." Indeed, he took pains to emphasize that he isolated necessary but *not* sufficient conditions (e.g., Janis 1972, pp. 198–201), and that he focused on tendencies rather than inevitabilities.

Many of Janis's critics have seen him as less-subtle on this crucial point and, on occasion, Janis often invited just this kind of criticism. For example, he too-sharply distinguishes "independent critical thinking," ostensibly only by individuals, from what too often (for him) occurs in groups. Indeed, at times, Janis comes close to allowing this view to creep into the minds of readers—that the only human aggregate really safe from groupthink are those sorry cohorts having a low degree of "amiability and esprit de corps."

Some Elaborations of "Groupthink"

Two elaborations of Janis's basic conceptual scheme may help in the sense of discouraging groupthink about groupthink. First, Janis's basic position is at least too broad, if not flat wrong. Ample evidence establishes that increasing cohesiveness *tends to be* associated with positive outcomes like productivity, creative ideas, and low absenteeism, *and strongly so*. Indeed, the association between high cohesiveness and favorable outcomes seems to occur in eight or nine of every ten cases, more or less. Groups seem to help more than they harm, in short. This conclusion was obvious some time ago (e.g., Golembiewski 1962, pp. 149–170), and remains so (e.g., Zander 1994; 1982, pp. 4–10). Janis implies that it is the other way around.

Second, Janis might well distinguish several types or kinds of groupthink. Strategic possibilities include at least three kinds of "crises of agreement," which could be included under the rubric "groupthink":

- the crisis of agreement among the "best and the brightest," based on a cohesiveness resting on high self-esteem as well as mutual regard, and with a confidence about future employment or life-chances. This seems to characterize most of those involved in Kennedy's Cuban missile crisis (e.g., Halberstam 1969).

- the crisis of agreement resting on an authoritarian cohesiveness based on seeing outsiders as "enemies" in a state of "war," with low self-esteem and fear dominating among members—fear not only concerning "enemies" but perhaps especially fear of losing their jobs, reinforced by low confidence about similar placements should that happen. This seems to have been the dominant case among Watergate Nixonians (e.g., Raven 1974).
- the crisis of agreement existing among persons having strong affective ties that are expected to continue, as in a family or a "close" work unit (e.g., Harvey 1988).

These three types differ in important ways. Thus, fear of exclusion because of expressing deviant opinions exists in all three cases, but is clearly apparent in the second. Moreover, conformity will exist in all cases, but the temptation will be strongest in the second type. Relatedly, different interventions seem appropriate for each of the three types of crises of agreement.

Bibliography

Golembiewski, Robert T., 1962. *The Small Group*. Chicago: University of Chicago Press.

Halberstam, David, 1969. *The Best and the Brightest*. New York: Random House.

Harvey, Jerry B., 1988. "The Abilene Paradox: The Management of Agreement." *Organizational Dynamics*, vol. 17 (Summer): 17–34.

Janis, Irving L., 1972. *Victims of Groupthink: A Psychological Study of Foreign-Policy Decisions and Fiascoes*. Boston: Houghton Mifflin.

Raven, Bertram, 1974. "The Nixon Group." *Journal of Social Issues*, vol. 30, no 2: 297–330.

Strachey, James, ed., 1955. *The Standard Edition of the Complete Psychological Works of Sigmund Freud*. London: Hogarth.

Zander, Alvin, 1994, 1982. *Making Groups Effective*. San Francisco: Jossey-Bass.

16

MILES'S LAW

Jeffery K. Guiler,
Robert Morris College

A maxim that evolved from a theory developed by Rufus E. Miles when he managed a branch of the Federal Bureau of the Budget responsible for labor and welfare in the late 1940s. Miles's Law states, "Where you stand depends on where you sit." The law theorizes that there is a direct correlation between the position an individual takes on a particular issue and the title or position that individual holds in the organization.

Development of the Theory

Although Miles himself admitted the "concept was as old as Plato," the "phraseology" evolved after a sequence of events that took place while Miles was supervising a group of middle-level federal employees at the Bureau of the Budget. One of Miles's employees, a budget examiner, was offered a position in a federal agency over which Miles's group had the power of budgetary review. The subordinate explained to Miles that he was concerned about working at a new agency that he did not perceive as very efficient. The subordinate also had been critical of this particular agency in his capacity as an examiner. The job, however, was a grade higher than the position of examiner the subordinate currently held and the income increase based on the job's higher grade was attractive to the employee. The employee informed Miles that he would like to remain in his current position as an examiner but with the increased salary of the position he had been offered at the other agency. Miles, while expressing appreciation for the employee's loyalty, refused to increase the individual's pay and the employee resigned his position with Miles to accept the position at the other agency. After the employee left the bureau, Miles remarked to his fellow workers that in a very short time, the former employee would become a defender of the very policies he had been critical of when he was in the position of an examiner because "where you stand depends on where you sit."

Lessons to Be Learned from Miles's Law

Miles determined there are three lessons that can be drawn from Miles's Law and its impact on organizations. The first lesson is that when individuals change positions in an organization, their position on issues impacting the area of their new area of responsibility will evolve to reflect the needs of that area. An example of such an evolution exists with the case of John Gardner, chairman of President Johnson's Task Force on Education. Gardner, president of the Carnegie Corporation, was asked to chair a task force on education in 1964. The task force under Gardner's leadership concluded that the Department of Health, Education, and Welfare (HEW) as constituted in 1964 could not adequately address the needs of education. The task force was split as to whether a separate cabinet-level Department of Education should be established. Less than a year later, Gardner accepted the position of Secretary of Health, Education, and Welfare. When asked in his new position if education should be removed from HEW, Gardner replied with an emphatic no. Now that Gardner was the secretary and no longer simply a detached evaluator, his position of the issue was reversed. He did not wish to see his responsibilities decreased or his opportunities limited. In the case of Gardner, where he stood on the issue was now a direct result of the perspectives of his new position at HEW.

The second more subtle lesson that can be learned is that no individual can serve objectively on a committee or task force that is called upon to evaluate the agency or commission of which the individual is an integral part. This is the problem that impacts internal committees that are called together to assess and evaluate their own agency's efficiency and effectiveness. Miles believes that no person from within the organization can "totally rise" above the individual concerns and issues of the agency they are called upon to evaluate if this individual is a part of the organization. Such individuals will be unable to make sound recommendations as they will always be concerned about the impact of their recommendations on the organization to which they eventually return. Miles feels that people should not be placed in a position where they are asked to render a recommendation or decision that will impact their own future.

The third implication of Miles's Law concerns communication. The head of an agency or organization must constantly evaluate the channels of communication from which data are received within the organization. No subordinate, according to Miles's Law, is able to give a superior information that is not partially biased in favor of the messenger's agenda. Even the most trustworthy subordinates cannot help but flavor their communications to their superior with the essence of their own opinions or biases. Miles noted that Franklin Roosevelt was an excellent user of the multichannel communication process, as he gathered information from many sources within his organization. Richard Nixon, on the other hand, drew his data from a select few with disastrous results.

Impact of Miles's Law

Miles's Law makes it clear that no individual can be divorced from the perspectives of the responsibilities of the position they hold. These perspectives will change when the individual assumes a new capacity in a different agency and these revised perspectives can legitimately be the opposite of previous positions taken by the individual because "where you stand depends on where you sit."

Bibliography

Miles, Jr., Rufus E., 1976. *Awakening from the American Dream*. New York: Universe Books.

______, 1978. "The Origins and Meanings of Miles's Law." *Public Administration Review* (September-October) 399–403.

______, 1979. "Miles Six Other Maxims of Management." *Organizational Dynamics* (Summer).

17

Parkinson's Law

Peter Foot,

United Kingdom Joint Services Command and Staff College

The proposition that work expands to fill the time made available for its completion. The idea was first set out formally by the British social theorist and political scientist, C. Northcote Parkinson, in his book *Parkinson's Law,* published in 1957. Like a number of popular studies, its main function is to suggest that the more severe theorists of management practice ought not to take themselves too seriously.

Parkinson was what used to be called an Admiralty civil servant: a British official seconded to the Royal Navy. It was during an investigation of work practices in the British Naval Service that he became impressed by the phenomenon expressed in the principle that was ever after to bear his name. Regardless of management structure or an incentive- or reward-based system, individuals seemed to make their own choices as to how fast a job could be completed. The work would be completed on time—the "time" being defined as the moment when adverse effects would be visited upon the employee for late delivery. As interesting is Parkinson's analysis of how employees respond to repeated difficulties in meeting deadlines. In effect, Parkinson argues that employees conspire against their employers by increasing the size of the hierarchy, aggrandizing their own position in the process, at the expense of those who pay them. He tended to assume that supervisors tended to conspire against the employer; that employees (acting individually or in concert) would injure themselves to the point where the paymaster is brought to the brink of bankruptcy; that less spent on wages will maximize profits. While challenging, none of these are self-evidently true.

Parkinson, as with many who have a particular insight—in this case the one that is encapsulated in the definition above—took the point too far in his published theoretical work, to the extent where other theorists had more to say on the questions that he was addressing. Unlike them, however, he has achieved his own immortality.

Bibliography

Parkinson, C. N., 1957. *Parkinson's Law and Other Studies in Administration*. Boston: Houghton Mifflin.

18

PETER PRINCIPLE

Susan C. Paddock,

University of Wisconsin, Madison

The concept originated by Laurence J. Peter and discussed in his book of the same name (Peter and Hull 1969) that "in a hierarchy, every employee tends to rise to his level of incompetence." Peter's Corollary is "in time, every post tends to be occupied by an employee who is incompetent to carry out its duties."

Based on his observations of schools, government organizations, and businesses, Peter hypothesized that employees are promoted to positions because of their competence in their current position, not because of the competence they might have in a future position. As a result, employees are promoted to positions where they might not have the necessary skills.

While a person might move from a level of competence to a higher level of competence—for example, from a line worker to a lead worker—ultimately, Peter claimed, the final promotion would be to a level of incompetence. As a result, hierarchies are staffed by people operating beyond their level of competence.

There are apparent exceptions to this rule. An incompetent person may be promoted, or a competent one not promoted. Peter argued that these are not exceptions but rather further proof that the Peter Principle is accurate. An already incompetent person who is promoted may be moved in such a way that the new position is outside the hierarchy, as in a promotion to a staff position, for example; or the individual may be "promoted" laterally.

Organizational rules and regulations rather than individual incompetence may seem to cause poor performance. For example, a functionary may refuse to give out information because it is "not in the job description" or may require the completion of multiple forms "because it is required." These bureaucratic behaviors, however, are ruses to mask individual incompetence.

When a supercompetent person is dismissed rather than promoted, the principle of incompetence is upheld. Supercompetence disrupts the hierarchy and interferes with the operation of the Peter Principle. Supercompetents who are dismissed from an organization often form their own businesses where their competence can be demonstrated. However, even the brightest supercompetent can fail when he or she moves into an area requiring new competence—for example, when an outstanding computer developer moves into management.

Peter argued that promotion to a level of incompetence not only inflicts damage on the organization, but also harms the physical and psychological health of the individual. Once promoted to a level of incompetence, the individual realizes that he or she is no longer able to meet or exceed expectations. This causes both diminished self-esteem and fear that someone might "find out" about one's incompetence. Thus, the person begins to work harder, and to pay more attention to sometimes inconsequential details. As the Queen in *Through the Looking Glass* (Carroll 1916) notes, "Now *here*, you see, it takes all the running you can do to keep in the same place." Being at one's level of incompetence causes the final placement syndrome, whose symptoms include such things as ulcers, alcoholism, insomnia, chronic fatigue, and even more serious medical problems.

Peter's cure for the Peter Principle was creative incompetence. He argued that it usually is not possible to refuse a promotion, even if one knows that the new position is beyond one's competence. Instead, Peter suggested one should develop strategies to disguise or camouflage competence. You must, Peter said, "create the impression that you have already reached your level of incompetence" but you must do it in such a way that it does not prevent you from carrying out your duties.

The term "Peter Principle" has come to mean any individual or organizational behavior which is irrational and inefficient, yet supported by the hierarchy. The term is widely used and now commonly accepted as a mark that an organization or system is characterized by incompetence and inefficiency.

Bibliography

Carroll, Lewis [pseud.], 1916. *Alice's Adventures in Wonderland and Through the Looking Glass*. Chicago, IL: Rand McNally.

Peter, Laurence J., and Raymond Hull, 1969. *The Peter Principle*. New York, NY: William Morrow and Company.

Part Six

Public Management

Public Management

19

Public Management

Mary E. Guy,
Florida State University

The application of the craft, art, and science of management to a context where political values govern the evaluation of success and where the rule of law dictates constraints on administrative discretion. Because political preferences bring policy shifts, the ability to navigate in politicized waters is a skill that is as essential to the public manager as the ability to plan, organize, staff, direct, budget, and perform other standard managerial duties. Public management means "doing" government. And, because politics is a key dimension to government, public management requires mastery of political as well as administrative skills.

Public managers work in city, county, state, and federal government, as well as special districts. They work in executive, judicial, and legislative agencies in roles as varied as the missions of those agencies. For example, missions range from wastewater treatment plants to foster care for children; from highway engineers to agricultural extension agents; from welfare services to weather forecasting; from public health services to law enforcement; from public education to firefighting; from national defense to economic development; from environmental protection to emergency preparedness; from tax collection to neighborhood zoning; from parks and recreation facilities to court administration; from public libraries to highway safety; from national research and development laboratories to regulatory commissions. Managing each of these enterprises requires substantive knowledge of the policy arena pertaining to the mission, mastery of generic managerial skills, a keen ability to maximize political values to advance the work of the agency, and an abiding respect for democratic policies and procedures.

Evolution of the Term

As the 1900s progressed, a bifurcation developed among those who wrote about the work of government (Ott, Hyde, and Shafritz 1991). While some wrote about the administrative side of the enterprise, others wrote about the policy side. Graduate programs developed that emphasized either the public policy aspects or the administrative aspects. In the meantime, those who were actively engaged in the work of government were wrestling with both sides of the coin: policy *plus* administration. As a corollary event, business administration programs made a transition from the word "administration" to the word "management," as public administration programs began to replace the term "administration" with "management." At the least, the term "public management" merely reflects the transition in popularity from the word "administration" to the word "management." At most, it reflects the appreciation that public managers must juggle both policy and administration to be effective.

By this time, the term "public management" is widely accepted and connotes an action orientation to the coordination and interconnectedness that is inherent in the operation of public programs. Its precedent "public administration" has not so much changed as it has fallen from favor as the more contemporary term "management" has risen in popularity. Some argue that "administration" reflects too much of a policy emphasis and too little of the management emphasis. Others argue that the term "administration" fails to reflect the convergence of policy and administration that marks the work of today's public manager. Still others view the focus of public "administration" as being too near the apex of public agencies and thus not cognizant enough of the many layers of managers in specialized units within public agencies.

While the focus of public management is on the efficient delivery of services, it is refined through the lens of public policy. Thus, subfields of public management include generic managerial components: budgeting and financial management, human resources, and information technology. Yet these are inextricably embedded in a democratic political context that radically alters the work of public management as contrasted to management in for-profit concerns.

Public Management vis-à-vis Partisan Politics

Public management requires balancing responsibility and action with political sensitivity and public service values. As a term, "public management" denotes the convergence of public policy analysis with administration and acknowledges that management and politics walk side by side in public management endeavors. While elected officials may want an agency to aggressively pursue the implementation of a given policy, the experience of career public managers may speak to the wisdom of maintaining a steady course between extreme interpretations of the policy. Since elected officials come and go and career managers remain, they function as conservers who straddle the extremes that are reflected in elected officials' priorities.

While some refer to "public management" as an inclusive term for all elected as well as appointed and career civil service posts, others reserve the term for only nonelected posts. In its most inclusive usage, public managers may include those who are elected, such as the president, governors, mayors, and some elected municipal and county executives; those who are political appointees, such as agency directors and city managers; plus those who rise to office through competitive civil service procedures, such as bureau chiefs and department heads. More often, the term "public management" is reserved for the activities conducted by career managers who gain their appointments through competitive civil service procedures. To the extent possible, these managers refrain from becoming actively involved in partisan campaigns and elections in order to remain as neutral as possible as they interpret and implement public policy.

Public Management vis-à-vis Public Policy

Public management is that aspect of public administration that is concerned with efficiency, accountability, goal achievement, and other managerial and technical questions (Graham and Hays 1993). The relationship between public management and the policy process is intertwined. Public management goes beyond simplistic mechanics of administration. It is about a dynamic multidisciplinary field that borrows from finance, human resources, planning, policy analysis, politics, and organization development. The public manager maintains a delicate balance:

- Between helping to make policy and to implement it;
- By facilitating the governing body's decisionmaking regarding policy initiatives;
- By resolving conflicts and building coalitions among groups with conflicting interests;
- By maintaining a steady course while managing change; and
- By enabling citizens to participate in government.

Contemporary public management as a field of endeavor reflects the changing emphasis from administrators who hold policy advocacy at arm's length to managers who, charged with responsibility for managing public programs, use policy advocacy to facilitate their program operations. This action orientation reflects the necessity for incorporating an appreciation of democratic theory and practice with efficient management (Waldo 1984). It merges a focus on policy with a focus on administration and reflects the interorganizational linkages, economic context, and partisan considerations that converge in the process of governance (Newland 1994).

Public management is an enterprise in pursuit of significance (Denhardt 1993). As a craft, it is reflective of the postmodernist age, where boundaries are fuzzy, the environment is turbulent, and the line between facts and values is often indistinguishable. Denhardt (1993) finds that contemporary public managers pursue their work through five means: a commitment to values, a concern for serving the public, empowerment and shared leadership, pragmatic incrementalism, and a dedication to public service.

Public managers report that they spend their time directing, organizing, coordinating, planning, managing people, managing money, and managing information. They describe themselves as leaders, administrators, implementors, coaches, and mediators (Bozeman 1993; Ingraham and Romzek 1994; Perry 1989; Rainey 1991). To succeed at public management, one must be a master of a number of topics, as the list in Table 19.1 shows.

Public management reflects a marriage between the policy process and policy implementation. The marriage commingles analytic fact, intuitive judgment, democratic values, and political reality to produce programs that fulfill legislative intent and satisfy citizen demands. Knowing how and when to intervene in the policy process is a required skill for public managers. In the early years of the twentieth century, it was generally as-

TABLE 19.1 Public Management Involves

Providing Leadership
Shaping Policy
Planning Programs
Designing Organizational Environments
Communicating with Constituencies
Budgeting Resources
Staffing
Directing Work Flow

sumed that public managers should follow behind the policy process, and refrain from exerting influence at any stage. Their purpose was thought to be the implementation of policy after it had been decided by elected officials. As the twentieth century draws to a close, contemporary thinking has changed. In order to do their job effectively, public managers are expected to know if, when, and how to affect the policy process. When managers have a hand in sculpting the policies that drive their programs, they increase their capacity to design programs that fulfill legislative mandates.

From a functional perspective, public organizations convert resources in the form of tax revenues and political capital into programmatic outputs. A review of the scholarship on public management reveals an evolution from a focus on economy in terms of eliminating waste and cutting cost (1880–1932) to improving efficiency through good management (1933–1960) to improving effectiveness through planning and policymaking to improving efficiency through improved management (1961–present) (Swiss 1991).

The bottom line for public management is that it must always carry out legislative intent, whether that intent is decreed by city councils, county commissions, state legislatures, or the U.S. Congress. Beyond the letter of the law, public managers seek to operate their programs so as to fill in the chinks left by policies that contradict one another, that leave gaps between services, or that fail to address public needs. The scope of a public manager's tasks depends on that person's position in an agency. At the lowest level, public management begins when a public employee has responsibility and authority that extends beyond discrete professional tasks to the supervision of others, and/or to the coordination of tasks.

Public Management Versus Business Management

It has been said that government and business are alike in all unimportant respects. To a degree this is true. Public management differs from private management primarily because the public sector is political. For this reason, management systems that work well behind the closed doors of business establishments are illegal through the open windows of government organizations. The following differences are significant in the impact they have:

Public agencies usually have a larger number of competing goals;
Public agencies operate under public scrutiny;
Public managers operate under fragmented authority structures;
Public organizations have more legal restrictions on their actions; and
Public organizations have more restrictions on their staffing—they cannot hire, fire, or promote as flexibly (Ott, Hyde, and Shafritz 1991; Swiss 1991).

Organizational leadership in public organizations differs from that in private organizations and thus causes the work of the public manager to differ from that of the private manager. In public organizations, leadership is shared between elected or appointed officials and career executives. Political executives are elected or appointed by elected officials and serve as change agents in the most fundamental sense: to make the work of government reflect the partisan ideology of the administration currently elected to office. The career executives are also change agents but are advocates for change that is in accord with their understanding of the need for, and the potential levers of, change initiatives. The typical appointed executive holds office for a relatively short time, usually around two years, thus causing their time horizon to be near term. Career executives, on the other hand, may hold office for many years and thus, their time horizon is substantially extended (Ingraham and Romzek 1994). This affects program planning as well as evaluation. It also creates a tension between appointed executives who want to make swift changes and career officials who have experienced the arrival and departure of numerous appointed officials.

Accountability structures also differ for those in public management. Public sector stakeholders are comprised of elected officials, agency superiors, professional peers, clientele groups, special interest groups, and citizens. The courts also play a significant role in holding public agencies accountable for performance and for adherence to law. Managerial discretion and authority is more limited in public management than in private business. The ability to hire, fire, and promote is constrained by job protections that are in place to free employees from partisan favoritism. The budgetary process is often complicated by real cracks in the theoretical connection between programmatic needs, constituent demands, and resource flow. Demands for government accountability inhibit flexibility and make reporting requirements onerous. These facts of life attenuate the ability to operate from what would otherwise be viewed as a sound managerial base (Ingraham and Romzek 1994).

Current thinking in public management is moving from earlier notions of neutral competence to current notions of the value of the public service as an instrument for advancing the public good. This requires a widespread commitment to competent and effective management on the part of both career and political executives in order to manage in the public interest (Ingraham and Ban 1986). This also requires an interdependence between the public and private sectors and an ability to build interorganizational and intersectoral linkages (Starling 1993).

Public management must respond to a number of constituents, including elected officials, taxpayers, and agency clientele, as well as subordinates, superiors, and peers within their agencies. The demands of these constituencies are often mutually exclusive and to satisfy one is to create another. Thus, the balancing act that is required in public management is never ending and rarely easy. The character of the polity affects the work of public managers, just as market mechanisms affect the work of business managers. As the market determines success or failure of business ventures, political values as well as market values determine the success or failure of public ventures.

The public interest model of public management requires a connection between professional concerns and social needs while avoiding partisan conflicts. Public managers are charged with the legitimate direction of society. Given the complexities of interorganizational linkages, rapid change, and economic restructuring, public managers must implement policies that are effective and legitimate and that are representative of society as well as fair (Uveges and Keller 1989).

Summary

Public management is the enterprise of doing the business of government. Public management cannot be properly understood without being placed in its political, economic, and constitutional context. Everything that government does must first pass through a sieve that blends connections between levels and branches of government, partisan politics with substantive mission, economic efficiency with constitutional freedoms, and a tacit agreement between business and government and nonprofit enterprises about the boundaries which surround them. Public management is complex and requires a sophisticated appreciation for the interconnections that exist between all segments of society.

Bibliography

Bozeman, Barry, ed., 1993. *Public Management: The State of the Art*. San Francisco, CA: Jossey Bass.

Denhardt, Robert B., 1993. *The Pursuit of Significance: Strategies for Managerial Success in Public Organizations*. Belmont, CA: Wadsworth.

Graham, Cole Blease, and Stephen W. Hays, 1993. *Managing the Public Organization*. Washington, D.C.: CQ Press.

Ingraham, Patricia W. and Carolyn R. Ban, 1986. "Models of Public Management: Are They Useful to Federal Managers in the 1980s?" *Public Administration Review* 46(2):152–160.

Ingraham, Patricia W. and Barbara S. Romzek, 1994. *New Paradigms for Government: Issues for the Changing Public Service*. San Francisco, CA: Jossey Bass.

Newland, Chester A., 1994. "A Field of Strangers in Search of a Discipline: Separatism of Public Management Research from Public Administration." *Public Administration Review*, 54(5):486–488.

Ott, J. Steven, Albert C. Hyde, and Jay M. Shafritz, eds., 1991. *Public Management: The Essential Readings*. Chicago, IL: Nelson-Hall.

Perry, James L., ed., 1989. *Handbook of Public Administration*. San Francisco, CA: Jossey Bass.

Rainey, Hal G., 1991. *Understanding and Managing Public Organizations*. San Francisco, CA: Jossey Bass.

Starling, Grover, 1993. *Managing the Public Sector*. Belmont, CA: Wadsworth.

Swiss, James E., 1991. *Public Management Systems: Monitoring and Managing Government Performance*. Englewood Cliffs, NJ: Prentice Hall.

Uveges, Jr., J. A. and L. F. Keller, 1989. "The First One Hundred Years of American Public Administration: The Study and Practice of Public Management in American Life." In J. Rabin, W. B. Hildreth, and G. J. Miller, eds., *Handbook of Public Administration*. Volume 35. New York: Marcel Dekker, pp. 1–42.

Waldo, Dwight, 1984. *The Administrative State: A Study of the Political Theory of American Public Administration*. 2d ed. New York: Holmes & Meier.

20

SCIENTIFIC MANAGEMENT

Judith A. Merkle,
Claremont-McKenna College

The name given to the Taylor System and related systems of shop management during hearings of the Interstate Commerce Commission on railroad rates in 1910. Other terms covering the same methods of quantified work study and management are "efficiency engineering," "industrial engineering," and, in the European context, "rationalization." All of these terms grew out of applications of the original Taylor System in ever wider contexts and include time and motion studies, the microdivision of labor, forward planning, and a system of strict labor discipline, usually backed by some variant on the piecework wage (see **Taylor, Frederick W.**).

The Taylor System itself, however, was not a single method of increasing productivity but was a collection of techniques that tended to be adapted and to evolve over time and depending upon circumstance. And it was not all the work of one man, Frederick Winslow Taylor, although his work was central to the scientific management movement. Associates such as Henry Laurence Gantt, Morris L. Cooke, Carl Barth, and Frank and Lillian Gilbreth, among others, made important contributions to Taylorism. What these techniques had in common was a strong bias toward the rational-utilitarian, the quantified, and the mechanistic. They tended to downplay the element of human nature and sought to control the results of the interaction of human beings as precisely as the output of a machine could be controlled. In the first half of the twentieth century, nearly all the formal management that was taught was Scientific Management: the increase of productivity through rational measurement, the elimination of waste and duplication, and the search for the "one best way."

The Popularization of Scientific Management in the United States

Just how did the U.S. government become involved in the christening of a system of machine-shop management? When the Interstate Commerce Commission held hearings to determine whether the Eastern railroads would be allowed to increase freight rates, Louis Brandeis (later a Supreme Court Justice, but then known as "the people's lawyer" and serving without pay on the case) determined that consumer interests could be upheld and rates kept low if it were shown that the railroads were inadequately managed. At that time, efficiency engineers were actively engaged in reorganizing industry, but their newly developing discipline was little known to the general public. Brandeis met with a group of them (including Gantt and Frank Gilbreth, but not Taylor) in Gantt's apartment in New York City, where he arranged for their testimony and they settled on an attractive new name for the methods of rational work study that they advocated.

The spectacular testimony of these industrial engineers, that the railroads, if properly managed, could save "a million dollars a day," brought headlines and set off an efficiency craze that swept the nation. Suddenly every problem, from governmental sloth to personal inadequacy, could be cured by the new methods if properly applied. Experts wrote popular articles, lecturers and training courses multiplied, and fly-by-night charlatans hastened to palm themselves off as efficiency consultants. President William Taft appointed a Commission on Economy and Efficiency to reform government. Housewives were informed how they might have efficient kitchens, and schoolchildren how they might study with greater efficiency. Efficiency was the virtue that could lead to national salvation. This typically American convulsion of popular enthusiasm set Scientific Management forever at the center of popular culture and the "American way."

The Components of Scientific Management

According to Taylor, the "Father of Scientific Management," Scientific Management was nothing less than a "mental revolution." Instinct and superstition, represented by the "rule of thumb," would be banished from the workplace, replaced by the precise quantification and written record keeping of science. There would be fewer mistakes, fewer false starts, and less time for training. What is more, the objective study of work would eliminate any differences between management and labor as to what fair pay ought to be. Scientific Management would reduce conflict, reduce unionization, and reduce the exploitation of labor. Taylor aimed to get rid of "systematic soldiering," the way in which workers concealed productivity and set their own pace at work. The new system, he promised, would bring about the increase of prosperity for both workers and owners, as well as a "diminution of poverty" in the community as a whole.

In *The Principles of Scientific Management*, Taylor (1911) stated that Scientific Management is "no single element," but a combination summarized as

> Science, not rule of thumb.
> Harmony, not discord.
> Cooperation, not individualism.
> Maximum output, in place of restricted output.
> The development of each man to his greatest efficiency and prosperity.

Yet, in the popular mind, Scientific Management was usually associated not with these generalizations, but with a set of very specific "efficiency" techniques. These techniques did not vanish, as some academics have suggested. A trip to most business schools, to any factory floor, or to the industrial engineering section of the library will show that many of these techniques are still in use today, having formed the foundation of modern management.

Time Study

The use of the stopwatch to time work is the element most commonly associated with Taylorism. Taylor began timing workers in the 1880s during his employment at Midvale Steel, and his development of time study is at the center of Scientific Management's efficiency methods. In popular lore, Taylorism "is" the stopwatch, and Taylor, in a poetic flourish, is said to have died with his watch in his hand.

Taylor's early time-based approach to the measurement of productivity was broadened by the inclusion of motion study, the microanalysis of motions developed by Frank and Lillian Gilbreth based on a unit of analysis called the "therblig" ("Gilbreth" spelled backwards). By examining and measuring the way in the which each part of a job was performed, the "one best way" (an early Scientific Management slogan coined by the Gilbreths) to do the work could be determined and made standard practice throughout an industry, thus increasing efficiency. Time and motion studies are still an important technique in current use. The Gilbreths' extension of this approach into "fatigue studies" (the study of the kinds of motions that tire or overextend the body) underlies much of modern ergometric and man-machine interface studies. The fatigue study approach also opened the way to the experiments of Elton Mayo and thus to the development of the Human Relations School of management.

Standardization

The approach of Scientific Management was to make the best practice standard practice. This included the standardization of tools and equipment for any given job and their provision to the working person by management. It also included the standardization of "acts or movements of workmen for each class of work" once time and motion studies had discovered the "one best way." Special equipment such as the Barth Slide Rule, developed by Taylor's associate Carl G. Barth, allowed for the optimization of technical tasks (in this case, metal cutting) on a standard pattern. The idea of standardization to increase the interchangeability of parts was taken up almost as a crusade by interested manufacturers. Yet, standardization was also seen as far more than a universal means to efficiency within and between industries; the world standardization movement, which still exists, was buoyed up in the time before World War I with the belief that international standardization would bring about world peace.

One of the great innovations of early Scientific Management was making standard practice a matter of written record. Craft skills were analyzed, measured, broken into their component parts, and stored in written form in the new "planning room" advocated by the Scientific Managers. Also kept there were work and wage calculations as well as newly developed forward planning and coordination devices such as flowcharts and Gantt's new planning bar chart, the "Gantt chart," a device not superseded until the development of computerized planning. The new standardized work process also involved giving each worker written instructions about a job. Printed work blanks were another novel element associated with the adoption of Taylorism. Both, once astonishing to contemporary observers, are now common practice. And Scientific Management, by making explicit, recording, and systematizing previously arcane skills, was the first step on the eventual road to automation.

Wage Incentives

From its very beginning, with the publication of Taylor's (1895) "A Piece-Rate System, Being a Step Toward Partial Solution of the Labor Problem," Taylorism was tied not only to technology, but to a specific wage incentive plan derived from a narrow view of human nature. For the success of the technical and standardization components of Scientific Management depended upon the idea of a powerful and precise incentive for laborers to work within the strict confines of the system. The incentive or motivator upon which Taylorism relied was the differential piecework wage, set at a "fair" level calculated by time study, with penalties for lagging behind and bonuses for overfulfillment of the work plan.

The most celebrated example of the differential piecework wage in action is given by Taylor in *The Principles of Scientific Management* when Schmidt, the ox-brained pig iron handler (Taylor's characterization), is induced to load 47 tons of pig iron per day, rather than the standard 12 1/2 tons, by being offered US $1.85 a day, rather than US $1.15 a day. (Taylor did not believe in excessive bonuses. He felt that any bonus over 60 percent would be spent on drink.) It was this element of Taylor's system, so perilously close to the classic "speed-up" and without apparent protection against physical overwork, that most excited the enmity of organized labor.

Money incentives were also applied at the managerial or supervisory level, the most well known being the Gantt task-and-bonus system. But behind the money incentives at every level was a sense that there were also spiritual rewards in Scientific Management, most notably, the uplifting virtue of serving scientific rationality instead of backwardness and superstition, as well as the "hearty teaching relationship" that Taylor advocated between supervisor and supervised. Even Schmidt is represented as being dazzled by the offer to make him a "first-class man," although he needs a great deal of coaxing and explaining to make the concept clear to him.

Accounting and Mnemonic Systems

The efficiency savings of Scientific Management could not be demonstrated without a different sort of accounting system, one that could demonstrate the costs of waste and "down time" effectively. Taylor advocated the use of the Taylor Accounting System as part of the Scientific Management reorganization package. According to Charles Wrege and Ronald Greenwood (1991), the Taylor Accounting System adapted the bookkeeping system developed by William Basley, accountant for the New York and Northern Railroad, later obscuring its origins. Also included in the reform package was the Taylor Mnemonic System, designed to label materials in storage, which considerably reduced the search-and-retrieval time for parts and replacements.

Functional Foremanship

Taylor believed that the increasing complexity of technical tasks at the shop level required the division of authority between several specialist foremen. This element of Scientific Management was the one most often discarded by industrialists who adopted other parts of the system. Functional foremanship violates the principle of the "unity of command" and a Bible quotation, "No man can serve two masters," was often pressed into service as the authority on the question. But with the increasing technological complexity of many tasks today, as well as the growth of teams and other forms of divided authority, there has been a reexamination of the once "impractical" functional foremanship as simply ahead of its time.

The Opposition of Labor

No account of Scientific Management would be complete without mentioning the strenuous opposition to the system mounted by organized labor. Early in his career at Midvale Steel, Taylor received death threats for trying to speed up work, and when he later worked at Bethlehem Steel, the planning room was mysteriously burned. Because Taylor's system replaced scarce craft labor with unskilled labor, he thought it would eliminate the possibility of strikes, since replacements could be easily trained. But Taylor's methods resembled the dreaded "speed-up" in which piece-rates could be lowered to drive workers to substandard wages and exhaustion, and strikes followed the system as it spread. Time study men were driven out of plants and work rates successfully concealed from them. The rumor was even spread, both in the United States and overseas, that Schmidt had died of overwork. In vain the real Schmidt, named Henry Knolle, was produced and shown to be living, indeed, to even have outlived Taylor. Labor activists the world over continued to tell the apocryphal tale of the advanced American industrialist who generously built a company cemetery for the laborers he had worked to death under the new efficiency system.

In 1911, strikes against the installation of Scientific Management in the Watertown Arsenal led to an investigation into the Taylor System by a committee of the House of Representatives. Taylor testified in the Capitol, confronting labor leaders in a session so stormy that it appeared as if blows might be struck. When the committee failed to recommend legislation against the Taylor System, legislators in the House passed a rider to attach to all appropriations bills forbidding the use of stopwatch timing in any government installation. But as Taylor had said, Scientific Management was not the stopwatch alone, and it continued to spread.

Over the next few decades, as Scientific Management became standard practice in industry, organized labor gradually accommodated to the changes involved, many of which were in fact improvements, although unions maintained bargaining leverage by shifting from a largely craft basis to an industry wide basis.

Scientific Management Outside of the United States

Frederick Taylor was convinced from the beginning that the principles of Scientific Management would come into general use "throughout the civilized world," and from the first, an active campaign to export Scientific Management was undertaken by its advocates, and many of them traveled abroad for that purpose. At the Paris Exposition of 1900, the Bethlehem Steel Exhibit demonstrated cutting tools made of Taylor-White steel running red-hot at unheard-of speeds. The European steel producers were stunned; when they made inquiries about the tool steel, they discovered that running lathes at that speed required the adoption of the techniques of the Taylor System of management. In this way Taylorism began its spread through the heavy industries of Europe.

In France, Scientific Management met with a great deal of enthusiasm from the technical elite. The distinguished metallurgical engineer Henri-

Louis Le Chatelier became an early and active advocate of the Taylor System. He was assisted in adapting Scientific Management to French industry by Charles de Fréminville, former chief engineer of the Paris-Orléans Railway, who was converted by a personal meeting with Taylor. The Michelin brothers, on reading Le Chatelier's articles on Taylorism, arranged a meeting with Taylor when he came to Paris, rushing out immediately afterward to buy a stopwatch for their factory at Clermont-Ferrand. By 1913, there were strikes against the Taylorized industries around Paris, but with World War I high productivity became essential, and Scientific Management was extensively adopted in French industry.

Foreign engineers and specialists descended on Taylorized plants in the United States, returning home to spread the system in their native countries. The Germans, despite an active labor movement that called Taylorism "murder-work," were quick to introduce Scientific Management into their industries, and a number of engineers became firm advocates of the system. However, to avoid the social opposition not only to the term "Taylorism" but also to "Scientific Management," they took their cue from the French, who had renamed the method *"l'organisation rationnel du travail,"* and coined the term *"die Rationalisierung"* (rationalization) to cover the campaign for reorganization. The emphasis on production planning blended well with the corporative state traditions of Germany; the great industrialist Walter Rathenau is counted among the number of Scientific Managers, as is Wichard von Moellendorf, author of a corporatist plan for the reconstruction of German industry between the wars. Other nations that showed an interest in early Scientific Management were the Japanese and the British, although labor and other troubles delayed the widespread application of the system in the latter case.

By far the strangest convert to Scientific Management was Vladimir Lenin, who in 1915 read an article by Frank Gilbreth on motion study as a means of increasing national wealth and brought emigré engineers trained in Taylorism back to the newly founded Soviet Union to improve the operations of industry. Under Lenin, the First Five-Year Plan was drawn up on Gantt charts, although the plan itself was not put into effect until Stalin took power. Echoes of a much distorted Taylorism are seen in some of the task and bonus systems of Soviet socialism, as well as in the strange practices of Stakhanovism (a bizarre and heavily publicized "speed-up" in which "labor heroes" performed humanly impossible tasks of overproduction) during the 1930s. Indeed, in the years between the two world wars, the practices of Scientific Management were established worldwide in industry, and management historians continue to unearth new examples of the diffusion of the system with some regularity.

Beyond Scientific Management

Scientific Management spread beyond the confines of the industrial establishment and was extended by its admirers to include earlier attempts to apply rational study and reform to work. For example, Lyndall Urwick, an important figure in British Scientific Management as well as one of the developers of the Administrative Management School of public administration, included the early management experiments and advanced practices of the British steam engine manufacturer Boulton and Watt a century before Taylor in his discussion of pioneers of Scientific Management. Likewise, he included the labor studies of Charles Babbage (1792–1871), although the celebrated inventor of the Difference Engine would seem to require no further laurels.

Scientific Management had a powerful impact on government administration, city management, and educational administration and was even the inspiration for the founding of an obscure American political party. For example, its work of seeking out and standardizing the best practice inspired the work of the New York Bureau of Municipal Research, whose director, Frederick A. Cleveland, was a friend of Taylor's. This approach to local government spread as similar bureaus were founded across the country in the teens of this century to improve administrative practice. Scientific Management's method of developing a single measure of production to calculate efficiency was adapted to education by Morris L. Cooke, who as early as 1910 proposed using the "student hour" to reform educational administration. Cooke, an associate of Taylor's, also directly intervened in the organization of the government of the city of Philadelphia, rationalizing its operations and publishing his observations on city management improvement methods in 1918.

The teachings of the Administrative Management School, many of which developed out of the work done in the New York Bureau, formed the basis for the teaching of public administration for many years. In addition, they provided the theoretical background for the work of the President's Committee on Administrative Management, which in 1937 proposed major reforms of the executive branch that included the establishment of the Executive Office of the President. These reforms, put in place for World War II, still undergird the modern presidency. At the opposite end of the political spectrum were the zany proposals of Technocracy, Incorporated, an obscure political party that rose to visibility during the Great Depression of the 1930s only to be suppressed and reduced to a handful of eccentrics in the decades that followed. Inspired by Scientific Management and the credo of efficiency bringing national happiness, the technocrats proposed to abolish the Constitution and replace it with a "technate" of engineers, who would restore national prosperity by eliminating energy waste and organizing all of national life along efficient assembly-line principles.

In the century since "A Piece-Rate System" first appeared, Scientific Management has worked its way into the fabric of all modern industrial societies, where it is now so common as to go unnoticed by most people. But its results were profound and lasting, encompassing a "second industrial revolution" of mass production and a "white collar revolution" of expanding middle management made possible by higher worker productivity and made necessary by the requirements of coordinating the new, microdivided labor that created that productivity. Even now, when many management texts, stressing teams and nonmaterial incentives, advocate the dismantling of certain outmoded structures of Scientific Management, they justify these changes with arguments rooted in the very methods of productivity measurement and work study first devised and applied by the Scientific Managers at the beginning of the twentieth century.

Bibliography

Aitken, A. G. H., 1960. *Taylorism at the Watertown Arsenal: Scientific Management in Action, 1908–1915*. Cambridge, MA: Harvard University Press.

Alford, L. P., 1932. *Henry Lawrence Gantt: Leader in Industry*. New York: Harper and Bros.

Cooke, Morris L., 1918. *Our Cities Awake: Notes on Municipal Activities and Administration*. New York: Doubleday.

Copley, Frank B., 1923. *Frederick W. Taylor: Father of Scientific Management*. New York: Harper and Bros.

Gilbreth, Frank B., 1917. *Applied Motion Study*. New York: Sturgis and Walton.

Gilbreth, Frank B., Jr., and Ernestine Gilbreth Carey, 1948. *Cheaper by the Dozen*. New York: T. Y. Crowell.

Gilbreth, Frank B., and Lillian M. Gilbreth, 1916. *Fatigue Study: The Elimination of Humanity's Greatest Unnecessary Waste*. New York: Sturgis and Walton.

Gulick, Luther, and Lyndall Urwick, eds., 1937. *Papers in the Science of Administration*. New York: Columbia University Press.

Haber, Samuel, 1964. *Efficiency and Uplift: Scientific Management in the Progressive Era, 1890–1920*. Chicago: University of Chicago Press.

Hoxie, R. F., 1921. *Scientific Management and Labor*. New York: D. Appleton.

Mayo, Elton, 1933. *The Human Problems of an Industrial Civilization*. New York: Macmillan.

Merkle, Judith A., 1980. *Management and Ideology: The Legacy of the International Scientific Management Movement*. Berkeley and London: University of California Press.

Nadworny, Milton J., 1955. *Scientific Management and the Unions 1900–1932*. Cambridge, MA: Harvard University Press.

Nelson, Daniel, 1980. *Frederick W. Taylor and the Rise of Scientific Management*. Madison: University of Wisconsin Press.

Taylor, Frederick W., 1895. "A Piece-Rate System, Being a Step Toward Partial Solution of the Labor Problem." Paper no. 647, *Transactions*, American Society of Mechanical Engineers, vol. 16: 856–903.

______, 1967 [1911]. *The Principles of Scientific Management*. New York: W. W. Norton.

______, 1919. *Shop Management*. New York: Harper Bros.

Urwick, Lyndall, 1949. *The Making of Scientific Management*. London: Management Publications Trust.

______, 1956. *The Golden Book of Management*. London: Newman, Neame.

Wrege, Charles D., and Ronald G. Greenwood, 1991. *Frederick W. Taylor: The Father of Scientific Management; Myth and Reality*. Homewood, IL: Business One Irwin.

21

Management Science

Dorothy Olshfski,
Rutgers, The State University of New Jersey

Michele Collins,
Rutgers, The State University of New Jersey

An interdisciplinary field comprising elements of mathematics, economics, computer science, and engineering. It is primarily concerned with the development and application of quantitative analyses to find solutions to problems faced by managers of public and private organizations.

History

Although quantitative analysis to solve managerial problems can be identified as having been used by very early civilizations, the generally agreed upon beginning of management science, as a field of study, dates to World War II. In the early 1940s, P. M. S. Blackett, a Nobel Prize–winning physicist, was asked by the British government to convene a group of scientists to study operational problems such as optimal deployment of convoy vessels, tactics of antisubmarine warfare, and strategies of civilian defense. This group included physicists, astrophysicists, mathematicians, physiologists, surveyors, mathematical physicists, and army officers. It was officially known as the Army Operations Research Group; unofficially the group was called Blackett's Circus. This diverse group successfully found solutions to complex military problems and led to the creation of similar "operations analysis" groups in all branches of the military in Britain and the United States.

Operations research was the original term used to describe the work of a group of mathematicians and scientists who collaborated in attempting to apply scientific principles to solve business and industrial problems. However, a division among the practitioners of this new discipline developed early in the life of the discipline between those who were oriented toward business and those who focused on industry or engineering. Consequently, two terms emerged to reflect the divergent applications. Management science emphasized the application of scientific principles to management problems, whereas operations research was grounded in civil and industrial engineering, thus emphasizing production problems and nonbusiness applications. Today the terms are used interchangeably.

After World War II, some of the scientists involved in the operations analysis groups began to apply the techniques, developed as part of those groups, to business and national security problems. However, their efforts did not really take off until computers became commercially available in the 1950s. In fact, industrial applications of operations analysis are largely attributed to two events: the availability of high-speed computers and the development of linear programming by George Dantzig.

The dependence of management science on computers cannot be underestimated. Solutions to complex business and industry problems frequently require the ability to perform numerous calculations and keep track of large data sets. The commercial availability of computers in the 1950s, even though these early computers were puny by today's standards, provided firms large enough to afford computers the ability to apply the advances in analytic decisionmaking developed to aid the war effort. Computers were an invaluable tool for management science and operations research as it developed into a profession.

In 1947, George Dantzig developed the simplex method of solving linear programming problems. This technique is an algebraic procedure that can be used to solve a system of simultaneous linear equations to determine the optimal allocation of resources. Dantzig's work gave business a powerful tool to analyze many large-scale resource allocation problems. When coupled with the rapid development of computers, linear programming applications spread throughout the private sector, and it became an important tool for business and industry. It exemplified the application of scientific techniques that supported the overwhelming success of American business after World War II.

Reflecting the wartime roots of management science, public sector development and application of management science was dominated by the military in the 1940s and 1950s. The navy, in cooperation with the consulting firm of Booz, Allen, and Hamilton, developed PERT (Program, Evaluation, and Review Technique) to assist in the planning and control of large-scale projects or networks. PERT is credited with delivering the navy's Polaris submarine two years ahead of schedule. This development exercise is an early example of successful public-private cooperation.

The nonmilitary public sector began to employ management science in the late 1960s and early 1970s. City governments perform tasks such as sanitation, fire, and police management that are particularly suited to the application of management science techniques. And as software packages became available, local governments increasingly took advantage of the opportunity to use linear programming, integer programming, and decision analysis to manage government operations more efficiently.

Management Science Techniques

Management science provides a methodology to assist managerial decisionmaking. The techniques used in management science help to provide a more rational and scientific basis for making these decisions. Over time the techniques that make up the field have grown to reflect the large-scale computing capacities available and to make use of the new communication and transportation technologies.

The content of the field in the 1950s was dominated by linear and dynamic programming, network analysis, inventory control, and queuing theory. The 1960s introduced decision analysis and goal and multiobjective linear programming. In the 1970s, the management science efforts focused on artificial intelligence and expert systems. Also during the 1970s, small computers became increasingly available to businesses and the general public and work began to focus on management information systems. Since the 1980s, with the increased availability of personal computers, management science techniques have not just been within the purview of business anymore. Increasingly, the tools of management science are available to anyone who wants to use them. Some emphasis has been placed on adapting the techniques to make them more user-friendly for general use.

Professional Associations

The establishment of operations research and management science as a profession was indicated by two events: the development of academic programs to train individuals specifically for management science positions and the formation of professional associations. Academic programs were developed in the late 1950s and early 1960s based on recommendations by the Carnegie and Ford foundations. The first graduate to receive a Ph.D. in Operations Research was Lawrence Freidman, who received his degree from Case Western in 1957. MIT, Stanford, UC at Berkeley, and Cornell were the early leaders in formalizing the study of operations research or management science.

The growth of professional associations to facilitate research and development, to enhance communication among members, and to act as advocate for the emerging profession occurred very early. In 1952, the Operations Research Society of America (ORSA) was formed, followed in 1953 by the creation of the Institute of Management Science (TIMS). The original membership of these two associations reflected the different types of application being emphasized. However, over time the distinction became less meaningful and the two groups merged in 1995. The new group is called the Institute for Operations Research and Management Science (INFORMS), and its mission is to "serve as an international network to facilitate improvements in operational processes, decision-making, and management by individuals and organizations through the use of operations research, the management sciences and related methods" (INFORMS brochure). Presently, the association consists of 135,000 members in more than 80 countries from a variety of fields such as government, computer science, engineering, and economics. INFORMS sponsors international meetings and publishes ten professional journals or magazines: *Interfaces, Management Science, Operations Research, Information Systems Research, Journal on Computing, Organizational Science, Marketing Science, Mathematics of Operations Research, Transportation Science,* and *OR/MS Today.*

22

Entrepreneurial Public Administration

Carl J. Bellone,
California State University, Hayward

A philosophical position and a managerial style that stresses innovation, the search for new opportunities, calculated risk taking, an emphasis on results and performance (such as outcome measurement, revenue generation, and profit making), rewards for merit, managerial autonomy, competitive market forces, and a future orientation. It is often contrasted with bureaucratic public administration, which is characterized by stability, standard operating procedures, monopolies, close limitations on authority, lack of measurable outputs, and a short-term orientation.

French economist J. B. Say (1767–1832) is credited with coining the term "entrepreneur" in about 1800 to refer to industrialists who shifted resources from areas of low yield to areas of higher yield. Early uses of entrepreneurial management referred to the expeditions of French military leaders and French businessmen who undertook major public works. The economist Joseph Schumpeter (1883–1950) described businessmen who took calculated risks with capital, increased profits and productivity, and opened new markets as entrepreneurs.

Entrepreneurship has been most associated with start-up ventures, innovation, risk taking, and profit making in the private sector. Although some of the elements of public entrepreneurship—such as municipal airports run as revenue-generating public enterprises—have been around for many years, it was not until the 1980s that a few public administrators began to refer to themselves as public entrepreneurs. The most notable of them, Ted Gaebler, former city manager of Visalia, California, went on to help establish the reinventing government movement with the publication of *Reinventing Government* (with David Osborne) in 1992. This book expanded the notion of entrepreneurial public administration to include a focus on the customer, decentralized government structures, empowerment of employees and communities, a catalyst role for government, and mission-driven organizations.

Types of Entrepreneurial Public Administration

Entrepreneurial public administration can be viewed as either economic entrepreneurship or political or policy entrepreneurship. The most widely referred to type is economic entrepreneurship, where public managers, under pressure to limit or reduce taxes, have developed clever means to increase nontax revenues. In 1983, the International City Management Association published a collection of readings entitled *The Entrepreneur in Local Government*, which detailed the activities of several public managers who practiced this economic entrepreneurial style of management. An example of an economic entrepreneurial project is a city using its powers to acquire and prepare land for a private developer's shopping mall and in turn receiving a share of the developer's profits. This is an instance of a public-private partnership. Another example is building a municipal facility with additional space that can be leased out to private sector businesses (a municipal leasing scheme) creating nontax income that can be used to pay off the original cost of the municipal facility. Other examples of public economic entrepreneurship include the following: user fees (charging individual users for the cost of the public service consumed), developer fees (charging developers for the public costs associated with housing or business development such as roads and schools), privatization (letting the private sector take over a previously publicly provided service such as garbage collection), load shedding (ceasing to provide a service such as a city library), creation of public enterprises (such as a city harbor), and selling a public service to another entity (such as providing fire protection services to another city for a fee). These activities are supported by budgetary processes that give project managers greater control and reward saving. Public entrepreneurship outside of the United States most often refers to public enterprise development.

A second type of entrepreneurial public administration described in the literature is political or policy entrepreneurship. Eugene Lewis and Jameson Doig have used the term "public entrepreneurship" to refer to leaders in the political arena who have developed new agencies or created new policy directions, such as J. Edgar Hoover's creation of the Federal Bureau of Investigation (FBI) and Gifford Pinchot's formation of the U.S. Forest Service. Political entrepreneurs are skillful at setting public agendas, creating new agencies, and implementing new policy directions.

Democratic Concerns

Some democratic theorists have argued that the philosophy of entrepreneurial public administration as well as some of the techniques of the entrepreneurial management style conflict with democratic values such as public accountability and citizen input. Autonomy and risk taking (even calculated risk taking) with public funds by public managers are causes for serious concern. Indeed, not all public entrepreneurial activities have been successful. In the 1980s, the City of San Jose, California, lost millions of dollars through failed arbitrage investments. The City of St. Petersburg, Florida, built a baseball stadium that as of yet has failed to attract a major league team. The plans that public entrepreneurs have and their strong determination to carry them out, sometimes in secrecy for competitive reasons, is also of concern to democratic theorists. The tenets of democratic theory require that public managers be held readily accountable and that the public has a right to meaningful input into the plans and actions of its public leaders and managers.

Entrepreneurial public administration's emphasis on economic rationality and market mechanisms—as well as problems with public accountability and citizen input—has resulted in criticism of entrepreneurship as an inappropriate model for a democratic public administration. Supporters, however, argue that the failures of traditional bureaucratic public administration and the public's desire for high service levels, coupled with their reluctance to pay for these services, makes entrepreneurial public administration attractive even if there are democratic concerns (which they propose can be mitigated) and a less than 100 percent success rate.

Bibliography

Bellone, Carl, and George Frederick Goerl, 1992. "Reconciling Public Entrepreneurship and Democracy." *Public Administration Review*, vol. 52 (March-April): 130–134.

Doig, Jameson W., and Erwin C. Hargrove, eds., 1990. *Leadership and Innovation Entrepreneurs in Government*. Abridged ed. Baltimore: Johns Hopkins University Press.

Lewis, Eugene, 1984. *Public Entrepreneurship*. Bloomington, IN: Indiana University Press.

Moore, Barbara H., ed., 1983. *The Entrepreneur in Local Government*. Washington, DC: International City Management Association.

Osborne, David, and Ted Gaebler, 1992. *Reinventing Government*. Reading, MA: Addison-Wesley.

Part Seven

Strategic Management

23

Leadership

Frederick W. Gibson,
Oppenheimer Funds

Fred E. Fiedler,
University of Washington

The actions of a person who, whether elected, appointed, or emerging by group consensus, directs, coordinates, and supervises the work of others for the purpose of accomplishing a given task. This excludes, for example, fashion or opinion leaders, and leaders of groups designed to enhance the growth or adjustment of their members, or to provide for the members' enjoyment. It has been said that there are as many definitions of leadership as people who write about it. Although this may be poetic license, there is no doubt that the number of definitions is considerable.

Leadership has fascinated humanity for at least as long as the existence of written records. Plato's *Republic* (about 500 B.C.E.) is an early example, but there are even earlier references to leadership in ancient Egyptian documents. The popular concern with leadership is perhaps best seen by the more than 7,500 empirical leadership studies that have been reported in the literature (Bass 1990). The reasons for the popularity of this topic are not difficult to find. Leadership is an ever-present social phenomenon in all cultures. Furthermore, the quality of leadership frequently determines the fate of a group or an organization. In addition, a leader is almost always required whenever a job cannot be done by one person alone. Leadership has been a peculiarly American concern, in large part because in most other countries, the question of who should be a leader was academic since higher management positions in government, business, and the military were automatically preempted by the aristocracy. Also, according to Meindl and Ehrlich (1987), Americans have a strong belief in the importance of leadership as a major force in the development and success of organizations.

Whether this belief is warranted is another question. Pfeffer (1977) has argued, for example, that so many factors influence organizational performance that leadership makes little or no additional contribution. He cites a study by Salancik and Pfeffer (1977), which showed that city mayors account for "only" about 10 percent of the city's performance. However, Pfeffer's interpretation cannot be supported. First, 10 percent is a rather sizable amount of the variance when we consider all the other extraneous factors that a criterion of this nature involves (Fiedler and House 1988). More to the point, a review by Hogan, Curphy, and Hogan (1994) cites evidence that leaders make a difference in samples as diverse as flight crews, United States presidents, and Methodist ministers. Most telling is a study by Thorlindsson (in Fiedler and House 1988) on over 100 trawlers in the Icelandic herring fishing fleet. These ships, usually staffed by a crew of 10 or 11, are highly comparable and fish under highly competitive conditions at times set by the Ministry of Fisheries. Thorlindsson found that the captains of these ships accounted for 35 to 49 percent of the variation in the yearly catch. These findings leave no doubt that the leader does affect performance.

What makes some leaders effective and others ineffective? One problem in answering this question is that studies often define leadership effectiveness quite differently. A leader may be effective on the basis of one criterion (profitability) but ineffective when we measure performance on a different criterion (e.g., satisfaction of followers). Compounding this complexity is that the current week's profits may be unrelated to the company's profitability over the next three years. Unfortunately, the more delayed the outcome, the more it is contaminated by extraneous events. One strategy is to use multiple criteria in order to assess the pattern of outcomes that result from leader actions. While this may sound good, such criteria as performance, job satisfactions, development of subordinates, and the like usually are not related and cannot, therefore, be combined into one single measure of performance. We shall here focus primarily on performance.

Major Approaches to the Study of Leadership

Leadership theories can be categorized roughly into two types. One type is based primarily on personal attributes and abilities. This includes the charismatic and transformational leaders and influence based on such attributes as intellectual abilities, expertise, and experience. The other type includes the so-called transactional theories of leadership, where influence is based on an explicit social contract, for example, an employment agreement with stated wages, salaries, and working conditions, or a labor contract. Needless to say, these two types of leadership frequently occur together, and there are few pure types. We begin with a brief historical overview and then discuss several transactional theories, followed by a discussion of the charismatic and transformational theories of leadership that more recently came to prominence. Given the limitations of space, we believe the reader will gain more if we discuss one or two examples of each class of theories in some detail rather than try to cover all the theories and empirical studies.

The "Great Man" Theories and Leadership Traits

In the minds of most people, the ability to lead is associated with personality. The view of trait theorists is that "great men" rise to leadership positions because of their superior abilities and attributes. The underlying basis of the "great man" theory is probably the oldest conception of leadership (Hollander 1985) and probably arose as a result of two converging forces. One was the physical, intellectual, and educational superiority of the aristocracy, who were able to enjoy better nutrition as well as educational advantages. The other was the close tie between religion and the ruling classes. Kings and nobles held their place by the grace of God, and every person was expected to be satisfied with the place in the social order to which one had been born. Attempts to rise above one's station were viewed with disfavor and generally discouraged and often regarded as treason. Early research focused on identifying the traits that differentiated leaders from nonleaders or effective from ineffective leaders. Hook, a prominent spokesman for this view, wrote that "all factors in history, save men, are inconsequential" (1955, p. 14).

The trait approach was the dominant research model until Stogdill (1948) reviewed 43 years of research and failed to find one single trait that identified a person as a leader regardless of the situation. While Stogdill's conclusion was interpreted too literally, it spelled the decline of research on leadership traits. Leadership research instead turned from personality variables to looking at the specific behaviors that would differentiate effective from ineffective leaders. The feeling was that if one could identify behaviors that resulted in effective leadership performance, one could then train leaders to use these effective behaviors.

Leader Behaviors

The most influential work on leader behaviors was conducted at Ohio State University. Researchers asked followers to rate their leaders on nine categories by rating the frequency with which the leader exhibited each type of behavior. An analysis of thousands of questionnaires identified two major factors in leader behavior (Stogdill and Coons 1957). These were labeled (1) "consideration" and included behaviors concerned with the well-being and esteem of followers, such as listening for followers' opinions and being friendly and approachable; and (2) "initiation of structure," which included behaviors designed to assign tasks and roles to group members and to focus the group on performing the task.

Unfortunately, the way in which leaders behaved had little to do with how they performed (Korman 1966). One result of these findings was the development of increasingly more complex category systems of leader behavior. For example, Yukl's (1994) Integrating Taxonomy of Managerial Behavior consists of 14 behavioral categories. This and similar taxonomies offer promising new insights of how leaders behave, but they have not radically affected leadership theory (Landy 1989).

Several prominent training programs were based on behavioral theories. One of the most popular was, and still is, the Managerial Grid (Blake and Mouton 1964), which categorizes leaders on concern for people and concern for production. Despite its acceptance by many business and industrial organizations there is little evidence in support of this model or of its effectiveness as a training device.

The Situational (Structural) Approach

The situation approach grew out of dissatisfaction with and the perceived limitations of the trait and behavioral approaches. The view of this school is that leaders are successful (or unsuccessful) because they happened upon the right (or wrong) circumstances at the right time.

Theorists here focused on the task as the primary relevant characteristic of leadership performance. Because the task is generally the most important element in leadership activities, early research focused on differences between tasks as a basis for determining who emerged as the leader (Carter and Nixon 1949). Structuralists saw performance as dependent on characteristics of the organization rather than those of the leader. The best-known researchers in this area include Woodward (1958) and Simon (1947).

The situational school served as a needed counterpoint to the overemphasis on traits and brought attention to another class of variables important in the leadership equation. However, by assuming that the individual is unimportant, it also failed to consider the effects of multiple factors as they interacted in effecting leadership. This final shift in thought was accomplished by the contingency approach.

Transactional Theories of Leadership

Transactional theories of leadership had early beginnings in the 1930s but did not emerge as the dominant theories of leadership until the 1950s. Two primary forces were behind the ascendancy: frustration and disappointment with the trait theories and dramatic post-World War II advances in the applied behavioral sciences.

Contingency Theories

Contingency theories assert that the effects of a leader's personality or behavioral style on performance depend on (are contingent on) the nature of the leadership situation. These theories therefore attempt to integrate the role of personality and situational factors in their predictions of leadership performance. The first theory to do so was the Contingency Model of Leadership Effectiveness (Fiedler 1967).

The Contingency Model of Leadership Effectiveness. This theory holds that the effectiveness of a group depends upon two interacting elements: (1) the leader's personality and (2) the degree to which the situation gives the leader control and influence over the group process and outcomes. The relevant personality component is the leader's motivational structure (the hierarchy of goals the leader seeks to satisfy at work). This variable is measured by the "least-preferred coworker" scale (LPC), which is obtained by asking leaders to think of all the people with whom they ever worked and to describe the one person with whom it was most difficult to get the job done. Low-LPC persons describe their least-preferred coworkers in highly negative terms. These leaders are primarily task-motivated and react emotionally to those who keep them from getting the job done. To these leaders, getting the job done is so important that poorly performing coworkers are seen not only as incompetent but as having generally undesirable personalities. On the other hand, high-LPC leaders describe their least-preferred coworkers in more positive terms. These leaders are relatively more concerned with interpersonal relationships than task accomplishment, so they can view their least-preferred coworkers more objectively, describing them as lazy but honest or incompetent but pleasant.

As we mentioned, LPC measures a motivational hierarchy—whether the leader sets a higher value on getting the job done or on interpersonal relations. The high-LPC leader places a higher value on relationships, while the low-LPC leader values the task more highly. However, leaders do not always behave in accordance with their primary goals. So, low-LPC leaders behave in a task-oriented way only as long as they feel there will be difficulty getting the task accomplished. Once they feel certain the task will be completed, they turn to their secondary goal of maintaining good relations. High-LPC leaders strive for good interpersonal relationships only as long as the situation makes them feel uncertain that good interpersonal relations can be reached. Once good relations with group members seem assured, these leaders turn their attention to the task.

A second major aspect of the contingency model is situational control, which indicates the perceived probability on the part of the leader that the task will get done. It consists of (1) leader-member relations, the degree to which the leader feels accepted by followers and the degree to which followers get along, (2) task structure, the degree to which the task is clear-cut, programmed, and structured, and (3) position power, the degree to which the leader's position provides power to reward and punish to obtain compliance. Basically, low-LPC leaders perform best when their situational control is either high or relatively low. High-LPC leaders perform best when their situational control is moderate.

The contingency model views leadership as a dynamic process. As situational control changes, so will the match between leadership style and situational control. It is therefore possible to predict the changes in leadership performance that are likely to occur as a result of changes in the leader's situational control. For example, training should increase the structure of the task and hence the leader's situational control. An experiment by Chemers, Rice, Sundstrom, and Butler (1975) found that training improved the situational control of teams from low to moderate, but training did not improve overall performance. Rather, training improved the performance of high-LPC leaders, but the same training was detrimental to the performance of groups with low-LPC leaders.

The contingency model is arguably the most tested leadership theory and the majority of studies support the model as well as Fiedler's interpretation of LPC. The theory is complex and does not provide easy answers. We shall discuss the training applications of this model in a later section of this entry.

Path-Goal Theory. This theory is an extension of expectancy theory, which states that individuals' actions or effort levels are based on their perceived probabilities that their efforts (or actions) will lead to outcomes they desire. According to House and Mitchell (1974), then, the leader's basic functions (in order to maximize follower performance) are to ensure that the outcomes followers desire (the goal) are available to them and to help subordinates reach that goal (the path). By doing these things, the effective leader strengthens the followers' beliefs that their efforts will accomplish the task and that task accomplishment will lead to valued outcomes. Effective leadership may lead to increased follower motivation, and also satisfaction, to the extent followers see the leader's behavior as an immediate source of goal attainment or a source of future goal attainment.

According to this theory, the most effective leadership style depends on follower and task characteristics. Essentially, the leader should provide whatever the situation (followers or task) does not. Conversely, leader behaviors seen as redundant are generally met with follower dissatisfaction and/or low motivation. In general, leader behavior should match the level of follower confidence; the lower the confidence, the more directive the leader should be. Mitchell, Smyser, and Weed (1975) found that followers with low confidence were most satisfied with directive leaders, and followers with high confidence were most satisfied with participative leaders. When the task is structured, follower confidence in accomplishing such a task is high. Under these conditions, the leader's directiveness seems redundant, or like an attempt to exert excessive control, and therefore results in subordinate dissatisfaction. When task structure is low, subordinates look to the leader for direction to clarify the path to the goal. Although path-goal theory has been more effective in predicting job satisfaction than performance, it has shed some light on potentially critical situational variables (Yukl 1994).

The Normative Decision Model. Vroom and Yetton (1973) proposed that leader effectiveness is a function of knowing when and how much to allow followers to participate in decisionmaking. Their model defines five levels of participation, from autocratic (leader solves the problem or makes the decision alone using information available) through consultative to joint (leader shares the problem with the group, and together they generate alternatives and attempt to reach a decision). The critical leader behavior consists of the level of participation the leader grants to followers. The key to effective leadership is to decide which behavior to exhibit and when; again, the answer depends on situational factors.

Before a recommendation is made on participation level, seven facets of the situation are considered, from the amount of information available to the likelihood that conflict among followers over the preferred solution will result. The situational factors are listed in the form of questions. Answering the questions leads to a set of alternatives regarding participation level. Once the set of alternatives is reached, the model supplies considerations for choosing among them. The predictions of this model have not yet been fully tested. Most studies examined only whether decisions made by leaders matched the prescriptions of the model; few attempts have been made to tie these decisions to organizational performance.

Life-Cycle Theory (Situational Leadership Theory, or SLT). Hersey and Blanchard (1982) relate the maturity of the group to prescribed leader behaviors. As in path-goal, SLT's leader behaviors are borrowed from the Ohio State dimensions. Unlike the Managerial Grid, however, which emphasized 9, 9 leadership (high concern for both the task and interpersonal relationships) as the most effective style, SLT asserts that no one behavior is appropriate for all circumstances; leaders must adjust their behavior to the maturity of the followers. Follower maturity consists of job maturity—the task-relevant knowledge, experience, and ability possessed by followers—and psychological maturity—the self-confidence and motivation relative to the task. Note that followers are described by their confidence (perceived ability to get the job done), much like path-goal theory and the contingency model's situational control. This confidence notion seems to be a common thread in many contingency models.

SLT predicts that with an immature work group, the appropriate leader behavior is to be directive with little concern for relationships. Again, note the similarity of this prescription to that of path-goal theory and the contingency model. As the group matures, the leader must maintain concern with the task but also increase considerate behaviors. As maturity increases further, the need for both structure and consideration decreases until, when the group is fully mature, the need for both subsides completely. Personnel turnover, reorganization, or change of mission may reduce group maturity, again requiring leader-specific action.

While SLT provides simplicity and a commonsense approach, there is little support for the model. Group maturity is left to the leader's judgment to determine. Further, the model provides little rationale for how or why follower maturity and leader behavior interact to effect performance. Finally, leadership effectiveness is defined as simply those behaviors that match the prescriptions of SLT; it is not linked to outside criteria of organizational performance. As a result, virtually no reported research supports the theory.

Multiple Linkage Model (MLM). Contingency theories have been criticized for being too simplistic, since they describe leader behaviors or the situation, for example, in terms of only one or two characteristics. The Multiple Linkage Model (Yukl 1989) is an example of a leadership theory that responds to such criticisms. The theory starts by detailing 14 behaviors that define possible ways for leaders to act, including supporting, delegating, rewarding, developing, clarifying, monitoring, representing, and networking. MLM states that such leader behaviors effect group processes, which in turn effect unit performance. In other words, according to MLM, group processes intervene between leader behaviors and unit outcomes. The use of such intervening variables in a leadership model helps explain why the effects of leader behaviors on performance are often delayed; leader actions must first affect the intervening variables before these can in turn affect group outcomes.

MLM consists of two basic propositions. First, in the short term, the leader best improves unit effectiveness by correcting deficiencies in intervening variables (the group processes). Leaders usually have a choice as to which variable to improve and which corrective behavior to use. This choice notion is a substantial departure from other models, which assumed that there was a best style of leadership for a given type of situation. Second, in the long term, effective leaders best increase unit effectiveness by improving the situation. In so doing, they indirectly influence the intervening variable.

The Multiple Linkage Model treats leaders and situations more comprehensively than other models. It also treats intervening variables explicitly, clarifying how leader behaviors affect unit performance. MLM also makes a valuable distinction between short- and long-term strategies for improving leadership effectiveness. Success in the long and short run is often brought about by different mechanisms, and the MLM provides prescriptions for addressing both concerns. However, the model does suffer some shortcomings. It ignores characteristics of followers that might effect their reactions to leader actions. For example, experienced followers may resent leaders who unnecessarily structure the work. Second, there is little explanation of the mechanisms that tie leader behaviors to the intervening group process variables. Third, given its complexity, the model may be difficult for practitioners and trainers to use. Nevertheless, the model must be viewed as an advance over previous contingency models.

Personality, Charismatic, and Transformational Leadership

In recent years, a significant number of leadership theorists have moved beyond the transactional approaches to focus on leadership from a variety of perspectives most notably personalities, charismatic, and transformational leadership.

Leader Personality Revisited

In the past, leadership trait research was often hard to interpret because studies used different terminology. For example, conscientiousness has been called conformity, constraint, and will to achieve, among other labels. Research tying together these and other such studies was therefore never properly integrated because of label confusion. Recently, these personality descriptors have been mapped onto the "big-five" model of personality (Hogan and Hogan 1992), which holds that personality can be described in terms of five broad dimensions: surgency (dominance), agreeableness, conscientiousness, emotional stability, and intellect. The model provides a common vocabulary for interpreting the results of personality research as it relates to leadership (Hogan, Curphy, and Hogan 1994).

Research using the model has been encouraging. Gough (1990), for example, found the dominance, capacity for status, sociability, and social presence (surgency), self-acceptance and achievement via independence (emotional stability), and empathy (agreeableness) scales of the California Psychological Inventory were correlated with ratings for leader emergence. Hogan, Curphy, and Hogan (1994) summed up the recent evidence by stating, "The big-five model provides a convenient way to summarize both leaderless group discussion and assessment center research. The results also suggest that measures of surgency, agreeableness, conscientiousness, and emotional stability can be used to predict . . . leadership potential" (p. 497). More supporting evidence for the role of leader personality should emerge in the future.

Charisma

Although the charismatic leader has long dominated the popular imagination, empirical study of charismatic leadership is relatively recent. The term charisma, coined by Weber (1946), is derived from the Greek word for gift and suggests that certain leaders have a divine gift that enables them to engender such loyalty and devotion that followers will not only obey unquestionably but sacrifice their possessions and even their lives at the leader's command. Such recent events as the 1978 Jonestown murder/suicide of over 800 people and the similar 1993 tragedy in Waco, Texas, dramatically attest to the charismatic leader's power. Thus, charismatic leadership is an important topic for study.

What makes leaders charismatic? First, charismatic leaders are able to articulate a clear vision of the future, often a reaction to perceived fundamental discrepancies between the way things are and the way they ought to be. In so doing, they offer to help a group move from their present circumstances to a "promised land." Second, charismatic leaders possess a gift for rhetoric—they are skilled communicators who heighten the emotions of followers and inspire them to embrace the vision. They have a strong and unshakable belief in their vision and the eventual achievement of their goals. Moreover, they are skilled image-builders and communicators who can give themselves the appearance of infallibility.

Leaders with these and similar characteristics will not necessarily be charismatic, however. As always, the followers and situation must be taken into account. Charismatic leadership is as much a function of follower reactions as it is the leader's traits. It might even be said that charismatic leadership is defined by these reactions: strong affection for the leader, heightened emotional levels, willing subordination to the leader and trust in the correctness of the leader's beliefs, and feelings of empowerment. Situational factors are equally important in determining whether leaders are seen as charismatic. Probably the most important is the presence or absence of a crisis. Followers who perceive crises are more willing to follow a leader who promises change and a vision to resolve the crisis. Sensing this, some leaders purposely create or accentuate the perceptions of crisis for their own ends. Apart from the power leaders enjoy, followers of charismatic leaders tend to be more satisfied and motivated with their participation, and the groups are more cohesive. However, there is not much evidence that charismatic leaders are necessarily more successful.

Transformational Leadership

Burns (1978) has postulated that some charismatic leaders are also "transformational," that is, able to raise the moral and ethical standards of their followers and to enlist them in actions that go beyond their own self-interest. Bass (1985) and others have supported Burns's theory and shown that transformational leaders also stimulate their group members to greater intellectual accomplishments and unselfish deeds. This is a relatively new development in the area of leadership and will, no doubt, become more developed and systematized in the years to come. Bass and his coworkers recently developed promising methods designed to help leaders become more transformational.

Cognitive Resource Theory

Although it is generally assumed that effective leadership requires a high level of intelligence, technical abilities, and experience, empirical research shows rather conclusively that these "cognitive resources" do not, by themselves, contribute to organizational performance. This conclusion is difficult to accept because many leadership functions involve intellectual abilities (e.g., planning, decisionmaking, and problemsolving).

In light of our experience with other leadership factors, and in light of the lessons of the contingency models, it seems likely that the effective contribution of cognitive abilities and experience also depends, or is contingent, on certain situational factors.

Cognitive Resource Theory, or CRT (Fiedler and Garcia 1987), attempts to discover the conditions under which leaders make effective use of their own, and their followers', intellectual abilities and job-relevant knowledge. CRT identified two major situational factors that affect how the leader's cognitive resources contribute to leadership and organizational performance. First, the leader has to be willing and able to direct and supervise the group. For example, Blades and Fiedler (1973) showed that the leader's intelligence and task-relevant knowledge correlated highly with group performance only if the leader was directive as well as supported by the group. Second, stress, especially caused by conflict with the immediate superior, strongly inhibits the leader's ability to make effective use of intellectual abilities and creativity. In somewhat oversimplified terms, leaders in stress-free situations use their intelligence and creativity but not their experience. Leaders in stressful situations use their experience but not their intellectual abilities. In fact, under high stress, leader intelligence correlates negatively with performance; under low stress, leader experience tends to correlate negatively with performance.

To explain these findings, CRT has advanced the hypothesis that experience represents overlearned behavior and that this type of behavior becomes dominant under stress and in emergency conditions (Gibson 1992). So, under stress the leader falls back on that previously overlearned behavior. Gibson, Fiedler, and Barrett (1993) showed that the language of comparatively more intelligent leaders became less intelligible and that they "babbled" more (more words—less content) in stressful than nonstressful conditions.

These finding are explained by noting that leaders who have experience tend to discourage thoughtful consideration of problems for which they think they already know the answer; hence, the more experienced they are, the less their intellectual abilities will be used. Intelligent or creative leaders are less likely to rely on their own and their group members' intuition and hunch (i.e., experience). This tendency (wanting to consider all options before making a decision) serves them well under low stress, but it seriously inhibits appropriate response under high stress.

Improving Leadership

One reason for the popularity of leadership study is its perceived impact on the bottom line. We also indicated factors associated with leadership effectiveness. Here these lines of discussion are integrated; one can use knowledge gained from research to improve leadership and in turn organizational effectiveness. This section reviews some approaches and major techniques.

Selection and Placement

Sometimes the best way to improve leadership is to match leader and job by hiring individuals to fill a position (selection) or assigning someone to a position (placement). For this approach to succeed, one must know the requirements of the job; this is accomplished through job analysis. Following a job analysis, the organization should assess the characteristics of prospective leaders. Some characteristics might derive from the big-five model, which indicates traits that predispose leaders to succeed across a range of positions. Specific skills and knowledge required are determined from the job analysis.

Often, organizations assess leaders through résumés and job interviews. A more comprehensive approach is the assessment center, the primary purpose of which is to provide in-depth descriptions of leaders or candidates using interviews, tests, role playing, and work samples. The measurements in most centers provide fairly accurate information about leadership motivation, personality traits, and skills. When this is combined with information about a candidate's prior experience and performance, assessment centers make reasonably good predictions about leadership potential in specific positions (Howard and Bray 1988).

Situational Engineering

One alternative to matching leaders and positions is changing the situation to make it more favorable for the leader, or to conduct situational engineering. The only formal program for doing so is Leader Match. Based on Fiedler's model, Fiedler and Chemers (1984) developed a self-paced training manual assuming it is difficult for leaders to change their leadership style every time their situation changes. It is easier to diagnose situations in which leaders are likely to perform best and to modify situations so they match the leader's style. The training first asks the individual to complete an LPC scale. The trainee is then taught how to measure situational control. The final sections provide instruction on modifying the situation so it matches one's leadership style.

Leader Match has been tested in several studies that concluded the program improved leader performance. A review of leadership training research (Burke and Day 1986) also concluded Leader Match increased leader effectiveness and recommended its use, based on its effectiveness and low cost.

Leadership Training

Another alternative is to change the leader to fit the requirements of the position—to train the leader. Given the perception that leadership affects bottom lines, billions of dollars are spent each year on leadership training and scores of programs are available. Leadership training programs most often develop knowledge and skills relevant for effectiveness in the short term, but newer programs train in areas from self-insight to visioning (Conger 1992). These skills are difficult to develop formally, so specialized techniques like case analyses and role playing are often used. Although research on the effectiveness of these techniques is sparse, initial results indicate promise, with the most supported techniques being role modeling and simulations. Future research will provide more definitive conclusions regarding which programs develop which skills and under which conditions.

To summarize, leadership is a vibrant and steadily growing area of research, with considerable potential for improving organizational performance. At this point, the most important need for the future is the development of sound theoretically based programs for selecting and developing leaders and managers.

Bibliography

Bass, Bernard M., 1985. *Leadership and Performance Beyond Expectations*. New York: Free Press.

_____, 1990. *Handbook of Leadership*. New York: Free Press.

Blades, Jon W., and Fred E. Fiedler, 1973. "The Influence of Intelligence, Task Ability and Motivation on Group Performance." In *Organizational Research Technical Report*, 76–78. Seattle: University of Washington.

Blake, Robert R., and Jane S. Mouton, 1964. *The Managerial Grid*. Houston: Gulf Publishing.

Burke, Michael J., and Russell R. Day, 1986. "A Cumulative Study of the Effectiveness of Managerial Training." *Journal of Applied Psychology*, vol. 71: 232–246.

Burns, James M., 1978. *Leadership*. New York: Harper & Row.

Carter, J., and M. Nixon, 1949. "Ability, Perceptual, Personality and Interest Factors Associated with Different Criteria of Leadership." *Journal of Psychology*, vol. 27: 377–388.

Chemers, Martin M., Robert W. Rice, Eric Sundstrom, and William M. Butler, 1975. "Leader Esteem for the Least Preferred Co-Worker Scale, Training, and Effectiveness: An Experimental Investigation." *Journal of Personality and Social Psychology*, vol. 31: 401–408.

Conger, Jay A., 1992. *Learning to Lead: The Art of Transforming Managers into Leaders*. San Francisco: Jossey-Bass.

Fiedler, Fred E., 1967. *A Theory of Leadership Effectiveness*. New York: McGraw-Hill.

______, and Martin M. Chemers, 1984. *Improving Leadership Effectiveness: The Leader Match Concept*, 2nd ed. New York: Wiley.

______, and Joseph E. Garcia, 1987. *New Approaches to Effective Leadership: Cognitive Resources and Organizational Performance*. New York: Wiley.

______, and Robert J. House, 1988. "Leadership Theory and Research: A Report of Progress." In Cary L. Cooper and Ivan Robertson, eds., *International Review of Applied Psychology*. New York: Wiley, 73–92.

Gibson, Frederick W., 1992. "Leader Abilities and Group Performance as a Function of Stress." In Kenneth E. Clark, Miriam B. Clark, and David P. Campbell, eds., *Impact of Leadership*. Greensboro, NC: Center for Creative Leadership, 333–343.

______, Frederick W., Fred E. Fiedler, and Kelley M. Barrett, 1993. "Stress, Babble, and the Utilization of the Leader's Intellectual Abilities." *The Leadership Quarterly*, vol. 4:189–208.

Gough, Harrison G., 1990. "Testing for Leadership with the California Psychological Inventory." In Kenneth E. Clark and Miriam B. Clark, eds., *Measures of Leadership*. West Orange, NJ: Leadership Library of America, 355–379.

Hersey, Paul, and Kenneth H. Blanchard, 1982. *Management of Organizational Behavior: Utilizing Human Resources*, 4th ed. Englewood Cliffs, NJ: Prentice-Hall.

Hogan, Robert, Gordon J. Curphy, and Joyce Hogan, 1994. "What We Know About Leadership." *American Psychologist*, vol. 49: 493–504.

______, Robert, and Joyce Hogan, 1992. *Hogan Personality Inventory Manual*. Tulsa, OK: Hogan Assessment Systems.

Hollander, Edwin P., 1985. "Leadership and Power." In Gardner Lindzey and Elliot Aronson, eds., *Handbook of Social Psychology*, 3d ed. New York: Random House.

Hook, Sidney, 1955. *The Hero in History*. Boston: Beacon Press.

House, Robert J., and Terrence R. Mitchell, 1974. "Path-Goal Theory of Leadership." *Journal of Comtemporary Business*, vol. 3: 81–97.

Howard, Ann, and Douglas W. Bray, 1988. *Managerial Lives in Transition: Advancing Age and Changing Times*. New York: Guilford Press.

Korman, Abraham K., 1966. "'Consideration,' 'Initiating Structure,' and Organizational Criteria—A Review." *Personnel Psychology*, vol. 10: 349–361.

Landy, Frank J., 1989. *Psychology of Work Behavior*, 4th ed. Pacific Grove, CA: Brooks/Cole.

Meindl, James R., and Sanford B. Ehrlich, 1987. "The Romance of Leadership and the Evaluation of Organizational Performance." *Academy of Management Journal*, vol. 30: 91–109.

Mitchell, Terence R., Charles M. Smyser, and Stanley E. Weed, 1975. "Locus of Control: Supervision and Work Satisfaction." *Academy of Management Journal*, vol. 18: 623–630.

Pfeffer, Jeffrey, 1977. "The Ambiguity of Leadership." *Academy of Management Review*, vol. 2: 104–112.

Salancik, Gerald R., and Jeffrey Pfeffer, 1977. "Constraints on Administrative Discretion: The Limited Influence of Mayors on City Budgets." *Urban Affairs Quarterly*, vol. 12: 447–498.

Simon, Herbert A., 1947. *Administrative Behavior: A Study of Decision-Making Process in Administrative Organizations*. New York: Macmillan.

Stogdill, Ralph M., 1948. "Personal Factors Associated with Leadership: A Survey of the Literature." *Journal of Psychology*, vol. 25: 35–71.

______, Ralph M., and A. E. Coons, 1957. *Leader Behavior: Its Description and Measurement*. Columbus: Ohio State University, Bureau of Business Research.

Vroom, Victor H., and Philip W. Yetton, 1973. *Leadership and Decision-Making*. Pittsburgh, PA: University of Pittsburgh Press.

Weber, Max, 1946. "The Sociology of Charismatic Authority." In H. H. Mills and C. W. Mills, eds. and trans., *Essays in Sociology*. New York: Oxford University Press.

Woodword, Joan, 1958. *Management and Technology*. London: Her Majesty's Stationery Office.

Yukl, Gary, 1989. *Leadership in Organizations*, 2d ed. Englewood Cliffs, NJ: Prentice-Hall.

______, 1994. *Leadership in Organizations*, 3d ed. Englewood Cliffs, NJ: Prentice-Hall.

24

STRATEGIC PLANNING

John M. Bryson,
University of Minnesota

A "disciplined effort to produce fundamental decisions and actions that shape and guide what an organization is, what it does, and why it does it" (Bryson 1988, p. 5). Strategic planning consists of a set of concepts, procedures, and tools developed primarily, but far from exclusively, in the private sector. This history has been amply documented by others (Ansoff 1980; Bracker 1980; Quinn 1980; Mintzberg 1994). The experience of the last fifteen years, and a growing body of literature, however, indicate that strategic planning approaches either developed in the private sector, or else strongly influenced by them, can help public organizations, as well as communities or other entities, deal in effective ways with their dramatically changing environments.

That does not mean, however, that all approaches to what might be called corporate-style strategic planning are equally applicable to the public sector. This entry, therefore, will compare and contrast six approaches to corporate strategic planning (actually eight approaches grouped into six categories), discuss their applicability to the public sector, and identify the most important contingencies governing their use.

Remember that corporate strategic planning typically focuses on an organization and what it should do to improve its performance and not on a community, or on a function, such as transportation or health care within a community, or marketing or personnel within an organization. Most of what follows focuses primarily on organizations and how they might plan to improve their performance. But applications to communities and functions will be discussed as well.

It should be noted that careful tests of corporate-style strategic planning in the public sector are few in number (Bryson 1988b; Boal and Bryson 1987; Boschken 1988, 1994; Bryson, Bromiley, and Jung 1990; Bryson and Bromiley 1993; Stone and Crittenden 1993; Mintzberg 1994). Nevertheless, there is enough experience with corporate strategic planning in the private sector, and increasingly in the public sector, to reach some tentative conclusions about what works under what conditions and why.

The remainder of this entry is divided into two sections. The first discusses the six approaches and compares and contrasts them along several dimensions, including key features, assumptions, strengths, weaknesses, and contingencies governing their use in the public sector. The second section presents conclusions about the applicability of strategic planning to public organizations and purposes. The principal conclusions are (1) that public strategic planning is well on its way to becoming part of the standard repertoire of public leaders, managers, and planners and (2) that, nevertheless, public personnel must be very careful how they engage in strategic planning, since not all approaches are equally useful and since a number of conditions govern the successful use of each approach.

Approaches to Strategic Planning

This section briefly sets forth six schools of strategic planning thought developed primarily, but by no means exclusively, in the private sector. The strategic planning process includes general policy and direction setting, situation assessments, strategic issues identification, strategy development, decisionmaking, implementation, and evaluation (Bryson 1988b, 1995, 1996). Attention will be given first to three approaches that cover more of the process and that emphasize policy and direction setting; then the discussion will move to approaches that focus more narrowly on elements in the later stages of the process.

Approaches That Cover Much of the Process and Emphasize Policy and Direction Setting

The Harvard Policy Model. The Harvard policy model was developed as part of the business policy courses taught at the Harvard Business School since the 1920s (Bower et al. 1993). The approach provides the principal (though often implicit) inspiration behind the most widely cited recent models of public and nonprofit sector strategic planning, including my own (Olsen and Eadie 1982; Barry 1986; Bryson 1988b, 1995; Backoff and Nutt 1992).

The main purpose of the Harvard model is to help a firm develop the best "fit" between itself and its environment; that is, to develop the best strategy for the firm. As articulated by K. Andrews (1980), strategy is "a pattern of purposes and policies defining the company and its business." One discerns the best strategy by analyzing the internal strengths and weaknesses of the company and the values of senior management and by identifying the external threats and opportunities in the environment and the social obligations of the firm. Then one designs the appropriate organizational structure, processes, relationships, and behaviors necessary to implement the strategy and focuses on providing the leadership necessary to implement the strategy.

Effective use of the model presumes that senior management can agree on the firm's situation and the appropriate strategic response and has enough authority to enforce its decisions. A final important assumption of the model, common to all approaches to strategic planning, is that if the appropriate strategy is identified and implemented, the organization will be more effective. Attention also is paid to the need for effective implementation.

In the business world, the Harvard model appears to be best applied at the strategic business unit (SBU) level. A strategic business unit is a distinct business that has its own competitors and can be managed somewhat independently of other units within the organization (Rue and Holland 1986). The SBU, in other worlds, provides an important yet bounded and manageable focus for the model. John Montanari and Jeffrey Bracker (1986) argued that the public equivalent of the SBU is the strategic public planning unit (SPPU), which typically would be an agency or department that addresses issues fundamentally similar to one another (such as related health issues, related transportation issues, or related education issues).

The Harvard model is also applicable at the higher and broader corporate level in the private and public sectors. The model probably would have to be supplemented with other approaches, however, such as the portfolio and strategic issues management approaches, to be discussed later. A portfolio approach is needed because a principal strategic concern at the corporate level is oversight of a portfolio of businesses, in the private sector, and a portfolio of agencies or departments in the public sector. Strategic issues management is needed because much high-level work typically is quite political and articulating and addressing issues is the heart of political decisionmaking (Bryson and Crosby 1992).

The systematic assessment of strengths, weaknesses, opportunities, and threats—known as a SWOT analysis—is a primary strength of the Harvard model. This element of the model appears to be applicable in the public sector to organizations, functions, and communities. Another strength is its emphasis on the need to link strategy formulation and implementation in effective ways. The main weaknesses of the Harvard model are that it does not draw attention to strategic issues or offer specific advice on how to develop strategies, except to note that effective strategies will build on strengths, how to take advantage of opportunities, and how to overcome or minimize weaknesses and threats.

Strategic Planning Systems. Strategic planning is often viewed as a system whereby managers go about making, implementing, and controlling important decisions across functions and levels in the firm. Peter Lorange (1980), for example, has argued that any strategic planning system must address four fundamental questions:

1. Where are we going? (mission)
2. How do we get there? (strategies)
3. What is our blueprint for action? (budgets)
4. How do we know if we are on track? (control)

Strategic planning systems vary along several dimensions: The comprehensiveness of decision areas included the formal rationality of the decision process and the tightness of control exercised over implementation of the decisions (Armstrong 1982; Goold, Campbell, and Luchs 1993a, 1993b), as well as how the strategy process itself will be tailored to the organization and managed (Chakravarthy and Lorange 1991). The strength of these systems is their attempt to coordinate the various elements of an organization's strategy across levels and functions. Their weakness is that excessive comprehensiveness, prescription, and control can drive out attention to mission, strategy, and organizational structure (Frederickson and Mitchell 1984; Frederickson 1984; Mintzberg 1994) and can exceed the ability of participants to comprehend the system and the information it produces (Bryson, Van de Ven, and Roering 1987).

Strategic planning systems are applicable to public organizations (and to a lesser extent communities), for regardless of the nature of the particular organization, it makes sense to coordinate decisionmaking across levels and functions and to concentrate on whether the organization is implementing its strategies and accomplishing its mission (Boschken 1988, 1992, 1994). It is important to remember, however, that a strategic planning system characterized by substantial comprehensiveness, formal rationality in decisionmaking, and tight control will work only in an organization that has a clear mission, clear goals and objectives, relatively simple tasks to perform, centralized authority, clear performance indicators, and information about actual performance available at reasonable cost. While some public organizations—such as hospitals and police and fire departments—operate under such conditions, most do not. As a result, most public sector strategic planning systems typically focus on a few areas of concern, rely on a decision process in which politics play a major role, and control something other than program outcomes (e.g., budget expenditures) (Wildavsky 1979a; Barzelay 1992; Osborne and Gaebler 1992; Bryson 1995). That is changing, however. For example, the U.S. federal government is now moving toward performance-based strategic management as a result of the Government Performance and Results Act of 1993 (Public Law 103-62) and a number of states are following suit (National Governors Association 1993).

Stakeholder Management Approaches. R. Edward Freeman (1984) stated that corporate strategy can be understood as a corporation's mode of relating or building bridges to its stakeholders. A stakeholder for Freeman is any group or individual who is affected by or who can affect the future of the corporation; for example, customers, employees, suppliers, owners, governments, financial institutions, and critics. He argued that a corporate strategy will be effective only if it satisfies the needs of multiple groups. Traditional private-sector models of strategy have focused only on economic actors, but Freeman argued that changes in the current business environment require that other political and social actors be considered as well.

Because it integrates economic, political, and social concerns, the stakeholder model is one of the approaches most applicable to the public sector. Many interest groups have stakes in public organizations, functions, and communities. For example, local economic development planning typically involves government, developers, bankers, the chamber of commerce, actual or potential employers, neighborhood groups, environmentalists, and so on. Local economic development planners would be wise to identify key stakeholders, their interests, what they will support, and strategies and tactics that might work in dealing with them (Kaufman 1979; Backoff and Nutt 1992). John Bryson, R. E. Freeman, and William Roering (1986) argue in addition that an organization's mission and values ought to be formulated in stakeholder terms. That is, an organization should figure out what its mission ought to be in relation to each stakeholder group; otherwise, it will not be able to differentiate its responses well enough to satisfy its key stakeholders.

The strengths of the stakeholder model are its recognition of the many claims—both complementary and competing—placed on organizations by insiders and outsiders and its awareness of the need to satisfy at least the key stakeholders if the organization is to survive. The weaknesses of the model are the absence of criteria with which to judge competing claims and the need for more advice on developing strategies to deal with divergent stakeholder interests.

Freeman has applied the stakeholder concept primarily at the corporate and industry levels in the private sector, but it seems applicable to all levels in the public sectors. Researchers have not yet made rigorous tests of the model's usefulness in the private, public, or nonprofit sectors, but several public and nonprofit case studies indicate that stakeholder analyses are quite useful as part of the strategic planning effort (Bryson, 1988b, 1995; Backoff and Nutt 1992; Bryson and Crosby 1992; Kemp 1993; Boschken 1992, 1994). If the model is to be used successfully, there must be the possibility that key decisionmakers can achieve reasonable agreement about who the key stakeholders are and what the response to their claims should be.

A number of other encompassing approaches to strategic planning have been developed primarily in the United Kingdom in the field of operations research. These include Strategic Options Development and Analysis (SODA) (Eden and Huxham 1988; Eden 1989; Bryson and Finn 1995), soft systems methodology (Checkland 1981, 1991), and strategic choice (Friend and Hickling 1987). They are used mostly in Europe but are finding application elsewhere as well.

Content Approaches

The three approaches presented so far have more to do with managing an entire strategic planning process than with identifying specific strategy content. The process approaches do not prescribe answers, although good answers are presumed to emerge from appropriate application. In contrast, the tools to be discussed next—portfolio models and competitive analysis—primarily concern content and do yield answers. In fact, the models are antithetical to process when process concerns get in the way of developing the "right" answers. Other important content approaches not covered in this entry, due to space limitations, include "reinventing government" (Osborne and Gaebler 1992; Gore 1993; Thompson and Jones 1994), systems analysis (Churchman 1968; Senge 1990), and "reengineering the organization" (Hammer and Champy 1993; Linden 1994).

Portfolio Models. The idea of strategic planning as managing a portfolio of businesses is based on an analogy with investment practice. Just as an investor assembles a portfolio of stocks to manage risk and to realize optimum returns, a corporate manager can think of the corporation as a portfolio of businesses with diverse potentials that can be balanced to manage return and cash flow. The intellectual history of portfolio theory in corporate strategy is complex (Wind and Mahajan 1981). For our purposes, it is adequate to use as an example the portfolio model developed by the Boston Consulting Group (BCG): the famous BCG matrix (Henderson 1979; Hax and Majiluf 1984).

Bruce Henderson, founder of the Boston Consulting Group, argued that all business costs followed a well-known pattern: unit costs dropped by one-third every time volume (or turnover) doubled. Hence, he postulated a relationship, known as the experience curve, between unit costs and volume. This relationship leads to some generic strategic advice: Gain market share, for then unit costs will fall and profit potential will increase.

Henderson said that any business could be categorized into one of four types, depending on how its industry was growing and how large a share of the market it had:

1. High growth/high share businesses ("stars"), which generate substantial cash but also require large investments if their market share is to be maintained or increased.
2. Low growth/high share businesses ("cash cows"), which generate large cash flows but require low investment and therefore generate profits that can be used elsewhere.

3. Low growth/low share businesses ("dogs"), which produce little cash and offer little prospect of increased share.
4. High growth/low share businesses ("question marks"), which would require substantial investment in order to become stars or cash cows. The question is whether the investment is worth it.

Although the applications of portfolio theory to the public sector may be less obvious than those of the three approaches described earlier, they are nonetheless just as powerful (MacMillan 1983; Ring 1988; Backoff and Nutt 1992). Many public organizations consist of "multiple businesses" that are only marginally related. Often resources from various sources are committed to these unrelated businesses. That means the public and managers must make portfolio decisions, although usually without the help of portfolio models that frame those decisions strategically. The BCG approach, like most private-sector portfolio models, uses only economic criteria, not political or social criteria that might be necessary for public applications. Private-sector portfolio approaches, therefore, must be modified substantially for public and nonprofit use. (Indeed, thoughtful critics argue that because private-sector portfolio approaches ignore the missions, values, cultures, and competencies of the companies that comprise the portfolios, they can do far more harm than good. Strategic management which relies only on economically based portfolio analysis can produce disastrous results and, therefore, is itself probably bankrupt; see Hurst 1986; Mintzberg 1994).

The strength of portfolio approaches is that they provide a method of measuring entities of some sort (businesses, investment options, proposals, or problems) against dimensions that are deemed to be of strategic importance (share and growth, or position and attractiveness). Weaknesses include the difficulty of knowing what the appropriate strategic dimensions are, difficulties of classifying entities against dimensions, and the lack of clarity about how to use the tool as part of larger strategic planning process.

If modified to include political and social factors, portfolio approaches can be used in the public sector to make informed strategic decisions. They can be used in conjunction with an overall strategic planning process to provide useful information on an organization, function, or community in relation to its environment. Unlike the process models, however, portfolio approaches provide an "answer;" that is, once the dimensions for comparison and the entities to be compared are specified, the portfolio models prescribe how the organization or community should relate to its environment. Such models will work only if a dominant coalition is convinced that the answers they produce are correct.

Competitive Analysis. Another important content approach that assists strategy selection has been developed by Michael Porter (1980, 1985, 1990, 1994) and his associates. Called "competitive analysis," it assumes that by analyzing the forces that shape an industry, one can predict the general level of profits throughout the industry and the likely success of any particular strategy for a strategic business unit.

Porter (1980) hypothesized that five key competitive forces shape an industry: relative power of customers, relative power of suppliers, threat of substitute products, threat of new entrants, and the amount of rivalrous activity among the players in the industry. Katherine Harrigan (1981) has argued that "exit barriers"—that is, the barriers that would prevent a company from leaving an industry—are a sixth force influencing success in some industries. Two of the main propositions in the competitive analysis school are as follows: (1) The stronger the forces that shape an industry, the lower the general level of returns in the industry; and (2) the stronger the forces affecting a strategic business unit, the lower the profits for that unit.

Two additional concepts are crucial in Porter's view. Competitive advantage grows out of the value a firm creates for its customers that exceeds the cost of producing it. Competitive advantage grows out of the value chain, the linkage of discrete primary activities (inbound logistics, operations, outbound logistics, marketing and sales, service) and support activities (firm infrasructure, human resource management, technology development, procurement) that create value for which the customer is willing to pay. Profits are found in the margin between what things cost and what their value is to the customer. Every buyer and supplier has a value chain, which leads to an additional important proposition: The more a supplier understands a buyer's value chain, the greater the firm's ability to create value for that buyer.

For many public organizations, there are equivalents to the forces that affect private industry. For example, client or customer power is often important; suppliers of services (contractors and the organization's own labor supply) also can exercise power. There are fewer new entrants in the public sector, but recently private and nonprofit organizations have begun to compete more forcefully with public organizations. Governments and public agencies often compete with one another (public hospitals for patients; state and local governments for industrial plants).

An effective organization in the public sector, therefore, must understand the forces at work in its "industry" in order to compete effectively and must offer value to its customers that exceeds the cost of producing it. On another level, planning for a specific public function (health care, transportation, or recreation) can benefit from competitive analysis if the function can be considered an industry. In addition, economic development agencies must understand the forces at work in given industries and on specific firms if they are to understand whether and how to nurture those industries and firms. Finally, although communities do compete with one another, competitive analysis probably does not apply at this level because communities are not industries in any meaningful sense.

By contrast, Porter points out in *The Competitive Advantage of Nations* (1990) that for the foreseeable future self-reinforcing agglomerations of firms and networks are crucial aspects of successful international economic competition. U.S. Secretary of Labor Robert Reich (1992), the German Marshall Fund (Widener et al. 1992), and Neal Pierce (1989) make the same point. In effect, not just firms, but metropolitan regions (Singapore, Hong Kong, the Silicon Valley, New York, London, Paris) are key economic actors. Regions interested in competing on the world stage, therefore, should try to develop the infrastructure necessary for virtuous (rather than vicious) cycles of economic growth to unfold. In other words, wise investments in education, transportation and transit systems, water and sewer systems, parks and recreation, housing, and so on, can help firms reduce their costs—particularly the costs of acquiring an educated labor force—and thus improve firms' abilities to compete internationally.

The strength of competitive analysis is that it provides a systematic way of assessing industries and the strategic options facing SBUs within those industries. Public organizations can use competitive analysis to discover ways to help the private firms in their regions. When applied directly to public organizations, however, competitive analysis has two weaknesses: It is often difficult to know what the "industry" is and what forces affect it, and the key to organizational success in the public world is often collaboration instead of competition. Competitive analysis for the public organizations, therefore, must be coupled with a consideration of social and political forces and the possibilities for collaboration (Huxham 1993; Winer and Ray 1994).

Another Process Approach

We now leave content approaches to focus again on a process approach—strategic issues management—that is less encompassing than the previous process approaches and typically is less encompassing than the content approaches as well.

Strategic Issues Management. Strategic issues management approaches are process components, pieces of a larger strategic planning process. In the private sector, strategic issues management is primarily associated with Igor Ansoff (1980) and focuses attention on the recognition and resolution of strategic issues—"forthcoming developments, either inside or outside the organization, which are likely to have an important impact on the ability of the enterprise to meet its objectives" (p. 133). In the public sector, strategic issue management is primarily associated with Douglas Eadie (1986, 1989), Bryson (1988, 1995), and Backoff and Nutt (1992).

The concept of strategic issues first emerged when practitioners of corporate strategic planning realized a step was missing between the SWOT analysis of the Harvard model and the development of strategies. That step was the identification of strategic issues. Many organizations now include a strategic issue identification step as part of full-blown strategy revision exercises and also as part of less comprehensive annual strategic reviews (Chakravarthy and Lorange 1991). Full-blown annual revision has proved impractical because strategy revision takes substantial management energy and attention, and in any case most strategies take several years to implement. Instead, most firms are undertaking comprehensive strategy revisions several years apart (typically four or five) and in the interim are focusing their annual strategic planning processes on the identification and resolution of a few key strategic issues that emerge from SWOT analyses, environmental scans, and other analyses (Hambrick 1982; Pflaum and Delmont 1987; Heath 1988).

In recent years, many organizations also have developed strategic issues management processes actually separated from their annual strategic planning processes. Many important issues emerge too quickly, with too much urgency, to be handled as part of an annual process. When confronted with such issues, top managers typically appoint temporary teams or task forces to develop responses for immediate implementation.

Strategic issue management is clearly applicable to public organizations, since the agendas of these organizations consist of issues that should be managed strategically (Backoff and Nutt 1992; Bryson and Crosby 1992). In other words, they should be managed based on a sense of mission and mandates and in the context of an environmental assessment and stakeholder analysis. The strength of the approach is its ability to recognize and analyze key issues quickly. The approach also applies to functions or communities, as long as some group, organization, or coalition is able to engage in the process and to manage the issue. The main weakness is that in general the approach offers no specific advice on exactly how to frame the issues other than to precede their identification with a situational analysis of some sort. Nutt (1992, pp. 119–145), and Nutt and Backoff (1995) have gone the furthest in remedying this defect. They argued that public organizations exist within "tension fields" comprised of often conflicting or contradictory pressures for equity, preservation of the status quo, transition to a new state, and productivity improvement. Nutt and Backoff argued that exploration of the various combinations of these tensions, as they apply in specific circumstances, can lead strategic planners to the wisest formulation of strategic issues and strategies.

Process Strategies

The final two approaches to be discussed are process strategies. They are logical incrementalism and strategic planning as a framework for innovation. Process strategies are approaches to implementing a strategy that already has been developed in very broad outline and is subject to revision based on experience with its implementation. Other important process strategies not discussed in this entry, due to space limitations, include total quality management (Coucheu 1993, pp. 173–186; Cohen and Brand 1993), strategic negotiations (Pettigrew 1977; Mintzberg 1983; Mintzberg and Waters 1985; Pettigrew, Ferlie, and McKee 1992; Susskind and Cruikshank 1987), collaboration (Gray 1989; Huxham 1991, 1993; Winer and Ray 1994), and the management of culture (Hampden-Turner 1990; Schein 1992).

Logical Incrementalism. In incremental approaches, strategy is a loosely linked group of decisions that are handled incrementally. Decisions are handled individually below the corporate level because such decentralization is politically expedient—organizational leaders should reserve their political clout for crucial decisions. Decentralization also is necessary since often only those closest to decisions have enough information to make good ones.

The incremental approach is identified principally with James Quinn (1980; Mintzberg and Quinn 1991), although the influence of Charles Lindblom (1959; Braybrook and Lindblom 1963; Lindblom 1965, 1977, 1980) is apparent. Quinn developed the concept of logical incrementalism—or incrementalism in the service of overall corporate purposes—and as a result transformed incrementalism into a strategic approach. Logical incrementalism is a process approach that, in effect, fuses strategy formulation and implementation. The strengths of the approach are its ability to handle complexity and change, its emphasis on minor as well as major decisions, its attention to informal as well as formal processes, and its political realism. A related strength is that incremental changes in degree can add up over time into changes in time (Mintzberg 1987; Bryson 1988a, 1995; Bryson and Crosby 1992). The major weakness of the approach is that it does not guarantee that the various loosely linked decisions will add up to fulfillment of corporate purposes.

Logical incrementalism would appear to be very applicable to public organizations, as it is possible to establish some overarching set of strategic objectives to be served by the approach. When applied at the community level, there is a close relationship between logical incrementalism and collaboration. Indeed, collaborative purposes and arrangements typically emerge in an incremental fashion as organizations individually and collectively explore their self-interests and possible collaborative advantages, establish collaborative relationships, and manage changes incrementally within a collaborative framework (Huxham 1993; Winer and Ray 1994).

Strategic Planning as a Framework for Innovation. The earlier discussion about strategic planning systems noted that excessive comprehensiveness, prescription, and control can drive out attention to mission, strategy, and organizational structure. The systems in other words, can become ends in themselves and drive out creativity, innovation, and new product and market development, without which most businesses would die. Many businesses, therefore, have found it necessary to emphasize innovative strategies as a counterbalance to the excessive control orientation of many strategic planning systems. In other words, while one important reason for installing a strategic planning system is the need to exercise control across functions and levels, an equally important need for organizations is to design systems that promote creativity and entrepreneurship at the local level and prevent centralization and bureaucracy from stifling the wellsprings of business growth and change (Taylor 1984; Waterman 1987).

The framework-for-innovation approach to corporate strategic planning relies on many elements of the approaches discussed earlier, such as SWOT analyses and portfolio methods. This approach differs from earlier ones in four emphases: (1) innovation as a strategy, (2) specific management practices to support the strategy (such as project teams; venture groups; diversification, acquisition, and divestment task forces; research and development operations; new product and market groups; and a variety of organizational development techniques), (3) development of a "vision of success" that provides the decentralized and entrepreneurial parts of the organization with a common set of superordinate goals toward which to work, and (4) nurture of an entrepreneurial company culture (Pinchot 1985).

Minnesota employed a framework-for-innovation approach, called Strive for Excellence in Performance (STEP), under Governor Rudy Perpich in the 1980s. The STEP steering committee, cochaired by the governor and the chair of the state's big-business association, provided legitimacy and access to resources to experiment with projects proposed by state employees. A number of useful changes in the way the state provided goods and services resulted (Hale and Williams 1989; Barzelay 1992).

The main strength of the approach is that it allows for innovation and entrepreneurship while maintaining central control. It also is quite compatible with other approaches, such as reinventing government, systems analysis, reengineering the organization, and total quality management. The weaknesses of the approach are that typically—and perhaps necessarily—a great many, often costly, mistakes are made as part of the innovation process and that there is a certain loss of accountability in very decentralized systems (Peters and Waterman 1982; Mintzberg 1994). Those weaknesses reduce the applicability to the public sector, in particular, in which mistakes are less acceptable and the pressures to be accountable for details (as opposed to results) are often greater (Barzelay 1992; Jackson and Palmer 1992).

Nonetheless, the innovation approach would appear to be applicable to public organizations when the management of innovation is necessary, as in the redesign of a public service. Innovation as a strategy also can and should be pursued for functions and communities. Too often a distressing equation has operated in the public sector: More money equals more service, less money equals less service. As public budgets have become increasingly strapped, there has not been enough innovation in public service redesign. The equation does not have to be destiny; it is possible that creative effort and innovation might actually result in more service for less money (Osborne and Gaebler 1992; Gore 1993). It is particularly interesting to note that private and nonprofit sector innovations may be the answer to many public-sector problems. For example, many governments rely on private and nonprofit organizations to produce essentially "public" services on a contract basis.

Conclusions

Several conclusions emerge from this review and analysis. First, it should be clear that strategic planning is not a single concept, procedure, or tool. In fact, it embraces a range of approaches that vary in their applicability to public purposes and in the conditions that govern their successful use. The approaches vary in the extent to which they encompass broad policy and direction setting, internal and external assessments, attention to key stakeholders, the identification of key issues, development of strategies to deal with each issue, decisionmaking, implementation, and monitoring and interpretation of results.

Second, a strategic planning process applicable to public organizations and communities will need to allow for the full range of strategic planning activities from policy and direction setting through monitoring of results. Such a process will contrast, therefore, with most private-sector approaches that tend to emphasize different parts of such a complete process. A further contrast would be that private-sector approaches typically are focused only on organizations and not on functions that cross governmental or organizational boundaries, or on communities or larger entities.

Third, while any generic strategic planning process may be a useful guide to thought and action, it will have to be applied with care in a given situation, as is true of any planning process (Bryson and Delbecq 1979; Christensen 1985; Chakravarthy and Lorange 1991; Nutt 1992; Sager 1994). Because every planning process should be tailored to fit specific situations, every process in practice will be a hybrid (Bryson 1988b, 1995).

Fourth, familiarity with strategic planning should be a standard part of the intellectual and skill repertoire of all public managers and planners. Given the dramatic changes in the environments of their organizations in recent years, we can expect key public decisionmakers and planners to seek effective strategies to deal with the changes. When applied appropriately, strategic planning provides a set of concepts, procedures, and tools for formulating and implementing such strategies. The most effective leaders, managers, and planners no doubt are now, and will be increasingly in the future, the ones who are best at strategic planning.

Fifth, asserting the increased importance of strategic planning raises the question of the appropriate role of the strategic planner. In many ways, this is an old debate in the planning literature. Should the planner be a technician, politician, or hybrid—both technician and politician (Howe and Kaufman 1979; Howe 1980)? Should the planner be a process facilitator (Schein 1988) or what Bolan (1971) calls an "expert on experts?" Or should the planner not be a planner at all, at least formally, but rather a policymaker or a line manager (Bryson, Van de Ven, and Roering 1987; Mintzberg 1994)? Clearly, the strategic planner can be solely a technician only when content approaches are used. When all other approaches are used, the strategic planner (or planning team) should be a hybrid so that there is some assurance that both political and technical concerns are addressed. (Obviously, the specific proportions of technical expertise and political or process expertise would vary depending on the situation.) Furthermore, since strategic planning tends to fuse planning and decisionmaking, it is helpful to think of decisionmakers as strategic planners and to think of strategic planners as facilitators of strategic decisionmaking across levels and functions in organizations or communities.

Finally, research must explore a number of theoretical and empirical issues in order to advance the knowledge and practice of public-sector strategic planning. In particular, strategic planning processes that are responsive to different situations must be developed and tested. These processes should specify key situational factors governing their use; provide specific advice on how to formulate and implement strategies in different situations; be explicitly political; indicate how to deal with plural, ambiguous, or conflicting goals or objectives; link context, content, process, and outcomes; indicate how collaboration as well as competition is to be handled; and specify roles for those involved in the process. Other topics in need of attention include the nature of strategic leadership; ways to promote and institutionalize strategic planning across organizational levels, functions that bridge organizational boundaries, and intra- and interorganizational networks; and the ways in which information technologies can help or hinder the process. Progress has been made on all of these fronts (Checkoway 1986; Bryson and Einsweiler 1988; Boschken 1988, 1994; Kemp 1993; Bryson 1995), but work clearly is necessary if we are to understand better when and how to use strategic planning to further public purposes.

Notes

Adapted from Bryson (1988b, P. 22–45) and from a paper prepared for presentation at the workshop on "Strategic Approaches to Planning: Towards Shared Urban Policies," Politecnico Die Milano, Facolta Di Architettura, Milano, Italy, March 16–17, 1995.

Bibliography

Andrews, Kenneth, 1980. *The Concept of Corporate Strategy*. Homewood, IL: R. D. Irwin.

Ansoff, I., 1980. "Strategic Issue Management." *Strategic Management Journal*, vol. 1, no. 2: 131–148.

Armstrong, J. S., 1982. The Value of Formal Planning for Strategic Decisions: Review of Empirical Research. *Strategic Management Journal*, vol. 3, no. 2: 197–211.

Backoff, Robert, and Paul Nutt, 1992. *Strategic Management for Public and Third-Sector Organizations*. San Francisco, CA: Jossey-Bass.

Barry, B., 1986. *Strategic Planning Workbook for Nonprofit Organizations*. St. Paul, MN: Amherst H. Wilder Foundation.

Barzelay, M., 1992. *Breaking Through Bureaucracy*. Berkeley: University of California Press.

Boal, K. B., and J. M. Bryson, 1987. "Representation, Testing, and Policy Implications of Planning Processes." *Strategic Management Journal*, vol. 8: 211–231.

Bolan, R. S., 1971. "Generalist with a Specialty—Still Valid? Educating the Planner: An Expert on Experts." *Planning 1971: Selected Papers from the ASPO National Conference*. Chicago: American Society of Planning Officials.

Boschken, H. L., 1988. *Strategic Design and Organizational Change*, London: The University of Alabama Press.

______, 1992. "Analyzing Performance Skewness in Public Agencies: The Case of Urban Mass Transit." *Journal of Public Administration Research and Theory*, vol. 2, no. 3: 265–288.

______, 1994. "Organizational Performance and Multiple Constituencies." *Public Administration Review*, vol. 54: 308–312.

Bower, J., C. Bartlett, C. Christensen, A. Pearson and K. Andrews, 1993. *Business Policy: Text and Cases*, 7th ed. Homewood, IL: Irwin.

Bracker, J., 1980. "The Historical Development of the Strategic Management Concept." *Academy of Management Review*, vol. 5, no. 2: 219–224.

Braybrook, D., and C. Lindblom, 1963. *A Strategy for Decision: Policy Evaluation as a Social Process*. New York: Free Press.

Bryson, J. M., 1983. "Representing and Testing Procedural Planning Methods." In I. Masser, ed., *Evaluating Urban Planning Efforts*. Aldershot, England: Gower.

______, 1988a. "Strategic Planning: Big Wins and Small Wins." *Public Money and Management*, vol. 8, no. 3: 11–15.

______, 1988b. *Strategic Planning for Public and Nonprofit Organizations*. San Francisco, CA: Jossey-Bass.

______, 1995. *Strategic Planning for Public and Nonprofit Organizations*, rev. ed. San Francisco, CA: Jossey-Bass.

______, 1996. "Understanding Options for Strategic Planning." In J. Perry, ed., *Handbook of Public Administration*. San Francisco, CA: Jossey-Bass, pp. 479–598.

Bryson, J. M., and P. Bromiley, 1993. "Critical Factors Affecting the Planning and Implementation of Major Projects." *Strategic Management Journal*, vol. 14: 319–337.

Bryson, J., P. Bromily, and Y. S. Jung, 1990. "Influences of Context and Process on Project Planning Success." *Journal of Planning Education and Research*, vol. 9, no. 3: 183–195.

Bryson, J. M., and B. C. Crosby, 1992. *Leadership for the Common Good*. San Francisco, CA: Jossey-Bass.

Bryson, J. M., and A. L. Delbecq, 1979. "A Contingent Approach to Strategy and Tactics in Project Planning." *Journal of the American Planning Association*, vol. 45: 167–179.

Bryson, J. M., and R. C. Einsweiler, eds., 1988. *Strategic Planning for Public Purposes—Threats and Opportunities for Planners*. Chicago, IL, and Washington, DC: Planners Press of the American Planning Association.

Bryson, J. M., and C. B. Finn, 1995. "Development and Use of Strategy Maps to Enhance Organizational Performance." In A. Halachmi, and G. Bouckaert, eds., *The Challenge of Management in a Changing World*. San Francisco, CA: Jossey-Bass, pp. 247–280.

Bryson, J. M., R. E. Freeman, and W. D. Roering, 1986. "Strategic Planning in the Public Sector: Approaches and Directions." In B. Checkoway, ed., *Strategic Perspectives on Planning Practice*. Lexington, MA.: Lexington Books, pp. 65–85.

Bryson, J. M., A. H. Van de Ven, and W. D. Roering, 1987. "Strategic Planning and the Revitalization of the Public Service." In R. Denhardt and E. Jennings, eds., *Toward a New Public Service*. Columbia: Extension Publications, University of Missouri, pp. 55–75.

Chakravarthy, B., and P. Lorange, 1991. *Managing the Strategy Rrocess: A Framework for the Multi-Business Firm*. Englewood Cliffs, NJ: Prentice-Hall.

Checkland, P. B., 1981. *Systems Thinking, System Practice*. Chichester, England: Wiley.

Checkland, P. B., and J. Scholes, 1991. *Soft Systems Methodology in Action*. New York: Wiley.

Checkoway, B., ed., 1986. *Strategic Perspectives on Planning Practice*. Lexington, MA: Lexington Books.

Christensen, K. S., 1985. "Coping with Uncertainty in Planning". *Journal of the American Planning Association*, vol. 51, no. 1: 63–73.

______, 1993. "Teaching Savvy." *Journal of Planning Education and Research*, vol. 12, no. 3: 202–212.

Churchman, C. W., 1968. *The Systems Approach*. NY: Dell.

Cohen, S., and R. Brand, 1993. *Total Quality Management in Government*. San Francisco, CA: Jossey-Bass.

Coucheu, T., 1993. *Making Quality Happen*. San Francisco, CA: Jossey-Bass.

Dutton, J., and S. Ashford, 1993. "Selling Issues to Top Management." *Academy of Management Review*, vol. 18, no. 3: 397–428.

Dutton, J., and S. Jackson, 1987. "Categorizing Strategic Issues: Links to Organizational Action." *Academy of Management Review*, vol. 12, no. 1: 76–90.

Eadie, Douglas, 1986. "Strategic Issue Management: Improving the Council-Manager Relationship." *ICMA MIS Report*, vol. 18, no. 6: 2–12.

______, 1989. "Building the Capacity for Strategic Management." In J. L. Perry, ed., *Handbook of Public Administration*. San Francisco, CA: Jossey-Bass.

Eden, C., 1989. "Using Cognitive Mapping for Strategic Options Development and Analysis (SODA)." In J. Rosenhead, ed., *Rational Analysis for a Problematic World*. New York: Wiley.

Eden, Colin, and Chris Huxham, 1988. "Action-Oriented Strategic Management." *Journal of the Operational Research Society*, vol. 39, no. 10: 889–899.

Fesler, J., and D. Kettl, 1994. *The Politics of the Administrative Process*, 2d ed. Chatham, NJ: Chatham House.

Frederickson, James, 1984. "The Comprehensiveness of Strategic Decision Processes," *Academy of Management Journal*. vol. 39 (10): 445–466.

Frederickson, James, and R. R. Mitchell, 1984. "Strategic Decision Processes: Comprehensiveness and Performance in an Industry with an Unstable Environment." *Academy of Management Journal*, vol. 27, no. 2: 399–423.

Freeman, R. E., 1984. "Strategic Management: A Stakeholder Approach." Boston: Pitman.

Friend, J., and A. Hickling, 1987. *Planning Under Pressure*. Oxford: Pergamon Press.

Goold, M., A. Campbell, and K. Luchs, 1993a. "Strategies and Styles Revisited: Strategic Planning and Financial Control." *Long Range Planning*, vol. 26, no. 5: 49–60.

______, 1993b. "Strategies and Styles Revisited: Strategic Control Companies." *Long Range Planning*, vol. 26, no. 6: 150–162

Gore, A., 1993. *The Gore Report on Reinventing Government*. New York: Times Books.

Gray, B., 1989. *Collaborating: Finding Common Ground for Multiparty Problems.* San Francisco, CA: Jossey-Bass.

Hale, Sandra, and Mary Williams, eds., 1989. *Managing Change: A Guide to Producing Innovation from Within.* Washington, DC: Urban Institute Press.

Hambrick, D. C., 1982. "Environmental Scanning and Organizational Strategy." *Strategic Management Journal,* vol. 3, no. 2: 159–174.

Hammer, M., and J. Champy, 1993. *Reengineering the Corporation.* New York: Harper Business.

Hampden-Turner, C., 1990. *Corporate Culture.* Hutchinson, Great Britain: Economist Books.

Harrigan, K., 1981. "Barriers to Entry and Competitive Strategies." *Strategic Management Journal,* vol. 2: 395–412.

Hax, A. C., and N. S. Majiluf, 1984. *Strategic Management: An Integrative Approach.* Englewood Cliffs, NJ: Prentice-Hall.

Heath, R. L., 1988. *Strategic Issues Management.* San Francisco, CA: Jossey-Bass.

Henderson, B., 1979. *Henderson on Corporate Strategy.* Cambridge, MA: Abt Books.

Howe, E., 1980. "Role Choices of Urban Planners." *Journal of the American Planning Association,* vol. 46: 398–409.

Howe, E., and J. Kaufman, 1979. "The Ethics of Contemporary American Planners." *Journal of the American Planning Association,* vol. 45: 243–255.

Hurst, D. K., 1986. "Why Strategic Management Is Bankrupt." *Organizational Dynamics,* vol. 15: 4–27.

Huxham, Chris, 1991. "Facilitating Collaboration: Issues in Multi-Organizational Group Decision Support." *Journal of the Operational Research Society,* vol. 42: 1037–1046.

______, 1993. "Pursuing Collaborative Advantage." *Journal of the Operational Research Society.* vol. 44, 44: 599–611.

Jackson, S. E., and J. E. Dutton, "Discerning Threats and Opportunities." *Administrative Science Quarterly,* vol. 33: 370–387.

Jackson, P. M., and Bob Palmer, 1992. *Performance Measurement: A Management Guide.* Leicester, England: Management Center University of Leicester.

Kaufman, J. L. 1979. "The Planner as Interventionist in Public Policy Issues." In R. Burchell and G. Sternlieb, eds., *Planning Theory in the 1980s.* New Brunswick: Center for Urban Policy Research.

Kemp, R. L., 1992. *Strategic Planning in Local Government: A Casebook.* Chicago, IL: American Planning Association.

______, 1993. *Strategic Planning for Local Government.* Jefferson: Mcfarland and Company.

Lindblom, C. E., 1959. "The Science of Muddling Through." *Public Administration Review,* vol. 19: 79–88.

______, 1965. *The Intelligence of Democracy.* New York: Free Press.

______, 1977. *Politics and Markets.* New York: Free Press.

______, 1980. *The Policy-Making Process.* 2d ed. Englewood Cliffs, NJ: Prentice-Hall.

Linden, R. M., 1994. *Seamless Government: A Practical Guide to Re-Engineering in the Public Sector.* San Francisco, CA: Jossey-Bass.

Lorange, P., 1980. *Corporate Planning: An Executive Viewpoint*. Englewood Cliffs, NJ: Prentice-Hall.

MacMillan, I., 1983. "Competitive Strategies for Not-for-Profit Agencies." *Advances in Strategic Management*, vol. 1: 61–82.

Mintzberg, H., 1983. *Power in and Around Organizations*. Englewood Cliffs, NJ: Prentice-Hall.

______, 1987. "Crafting Strategy." *Harvard Business Review*, vol. 87, no. 4: 66–75.

______, 1990. "The Design School: Reconsidering the Basic Premises of Strategic Management." *Strategic Management Journal*, vol. 11: 171–195.

______, 1994. *The Rise and Fall of Strategic Planning*. New York: Free Press.

Mintzberg, H., and James Quinn, 1991. *The Strategy Process*, 2d ed. Englewood Cliffs, NJ: Prentice-Hall.

Mintzberg, H., and J. A. Waters, 1985. "Of Strategies, Deliberate and Emergent." *Strategic Management Journal*, vol. 6: 257–272.

Montanari, J. R., and J. S. Bracker, 1986. "The Strategic Management Process." *Strategic Management Journal*, vol. 7, no. 3: 251–265.

National Governors Association, 1993. *An Action Agenda to Redesign State Government*. Washington, D.C.: National Governors Association.

Nutt, Paul, 1992. *Managing Planned Change*. New York: Macmillan.

Nutt, Paul, and R. W. Backoff, 1987. "A Strategic Management Process for Public and Third-Sector Organizations." *Journal of the American Planning Association*, vol. 53 : 44–57.

______, 1993. "Organizational Publicness and Its Implications for Strategic Management." *Journal of Public Administration Research and Theory*, vol. 3, no. 2: 209–231.

Nutt, Paul, and R. W. Backoff, 1995. "Strategy for Public and Third Sector Organizations." *Journal of Public Administration Research and Theory*, vol. 5, no. 2: 189–211.

Olsen, J. B., and D. C. Eadie, 1982. *The Game Plan: Governance with Foresight*. Washington, DC: Council of State Planning Agencies.

Osborne, D., and T. Gaebler, 1992. *Reinventing Government*. Reading, MA: Addison-Wesley.

O'Toole, J., 1985. *Vanguard Management*. New York: Doubleday.

Peters, G., 1995. *The Politics of Bureaucracy*, 4th ed. New York: Longman.

Peters, T. J., and R. H. Waterman, Jr., 1982. *In Search of Excellence: Lessons from America's Best-Run Companies*. New York: Harper & Row.

Pettigrew, A., 1977. "Strategy Formulation as a Political Process." *International Studies in Management and Organization*, vol. 7, no. 2: 78–87.

Pettigrew, A., E. Ferlie, and L. Mckee, 1992. *Shaping Strategic Change*. Newbury Park, CA: Sage.

Pflaum, A., and T. Delmont, 1987. "External Scanning—A Tool for Planners." *Journal of the American Planning Association*, vol. 53, no. 1: 56–67.

Pierce, Neal, 1989. *Urban Challenges: A Vision for the Future*. Phoenix, AZ: Arizonel Republic, Phoenix Gazette.

Pinchot, G., III, 1985. *Enterpreneuring*. New York: Harper & Row.

Porter, M., 1980. *Competitive Strategy: Techniques for Analyzing Industries and Competitors*. New York: Free Press.

______, 1985. *Competitive Advantage: Creating and Sustaining Superior Performance.* New York: Free Press.

______, 1990. *The Competitive Advantage of Nations.* New York: Free Press.

______, 1994. *Competitive Strategies for Changing Industries.* Boston, MA: Harvard Business School Management Productions.

Quinn, J. B., 1980. *Strategies for Change: Logical Incrementalism.* Homewood, IL: R. D. Irwin.

Reich, R. B., 1992. *The Work of Nations.* New York: Vintage.

Ring, Peter, 1988. "Strategic Issues and Where Do They Come From?" In John Bryson and Robert Einsweiler, *Strategic Planning for Public Purposes—Threats and Opportunities for Planners.* American Planning Association, pp. 69–83.

Rue, L. W., and P. G. Holland, 1986. *Strategic Management: Concepts and Experiences.* New York: McGraw-Hill.

Sager, T., 1994. *Communicative Planning Theory.* Aldershot, United Kingdom: Avebury.

Schein, E., 1988. *Process Consultation. Vol. 1: Its Role in Organization Development.* Reading, MA: Addison-Wesley.

______, 1992. *Organizational Culture and Leadership,* 2d ed. San Francisco, CA: Jossey-Bass.

Senge, P. M., 1990. *The Fifth Discipline: The Art and Practice of the Learning Organization.* New York: Doubleday.

Stone, M., and W. Crittenden, 1993. "A Guide to Journal Articles on Strategic Management in Nonprofit Organizations." *Nonprofit Management and Leadership,* vol. 4: 193–213.

Susskind, L. E., and J. Cruikshank, 1987. *Breaking the Impasse: Consensual Approaches to Resolving Public Disputes.* New York: Basic Books.

Swanstrom, T., 1987. "The Limits of Strategic Planning for Cities." *Journal of Urban Affairs,* vol. 9: 139–157.

Taylor, B., 1984. "Strategic Planning—Which Style Do You Need?" *Long Range Planning,* vol. 17: 51–62.

Thompson, F., and L. R. Jones, 1994. *Reinventing the Pentagon: How the New Public Management Can Bring Institutional Renewal.* San Francisco, CA: Jossey-Bass.

Waterman, R. H., 1987. *The Renewal Factor.* New York: Bankam.

Waterman, R. H., Jr., T. J. Peters, and J. R. Phillips, 1980. "Structure Is Not Organization." *Business Horizons,* 14–26.

Widener, R., et al., 1992. *Divided Cities in the Global Economy: Human Strategies.* Columbia, SC: PASRAS Fund.

Wildavsky, A., 1979a. *The Politics of the Budgetary Process.* Boston, MA: Little, Brown.

______, 1979b. *Speaking Truth to Power.* Boston, MA: Little, Brown.

Wind, Y., and V. Mahajan, 1981. "Designing Product and Business Portfolios." *Harvard Business Review,* vol. 59: 155–165.

Winer, M., and K. Ray, 1994. *Collaboration Handbook.* St. Paul, MN: Amherst H. Wilder Foundation.

25

Mission Statement

Kevin P. Kearns,
University of Pittsburgh

A brief written statement of an organization's purpose, goals, operating philosophy, and aspirations—hence, the mission statement provides a guide for decisionmaking and planning within the organization and also can be used as a contract of accountability for citizens, clients, and other external constituencies.

Purposes of a Mission Statement

An effective mission statement should serve three essential purposes. First, it should provide constituencies inside and outside the organization with a commonly understood interpretation of the organization's legal mandate.

The mandate and the mission statement, while related, are not the same (Bryson 1991, pp. 93–95). The organization's mandate specifies the obligations to which it is legally bound and often is expressed in the form of a charter, articles of incorporation, bylaws, authorizing legislation, statutes, ordinances, or administrative regulations. Often, the mandate will outline in excruciating detail nearly all facets of the organization's functions, its structure, its policymaking procedures, and the sources of its revenue. For example, the Borough Code for the Commonwealth of Pennsylvania—a typical mandate—is a document of several hundred pages covering everything from the allowable sources of tax revenue to procedures for awarding public contracts.

Technically, the mandate is a public document, but generally it is not widely distributed and is not expressed in terms that the general public can understand. The mission statement, therefore, should provide a concise interpretation of the mandate in terms that people can easily understand. What business are we in? What are our principle products and services? Who are our primary clients or beneficiaries? What needs do we fill? What operating philosophies do we follow? What are our priorities for the future? As such, the mission statement should dwell less on technical or legal obligations and more on what the organization is committing itself to do within whatever discretionary authority is granted by the mandate.

Second, the mission statement should provide a guide to daily decisionmaking and long-term planning. In other words, an effective mission statement should provide much more than eloquent, but meaningless, rhetoric about the organization's purpose. Rather, it should provide an explicit statement of the organization's operating philosophy and core values. For example, the mission statement of a prestigious research university contains a section that states, among other things, that the institution will pursue only those initiatives in which it has a "comparative advantage" and that all of its activities in teaching and research will be designed to enhance its position of national leadership by influencing the behavior of other institutions. In other words, the institution is publicly stating, to both internal and external audiences, that it will not attempt to be all things to all people. Such an explicit operating philosophy clearly can have a powerful impact on strategic decisionmaking and long-term resource allocation.

Some operating philosophies may have immediate effects on short-term (versus long-term) decisionmaking. For example, the mission statement may say something about the organization's commitment to employee development, to measuring the quality of client services, or to a certain philosophy of resource management.

Third, and finally, the mission statement should be linked to the organization's strategic plan by providing a concise and general statement of the organization's goals and aspirations for the future. Often, the strategic direction of the organization is expressed in a separate vision statement appended to the mission. Whether as a separate vision statement or incorporated into the mission statement, the organization should publicly state its priorities and the strategic direction in which it is heading.

Thus, the mission statement should include at least three distinct sections as follows:

1. the purpose of the organization expressed in terms of products, services, targeted customers, and needs filled;
2. the operating philosophies and values expressed in terms of the organization's self-image, how it perceives its niche or distinctive characteristics in the marketplace, how it makes decisions and manages resources to preserve or enhance its self-image; and
3. the aspirations for the future, expressed in terms of broad strategic goals and priorities.

Developing a Mission Statement

Occasionally, decisionmakers express skepticism about the value of mission statements, especially in government organizations where the prevailing belief may be that the mandate is the mission. "Why should we develop a mission statement when everything we need to know is contained in our authorizing legislation or in the administrative regulations which guide us?" Missions are slightly more fluid and dynamic than mandates because they reflect the organization's interpretation of its role in society, its relationship to its constituents, its position in the marketplace, and its aspirations for the future. Also, old missions can be accomplished and new missions can be formulated to take their place, all within the context of an unchanging mandate.

Additionally, there are several "triggers," or symptoms, that may suggest that the mandate alone is not sufficient and, therefore, that effort should be invested in the development of a mission statement:

1. recurring and unproductive debates within the organization (e.g., line versus staff, headquarters versus field offices) regarding interpretation of the mandate—core purpose, resource allocation, operating philosophies, and goals;
2. a pattern of apparently *ad hoc* decisionmaking at the top of the organization or "goal displacement" in the middle of the organization wherein key decisions do not seem to be guided by an overarching purpose or vision;

3. a portfolio of services or products, with shifting priorities among them, which appear haphazard or disjointed; and
4. a pattern of confusion or misunderstanding among key constituencies—elected officials, oversight agencies, citizens, and funders—regarding the core purpose and goals of the organization.

Any of these symptoms may suggest that the organization should develop or refine its mission statement. The process of developing a mission statement should include a variety of stakeholders—executive staff, middle management, and key external constituencies. In general, the following steps will provide useful input in the development of a mission statement (see also Bryson 1991, pp. 106–116; Espy 1986, pp. 21–41):

1. a thorough review of the organization's mandate—what it is legally obligated to do—and how that mandate has evolved since its inception;
2. a survey of key stakeholders regarding their expectations of the organization, which may or may not be perfectly consistent with its mandate;
3. an assessment of external trends, which present either opportunities or challenges for the organization, accompanied by an evaluation of the organization's current strengths and weaknesses in responding to those trends (Kearns 1992);
4. a list of operating philosophies and values, generated by executives and staff, which they believe should guide the organization; and
5. a summary statement of the strategic goals derived from the long-range plan of the organization.

Although the process of gathering and interpreting this information should involve a diverse set of stakeholders, the task of actually drafting the mission statement should probably be assigned to one person or a small team of people. The drafts should then be circulated, edited, and finalized with input from the broader set of stakeholders.

Generally, the mission statement should be formally reviewed every five years or so, consistent with the organization's strategic planning cycle. Often it is suggested that the mission statement be drafted as the first step in the strategic planning process. But decisionmakers should keep in mind that certain portions of the mission statement (e.g., priorities and aspirations) cannot be drafted until the strategic plan is nearly complete. Clearly, there is a delicate trade-off between a mission statement that is so broad and general that it is never changed and one which is so specific and focused that it quickly becomes obsolete. This trade-off can be addressed by asking, "Is this draft mission statement capable of providing a useful, but not overly confining, guide to decisionmaking over the next five years or so?"

Mission Statements, Performance, and Accountability

Like the mandate, the mission statement is a powerful instrument of accountability. Peter Drucker (1990) goes further by suggesting that the mission statement is the instrument of accountability for nonprofit organizations, since they do not have a "bottom line" of performance like profit and loss: "(Nonprofits) must therefore have a clear mission that is translated into operational goals and provides guides for effective action. Of course, businesses also deteriorate if they do not have a clear mission. . . . But, in good times a business can muddle through for a while with no other lodestar than the financial bottom line. A nonprofit institution will start to flounder almost immediately unless it clearly defines its mission and emphasizes that mission again and again" (p. 8).

Consequently, the mission statement may be the organization's primary accountability contract with the public. It is the document in which we essentially say to the public, "Here is what we promise to do for you. You may hold us accountable for this."

Bibliography

Bryson, John M., 1991. *Strategic Planning for Public and Nonprofit Organizations.* San Francisco: Jossey-Bass. (See especially Chapter 5, "Clarifying Organizational Mandates and Missions.")

Drucker, Peter F., 1990. "Lessons for Successful Nonprofit Governance." *Nonprofit Management and Leadership*, vol. 1, no. 1: 7–14.

Espy, Siri N., 1986. *Handbook of Strategic Planning for Nonprofit Organizations*. New York: Praeger. (See especially Chapter 3, "Corporate Identity and Directions.")

Kearns, Kevin P., 1992. "From Comparative Advantage to Damage Control: Clarifying Strategic Issues Using SWOT Analysis." *Nonprofit Management and Leadership*, vol. 3, no. 1: 3–22.

Part Eight

Performance Management

26

PRODUCTIVITY

Marc Holzer,
Rutgers, The State University of New Jersey

The ratio of outputs (work done, products distributed, services rendered) and outcomes (impact achieved) to inputs (labor, capital, materials, space, energy, time, etc.). Productivity improvement represents favorable changes in that ratio. Thus, it is important to recognize the differences between various ratios of improvement.

- *Inputs decline, outputs/outcomes remain constant.* This ratio represents a cutback management situation in which management is forced to respond productively. For example, faced with a cutback in staff, a state mental health facility may reorganize, allowing for the same level of services with more efficient use of remaining staff.
- *Inputs remain constant, outputs/outcomes improve.* Many critics advocate this case. They often expect "quick fixes" based on limited perspectives or critiques by groups external to the agency. For example, they might propose that each social services worker increase applications processed by 25 percent. This might be a reasonable goal, but only in the long run as better management of inputs improves outputs. But still, without the capacity to invest in better management, and to provide adequate services to more applicants, this case is less reasonable than the next.
- *Inputs decline substantially, outputs/outcomes improve substantially.* Some elected officials and private sector critics advocate this

scenario. It is, however, almost always based upon unreasonable and naive assumptions, for example that waste is of enormous proportions.

- *Inputs increase moderately, outputs/outcomes improve substantially.* This is a more likely case, as it allows for continued modest investments in improved productive capacity. But in the short run, a true productivity program is more likely to experience temporarily decreasing productivity—constant outputs while inputs increase modestly to allow for improved internal capacities, which will then increase outputs at a later stage. For example, in a state correctional facility investments in training, buildings and equipment may be necessary in year 1 prior to improved correctional services in year 2.
- *Inputs decline substantially, outputs/outcomes decline less rapidly.* Although the output to input ratio is apparently increasing, drastic cutbacks in resources often result in cutbacks in services which fall most heavily on those citizens least likely to have alternatives. In a situation of deep cutbacks a municipal college, for example, may be forced to cut psychological counseling services to students—most of whom are unlikely to be able to purchase such services privately and will therefore be less likely to graduate.

Producing Public Services

Productive management, public and private, has evolved from simple "common sense" in the late nineteenth century to complex systems in the late twentieth century (Holzer 1992). Today, to produce public services, the best public organizations have developed multiple, reinforcing capacities, as summarized in "An Overview of Productivity and Performance" (in Holzer and Gabrielian 1995). Government agencies which have been formally recognized as high achievers, as state-of-the-art

- apply quality management principles;
- use measurement as a decisionmaking tool;
- work hard to motivate employees;
- adapt new technologies; and
- develop public-private partnerships.

FIGURE 26.1 How Is Productivity Improved?

1. Same output/outcomes
   - Less input
2. More output/outcomes
   - Same input
3. Much more output/outcomes
   - Much less input
4. Much more output/outcomes
   - More input
5. Less output
   - Much less input

FIGURE 26.2 Productivity Improvement: A Multifaceted Approach

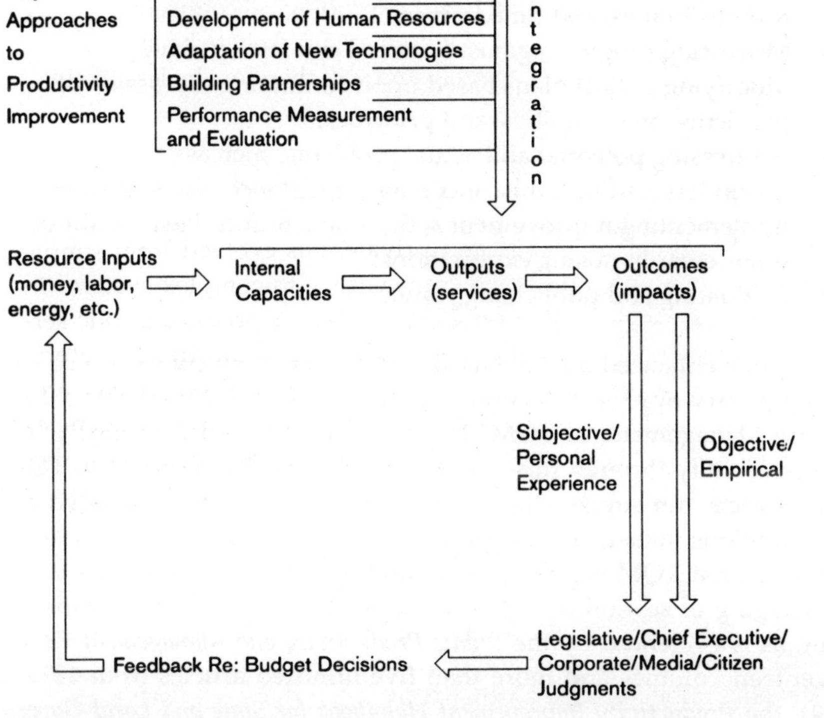

In government, management improvement programs operate under many labels. The program's name, however, is less important than its substance: comprehensive, quality-oriented productivity improvement in an environment of increasing demands and reduced resources (Poister 1988). Such programs improve performance systematically. Typically, they follow multiple steps:

- Clarifying goals with, and obtaining support from, top management and elected officials;
- Locating models as successful blueprints to modify, and as warnings of potential mistakes;
- Identifying promising areas, such as those functions faced with large backlogs, slipping deadlines, high turnover, or many complaints;
- Building a team through which all interested parties—particularly management, labor, and clients—can identify obstacles and suggest improvements;
- Planning a well-managed project, including objectives, tasks, responsibilities, and time frames;
- Measuring progress against financial and service data;
- Modifying project plans based upon continuing discussion of problems, opportunities, and priorities;
- Addressing potential and actual problems, such as misunderstandings, misconceptions, resistance, and slippages;
- Implementing improvement actions on a routine basis, without unnecessarily raising expectations;
- Evaluating and publicizing results.

Although enhanced quality has always been a productive concern, one contemporary approach to public productivity improvement is Total Quality Management, or TQM. The opportunities and problems which we can identify through this lens are not necessarily confined to TQM-type projects, but suggest the subtleties of systemic problem solving in any ambitious management capacity-building project. It is important to recognize that TQM is not a new invention. Rather, it is an innovative repackaging of several decades of public sector productivity improvement, as is evidenced by the *Public Productivity and Management Review* (seventeen volumes and more than five hundred articles from 1975 to 1994), the *Productivity Improvement Handbook for State and Local Govern-*

ment (Washnis 1980, 1,492 pp.) and the *Public Productivity Handbook* (Holzer 1992, 705 pp.). The TQM movement in government also draws heavily on decades of industrial quality improvement work in the private sector, such as that of Deming and Juran. Although neither "TQM" nor "quality improvement" were terms generally found in the public sector literature as late as 1988, the past several years have witnessed an accelerated improvement and publication movement under this terminology. In many cases, what were formerly "productivity" projects are now redescribed as "quality" efforts.

Performance Measurement and Evaluation

Productivity measurement is not new. Concerns with public sector productivity measurement have been as constant as concerns with high taxes, corruption, or incompetence. Measurement is implicit in questions from all parts of the political spectrum, in discussions among business people and union people, in analyses by reporters and academicians: "Is crime up?" "Are the streets cleaner?" "What benefits will a new building produce?" "Is the air quality better?" "How well are our children doing in school?"

Productivity measurement is continually evolving. A century ago efficient production of outputs was paramount; in the public sector such outputs are normally services. But we have since added concerns as to outcomes or impact—public sector performance—to our measurement agendas.

Managers who are responsible for day-to-day management (Hatry and Fisk 1992) now often have access to information with which to implement public policy, and often use that data to

- Make more productive resource allocation decisions, tying spending to problem solving;
- Hold programs accountable;
- Match results with plans;
- Compare agencies or subunits to similar entities or to past levels of achievement;
- Question the causes for apparent progress or lack thereof;
- Predict periods of work overload or underload;
- Evaluate benefit-cost linkages.

Data about inputs, outputs, and outcomes can help defend or expand a program, rather than let it suffer from relatively subjective, political decisions. Measures help answer such questions as: Is an organization doing its job? Is it creating unintended side effects or producing unanticipated impacts? Is it responsive to the public? Is it fair to all, or does it favor certain groups, inadvertently or deliberately? Does it keep within its proper bounds of authorized activity? In short, is it productive?

Although multiple measures of public sector services cannot usually be aggregated as productivity "indexes" (analogous to the bottom line of profit in the private sector), it is possible to measure public sector performance given certain guidelines:

1. If service quality is to be maintained or improved, a measurement program must be oriented to effectiveness, rather than just quantity or efficiency.
2. Management's uses of productivity measures are often in the budgeting and fiscal area: estimating resource requirements, justifying budgets, reducing costs, reallocating resources, investing increased resources, and improving benefit-cost linkages.
3. A measurement program, which requires substantial expertise and careful planning, should ask and begin to answer the following questions:
    - In terms of program performance: How much of a service is provided? How efficiently are resources used? How effectively is a service provided?
    - In terms of effectiveness indicators for performance: What is the intended purpose of the service? What are the unintended impacts of the service? How effective is the service in prevention of problems before they arise? Is the service adequate? Is the service accessible? Are clients satisfied with services? Are services distributed equitably? Is a product durable? To what extent is a service provided to clients with dignity?
    - In terms of desirable characteristics of performance measures: Is a service significant? Is the service appropriate to the problem being addressed? Is performance quantifiable? Are services readily available? Are services delivered in a timely manner? Are services delivered in a relatively straightforward manner? Is a measure of performance valid? Is a measure

acceptable? Is performance measured completely? Are measures accurate? Are measures reliable?

- In terms of management's uses of productivity measures, are measures used to help: Set goals? Estimate resource requirements? Develop budget justifications? Reduce costs? Develop organization improvement strategies? Control operations? Reallocate resources? Hold individuals or organizational units accountable? Motivate employees to improve performance? Compare agencies or subunits to similar entities or to past levels of achievement? Predict periods of work overload or underload? Link increased resources to policy outcomes or to systemwide problems? Improve benefit-cost linkages? Develop more sophisticated capacities for measurement?
- In terms of data collection: Are existing records analyzed? Are clients surveyed? Are taxpayers surveyed? Are services rated by professional or trained observers? Are special data collection techniques utilized?
- In terms of the analysis of productivity data: Are before versus after comparisons made? Are measures displayed in a time series? Are comparisons made with other areas, jurisdictions, or client groups? Are comparisons made with targets?

Development of Human Resources: Motivating Employees

Turn-of-the-century scientific management assumed that in exchange for a fair day's pay someone competent could always be found to fill any vacant slot in the organization, to complete any task. Money would be a sufficient motivator; personality, individuality, and social interests were irrelevant to job performance.

But research in private firms and public agencies made it clear that such assumptions were not valid: People remained individuals, even in the workplace, and were affected and moved by many forces, of which money was only one. As individuals, they could be "turned on" or "turned off" by their organizational roles, depending on what the situation offered them psychologically, and whether the organization treated them as mature, vibrant adults or as lazy, dependent drones. Managers began to realize that people tend to join social groups on the job, and these groups develop production-oriented norms of their own to which the individual is expected to adhere. Human behavior, therefore, reflects not only organizational, but personal and group, pressures. A productive organization is humane, structured around not only the task but its members and their human needs. The art of leadership inheres in getting people to work well for the organization by understanding and responding to their needs—by motivating them. Guy (1992), for example, points out that many interdependent factors contribute to creating a productive work environment: organizational culture, team-building that maximizes the strengths of employees while compensating for their weaknesses, open communication channels, flexibility in the midst of predictability, and balancing of the needs of the organization with the needs of employees.

Government's most extensive and expensive investments are people—most public organizations devote from 50 to 85 percent of their budgets to employee salaries and benefits. Because those "human resources" have complicated needs, the most progressive public organizations have adopted enlightened human resource practices, rejecting an authoritarian, bureaucratic style. Typically, they

- Recognize that motivation requires management of many, interrelated elements. Ban, Faerman, and Riccucci (1992) hold that to achieve their goals, public organizations need to take an integrated approach to personnel management, linking workforce planning, recruitment, hiring, training, and other personnel policies. Building and maintaining a productive work force includes (1) developing a formal workforce plan; (2) actively recruiting job applicants; (3) redesigning tests or developing creative alternatives to written tests; (4) linking training and development activities to organizational mission; and (5) revising personnel policies to meet the needs of employees.
- Understand that money can be an important motivator, but is not the only motivational option. A sense of being able to make a difference in the organization is more important to the job satisfaction of public sector managers than to that of private managers (Balfour and Wechsler 1991).
- Carefully apply performance appraisal systems. Daly (1992) points out that productivity is a function of motivation, and motivation—extrinsic or intrinsic—is itself a function of the

recognition of an individual's work effort. Such recognition can come from a well-conceived and well-managed system of performance appraisal.

Adaptation of New Technologies

Advanced technologies are as important to the public as to the private sectors, and the public sector has often pioneered new systems. Government employees have invented lasers, solid state technology, the basic design of most commercial and military aircraft, instrument landing systems, the first modern computer, titanium (and other stronger and lighter materials), the CAT scan, plastic corneas, advanced fishing nets, nuclear power, Teflon, wash and wear fabric, resuscitation devices, and plastic wrap (Public Employees Roundtable 1990). Public Technology, Inc. is devoted to the development and diffusion of productive technologies for the public sector. NASA has a continuing program to help the private sector exploit innovations resulting from the space program.

Technology is not limited to computer applications. In as mundane an area as refuse collection, for example, departments of sanitation in New York City, Scottsdale, Arizona, and other localities have developed and applied technological changes:

- Trucks designed specifically for operation by two people, rather than the traditional three-person team.
- Remote-control arms which allow the driver to lift and empty large containers of refuse.
- Robotic truck painters, which a management-labor team approached the private sector to design.
- Tire-changing machines designed specifically to the agency's standards and intended to alleviate the high degree of manual work in the operation.
- Purchase of "high dump" street cleaning brooms, which are faster, safer, and can dump refuse into another vehicle.
- Comparison testing of refuse collection equipment from different manufacturers.
- Redesign of the equipment used to transport refuse from barges to landfills.

Partnerships: Multiple Tenets of Cooperation

Privatization has gained momentum. Touted regularly by politicians and emphasized by the media, it may now be the most popular argument for public sector productivity improvement. Their logic is that contracting out or turning over services to the private sector produces large savings with virtually no loss of quality or reduction in service levels (Savas 1992). Thus, advocates hold that outsourcing or privatization can deliver a much greater portion of services which are now public. But skeptics hold that many services are necessarily government's responsibility, and that a public to private shift will not automatically enhance productivity in a jurisdiction or department (Barnekov and Raffel 1992). A recurring theme in the privatization literature is that what makes a difference is competition, not the fact of privatization by itself, and that private monopolies are no better than the public ones. Thus, privatization is productive as long as it assumes competition.

While competition is certainly important, cooperation is also an essential productivity enhancement strategy that is very often overlooked. Cooperative arrangements of service provision today may be a more accurate characterization of emerging day-to-day relationships. Joint public-private initiatives are options to which innovative public officials often turn. Rather than privatizing, raising taxes, or soliciting donations for visible projects (i.e., tax supplements), these new relationships are joint problem-solving efforts which may be initiated by either "side." Cooperation between labor and management, different public agencies, neighboring local governments, government and voluntary organizations, executive and legislative branch, or governmental entities of different levels have proven to be effective arrangements aimed at improving government service and cutting costs. The ability to think and act outside the rigid but familiar "bureaucratic box" can be essential for pooling resources and improving productivity in an increasingly resource-scarce atmosphere.

Different forms of partnerships may enhance productivity improvements in public organizations. In the New York City Transit Authority an independent labor-management consulting institute facilitated solutions to problems that government agencies and labor unions faced. The case of the Small Business Administration and the Service Corps of Retired Executives demonstrates a coproduction model that has proven effective in the link between a federal agency and a group of citizen-volunteers. Cooperation between the Delaware Public Administration Institute and the state legislature showed how all sides benefited from such cooperation; for public administrators it resulted in vastly improved knowledge of the legislative environment, and for the legislature it resulted in greater professionalism of their work.

Conclusion

The most innovative and productive public agencies do not simply execute one good program. Rather, they integrate advanced management techniques into a comprehensive approach to productivity improvement. They institutionalize productivity improvements by identifying, implementing, measuring, and rewarding major cost savings and performance enhancements in their agency. They benchmark their efforts against similar organizations across the nation. They have a client orientation. Perhaps most important, productive programs are built on the dedication, imagination, teamwork, and diligence of public servants.

Bibliography

Balfour, Danny L., and Barton Wechsler, 1991. "Commitment, Performance, and Productivity in Public Organizations." *Public Productivity and Management Review,* 15 (1): 355–368.

Ban, Carolyn, Sue R. Faerman, and Norma M. Riccucci, 1992. "Productivity and the Personnel Process." In Marc Holzer, ed., *Public Productivity Handbook.* New York: Marcel Dekker, pp. 401–423.

Barnekov, Timothy K., and Jeffrey A. Raffel, 1992. "Public Management of Privatization." In Marc Holzer, ed., *Public Productivity Handbook.* New York: Marcel Dekker, pp. 99–115.

Daly, Dennis M., 1992. "Pay for Performance, Performance Appraisal, and Total Quality Management." *Public Productivity and Management Review,* 16:2 (Fall) 39–52.

Epstein, Paul, and Alan Leidner, 1990. "Productivity Forum for Computer Technology." *Public Productivity and Management Review,* 14:2 (Winter) 211–220.

Guy, Mary E., 1992. "Productive Work Environment." In Marc Holzer, ed., *Public Productivity Handbook.* New York: Marcel Dekker, pp. 321–335.

Hatry, Harry P., and Donald M. Fisk, 1992. "Measuring Productivity in the Public Sector." In Marc Holzer, ed., *Public Productivity Handbook.* New York: Marcel Dekker, pp. 139–160.

Holzer, Marc, ed., 1992. *Public Productivity Handbook.* New York: Marcel Dekker.

Holzer, Marc, and Vatche Gabrielian, eds., 1995. *Case Studies in Productive Public Management: Capacity Building in Government*. Burke, VA: Chatelain Press.

Hyde, Albert C., 1992. "Implications of Total Quality Management for the Public Sector." *Public Productivity and Management Review*, 16:1 (Fall) 23–24. Also see Hyde, "The Proverbs of Total Quality Management," pp. 25–38.

Keehley, Pat, and Steve Medlin, 1991. "Productivity Enhancements Through Quality Innovations." *Public Productivity and Management Review*, 15(2): 217–228.

LOGIN (Local Government Information Network). St. Paul, Minnesota: The Norris Institute.

Milakovich, Michael E., 1996. "Total Quality Management for Public Service Productivity Improvement." In Marc Holzer, ed., *Public Productivity Handbook*. New York: Marcel Dekker, pp. 577–602.

Mizaur, Donald, 1992. Unpublished paper presented to the Fifth National Conference on Public Sector Productivity in Newark, New Jersey. Charlottesville, Virginia, Federal Quality Institute.

Poister, Theodore H., ed., 1988. "Success Stories in Revitalizing Public Agencies." *Public Productivity Review*, 11:3 (Spring) 27–104.

Public Employees Roundtable, 1990. "Unsung Heroes" (newsletter 1987–1990) and brochures. Washington, DC.

Public Productivity and Management Review. Thousand Oaks, CA: Sage Publications.

Savas, E. S., 1992. "Privatization and Productivity." In Marc Holzer, ed., *Public Productivity Handbook*. New York: Marcel Dekker, pp. 79–98.

Taylor, Paul W., 1991. "Working with Quality at the New York State Department of Transportation." *Public Productivity and Management Review*, 15:2 (Winter) 205–212.

Washnis, George J., ed., 1980. *Productivity Improvement Handbook for State and Local Government*. New York: John Wiley and Sons.

27

Reengineering

Albert C. Hyde,
The Brookings Institution

A management approach to change for organizations that revisualizes and redesigns an organization's core work processes to achieve dramatic improvements in organizational performance by significantly decreasing operating and support costs, improving production and service cycle time frames, and increasing customer satisfaction with the product and the service quality and value.

Reengineering, perhaps better termed Business Process Reengineering (BPR), has become the 1990s change management method of choice. Although definitions abound, there is a general understanding that reengineering involves revisualizing and redesigning an organization's core work processes to accomplish very dramatic and rapid improvements. Such redesigns focus primarily on (1) lowering operating and support costs, (2) improving service delivery time and response levels, (3) increasing product and service quality levels, and (4) enhancing employee involvement in reaching organizational goals.

Reengineering as a change strategy assumes that organizations must have lower costs, faster service, more innovative products, and are beyond trading off one facet against the other. Most organizations have used various forms of cutback management to reorganize or realign resources to handle increased workloads or to speed up service response times by reassigning staff or adding more personnel. But to cut costs by increasing levels of productivity by 50 percent, speed up product completion or service delivery (what is referred to as "cycle time") by 75 percent to 100 percent, or create entirely new service features or products for customers goes considerably beyond reorganizing, simplifying, and streamlining work activities. A central premise of reengineering is that the goals are so ambitious that they can only be accomplished by completely rethinking and redesigning the way work is performed and the methods by which outputs are delivered.

Reengineering as a Management Strategy for Change

Most of the methods and techniques used in BPR are not new. In fact, many organizations have used variations of reengineering as part of their strategic or breakthrough planning or quality management efforts. Among the more advanced organizations which have pioneered in quality management, reengineering was an innovation strategy to be applied selectively to redesign processes for breakthroughs while the rest of the organization continued its overall pursuit of continuous incremental improvement.

The term "reengineering" emerged in the early 1990s. Credit is usually given to Boston-based consultant Michael Hammer for his description of the concept in a 1990 *Harvard Business Review* article entitled "Reengineering: Don't Automate; Obliterate." In 1992, Hammer and James Champy coauthored *Reengineering the Corporation*, popularizing the concept.

Hammer and Champy are not the only notables who have developed reengineering as a management concept. James Harrington published *Business Process Improvement* in 1991, which is a comprehensive guidebook to the techniques and methods that organizations can use to modify and redesign their business processes. In 1993, Thomas Davenport published *Process Innovation*, which remains one of the most in-depth studies of reengineering methods. Davenport sees reengineering as a radical strategy for change that must carefully consider complex implementation issues involving the workforce, technology, and organizational culture.

Of course, the reengineering bookshelf has grown demonstrably in even the short span of two to three years. These three works are notable because they were among the first volumes, they were written by major names in the consulting field, and—for purposes here—they nicely illustrate the continuum of change that organizations must address, as follows: Reorganization; Total Quality Management (TQM); Business Process Improvement (BPI); Business Process Reengineering (BPR); minor change; and, finally, major change.

Reengineering is the far point, and, as Hammer and Champy and Davenport have noted, it requires the highest degree of top management commitment because of its high-risk and its ambitious goals. Business Process Improvement (Harrington's term) is more modest: it might involve undertaking major streamlining, removal of major barriers, and reworking delays or problems in core work processes, or BPI may even be accomplished through a redesign of an entire process; but the goals are usually couched in such terms as a 20 percent to 30 percent improvement in cost reduction or productivity enhancement levels. TQM aims for modest but sustainable improvements of 10 percent to 15 percent each year, primarily by reducing revisions and improving reliability.

There are a host of management strategies for change that can be used to achieve reorganization or incremental improvement. The key point of this continuum is that an organization chooses a BPR approach when only "radical change" will do. When major innovation and radical redesign are required, reengineering is the appropriate choice. Davenport would add, however, that reengineering also requires rethinking the *level of innovation* required for organizational-wide culture change and realignment of the organization infrastructure (people, technology, and management systems).

Reengineering is so different from other strategies because it is premised on major levels of top management involvement and commitment. It is a high-risk strategy, by definition, because its assumption is that both *what* the organization is doing and *how* it is doing it *can and must be radically altered*.

Top management involvement requires the complete participation of a firm's managers. (One recent *Harvard Business Review* article estimated that in successful BPR efforts, top managers had to commit 20 to 30 percent of their time personally to champion the efforts to change and to carry them through.) Management must also want the change effort. Unlike other change strategies, reengineering will not be accomplished without the total support of the people at the head of the company.

Relating Reengineering to TQM and Downsizing

What does reengineering have to do with total quality management? Everything; but, unfortunately, there is a growing dispute between TQM and BPR advocates over how organizations should change and whether an organization can sustain a BPR effort without having created a quality management base. This dispute is partly a disagreement among consultants who are looking for market share and partly a difference between the views of quality proponents, who see nothing new in BPR, and those of BPR proponents, who see everything related to TQM as being too old. This conflict is understandable, given that BPR is a highly selective, fast-paced, innovative, top-down-driven change approach and that TQM is just the opposite. TQM emphasizes a broad-based, slow (but sure) cumulative improvement, with a bottom-up approach. The two systems do share all of the important things, however, such as emphases on management by process, concern for customers, extensive use of work teams, and decisions based on performance results data.

Quality management provides an effective foundation for best management practice, and BPR may be used selectively to drive radical change efforts where needed. (And it would be nice to think that BPR advocates would want to learn from the many mistakes made in implementing TQM).

But what is the relationship between reengineering and downsizing? Business Process Reengineering done incorrectly is downsizing. When BPR is done correctly, however, the two methods should be totally different.

Typically, a corporation (or a government) reassesses its financial position when it is facing a crunch. It may subsequently announce a series of layoffs or workforce cuts that are needed to meet a financial objective. The organization then sets up some sort of personnel scheme to get people to leave their jobs so it can realize the necessary savings. It then waits for the next crisis. (It is no wonder that downsizing is derisively called "dumbsizing.") If the organization is grossly overstaffed, then the personnel cuts cause no problems in terms of the company coping with a reduced staff. If it is understaffed, however, the organization may experience significant performance problems and may have to rethink its cutback strategy.

When reengineering is used correctly, it is focused on targets selected by the strategic planning process. What is important is to change the way work is done, not just how many are doing it. The redesign effort itself might require more resources (not less) to accomplish. Although the implementation effort might result in significant cuts in the workforce responsible for that process, there are major implications for the firm with regard to retraining and reinvestment in the employees that are retained (what is often called "upskilling") and for rethinking the management of work teams.

In reengineering, the workforce and cost reductions come after the target is selected and the redesign is accomplished. In downsizing, the workforce and cost reductions often are announced before any redesign has been accomplished.

The Heart of the Matter: Managing by Process

There is one area in which quality and reengineering methods agree, and that is the importance of process management. A process is a sequence of related activities that begins with some type of input, has some value added, and results in some type of output. For example, it is a series of actions that begins with a customer need and is done only when customer expectations are satisfied. But managing by process has immense implications for organizations.

Both TQM and BPR advocates recognize that the change that must be made in organizations must be the movement away from a vertical (hierarchical), or functional, management to horizontal, or process, management.

Most organizations manage by functions. Their structure, lines of communication, and their allocation of resources are all vertically aligned. Indeed, functional management even has functional performance criteria in place to ensure that the organization meets these specialized goals. The first assumption is that if each function meets its targets, the organization will meet its objectives. The second assumption is that strong functions will define organizational excellence.

Of course, for years management theorists have argued that there is a downside to strong functional management. For example, functional management can be highly competitive, to the point that "turf-protection" is equated to any organizational resistance to change. But functional management is also very risk-aversive. Most managers would recognize the following functional management strategies as prudent steps to ensure that the organization has the capability to react and solve any and all problems.

1. *Build in redundancy.* Add extra steps to verify work done by someone else; inspect for quality defects.

2. *Strive for self-containment*. Dedicate extra resources to fix other units' mistakes or to redo work, instead of having to rely on others' inputs.
3. *Inflate work time for tasks*. Add extra time requirements to permit grouping of work tasks to achieve economies of scale; add lead time to allow for more planning; and create backlogs to allow for economies of scheduling or to discourage work requests.
4. *Increase supervision and lower span of control*. Add extra supervision or create additional layers of supervision and coordination that can be dedicated to firefighting, managing reports, inspection, and coordination between units.

Perhaps the biggest problem with functional management is that firms that use it may too easily lose sight of the customer. With this method, dealing with customers, primarily through handling their complaints, is relegated to some form of customer service unit or to the marketing department. Important information from the customer's perspective about how products and services could be better designed, developed, delivered, and supported is not shared throughout the organization, nor is it systematically developed to guide the growth of new products and services. With functional management, only one part of the organization truly focuses on what is its most significant priority—serving customers.

If the organization were structured more with the customer in mind, it would act horizontally. Indeed, process management is structured horizontally. The company would seek to lower, if not tear down, organizational walls and create work teams that were cross-functional, that would have more direct contact with their customers (and their suppliers), and that would be better able to cooperate with other units. Process management encompasses a very different set of performance criteria.

Most important, process management methods place a premium on cycle time and on choice. *Cycle time* is defined as the real time measurement from start to finish for the completion or delivery of a product or service. This time period is different than an organization's productivity time, which is how long it takes to do a task. For example, if it takes an organization twenty minutes to process an order, but it waits fifteen days for the financial transaction to clear and another five days to have the order delivered by the postal service, then the total cycle time is over 20 days. (The cycle would actually begin the day the order was sent by the customer.) The organization may be proud of its fast productivity and work accuracy levels, but the customer may view the final product quite differently.

Choice is another critical variable for process management. A utility may pride itself on having a 24-hour response time for its repair service, but the customer who is pinned down at home, having to take a day off from work, waiting for the service person to show up may be considerably less pleased. Given a choice, the customer might prefer getting his or her service fixed within 48 or 72 hours, *if* the utility would guarantee a specific appointment time and arrive within 30 minutes of the time promised. Thus one of the most powerful reasons to adopt process management is the capability it creates for the company to focus on customers.

Process Management and the End of Supervision?

The use of process management also has major implications for managers and workers. Managing by process means creating a whole new approach for supervision. Process management assumes that the old job of the supervisor (to inspect work, respond to emergencies, and control the work environment) is a non-value-added position (to use the reengineering term). The process management supervisor is a "process owner" who sets team goals, coaches team members, and facilitates team cooperation and organizational communications. The process team itself consists of workers who are rewarded, trained, and developed to work for group goals such as customer satisfaction, problem prevention, lower cost and faster cycle time, and so forth.

Something should be said about the link between process management and participative management. With the latter method the firm tries to empower its employees in order to solve problems and improve performance. Few could argue that more empowerment is important, but process management, especially when accomplished through reengineering, is more than new uses for teamwork. In fact, the cross-functional team envisioned in process management may not at all resemble the self-directed work team of the 1990s. Self-directed work teams manage their work without supervisors, for the most part. Process teams push decisionmaking down to the problem source, but they carefully think through internal and external communication, working in a parallel, not serial, information sharing and developing metrics (work group measurements).

Special attention must also be given to new advances in technology. Greater technology will alter work performed and the ability to monitor and coordinate work, substantially enhancing the abilities of organizations to enlarge unit sizes, reduce direct supervision, and promote cross-functional and cross-organizational communication. Increasingly, decentralized decisionmaking with autonomous work groups and project teams that are supported by information management systems will prevail as dominant organizational structures. This trend toward participative management reduces organizational layers and changes supervision to facilitation and coordination. This requires that organizations reconceptualize the roles of supervisor and employee (through cultural change, education, or process reengineering strategies). However, for any type of work team to be effective, major obstacles must be dealt with that require careful planning, training, and preparation.

There is a distinction between the practice of what is often called "self-declared work teams" and that of "self-directed teams," or process teams. Teams need more than cheerleading from top management. Telling workers that they now have the freedom to go out and meet with customers, solve problems, and schedule their own work is not enough.

Process management lies at the core of what reengineering seeks to change most in bureaucratic organizations. This change goes well beyond the more simplistic goals touted in most management reform movements; that is, less administrative regulation, reduction in hierarchy and regional structures, broader span of control, and systems' streamlining and simplification. Process management offers a very different structure and alignment of work activity, with better customer (and supplier) communication.

Seven Questions for Would-Be Reengineers

Brief answers are provided to seven questions often asked about reengineering. The point is that if management cannot answer these basic questions, it is not ready for reengineering.

Why Is Reengineering Important?

Reengineering assumes that current work organizational systems are outmoded and badly in need of significant change to meet current economic needs and future environmental realities. In addition, reengineering also seeks to take advantage of major information and communication technology advances that make possible vastly different approaches to doing work. (Although it is critical to avoid simply applying technology to existing processes to speed up production times—commonly referred to as "paving the cow path.")

What Does Reengineering Seek to Change?

Reengineering focuses on the organization's key work processes and redesigns organizational management and support systems to fit external, not internal, requirements. The emphasis is on reducing processes; producing work products and services that are value-added from a customer perspective; realigning technology and communications to link suppliers, producers, and customers more directly; creating work teams that are cross-functional; and restructuring administrative support so that it is an enabling rather than a regulatory activity.

For Whom Is Reengineering Done?

Reengineering focuses on customers, emphasizing "value-addedness" from their perspective as the key to remaining competitive. Some reengineering methods push distinctions between external customers (value-added by definition) and internal customers (where benefits must outweigh costs). Such distinctions help firms to identify waste (defined as working for no one) and subject all internal customers to special scrutiny, such as having units calculate and send bills to "customers" for reports generated or services performed.

Reengineering also emphasizes employees and their roles in resolving problems. This is much more than only training workers to handle customer complaints. Reengineering seeks solutions through process management, by which the workforce is actively engaged in measuring quality and customer satisfaction levels, assessing cycle time and costs, and reviewing customer complaints and market data. Process team members are expected to review these metrics and propose solutions and design changes to meet organizational performance goals.

When Should Reengineering Be Started?

Reengineering should begin after the organization recognizes that to maintain the status quo is unacceptable and that innovative change is more desirable than is improving business as usual.

In the early years of BPR, most organizations pursued reengineering because their survival was threatened. (This is usually called a "burning platform.") One advantage of the burning platform is that employees do not have to be convinced that there is a compelling reason to change or that the pain of change is unavoidable.

There are now numerous organizations that pursue reengineering from a "position of strength"; using the adage that the best time to fix something is when it is not broken. Increasingly, the initiating factor is less relevant; the key lesson learned is not to undertake any change effort unless the organization has prepared for it by laying the foundation, creating and communicating a vision for change, and clearly articulating the change priorities tied to the vision.

How Is Reengineering Accomplished?

Three requirements seem critical for reengineering:

1. *Commitment from top management* is necessary to ensure that reengineering is aimed at management's top priorities. This action runs counter to many of the lessons learned in quality management, which argues the case for beginning change by generating small successes. In reengineering there are two slogans that speak to this requirement: "If we are going to fail, then fail over something really important"; and "If we are going to fail, then fail quickly."
2. *Use of good methodologies* is required that compare current state problems and customer limitations with future state requirements and market expectations. Use of good methodologies also means providing redesign models that can be tested to prove how well they work and how easily they can be implemented.
3. *Involve the best experts across functions* in the redesign effort. Reengineering is fast-paced, full-time work. It should not be seen as only another task force meeting to attend or another competing work priority on an already overfilled agenda. If the organization wants a new and radical solution to change it will chose its best people and its most innovative thinkers to be on the redesign team. Above all, the reengineering group must have the resources, time, information, and training if it is to succeed.

Who Does What to Implement Reengineering?

Usually, top management establishes a *steering committee* at a high level to coordinate the overall reengineering efforts. This group has major ongoing responsibilities for coordination and communication. To accomplish the reengineering work itself, some type of high caliber work group or *reengineering team,* consisting of internal and external experts, does the analysis and new design. In addition, there is some type of internal *implementation team* that oversees the conversion and translation of the change effort. Often, the implementation issues are so difficult that organizations will resort to a transition step that creates a conversion and integration team. Such a team plans out the necessary changes in work policies, training, workforce reinvestment, customer, communications, and so on.

How Long Does Reengineering Take?

Fast-track reengineering efforts can produce studies and new proposals in 3 to 6 months and implement changes in 9 to 18 months. Normally, organizations use 6 to 12 months for analysis and redesign, with 12 to 18 months for conversion and complete implementation. An entire reengineering project might span 24 to 30 months in terms of total cycle time. But, since many of the reengineering stages can be done in overlapping and parallel sequence, results can be produced much more quickly.

These long time frames to complete implementation are also balanced with 3-month (or shorter) "deliverables." Deliverables are measurable improvements or milestones that are reached at regular intervals to demonstrate success (or "fast" failure, if that is the case). Implementation plans try to create fast returns up front in the planning process.

Reengineering as Process and Methodology

There is both a process of reengineering and a methodology that are vital to making reengineering change efforts work. The process guides how an organization (1) selects the targets for reengineering; (2) creates and communicates the vision for change; (3) redesigns and validates the new process; (4) transitions from the old ways to the new; and (5) implements and improves the new process.

There are also very distinct methodologies behind BPR that usually involve a linked three-pronged approach, consisting of

1. *process mapping*: the flowcharting (and cost and cycle time measurement) of how an organization currently delivers services and products as a process (often called a current state analysis) and detailing what technology support is used;
2. *customer or stakeholder assessments*: evaluating customer current needs and market future expectations through focus groups, surveys, and meetings with consumers to determine product and service requirements and needs; and
3. *process visioning*: rethinking how work processes ought to work and generating new models for innovation and radical improvement (often called a future state analysis).

Of course, different organizations will tackle different process reengineering projects in different ways. But unlike quality management, which was often criticized for lack of guidance about how to do TQM and how long it would take to see results, reengineering is very specific about what has to happen. Each of the major phases is discussed in the five sections that follow:

Phase One: Preplanning—Is the Organization Ready?

An organization's decision and commitment to start change through reengineering is not easily achieved. In most organizations, top management is constantly looking for feasible approaches to make change work. The problem is how to lead that process to ensure that management's resolve to push through change is not doubted and to ensure that change will work as intended.

Skepticism about change runs deep in most managers, especially in mid-level managers and supervisors. Their belief, as more than one manager has remarked, is that change is constant; organizations seem always to be changing. The problem is how to make things better, to translate change into performance improvement.

So, before choosing reengineering as the change strategy, top management has to think through the need to change and the timing of change. Typically, top managers conduct a policy and planning review of where the organization is headed in terms of political environment and organizational culture. If there are unions involved, labor-management relationships must also be assessed.

This review tries to gauge the "window for change" to create a workable schedule to orchestrate the change process. Nothing makes top management look worse than to produce an innovative and bold reengineering effort that sits on the desk waiting for executive review and legislative approval—the reengineering team feels betrayed and the workforce becomes more frustrated over the delays and uncertainty.

Top managers are not going to do the actual redesign; but they do need to ensure that certain resources are in place and that preparatory actions have been taken to launch the effort when the time is right. For starters, top managers need to assure the organization that there will be some continuity and that they will see the effort through at least to the transition stage. This assurance may be less of a problem than one might suspect, given the fast time frames for the first three phases of reengineering—preplanning, vision, and redesign.

Part of the appeal of reengineering is that the change is rapid enough that the leadership will actually see something in place before their tenure is up (usually between 18 months and two years).

The organization's other major activity in the preplanning stage is making sure that resources are in place and that players have been selected to drive the change effort. Most organizations use some form of consulting intervention to start, so the most problematical task is to find a reasonable external consultant or a capable internal consultant, or a blend of both.

The services of external consultants with experience and expertise are expensive. Internal consultants, however, may be suspected of not being impartial or may be seen as inexperienced. Obviously, there are no easy ways out of this dilemma, but top management has to choose the project and then balance the needs for facilitation, analysis, and perspective.

Preplanning ends with a go-ahead decision. An announcement has to be made explaining to the organization the importance of the project and the choice of a radical change methodology. Above all, top management needs to communicate to the workforce, customers, suppliers, and all stakeholders that it is aware of the "pain" of change, (even though consultants may disagree over how high that pain threshold really is). The case for change has to be made from the start and recommunicated at every stage in the process of reengineering.

Phase Two: Strategic Planning—Is There a Vision?

Reengineering objectives are set by top management and some form of steering committee. Therefore, the first task is to appoint a top-level working group or committee, which previews and selects core process "targets" for innovation and redesign. This group plays a key role as "process sponsor." It is responsible for creating internal work groups to conduct the process reengineering analysis and make recommendations for redesign and restructuring. If consultants are to be used, they are also managed by the steering committee, which monitors requirements, schedules, and time frames.

The first step in BPR is the selection of projects. Top management and the steering committee are expected to *determine the priority (or sequence) for reengineering*, based on current and future needs. (In fact, some theorists and consultants hold that this selection process should be conducted as a part of a "portfolio," with the list of projects being reevaluated periodically.)

When a project is selected, as the second step, managers and the steering committee *should provide some form of initial "strategic direction,"* what is often called "the business case" or "compelling case for change." This case reviews where the process is going in the organization's future, how important it is, what values and characteristics should define it, what old and new customer groups and expectations are involved, and so forth. It also provides a frank review of current budget realities in terms of workload, operating costs, administrative support, and future budget cuts.

The case for change ends with determining what some call "stretch objectives": How much should this process improve in the future; how good should it seek to be? Can it be the best, or is better-than-average sufficient? (This is what some call "best practice" versus "leading practice.") Should it seek to be so?

The stretch objectives need to be very specific. They should enumerate the quality levels, how much the cycle time should improve, how efficient costs should be, and how satisfied customers (and even employees) should be with the process results.

All in all, BPR requires a vision, but it also requires appropriate methodologies, tools, people's competence, planning, and so on.

Of course, the steering committee does not give the go-ahead until it has properly laid the foundation. When commissioning the reengineering team that will redesign the process, the steering committee will ensure that some form of basic measurements are in place to set baselines and or benchmarks for change. (In this case, a baseline is some form of current measurement of cost, quality, cycle time, productivity, and customer satisfaction, to be used to make interval comparisons of progress. Benchmarking refers to collecting the same types of information, but comparing it to other organizations with the same process.)

To keep the reengineering effort focused, the steering committee should be assured that the organization has a good understanding of the core business processes and the boundaries for the current redesign effort. To round out the view of processes the organization should provide the committee with preliminary listings of customers and suppliers to be included in the redesign. Clear statements about what the process entails, what resources are used, and what products and services are given to which customers are invaluable to the reengineering team.

Last, and most important, the steering committee completes its strategic planning phase by selecting the redesign team. Depending upon the size and complexity of the processes to be changed, these teams will be made up of 6 to 10 or 12 to 25 individuals chosen for their knowledge and expertise and also for their willingness to function as change agents and innovators. In the next phase, the rules for how a redesign team operates are discussed, but there are two major considerations: First, to the extent possible, reengineering work is full time (or at least the highest priority of the team members' work responsibilities); second, reengineering teams are almost always cross-functional—they require a range of perspectives that cannot be provided by a single unit or function, no matter how narrow the process.

Phase Three: Process Redesign— Is There a Methodology?

Reengineering analysis is usually carried out by some group of individuals chosen specifically to pursue process innovation or reengineering. These teams document, chart, and analyze existing process, explore ideal models or new visions of processes, oversee customer surveys, and redesign core processes or new process innovations. Once a team has been selected and given a process to redesign, it must choose some type of measurement approach.

Process reengineering requires considerable information, both to analyze proposed design changes and to validate that the changes work. In terms of skills (and potential training) reengineering teams should have expertise in the following areas: process flowcharting, cycle time metrics, defect- and rework-level measurements, resource requirements planning and review, customer satisfaction measurements, and market share and other performance indicators.

In addition, major consideration of the information technology dimensions of process reengineering is vital. Information (and communications) technology plays a pivotal role in determining process cycle time, connectivity, and control, but information management is vital to the redesign effort. Software applications and models can be quite effectively used to track various process metrics, to plan and test prototypes for redesign models, and to validate conversion and implementation efforts. Therefore, reengineering teams may require special training in software applications or modeling and simulations.

Reengineering teams also require supplemental training and preparation. Once selected, the participants should be trained as a team in reengineering methodology, teamwork, decisionmaking, and communication skills. Attention must be paid to the training and education needs of team members over the course of their group effort.

But at the core of the reengineering apple, so to speak, are the methodologies that produce the redesign. Three methodologies were referred to previously: process mapping, customer assessments, and process visioning. This review will only outline some of the key steps that a reengineering team might take when it uses these methodologies. There is considerable flexibility in how the team divides up and sequences the work assignments, of course. Some organizations construct three separate subteams and conduct three different inquiries. The teams reassemble, present their findings, and create the new redesign.

Another model is to have the whole team undertake a part of each methodology and then to build a cumulative analysis that creates the new redesign.

Redesign, Step One: Process Mapping—What Is Wrong with It and How Is It Done?

There are a variety of techniques that can be used to review how the organization works, such as activity-based costing and value-added assessments, but most reengineering starts with a basic documentation step called process mapping. Process mapping is little more than horizontal flowcharting—tracking what work activities are performed, by whom, when, and what decisions are made in delivering the final product or service to a customer.

The purpose of mapping is always related to the objective of showing how work gets done in an organization. The vantage point is the customer's; so when work crosses organizational boundaries (commonly referred to as "hand-offs" or "linkage of process") this objective must be clearly identified.

Other factors shown when making process maps include all activities within blocks in sequence as stages, all hand-offs (crossing organizational units), decision points (and especially rejects or rework), suppliers (contractors), if involved, and the final product of service going to the customer.

A major dimension of the process map is its metrics, or completion time and productivity measurements. Each process map should provide data or estimates of the following:

quality rate, the accuracy or reject rates of output;
cycle time, how long the process takes from start to finish;
productivity, how long it takes to accomplish each work task; and
cost, levels of labor and capital used in completing work tasks.

Many reengineering consultants provide a note of caution before starting process mapping. Remember that the purpose is to get a better understanding of the current limitations, problems, and barriers in the process in order to change it. Extensive documentation and complex measurements should be kept to a minimum. The reengineering team will normally map out the key subprocesses, devoting most of its effort to activities that use the most resources or take the longest time to complete.

Redesign, Step Two: Customer/Stakeholder Assessments—What Is Value-Added?

Next is a detailed analysis of how customers and their needs are changing. This can be compiled informally through meetings or visits. But, increasingly, reengineering teams are turning to more formal methods such as customer satisfaction and expectation surveys or focus groups. Whether the analysis is informal or formal, the teams' goal is to produce a detailed assessment of the customer's environment, which can be translated into product and service design and delivery that will exceed customer expectations and future market needs. Sometimes this information can be obtained through face-to-face sessions with customers, asking them to detail their current requirements and then to project their requirements for the future.

Another important technique is to compare the current customer base and project how the base will change in terms of size, demographics, and other vital characteristics (such as use and access to technology).

Reengineering teams must be wary of competing or conflicting interests of different customers and factor this aspect into their customer review. A useful by-product of the customer assessment can also be new customer service standards and customer satisfaction measurement surveys.

Recently, a new model for customer assessments has emerged that will be of increasing interest to reengineering teams. The model—called "concept engineering" because it tries to impart customer information into initial design stages—uses five core steps of diagnosis, as outlined:

1. *environment scan*: understanding the consumer's environment by surveying market demands and customer expectations from both current customers and noncustomers;
2. *customer requirements*: translating market dynamics to customer needs after analyzing customer base projections and feedback;
3. *operational requirements*: operationalizing customer requirements by creating specific measurements of customer requirements and priorities;
4. *design options*: generating design concepts and design alternatives by brainstorming design ideas and creating design solutions; and
5. *design specifications*: selecting solutions and designs by assessing options, choosing the solution, and listing all specifications for product, service delivery, and feedback.

All this may sound very complicated, but it does illustrate the point that there is more to customer assessment than simply asking the customer questions. Too many times, organizations have learned the hard way that customers often do not know what they want, sometimes they have expectations that are too low, and, even occasionally, they do not trust the organization to use customer feedback constructively.

Redesign, Step Three: Process Visioning—How Should It Work?

Last, but not least, there remains the task of creating the new model. To capture the spirit of this approach the term "clean sheet of paper" is often used. The idea is for the team to think as if it could start over, that is, ignore the current system and design it all over again. This idea may sound attractive, but, as many teams will discover, the jump from "what the system does not do" to "what it needs to do" may be immense.

When a firm is facing the redesign or process visioning phase it may be more useful to begin with a simple description of an ideal model—how this process should meet customer needs and how it should provide a "competitive niche" for the organization. This first link (called the *process vision ideal*) leads to a definition of the internal process steps, resource usage, and performance levels that the organization should commit to in order to make this new process work (called the *process attributes*). A third link incorporates the external attributes, that is, what levels of quality are required to satisfy customer requirements and expectations. But this link also includes a review of values, such as choice and cycle time, and ensures that they are fully considered (called the *customer attributes and values*). The new redesign must be supported by technology, resources management, workforce training, and other *renewal processes*, which complete the institutional support part of the reengineering process.

In the final analysis, process visioning requires innovative ideas and creative brainstorming. Often, the team may invite suppliers, customers, and other stakeholders to attend the sessions and help create the new redesign. As tempting as it is to think that the best solutions are just lying out there, waiting to be implemented, this is just not the case. Innovation for new processes is no different than any invention; it requires creative, talented people who have a thorough knowledge of what is required for major change and a commitment to accomplish that change.

Once the redesign has been created and documented, it should be validated and tested. A follow-on step is to provide a flowchart of the new process, specify the desired performance and process metrics, and confirm the technology, workforce, and budget impacts. If possible, the performance of some form of test, or the construction of what is generally called a prototype, is an important step. For example, the firm could work with a limited number of customers and employees and test the new process (simulating the technology if necessary). Top management may then be more receptive to the new design, given the nature of its involvement; and prototyping will help prove the new design to those in the organization whose jobs are going to change and to those who are soon to be called upon to implement the new system and improve upon it.

Phase Four: Conversion—Is There a Transition Strategy?

Assuming acceptance of the new design by management, there remains the task of implementation planning. There must be some sort of organizational hand-off from the steering committee and the reengineering team to the actual unit implementation team that represents "the process owners." The more complex and far-reaching the redesign, the more likely the organization is to create a special team to handle the transition. This group is generally called the conversion team. It plans the transition process by considering, for example, how the organization will get its current work done while it is installing the new process design, and what will happen as the organization makes the process redesign work.

Once the organization initiates and makes a process reengineering decision, it must develop an overlapping implementation and conversion process. Process redesign and innovation, by definition, require major changes in all aspects. This redesign will impact many areas, including converting old policies to new policies, changing work assignments, retraining employees, realigning organizational structures, reconfiguring information technology, and reaffirming customer interfaces and requirements.

Perhaps the most difficult task facing the conversion team is dealing with the redesign's impact on the workforce. No matter how much of an improvement the new redesign is, many people in the workforce will be suspicious and resentful of it. They will want answers to three questions: Will I still have a job? How is my job going to change? Will I be able to do my new job with my current skills?

The conversion team leads what is called the "upskilling" effort to deal with these fears. For starters, there is a workforce planning review—what jobs are needed, where, and with what skill requirements. Then training and development plans must be created for process workers—those who will now require cross-functional training, new technology skills, and other competencies. Finally, if the redesign features self-directed work teams, plans must be laid to convert work groups into work teams by training workers in teamwork, meeting skills, cooperation and coaching, and so on. The transition is completed when all of these steps are included in a formal implementation plan, which is then passed on to the firm for the last stage of the reengineering process.

Phase Five: Implementation—Is There a Commitment for Real Change?

Organizations must be made aware of the high failure rate of reengineering efforts. Estimates of failure range from 50 to 60 percent.

Perhaps the most critical success factor impacting the future effectiveness of the redesign concerns communications. The effects of reengineering are large; it reorganizes unit structures, realigns technology usage, redesigns workforce roles, and even reshapes organizational culture. Normal lines of communication (effective or ineffective) are by definition uprooted. This dimension is so vital that the entire process of reengineering itself is dependent on enhanced communication before, during, and especially after the conversion and implementation processes. If the organization is going through any level of downsizing, there may be even more resistance from managers and employees and substantial communications problems between them when trying to understand the new process designs.

Understanding the reasons for failure of reengineering should not be too difficult. To begin with, the extensive use of process metrics and activity cost and results data makes it easy to see where the problems are and what is not being accomplished as planned. Therefore, the first rule of planning implementation is to make sure that the redesign has been properly tested and has the necessary metrics to show degree of success or failure.

Nevertheless, even the best redesigns and prototypes have fallen prey to a variety of conversion and change problems that should have been anticipated. Typically, the biggest problem is starting the implementation process too late. The larger the implications of change, the greater is the necessity to form an implementation team that overlaps the redesign phase. In some respects, there is a tendency for organizations to use a conversion or transition stage (phase four) as a way to correct for not having planned the implementation process early enough.

Implementation should also include active roles for administrative support staffs, customer representatives, suppliers, and contractors.

Internal resistance to the new redesign has to be anticipated and not simply reacted to after the plan has been put forward. No matter how much communication occurs, opponents can be expected to be passive before the redesign occurs. Indeed, their arguments gain additional credibility if they can claim they were not consulted.

No matter, there is only one unforgivable failure when confronting inside critics; this is having to admit that the team failed to consider something.

Reengineers should never be taken by surprise by the level of opposition and the emotional strength of criticisms of the redesign. After all, the old organization has huge investments in the old way of doing things. Entire careers were built on the basis of expertise and knowledge of how to make the old system perform (perhaps cope is the better word).

Finally, there is a team approach in process management that may be perceived by many middle managers as threatening to their control and to their primary role in the old organization—mainly that of supervision.

If firms want their engineering efforts to be successful they must have a realistic plan that integrates workforce involvement, upskilling, team development, changing human resources, and budget supporting processes, and they must systematically address how the organizational culture will be transformed. Of course, the key to making BPR work is to communicate, before, during, and after every phase of the reengineering effort.

Summing Up

As powerful as reengineering is as a change methodology, it will not succeed without extensive planning, measurement, analysis, and, above all, talent. If there is one way to convey to everyone in the organization the commitment to change and management's resolve to sustain change through reengineering, it is to assign the organization's best and brightest to the redesign effort. The workforce and future managers will not only take notice of who is leading the change effort but will also understand that this level of investment can only mean that the old ways must finally give way.

The premise of reengineering is that organizations can change in ways and at speeds previously thought impossible. Reengineering can help make that happen if there is a clear vision of the future, a plan to get there, a methodology to accomplish the journey, and a purpose important enough to capture the imagination and best talent of the organization.

28

Quality Circles

Ann-Marie Rizzo,
Tennessee State University

Problem-solving tools to improve productivity and job performance in business, industry, and government work settings. Quality Circle (QC) experiments enjoy a rich history, dating back more than 30 years. Conceived for Japanese industry, QCs are now common in business, government, and nonprofit organizations throughout the industrialized world. Circles have been used in South Africa, Colombia, Singapore, the United Kingdom, and the United States. Although QCs were originally designed as a stand-alone innovation, most current approaches to improve worker productivity have assimilated circles as major elements in more inclusive Total Quality Management (TQM) strategies.

In their most common form, many circles convene within an organization, each group charged with addressing problems in similar jobs or related work. Circle members may range from three to twelve employees, although, typically, groups include six to twelve people. These employees voluntarily join teams, which regularly address problems in individual job performance as well as whether jobs mesh in a given process (for example, personnel staffing). Primary activities involve revisiting job design and work flow continually and comparing these methods and approaches with eventual outcomes.

By virtue of their assignment to find new problems and long-term solutions, teams possess comparatively sweeping authority. QC advocates reason that day-to-day job experience promotes unique insight into how jobs and the work environment can be improved and how job tasks and the overall work process can be redesigned. Because job knowledge is valued over hierarchical status, in theory, QCs illustrate bottom-up innovations in productivity improvement. Communication and problem solving is directed from the lowest rungs of the organizational ladder to the top. This implicit trust in workers as authors of change means that, in principle, QCs challenge most traditional or classical approaches to organization in which control over such issues was concentrated at the top. Even though hierarchical authority appears undermined by this philosophy, extensive research has found that successful QCs rely heavily upon executive support. Effective implementation of quality circles, accordingly, begins and ends at the top.

The Quality Movement and Japan's Economic Transformation

Quality Circles trace their origin to postwar Japan's industrial recovery, through systematic efforts to build quality into goods manufactured for world trade. The Japanese Union of Scientists and Engineers was charged with finding a method to bridge the gap between job design and how work was actually produced. An American named W. E. Deming assisted the Japanese Union's efforts. Deming had long promoted the use of statistical tools in solving quality problems but met with enthusiastic audiences only in Japan (Fitzgerald and Murphy 1982). Although quality improvement strategies in general owe much to Deming's lessons about objective-setting and measurement, QC philosophy and practices were also subtly and powerfully shaped by Japanese cultural characteristics.

In one sense, the foundation for Quality Circles was set centuries ago in the strong Japanese work ethic and related values of collectivism and collaboration. Unlike American society, in which individuals compete to distinguish themselves from the group, the Japanese worker is expected to collaborate for the betterment of the larger community. Though French, Italian, and Spanish organizations have been described as highly centralized and marked by status distinctions, Japanese companies often are less concerned with rigid lines of authority (Lammers and Hickson 1979). Japanese workers are more respected for their expertise than their status or official position alone. Accomplishment for their team is frequently met with company approval via social recognition; development and educational opportunities; frequently, lifetime employment; and, not to be downplayed, economic rewards (Watanabe 1991). With a company's focus often fixed on long-term results rather than short-term profits, a circle's constant fine-tuning of a work process (known as *keisen*) is tolerated, even encouraged, if ultimately it means a better product.

By 1982, Quality Circles had become so embedded in Japanese corporations that five of every six Japanese workers were said to belong. Roughly two million QCs are now estimated to be active, representing substantial worker influence and involvement in the work-improvement process. Each circle member contributes an average 55 recommendations per year, which boosted Japanese productivity and quality steadily and substantially throughout the 1980s (Fitzgerald and Murphy 1982).

By the end of the decade, these achievements catapulted Japan into a new role as a leader in world trade. According to one perspective, Japan's "overnight success" can be explained by its singular focus on quality. Good pricing and other factors are clearly secondary. Product quality and the Japanese economic miracle, consequently, owes more to the "continuous improvement" doctrine than other contributing factors, such as technological innovation in the workplace (for example, industrial robotization). As such, the Japanese experience serves as testimony to the vigor of Quality Circles—at least as employed in Japan—to transform not just the workplace but an entire economy.

Quality Circle Accomplishments: What Research Tells Us

As word of QC accomplishments spread beyond Japan, work institutions elsewhere in Asia and in the West asked how they could adopt Quality Circles. In many cases, the manner of implementation was irrelevant, as long as it was timely: Executives and leaders wanted quick returns on QC's extraordinary promise. Researchers asked different questions. Some inquired as to the transferability of QCs to non-Japanese settings; others considered the factors and conditions behind circle effectiveness.

In comparisons of effective circles in Japan, the United States, and Singapore, size emerged as a critical factor. Groups should be limited to six to ten members. To a lesser extent, successful QCs are more likely voluntary and highly participative. They tended to enjoy a "people-building philosophy," top management commitment, union support, and a climate conducive to creativity and a continuous study process (Gosh and Song 1991).

With regard to outcomes, even though QCs have been cited as good examples of worker empowerment, some studies of Western industrial QCs indicated that they may not improve worker attitudes. Circles may, however, help to improve product quality, efficiency, cost savings, and work conditions (Adam 1991). But in other studies, QC members enjoyed higher performance ratings and were promoted more often than other employees. Presumably, QCs were a major factor insofar as they offered development opportunities and increased individual visibility and positive regard for their members (Buch and Spangler 1990).

Elsewhere, a comparison of QC members with nonmembers revealed that QC members submitted more suggestions but showed little difference from other employees on key organizational outcomes such as productivity (Steel et al. 1990). In a wide variety of organizations, QC employees registered reduced turnover and at least stabilized absenteeism. In addition, QCs appear to bond members to the overall organization (Buch 1992), a finding that on its face contradicts earlier speculation (by Adam 1991) that QCs fail to change worker attitudes or integrate employees.

Most QC writers agree, however, that to a great extent a circle's effectiveness rests on the quality of members' participation and commitment to its purposes. Often, the nature and quality of employee involvement depends upon whether their observations and suggestions are respected and acted upon by higher-ups. Where superiors are threatened by sharing information, decisionmaking authority, and job responsibility with circle members, QCs have generally been short-lived (Brennan 1992). Even high-performing workers reject QCs if adequate training in problem solving and group dynamics has not been provided or first-line supervisors and other hierarchical superiors fail to act on QC solutions. As QCs have been tried and refined in many settings across many cultures, one general rule appears consistently: Those that have produced the greatest successes have tended to be part of a planned, systemwide change effort (Heath 1990).

For these and other reasons, QCs have gradually become incorporated into system- or organization-wide quality improvement efforts, generally known in the U.S. as Total Quality Management (TQM). In many accounts of TQM, Quality Circles have largely evolved into self-directed work groups, which target tactical issues in getting the work done. Worker empowerment, formerly a critical implementation issue in QCs, has become part of an overall program to promote employee development and training and to encourage participation in decision-making.

Quality Improvement Efforts in the Public Sector: U.S. Governmental Bodies as Case Studies

Governmental institutions have been particularly receptive to quality and productivity improvement strategies inasmuch as they promise remedies for bureaucratic inefficiency and waste, and customer dissatisfaction, as well as help for shrinking budgets. The U.S. federal government reportedly loses an estimated US $400 billion annually to quality problems (McKenna 1993). TQM and Quality Circles have been adopted in U.S. federal agencies, including the Forest Service, the National Aeronautics and Space Administration, and the Air Force Systems Command.

Leading this assault on waste and inefficiency is the U.S. Federal Quality Institute, founded in 1988 and comprising a revolving group of 35 representatives from federal agencies. It has assisted the federal quality effort through training and technical assistance and has organized model TQM projects. Successful ventures reported reduced cost in airplane repairs for the Navy, lower labor cost at the Johnson Space Center, and greater accuracy in processing income tax returns at the Internal Revenue Service (Reynolds 1992).

Thirty-six out of the 50 states report some type of quality improvement activity, including Arizona, Arkansas, Pennsylvania, and Ohio. Cities from Portland, Oregon, and Austin, Texas (U.S.), to Ottawa-Carleton (Ontario, Canada) have turned to TQM to cope with fiscal stress, improve the delivery of services, and improve efficiency. These experiments report not only financial savings but also improved morale, faster service, and improved customer communication and service satisfaction (Kline 1992).

In some respects, quality innovations are the latest catchword or trend in business and government: Quality Circle managers like to say that they are contributing to a popular movement. However, systematic research suggests that Quality Circles are better understood as an umbrella label, tying together a vast array of approaches differing not only in design but also in execution and results. Researchers have yet to agree as to what works and why, and whether a particular tool such as QCs will produce the same results across work and national cultures.

Quality Circles: Form and Functions

Though Quality Circles vary in form across work institutions as well as cultures, some fundamental shared characteristics can describe a typical QC's organization and roles. The map of a QC's structure in many cases mimics a traditional organizational pyramid. At the top is the steering or executive committee, composed of representatives of upper management, human resource staff, and the individual(s) in charge of the QC program. This group generally serves as the policymaking body, overseeing and coordinating the QC effort. Committee members may be permanent or serve a fixed term. The steering committee typically meets at least monthly.

The QC administrator usually represents the single point of authority for the QC program. In this capacity, he or she maintains records of circle activities and works to ensure good communication within and between circles. The administrator also serves as a linchpin or liaison between circles and the executive committee. Typical additional functions include training, budgeting, public relations, and coordination.

The next role in the chain of command is the QC facilitator, who monitors circle progress on a routine basis. The facilitator provides direction in the appropriate use of QC tools and techniques and, like the administrator, also attends to communication between and among QC parties. More so than the administrator, a facilitator tends to focus on QC *process*, or how each circle accomplishes goals and solves problems. In larger companies, the facilitator may be independent of the administrator and this position tends to be filled by many individuals who facilitate a large number of circles; in smaller systems, one individual may wear both hats. In either case, this individual serves to link both the day-to-day work of the circles with policymakers by facilitating communication.

QC leaders are supervisors or workers trained in the QC process who help to coordinate a circle's work. They keep meetings on task and monitor their progress often, depending on a recorder who maintains the circle's written records. They may also consult with the facilitator, attend to feedback about prior suggestions, schedule special consultations, and arrange for presentations by outside experts.

Circle members are instrumental to its effectiveness. They must regularly attend, contribute ideas to, and "own" the circle's work. At a minimum, the following conditions appear necessary for QC effectiveness (for extensive coverage on circle implementation, see Fitzgerald and Murphy 1982). At a minimum members must:

- voluntarily join QCs;
- agree to basic QC ground rules and norms;
- accept and assist the circle leader;
- complete training in the QC process, group dynamics, and problem solving; and
- learn and apply QC tools and techniques to measure and track quality defects and sticking points.

QC tools include flowcharts, control charts and cause-and-effect diagrams. Flowcharts help to determine quality costs, which are divided into prevention, inspection and appraisal, and internal failure and external failure costs. Control charts can determine random or particular variation in processes, and cause-and-effect diagrams present how a work process assumes its shape (Kline 1993).

Quality: A New Direction for Governments?

The cornerstone of both Quality Circle and TQM philosophy is continual improvement, building quality into a service process or manufacture so that "zero defects" mark the outcome. The aim is to provide the customer, client, or public with an ever-higher quality of service, however the citizen-consumer defines it. By and large, a quality improvement agenda represents a new direction for government organizations. Circles and other tools depart from traditional ways of conducting the public's business, in which evaluating an organization's performance meant reliance on efficiency criteria—abandoned long ago by most business and industry—and greater embracement of outcome-based measures. Whether citizens will see great changes from these innovations or will support the use of such tools on a grand or national scale is an unanswered question. Whether legislatures and other elected officials will continue this experiment long enough for adequate testing of quality improvement techniques also remains to be seen (see also **Total Quality Management, productivity and quality improvement**.)

Bibliography

Adam, Everett E., Jr., 1991. "Quality Circle Performance." *Journal of Management*, vol. 1, no. 1 (March): 25–40.

Brennan, Maire, 1992. "Mismanagement and Quality Circles: How Middle Managers Influence Direct Participation." *Management Decision*, vol. 30, no. 6 (November): 35–46.

Buch, Kimberly, 1992. "Quality Circles and Employee Withdrawal Behaviors: A Cross-Organizational Study." *Journal of Applied Behavioral Science*, vol. 28, no. 1 (March): 62–74.

Buch, Kimberly, and Raymond Spangler, 1990. "The Effects of Quality Circles on Performance and Promotions." *Human Relations*, vol. 43, no. 6 (June): 573–583.

Fitzgerald, Laurie, and Joseph Murphy, 1982. *Quality Circles: A Strategic Approach*. San Diego: University Associates.

Gosh, B. C., and Lim Kia Song, 1991. "Structures and Processes of Company Quality Control Circles (QCCs): An Explanatory Study of Japan, the USA and Singapore." *Management Decision*, vol. 29, no. 7 (December): 45–54.

Heath, Phillip M., 1990. "Quality—And How to Achieve It." *Management Decison*, vol. 28, no. 8: 42–47.

Kline James J., 1992. "Total Quality Management in Local Government." *Government Finance Review*, vol. 8, no. 4 (August): 7–12.

______, 1993. "Quality Tools Are Applicable to Local Government." *Government Finance Review*, vol. 9, no. 4 (August): 15–20.

Lammers, Cornelis J., and David J. Hickson, 1979. "A Cross-National and Cross-Institutional Typology of Organizations." In Cornelis J. Lammers and David J. Hickson, eds., *Organizations Alike and Unlike: International and Interinstitutional Studies in the Sociology of Organizations*. London: Routledge and Kegan Paul.

McKenna, Joseph P., 1993. "Total Quality Government: More than Political Fashion." *Industry Week*, vol. 242, no. 12 (June 21): 44–46.

Reynolds, Larry, 1992. "The Feds Join the Quality Movement." *Management Review*, vol. 81, no. 4 (April): 39–41.

Steel Robert P., Kenneth R. Jennings, and James I. Lindsey, 1990. "Quality Circle Problem Solving and Common Cents: Evaluation Study Findings from a United States Mint." *Journal of Applied Behavior Science*, vol. 26, no. 3 (August): 365–382.

Watanabe, Susumu, 1991. "The Japanese Quality Control Circle: Why It Works." *International Labour Review*, vol. 130, no. 1 (January-February): 57–81.

29

PUBLIC ENTERPRISE

Roger Wettenhall,
University of Canberra

A business owned and operated by government.

For some, the whole process of development—of creating, fostering, and guiding the necessary social and economic forces for development, for which usually only the state has adequate resources and power—may be regarded as public enterprise. Mostly, however, the term is used within the discipline of public administration with a rather more precise meaning. A. H. Hanson (1959) was codifying from an already long tradition of scholarship, and from a series of significant United Nations documents in the early post–World War II period, when he offered this definition: "in a more restricted and more familiar sense . . . (public enterprise means) state ownership and operation of industrial, agricultural, financial and commercial undertakings" (p. 115).

Although the idea of public enterprise has taken a battering in recent years, the practice is as old as civilization itself. In the more general sense, it was responsible for the planning and construction of vast schemes of flood control and irrigation along the major waterways around which the early civilizations developed; it built the Great Pyramids of Egypt and the Great Wall of China. In the more limited sense, it stored and distributed the grain, salt, and other staple foods on which those civilizations depended. Such enterprise was associated with systems of "hydraulic agriculture," or agriculture involving the control of water on a large scale: those were systems which both permitted and demanded intensive cultivation, clear division of labor and social coordination on a massive scale. The works already indicated were often accompanied by the development of major highway and canal networks, and they were integral to the development not only of civilized society but also of organized government.

Later, when the new technologies spawned by the Industrial Revolution and associated developments in law and commerce made large-scale private enterprise possible, a major question for society became that of charting the appropriate roles of public ownership and public regulation. Early attempts to promote the public interest through unregulated private competition were generally unsuccessful, leaving governments, parliaments, political parties, and ideologies to contest whether the public interest was better protected from the greed of profit-seeking private entrepreneurs by public ownership and operation of basic services (which we would now call infrastructure services) or by public regulation of services owned and operated privately. In developing countries, however (and this category long included smaller European countries such as Norway and Sweden and "New World" countries like Australia, Canada, and New Zealand, as well as countries emerging from mid-twentieth century decolonizations), this choice was often simply not available: in the virtually total absence of a private market (not its failure, as many modern would-be rewriters of history would have it), the only capacity for the initiation, development, and operation of services rested in the institutions of the state.

One of the most surprising elements of late twentieth century ideology-making is the strength of the view that neither public ownership nor public regulation is necessary, that "the market" will provide the level playing field needed to ensure that public (consumer?) interests are protected. But there are also numerous critics of this ideology who are convinced that the market alone cannot do this, and some grounds for believing that most societies will return before long to the more traditional liberal stance that either public ownership or public regulation is necessary to ensure a tolerable degree of concern for public interest issues. In such societies, it is likely that a significant public sector will be maintained, with public enterprises functioning alongside private enterprises in the "mixed economy" style familiar through most of the non-Communist world for much of the twentieth century. Indeed, one of the rather spectacular results of the commercializing, corporatizing, and privatizing drives that have affected so many public sectors in the closing decades of the twentieth century is that new organizational forms are emerging which are neither fully private nor fully public. While these forms of public-private mix present a new fascination for public administration scholarship, they provide a very clear indication that the mixed economy is alive and well.

Roughly since the advent of the Thatcher government in Britain in 1979 and the enthusiasm of international financial agencies such as the World Bank and the IMF thereafter in pushing Thatcherite ideology in other countries, aided and abetted by the now-strident "public choice" school of economics, public policymaking in the area of public enterprise has divided into two strands. One, associated with all the rhetoric of smaller government and the beauty of market solutions, has aimed at shifting publicly owned enterprises to the private sector, or simply abandoning them. The other, accepting realistically that public sectors will remain even if somewhat reduced in size, has seen the introduction in a great many countries of reform programs designed to increase the efficiency of enterprises remaining in public ownership. Privatization is dealt with elsewhere in this encyclopedia; the remainder of this article is concerned with ongoing public enterprise systems, and the reform drives of the recent period.

Understanding Public Enterprise Systems

The study of public enterprise has focused almost exclusively on developments of the post–Industrial Revolution period, and has been concerned with exploring several main themes. These relate particularly to the reasons for establishing public enterprises, the functions they perform, how they are organized, how they obtain staffing and financial resources, how profits and losses are handled, and the patterns of relationships operating between them, their supervising ministers, the creating legislatures, and other "stakeholders" such as clients, employee groups, auditors, and (where relevant) official regulators. The degree of managerial autonomy they exercise is another important theme: it flows out of a consideration of these relationship patterns, and it leads to the further important issue of the extent to which they are subject to "community service obligations" which may be in conflict with primary commercial objectives.

Why Public Enterprise?

In addressing this question, we are, of course, concerned with the activity—why governments go into business—rather than forms of organization. Decisions about structures come later, after activities have been determined. While triggers for the activity have been extremely varied, a classification suggested in a study of the Swedish experience is nevertheless very useful in providing a framework for understanding the process at work. Thus Verney (1959) contrasted the "natural growth" character of Sweden's public enterprises with the "nationalization" character of Britain's (p. 7).

In the first, the enterprises grew from their birth under public ownership in a relatively sparsely populated country with an undeveloped capital market. This is a classic situation repeated so often in "young" economies, where public enterprise is necessarily the primary engine of development. While there is no known count of public enterprises so established, the number is very considerable; it is clear that in many developing countries (including earlier developers such as Australia, Canada, and the United States) most public enterprises fall into this category. Even where strong capital markets exist, projects may be simply too big or (in federations) too constitutionally complicated for any but governments to undertake them. Often intersector accommodations have emerged whereby it is tacitly agreed that it is appropriate for the public sector to provide the infrastructure services needed to enable the private sector to establish and operate production industries.

In the second, enterprises are already operating under private ownership, but for one reason or another they are then brought into public ownership through acts of nationalization. The reasons for such acts may be political or ideological, ranging from the fairly moderate belief that, if there has to be monopoly, accountability is better served if it is to a public ownership rather than left in private hands, to the more radical Marxist conviction about the virtue of socializing "the means of production, distribution, and exchange." Alternatively, they may be economic or strategic, ranging from a belief that "commanding heights" industries should remain in public hands to a need to "rescue" industries self-destructing in private hands. Around the world, many public enterprises have had this "ambulance for sick industry" guise, and in some a period in public ownership has revived them sufficiently to allow governments to contemplate next-stage privatizing action. Again, enterprises shift to public ownership for nationalistic and foreign-policy reasons, as in the desire of newly independent countries to substitute domestic for foreign control of major industries, and in the punitive confiscations of properties of enemy countries or their nationals, of collaborators of former occupying forces, and of unpopular racial or ethnic groups.

All these reasons, and more, explain why public sectors have grown to the proportions familiar in the 1960s and 1970s, before the small government movement got under way. And, even in the late twentieth century as many acts of privatization are taking place, some new public enterprises are appearing for reasons consistent with those summarized above, and others are emerging as part of the late twentieth-century administrative reform movement itself. The commercializing drives that are an important part of that movement are, in many countries, moving what have long been budget-funded activities into self-funding off-budget units operating on user-pays principles, and so new public "businesses" arise. As has been argued elsewhere, while the boundaries of the public sector are always changing and we are certainly experiencing contractions in many countries today, we are a long way from witnessing the death of public enterprise (Wettenhall 1983, 1993).

The Functions of Public Enterprise

Within the group of "industrial, agricultural, financial, and commercial undertakings" identified by Hanson in the definition of public enterprise given at the beginning of this article, enterprise managements will normally be seen organizing and operating ongoing public business concerns. Often also, notably where the enterprises are of the "natural growth" kind, they will be involved in the planning and construction work that goes on before business operations can be commenced.

In most mixed-economy countries, public utility industries such as water supply, sewerage, power (electricity and gas), communications (posts, telephones, broadcasting) and transport (rail, bus, shipping, ports, airlines, airports) have long been candidates for public ownership, either as monopolies or (as in the United States) in some kind of competition with private operators. Often—and particularly in developing countries—extractive and manufacturing industries such as oil, minerals, forest products, fertilizers, pharmaceuticals, automobiles, and farm machinery will also be, all or in part, in public ownership. As a rough measure of their economic contribution we are told that, for many such countries, these enterprises take up about 20 percent of capital investment. In the centrally planned economies the proportion of public to private enterprise will be very high: in Romania in the 1960s, for example, 96 percent of industrial output came from public enterprises (Hanson et al. 1968, p. 2).

Some writers separate the large group of commodity marketing undertakings, which are found in many countries, from the generality of public enterprise. But for our purposes this is scarcely necessary. It may be that mostly they do not actually produce the relevant commodities, but they acquire these commodities from the producers and thereafter have commercial responsibility for their sale and for distribution of proceeds to the producers. Some of them are indeed big businesses, and they share many of the characteristics of other public enterprises. Similarly the public financial institutions—insurers, banks, and other lending agencies—cannot be said to produce in the industrial sense; rather they are facilitators of the productive work of others, but in doing this they are commercial enterprises in the fullest sense.

A bigger complication occurs when a public enterprise management engaged in producing a good or service for sale is required by its sponsoring government to regulate the work of others engaged in productive activity in the same industry. Though not uncommon, this functional duality has often proved troublesome, and it certainly offends late twentieth-century notions of establishing competitive "level playing fields." A significant item in the modern reform agenda therefore seeks the clear organizational separation of productive and regulatory functions.

How Public Enterprises Are Organized

What public enterprises do and how they are organized are questions which are both conceptually and practically distinct. Experience shows that there is no single way of organizing such enterprise, and discourse that seeks to establish an identity between one such way and the activity of public enterprise (such discourse is fairly common) is less than helpful.

The theory of the evolution of public enterprise organization formulated by leading U.S. scholar Harold Seidman (1954, pp. 183–185) postulates that, in a first stage, advocates and designers of public enterprise systems believed that the ordinary machinery of the state was all that was required. Thus public enterprises would be vested in departments of the central government or, where the scale was appropriate, established local governments. It was only after considerable experience was acquired in running public enterprises in this way—here the Australian state railway systems in the period 1850–1880 provided an important laboratory (see Wettenhall 1990, pp. 3–5)—that it came generally to be appreciated that special administrative arrangements were needed for government-in-business. In their study of the German railways, Macmahon and Dittmar (1939) spoke of "a vast amount of spontaneous experimentation" going on to discover a suitable managerial instrument. Most countries entered Seidman's second stage when they "hived off" public enterprise activity from the central departments to specially incorporated bodies (usually termed boards, commissions, or authorities) with commercial and managerial autonomy to conduct the enterprises according to the standards of the commercial world. Later, some discovered that they had conferred too much autonomy; some of their public (or statutory) corporations had defied properly constituted governments on policy questions, and it was felt that accountability to those governments had to be restored. At this point, many countries moved to Seidman's third stage, involving a deliberate search for a formula that would allow entrepreneurial commercially oriented management and at the same time ensure ultimate accountability of those managements to government.

This is of course a global theory, digesting from the experience of many countries. Across countries, movement happened at different times and at different paces. Thus Canada and Australia were leaders in the widespread use of the device of the public corporation (usually termed crown corporation in the first, statutory corporation in the second; see Dawson 1992, Musolf 1959, Eggleston 1932, Wettenhall 1990); perhaps surprisingly, Australia's near neighbor, New Zealand, mostly remained faithful to departmental organization of public enterprises (Mascarenhas 1982). Even within single countries there can be inconsistency; in many, public enterprises can still be found within departments, within municipal structures (local government), and hived off to autonomous corporations. Almost everywhere, the post office was late to fall into line: the conversions from first-stage postmaster general departments to third-stage corporations did not occur until well into the second half of the twentieth century.

A variant form of public sector corporation has long been known, and has become increasingly popular in the recent reform period. This is the government-owned (or state-owned) company, formed when a government opts to use the standard companies act registration procedure to bring a new managing organization into being instead of enacting special legislation, which is the method traditionally used to create public, statutory, or crown corporations. Only in the company form is the capital organized in the form of shareholdings. This form thus facilitates joint ownership arrangements whereby government participates with private interests in the formation and/or management of an enterprise; where the government shareholding is greater than 50 percent, the enterprise is normally considered to be public.

The internal organization of public enterprises arranged departmentally or municipally is normally assimilated into the regular structures of the relevant public/civil or local government service. However, in the corporate public sector—whether statutory corporation or government-owned company—the organization is usually marked by the existence of a governing board as the top organ of the enterprise, with the enterprise's executive management answering to that board.

Staffing and Financial Resources

Where the enterprises are arranged departmentally or municipally, staffing and financial regimes again usually follow those of the relevant central or local government service. Minor adaptations may be made, such as the use of trust funds to provide greater financial flexibility than is possible through full subjection to regular central budget processes.

Enterprises in the corporate public sector are characterized by their separation from these central processes. While exceptions can be found, the general rule is that they have their own employment services and budgetary systems separate from those of their sponsoring governments. Thus they will recruit their own staffs independently of the central staffing system, and these staffs will not be civil/public servants in the generally accepted sense. Also they will draw most or all of their funds from charges for the goods and services they provide rather than from taxation revenues, they will often undertake their own borrowing, and they will be noted in central budgets only in so far as it is necessary to register transactions between them and government.

Profits and Losses

The transactions referred to in the last paragraph above are of several kinds. Since there are many profitable public enterprises, dividends and interest payments on loans from government flow back into central consolidated revenue funds. Conversely, there are also loss-making public enterprises—it is sometimes necessary for governments to make transfers to fund these losses, and monies then flow out of consolidated funds to the accounts of corporate managements. Outflows occur also where governments have commitments to fund the costs of noncommercial community service obligations imposed on corporate managements, and—usually in establishment phases—where governments advance funds for the development of corporate enterprises; such funds may be by way of investment (to acquire equity, on which dividends are payable) or loan (on which interest is repayable, together with eventual repayment of capital). Last but by no means least, a great many corporate public enterprises are subject to taxation as are private enterprises, and so the taxes they pay also take the form of transfers into consolidated revenue.

The earnings of public enterprises go first to covering their operating expenses, and then to payment of essential outgoings such as interest on loans and taxation. Surpluses are then applied variously to payment of dividends, to building up financial reserves, and to reinvestment in the enterprise itself, such as acquisition of new technology or enlargement of facilities.

Relationships and Autonomy

Where public enterprises have been vested in corporate bodies, a complex pattern of relationships exists. These relationships are often discussed in terms of accountability, and it is now customary to acknowledge the existence of a network of stakeholders. The sponsoring government is clearly the preeminent stakeholder (and, in the companies, the sole or majority shareholder). Maintenance of a positive, constructive link with the relevant portfolio minister must therefore be high on the corporate agenda: this minister will have certain formal powers in relation to the corporation laid down in the creating statute or in the articles of association registered under the companies act. Maintaining such a link also means maintaining good relations with senior officials in the minister's department and, in some countries, in special "focal points" established to coordinate the activities of a range of ministries in relation to their constituent public enterprises. Others within the government system with formal power or influence in relation to the corporation are likely to be the minister for finance, the auditor-general, and regulatory agencies such as planning, monopolies, and price surveillance commissions. Where strong parliamentary systems exist, there will also be a strong link to the legislature and to relevant investigating committees that it may have established—the corporations may sometimes find the requirements of accountability to the legislature and to the executive government to be in conflict. The list of stakeholders includes also customers, employee unions, special interest groups (who may on occasions have representation on the corporation board), suppliers of essential materials, and other operators in the industry with whom a degree of cooperation is necessary. The corporate management needs to cultivate good relationships with all these groups.

Recent research has indicated also that "corporate management" is something less than a unit. There are often tensions between governing boards and executives, who may be developing separate linkages with various stakeholders; the role of the board in particular is in need of clarification (Corkery et al. 1994).

Traditional scholarship has seen the enjoyment of a considerable measure of corporate autonomy as a sine qua non for successful public enterprise operation, and there can be little doubt that capricious political interventions in matters of managerial detail (e.g., staff appointments) have been ruinous for many public enterprises. The modern approach tends to be more sophisticated: it certainly wants to protect enterprises from interventions in matters that are properly the prerogative of corporate managements, but it also asserts that ultimate, strategic, broad policy responsibility must remain with governments.

Community Service Obligations

It has long been recognized that there will be tension between two expectations that governments and parliaments have about public enterprises. The first is that they should behave commercially, seeking to earn sufficient revenues at least to cover all expenses, and more recently, with the decline of socialist ideology, to earn surpluses to be applied to the purposes indicated under "Profits and Losses" above. The second is that, since they are part of the public sector, they should be available for use as required as instruments of social policy. In furtherance of the second, they have been required from time to time, usually by ministerial direction, to do things (like keeping unproductive coal mines open in order to provide continued employment in depressed regions) which would never be tolerated by commercially driven private enterprise. In consequence, their profitability suffers and often disappears, and their managements are unjustly accused of gross inefficiency.

At least since 1896 in the Australian state of Victoria (Wettenhall 1987, ch. 7), the need has been seen for a mechanism to allow governments to direct public enterprise managements in such ways but to ensure that, at the same time, their accounts and their business reputation do not suffer. This has involved transfer payments from the treasury (or other relevant ministry) to the corporate account, or other form of adjustment, commensurate with the degree of financial loss caused by the need to discharge the relevant community service obligation (CSO).

The Reform Movement of the Later Twentieth Century

This movement has been virtually universal in its effects, and several beginning "models" have been suggested. They mostly have it in common that they seek to substitute new "strategic" forms of accountability and control for the trivial, destructive forms of political control that so often damaged older public enterprises, and to recreate conditions for bold entrepreneurial action by enterprise managements. The reform agenda includes clarification of corporate objectives and removal of noncommercial tasks from enterprise corporations, regular corporate planning, better reporting and accounting systems, precise performance indicators and setting of corporate performance targets, identification and separate funding of CSOs, and executive salaries and benefits closer to those of private enterprise.

One of the earliest expressions of this reform agenda was contained in the 1968 report of France's Nora Commission, and it led to wide acceptance of a system of contracts binding governments and the corporate bodies managing public enterprises as their agents: the corporations are bound to achieve stated goals and objectives, and governments to keep faith with enterprise managements in providing facilitative operating environments, making adjustments for those CSOs, and so on. Agreements of this sort have appeared in many countries, called variously performance contracts (in France and Francophone countries), memoranda of understanding (India), statements of corporate intent (New Zealand), and the like. Others have added the notion of a "signaling system," among other things locating signals in the performance data coming forward that point to significant departures from plan, and so trigger quick remedial action. And the economic rationalists who have been particularly active through the 1980s and early 1990s in Britain, New Zealand,

Australia and some other countries and in the big lending agencies, which are themselves mostly multinational public enterprises, have pushed massively for market solutions and level playing field competition—often leading toward privatization and, where that is not wanted or not feasible, almost always moving public enterprises closer to commercial, market-oriented styles of behavior.

There has been a tendency in the modern reform period for (some) reformers to coin new terms like state-owned enterprise, government business enterprise, and government trading enterprise, and then to deny any connection between their creations and reconstructions and the much longer public enterprise tradition. To the extent that they do this, they also deny themselves the ability to profit from the many useful lessons contained in past public enterprise experience.

Cross references: **government corporation, privatization, stautory corporation.**

Bibliography

Aharoni, Yair, 1986. *The Evolution and Management of State-Owned Enterprises*. Cambridge, MA: Ballinger.

Corkery, Joan, Colm O Nuallain and Roger Wettenhall, eds., 1994. *Public Enterprise Boards: What They Are and What They Do*. Hong Kong: Asian Journal of Public Administration for International Association of Schools and Institutes of Administration.

Dawson, R. MacG., 1992. *The Principle of Official Independence*. London & Toronto: King.

Eggleston, F. W., 1932. *State Socialism in Victoria*. London: King.

Einaudi, M., M. Bye and E. Rossi, 1955. *Nationalization in France and Italy*. Ithaca: Cornell University Press.

Fernandes, Praxi and Pavle Sicherl, eds., 1981. *Seeking the Personality of Public Enterprise*. Ljubljana: International Center for Public Enterprises in Developing Countries.

Floyd, Robert H., Clive S. Gray and R.P. Short, 1984. *Public Enterprise in Mixed Economies: Some Macroeconomic Aspects*. Washington: International Monetary Fund.

Friedmann, W. and J. F. Garner, eds., 1970. *Government Enterprise: A Comparative Study*. London: Stevens.

Glaeser, Martin G., 1957. *Public Utilities in American Capitalism*. New York: Macmillan.

Goodman, Edward, 1951. *Forms of Public Ownership and Control*. London: Christophers.

Hanson, A. H., 1956. *The Management of Public Utilities by Local Authorities*. The Hague: Nijhoff for International Union of Local Authorities.

______, 1959. *Public Enterprise and Economic Development*. London: Routledge and Kegan Paul.

Hanson, A. H,. et al., 1968. *Organization and Administration of Public Enterprises: Selected Papers*. New York: United Nations.

Jones, Leroy P., ed., 1982. *Public Enterprise in Less Developed Countries*. Cambridge: Cambridge University Press.

Kaul, Mohan, et al., 1991. *Public Enterprise Management: Strategies for Success*. 2 vols. London: Commonwealth Secretariat.

Khera, S. S., 1963. *Government in Business*. Bombay: Asia Publishing House.

Lilienthal, David E., 1944. *TVA: Democracy on the March*. Harmondsworth: Penguin.

Macmahon, A. W., and W. R. Dittmar, 1939. "Autonomous Public Enterprise: The German Railways." *Political Science Quarterly*, vol. 54 (December): 481–513.

Mascarenhas, R. C., 1982. *Public Enterprise in New Zealand*. Wellington: Institute of Public Administration.

Mishra, R. K., and S. Ravishankar, eds. 1986. *Public Enterprises in the World*. Bombay: Himalaya.

Mitchell, Jerry, ed., 1992. *Public Authorities and Public Policy: The Business of Government*. New York: Praeger.

Musolf, Lloyd D., 1959. *Public Ownership and Accountability: The Canadian Experience*. Cambridge, MA: Harvard University Press.

Powell, Victor, 1987. *Improving Public Enterprise Performance: Concepts and Techniques*. Geneva: International Labour Office.

Ramamurti, Ravi, and Raymond Vernon, eds., 1991. *Privatization and Control of State-Owned Enterprises*. Washington: World Bank.

Ramanadham, V. V., 1984. *The Nature of Public Enterprise*. London: Croom Helm.

______, ed., 1986. *Public Enterprise: Studies in Organizational Structure*. London: Cass.

Robson, W. A., 1962. *Nationalized Industry and Public Ownership*. 2d ed. London: Allen & Unwin.

Sadique, Abu Sharaf H. K., ed., 1976. *Public Enterprise in Asia: Studies on Coordination and Control*. Kuala Lumpur: Asian Centre for Development Administration.

Seidman, Harold, 1954. "The Government Corporation: Organization and Controls." *Public Administration Review*, vol. 14 (Summer): 183–192.

______, 1983. "Public Enterprise Autonomy: Need for a New Theory." *International Review of Administrative Sciences*, vol. 49: 65–72.

______, 1988. "The Quasi World of the Federal Government." *The Brookings Review*, vol. 6 (Summer): 23–27.

Sharkansky, Ira, 1979. *Wither the State: Politics and Public Enterprise in Three Countries*. Chatham, NJ: Chatham.

Shirley, Mary, and John Nellis, 1991. *Public Enterprise Reform: The Lessons of Experience*. Washington, DC: World Bank.

Suarez, Ricardo Acosta, ed., 1985. *The Management of Interlinkages*. Ljubljana: International Center for Public Enterprises in Developing Countries.

Thurston, John, 1937. *Government Proprietary Corporations in the English-Speaking Countries*. Cambridge, MA: Harvard University Press.

UN Development Administration Division, 1986. *The Role of the Public Sector in the Mobilization of Domestic Financial Resources in Developing Countries.* New York: United Nations.

UN Technical Assistance Administration, 1954. *Some Problems in the Organization and Administration of Public Enterprises in the Industrial Field.* New York: United Nations.

Verney, D. V., 1959. *Public Enterprise in Sweden.* Liverpool: Liverpool University Press.

Vintera, Jan, et al., 1967. *The Role of Public Enterprises in the Formulation and Implementation of Development Plans in Centrally Planned Economies.* New York: United Nations.

Vratusa, Anton, et al., 1985. *Essays on Relations Between Governments and Public Enterprises.* Ljubljana: International Center for Public Enterprises in Developing Countries.

Walsh, Annmarie Hauck, 1978. *The Public's Business: The Politics and Practice of Government Corporations.* Cambridge, MA: MIT Press.

Wettenhall, Roger, 1983. "Privatization: A Shifting Frontier Between Private and Public Sectors." *Current Affairs Bulletin* (Sydney), vol. 60 (November): 14–22.

______, 1987. *Public Enterprise and National Development: Selected Essays.* Canberra: Royal Australian Institute of Public Administration, Australian Capital Territory Division.

______, 1990. "Australia's Daring Experiment with Public Enterprise."' In Alexander Kouzmin and Nicholas Scott, eds., *Dynamics in Australian Public Management: Selected Essays.* Melbourne: Macmillan.

______, 1993. "Public Enterprise in an Age of Privatization." *Current Affairs Bulletin* (Sydney), vol. 69 (February): 4–12.

Wettenhall, Roger, and O Nuallain, Colm, eds., 1990. *Public Enterprise Performance Evaluation: Seven Country Studies.* Brussels: International Institute of Administrative Studies.

Part Nine

Human Resources Management

Conceptual Approaches

Descriptive analyses of the features and practices of intergovernmental relations in a given country represent one prominent approach to this topic. Wright (1988, pp. 14–26) sets out a list of items that is commonly used to guide studies of IGR. Five distinctive features are identified: (1) number and types of governmental units, their legal status, and changes over time; (2) the number and types of public officials by jurisdiction and unit, their backgrounds and training, the attitudes and perceptions of their roles and responsibilities, and the actions they normally pursue; (3) the patterns of interaction among and between officials representing various jurisdictions and governmental units; (4) the range of involvement by all public officials—elected and appointed, national and local, executive, legislative, and judicial—especially in the formulation of policies and programs that have impact on more than one unit; and (5) the policies and programs implemented through intergovernmental arrangements, with particular concerns about administrative discretion by official and by unit, control over and flow of fiscal resources, and differential effects of policies and programs delivered via different intergovernmental routes. Typically, descriptive studies of IGR focus on one or more of the above features.

In contrast to the focus on structure common to descriptive studies of IGR, a second analytic strategy, which in the United States of America is one of the most characteristic styles of analyzing IGR, classifies changes and trends in the relations among governments by historical eras or phases. Analysis proceeds by describing the main problems, the most commonly used mechanisms of public action, and the attitudinal and behavioral shifts that typify a given time period. Some analysts use presidential terms (e.g., Nixon's New Federalism, Reagan's New-New Federalism) to characterize changes in IGR (Conlan 1988). Other analysts utilize metaphors to portray the distinctive features of a given phase; for example, one finds references to "layer-cakes" and "marble-cakes," even "fruit cakes," as well as references to "picket-fences," "whiplashes," and "fending-for-yourself" (Grodzins 1966; Stewart 1984). While highly informative about the details of change from one time period to the next, this historical or metaphorical approach to IGR is of limited use as a framework for theory building.

European scholars have adopted a focus on decentralization issues as an analytic approach in keeping with the context of a unitary government

30

Public Personnel Administration

Ronald D. Sylvia,
San Jose State University

The management of a system whereby public agencies recruit, compensate, and discipline their employees. The system is normally characterized by a watchdog differentiation between the structures that perform personnel tasks and structures that protect employee rights and insulate the process from politics.

Wallace Sayre, an expert in public administration, is widely cited as the source of the comment: public and private management systems are fundamentally alike in all unimportant ways (Henry 1995). Public personnel administration is illustrative of this truism because agencies must seek to sustain the highest levels of professionalism in their operations and yet be responsive to the desires of the elected officials whom they serve. Furthermore, the U.S. business culture produces ongoing pressures for government to be more efficient and effective according to the management trends of a particular era. Finally, government agencies must be more responsive than their private sector counterparts in removing any barriers to equality of opportunity because, like the majority, minority citizens are entitled to reasonable access to positions in government. These three themes of balancing merit and accountability, efficiency, and equity have shaped public personnel administration in the United States.

Professionalism Versus Politics

The German sociologist Max Weber (1946) noted in his writing on bureaucracy that a professionally trained administrative corps selected on the basis of individual merit is highly preferable to more traditional systems in which officials gain and retain their positions by virtue of birth or political sponsorship. Western nations began the conversion to professionalism during the nineteenth century. Great Britain undertook its administrative reforms in the 1850s. United States reform efforts in the 1880s were modeled on the British example. France embraced professionalism beginning with the rule of Napoleon. Ferrel Heady noted, in his work on comparative administration (1991), that the career civil service in France has sustained the nation through multiple political and social upheavals. German professionalism was set in place during the Bismarck period in the nineteenth century. German career professionals have served each successive regime regardless of the morality of its guiding ideology.

Patronage and Merit Systems

Because the United States lacked a nobility whose members assumed hereditary positions, the principal obstacle to professionalization was the patronage system of rewarding faithful party members with jobs in government with little regard to their qualifications. Once in place, these patronage appointees engaged in widespread fraud, waste, and abuse. At the extremes, they would authorize payments for equipment and supplies that were never delivered. Another common practice was to pay inflated prices for shoddy work from contractors with whom they were politically affiliated. At the very least, the system often led to the appointment of unqualified persons who would collect government salaries for work that was done poorly or not at all.

To overcome the evils of patronage government adopted merit systems of selection. Under merit, administrative agencies recruit, screen, and appoint employees on the basis of their abilities and training. Merit systems explicitly prohibit the use of political affiliation in the selection of career employees. In Europe, especially France and Germany, this has led to an administrative corps recruited into the lowest professional echelons of the bureaucracy; they then spend their entire careers in government service. France has professional schools which train many of its professional bureaucrats. In both France and Germany, career officials enjoy exceptional levels of authority. In France, bureaucrats are even considered members of the ruling elite and often seek elected office upon retirement.

By contrast, the U.S. civil service was influenced by the Jacksonian notion that any person of normal intelligence was capable of successfully running the government. U.S. civil service systems, therefore, were characterized early on by provisions for persons to enter the bureaucracy laterally at the middle or upper echelons rather than serving their entire careers in government. As a practical matter, however, most current U.S. bureaucracies recruit at the entry level and then promote from within. Generally speaking, the only career professionals in the United States who have sought national elective office upon retirement have come from the military bureaucracy.

Civil Service Systems

U.S. bureaucracies at all levels of government are characterized by the existence of independent citizen commissions that are created to insulate the recruitment process from political interference. Frequently, these commissions oversee personnel bureaucracies that are responsible for all phases of the human resource management. Beginning in the 1970s, however, the merit system protection function frequently was separated from the administration of other personnel functions better to police the process.

The federal government created the United States Civil Service Commission in 1883 to insulate federal recruitment from political interference. The three members of the commission served overlapping terms and no more than two of them could be from a single political party. The object was to replace partisanship with merit in the recruiting process. Soon after, however, the reformers realized that satisfactory employees needed protection from arbitrary discharge if there was to truly be a merit system of government employment. Otherwise, a merit-protected employee could be removed for any reason other than politics and replaced with a partisan of the manager's choosing. This led Congress to adopt the principle of discharge only for cause in 1897 and strict due process protection in 1912 (Sylvia 1994).

The Second Civil Service Act of 1897 defined discharge for cause as removal only for misfeasance (doing the job incorrectly), malfeasance (violations of law or agency policy), or nonfeasance (not performing the duties of the job). Of course, any employee can be terminated if the agency must engage in layoffs to balance its budget. During layoffs, however, agencies must strictly adhere to the principle of seniority. Thus, a more senior satisfactory employee may not be laid off to preserve the employment of a less senior person. The rule is popularly known as "last hired first fired."

Due Process

The Fifth Amendment of the Constitution of the United States specifies that the government of the United States may not deprive citizens of life, liberty, or property without due process of law. Government employees who work under merit systems have been granted a property interest in their jobs by civil service legislation. Federal employees were granted due process protection in 1912 with the Lloyd-LaFollette Act. State and local governments have also adopted rigorous due process standards which have been upheld by the courts. When a supervisor is so dissatisfied with an employee that discharge is believed to be warranted, the supervisor must adhere to the agency's discharge procedures, which must meet certain legal standards prescribed by the courts. This protection is extended to state and local government employees by the Fourteenth Amendment. Because public agencies are also the government, their due process procedures must meet a much higher standard than any private employer.

The due process to which public employees are entitled covers agency actions before as well as after discharge. Before a tenured civil servant can be removed, he or she must receive notice of the impending discharge, an explanation of the reasons for it, and the opportunity to respond to the charges. Thus, a state's civil service rules might specify that an employee must be given a written notice of an impending discharge ten days in advance of a meeting with the supervisor at which time the employee would be given a chance to explain why the discharge should not take place. These predischarge procedures are a check against making a mistake on the part of the supervisor who is acting for the agency. Post-discharge due process protections are even more elaborate.

Tenured employees are generally entitled to post-discharge hearings by an independent hearing examiner when they believe that the discharge was for a reason other than cause or that they did not receive appropriate pre-discharge protections. Some jurisdictions allow for an external review for suspensions and demotions as well as discharge.

Public employees paid a price for these elaborate protections from partisan political manipulations. Under the provisions of the Hatch Act of 1939, federal employees are prohibited from seeking partisan political office while employed by the government. They were prohibited from holding office in a political party and from giving funds to partisan political candidates. These so called Hatch prohibitions were subsequently adopted by state and local governments. Such insulation from partisan concerns was, in some cases, the result of the states own desires to root out the spoils system from program administration. Others passed legislation modeled on the federal Hatch prohibitions to comply with federal requirements that state agencies that expend federal funds must operate under merit systems. More recently, a number of states and the federal government have modified their Hatch rules to enhance the opportunities of public employees to participate in the political process.

Efficiency and Effectiveness

Governments reflect the values of the cultures that produce them. The founders, for example, believed strongly in representative democracy and limited government. The emergence of the industrial U.S. in the second half of the nineteenth and the early twentieth century led to the institutionalization of efficiency and effectiveness as the twin values against which U.S. bureaucracy would thenceforth be judged.

Merit systems have as their goal the selection of the best possible civil service corps (effectiveness). To achieve this, elaborate selection processes that include pencil and paper tests and extensive reference checks were developed that are to screen out the unworthy while searching for the one best person to do the job. These selection systems parallel industry's wholesale adoption of the methods of Frederick Taylor, who believed there was one best way to perform every task. In merit systems, by extension, there must be one best person, if we can only develop systems to find him or her.

The efficiency value was reflected in the development of government classification systems that determine the value of an employee according to the duties, qualifications, and responsibilities prescribed for the position he or she occupies. Duties and responsibilities can be shifted, reassigned, or deleted as necessary to obtain the most efficient configuration to perform a given government function. The federal government undertook uniform classification of employees in 1923.

The selection and classification systems of the federal government were the responsibilities of the Civil Service commission until the government had grown so complex as to render a centralized classification system no longer efficient. The classification act of 1949 delegated the function to the agencies, although the commission retained oversight authority. The commission retained hegemony over the selection process until the Civil Service Reform Act of 1978, when selection too was delegated to the agencies.

Equal Employment Opportunity

The quest for social justice for African Americans, other minorities, and women led to fundamental legislative changes that impact on all phases of public intercourse including political participation and representation, housing, education, and employment. In addition to race, the 1964 Civil Rights Act prohibited discrimination on the basis of religion, ethnicity, color, and gender. Title VII of the Act specifically prohibits discrimination in any phase of employment. Title VII combined with various presidential orders to profoundly alter civil service systems in the United States.

In 1961, newly elected President John Kennedy issued an executive order instructing agencies to engage in self-examination to identify any artificial or fundamentally unfair barriers to minority employment in government. Agencies were also instructed to engage in affirmative action to remove barriers and to reach out to minority communities through such activities as offering the civil service entrance examination on the campuses of predominantly black colleges. President Johnson issued an executive order in 1965 that required government contractors to give assurances that they were equal employment opportunity employers as a condition in the contracting process. The Office of Contract Compliance was created within the Department of Labor to enforce the order.

Oversight of federal agency compliance was assigned to the Civil Service Commission in 1965 even though the Equal Employment Opportunity Commission (EEOC) existed to enforce laws against employment discrimination in the rest of society. The Commission accepted the responsibility reluctantly to keep it out of the hands of the EEOC.

Responsibility for equal employment opportunity and affirmative action provided a built-in contradiction for the commission, which defined its mission as preservation of merit. While the commission struggled with its dilemma, line agencies moved more aggressively to enhance minority employment opportunities. In 1972, the commission reluctantly approved the first use of goals and timetables by the United States Army to increase minority employment. All in all the commission was never comfortable with its role in affirmative action, which in many ways conflicted with its more traditional role as protector of merit. Ultimately, equal employment opportunity enforcement was transferred to the Equal Employment Opportunity Commission under the provisions of the 1978 Civil Service Reform Act.

Affirmative action was for the commission another responsibility that asked it to police itself. Previously, responsibility for recruitment and merit protection had been identified as problematic for the Civil Service Commission by various blue ribbon groups as early as 1936. When it was revealed that commission staff had colluded with officials of the Nixon administration to circumvent the merit selection process, policymakers undertook the most sweeping reforms in almost one hundred years.

The 1978 Civil Service Reform Act

First and foremost, the act expanded the definition of merit. Originally, merit meant selection on the basis of qualifications and prohibited politics as a criterion for selection or discharge. In 1978, the definition was expanded to include equal employment opportunity, equal pay for equal work, efficiency and effectiveness in the use of the federal workforce, and whistleblower protection for those who report fraud, waste, abuse, or gross mismanagement. The act specified a number of structural reforms as well.

The Civil Service Commission was abolished. In its place, the act created an Office of Personnel Management that was directly accountable to the president. This office oversees the personnel process government wide. The act created a Merit System Protection Board to hear complaints of merit violations and employee appeals from adverse personnel actions. An Office of Special Counsel was created to investigate whistleblower charges of fraud, waste, and abuse or gross mismanagement. The act also created a federal Labor Relations Authority to oversee union management relations in the federal government. Significantly, enforcement authority for equal employment opportunity in federal agencies was transferred to the Equal Employment Opportunity Commission, which had enforced the various civil rights acts in the private sector since 1964. The goal of these changes was to create a government employment system that reflected modern U.S. values in employment fairness and government efficiency. In the latter regard, Congress sought to reassert authority over the bureaucracy by making top career officials directly accountable to the elected administrations for whom they work.

Senior Executive Service

The creation of the Senior Executive Service in 1978 may be the most significant alteration of relationships between career civil service employees and their politically appointed overseers in this century. Previously, the top three career grades were divided into ten steps much like lower level grades. Each year, satisfactory employees would advance a step within their grade.

Political appointees of an incoming administration would find themselves in what Hugh Heclo called "a government of strangers." Prior to 1978, new administrations would appoint secretaries and undersecretaries who were eager to put forward the administration's agenda. Their goals, however, could be frustrated by career officials at the top of the bureaucracy who did not agree with the administration. Career officers could frustrate political administrators, not by refusing to perform, but by doing so with an excruciating attention to detail and adherence to bureaucratic rules and procedures. Minimally sufficient compliance was protected by a myriad of civil service regulations that made it virtually impossible to remove them or to withhold merit pay increases.

Since the 1978 reforms, senior executives are collapsed into a single class in which pay is based upon performance and exceptional performers may receive one-time bonuses amounting to many thousands of dollars. To be eligible for these rewards, senior executives must distinguish themselves as program administrators and innovators of extraordinary abilities. Those who do not perform satisfactorily are subject to transfer or demotion back into the lower grades. This ability to remove substandard performers enables policymakers to carry out the mandates that brought their administration to power.

Maintaining one's place in the Senior Executive Service requires career officials to come up with policy initiatives and creative ways for achieving administration goals. When an administration's policies differ dramatically from the values of senior career executives, wholesale turnover in senior positions may occur. Such was the case, for example, when the Reagan administration attempted to depart dramatically from long established policies in the Department of Agriculture.

The blending of professionalization and policy accountability is not unique to the federal government. States such as California adopted systems to make senior career officials accountable to elected leaders years before the federal government. State level systems, moreover, make it easier to remove an uncooperative career official than the federal system. In California, for example, ten days' notice is all that is necessary to reassign a policymaking career official to a lesser position. Federal administrators, by contrast, cannot remove recalcitrant bureaucrats for the first 180 days of the administration.

Recent Events

For 12 years from 1976 to 1988 Presidents Carter and Reagan consistently criticized the federal government, and by extension federal employees, for bureaucratic waste and inefficiency. The 1978 reforms of the civil service system were, in part, a reflection of President Carter's cynicism about government. The Reagan presidency made broadbased attacks on domestic programs with which it disagreed. These resulted in accelerated retirements among senior career employees. And the Office of Personnel Management dramatically reduced federal retirement benefits, making the public service much less appealing than it had been previously.

President George Bush, a long-time public servant, recognized the need to reinvigorate the public service. To this end, he appointed a blue ribbon commission to address the problem. The Volker Commission on the Status of the Public Service reported in 1989 that morale was low and retirements were high. The best and the brightest were leaving government service and recruiting talented young people would prove problematic in the existing negative climate. The Volker Commission was particularly concerned about the ability of agencies to recruit Senior Executives from the ranks of midlevel career officials. The commission noted that continued shortages may cause a reconsideration of the program because, under current rules, 90 percent of an agency's senior executives must be recruited from the career service. Subsequent reforms undertaken by the Clinton administration sought to empower rank and file federal employees.

Reinventing Government

The U.S. fixation with efficiency and effectiveness again manifested itself in the Clinton administration's efforts to reinvent government. In 1993, President Clinton announced that Vice President Al Gore would personally lead a task force that would undertake a "National Performance Review." Among its goals were to hold public employees responsible for program outcomes. The administration also sought ways to cut cumbersome regulations and procedures that serve only to impede efficient program administration. The review also recommended the adoption of customer service orientations by agencies and, wherever practicable, the utilization of market dynamics to enhance agency performance.

An early and logical target for the review team was the cumbersome personnel policy and procedure manual of the federal service. During a hundred-odd years of civil service, the Civil Service Commission and the Office of Personnel Management created volumes of rules regulating every phase of personnel management. The result was thousands of pages of regulation that challenged the patience of administrators seeking to recruit, train, manage, and discipline career employees.

The Gore report proposed to replace the detailed regulations with broad standards that would allow agencies to develop their own procedures. The report recommended that OPM assist agencies as they seek to develop their own examinations and selection processes. The report further recommended that agency classification systems be streamlined. Finally, the report recommended that the rules whereby unsatisfactory employees are removed also be streamlined.

Delegation of selection procedures to the agencies was intended by the 1978 act. The adoption of standards that would allow agencies to develop their own policies and procedures could be accomplished by a presidential order. Altering the classification system or significantly changing the due process protections due federal employees both would require actions by Congress, which have not occurred at this writing.

Reforms of personnel systems have not been unique to the federal government. Many states have also taken the step of separating the personnel administration function from merit protection. Much of the movement to enhance managerial discretion and flexibility through a reduction in rules and regulations was initiated at the local level.

Future Trends

Public personnel systems have been periodically reexamined since their inception. In the future we can anticipate further modifications as professionalism continues to grow as a value regarding government. As the threat of patronage style corruption declines, administrators at all levels of government will be given additional flexibility in how they manage all segments of the people's business including how career employees are recruited.

The decline of patronage, moreover, has led to a reenfranchisement of federal employees who may take a much more active role in politics than was possible under traditional civil service systems. In 1993, President Clinton signed into law legislation which greatly enhances the opportunities for federal employees to participate in the political process short of seeking partisan political office. While they must resign their positions before seeking partisan office, federal employees may contribute to candidates and participate in political campaigns. Much the same phenomenon has transpired at the state and local level, where career employees take an active part in the public lives of their communities.

We also can anticipate continuing pressure from those who seek further modification and expansion of equal employment protections for various groups who will organize and pressure legislatures at various levels to include their members under equal employment opportunity laws. Persons with disabilities, for example, gained such protections under the 1991 Americans with Disabilities Act. Also in the 1990s, gay and lesbian groups gained state-level employment protections under California's equal employment statute. The public debate of the 1990s will doubtlessly continue to focus on affirmative action as those interests who oppose its additional expansion mobilize politically. In short, public personnel systems will continue to evolve along with the values of the culture in which the systems operate.

Bibliography

Ban, Carolyn, and Norma M. Riccucci, eds., 1991. *Public Personnel Management*. New York: Longman Publishing.

Executive Office of the President, National Performance Review, 1993. *From Red Tape to Results: Creating Government That Works Better and Costs Less*. Washington, DC: U.S. Government Printing Office.

Heady, Ferrel, 1991. *Public Administration: A Comparative Perspective*. 4th ed. New York: Marcel Dekker.

Heclo, Hugh, 1977. *A Government of Strangers*. Washington, DC: The Brookings Institution.

Henry, Nicholas, 1995. *Public Administration and Public Affairs*. 6th ed. Englewood Cliffs, NJ: Prentice-Hall.

Ingraham, Patricia W., and David H. Rosenbloom, eds., 1992. *The Promise and Paradox of Civil Service Reform*. Pittsburgh, PA: University of Pittsburgh Press.

Klingner, Donald E., and John Nalbandian, 1993. *Public Personnel Management: Contexts and Strategies*. 3d ed. Englewood Cliffs, NJ: Prentice-Hall.

National Commission on the Public Service Task Force, 1989. *Rebuilding the Public Service*. Washington, DC: National Commission on the Public Service.

Sylvia, Ronald D., 1994. *Public Personnel Administration*. Belmont, CA: Wadsworth.

Taylor, Frederick W., 1967. *The Principles of Scientific Management*. New York: Norton.

Thompson, Frank J., ed., 1979. *Classics of Public Personnel Administration*. Oak Park, IL: Moore Publishing.

Weber, Max, 1946. *Essays in Sociology*. Trans. by H. H. Gerth and C. Wright Mills. New York.: Oxford University Press.

31

MENTORING

Steven W. Hays,
University of South Carolina

The use of more experienced employees to assist with the orientation, training, and career advancement of newer workers. A "mentor" is "someone with whom you had a relationship at any stage of your career in which he or she took a personal interest in your career and helped to promote you and who guided or sponsored you" (Roche 1979, p. 14). As such, mentoring is an inexpensive and relatively unstructured means of career development. Understandably, it is extremely commonplace. One survey found that over 70 percent of all public managers benefit from two or more mentors during their careers (Henderson 1985).

The vast majority of mentoring relationships arise spontaneously. Older workers take younger workers "under their wings" in order to "show them the ropes." This approach is called informal mentoring; it probably occurs every day in every organization. Often, the contact is so subtle that one or even both of the participants may not recognize that mentoring is taking place. Helpful information concerning organizational norms and professional expectations is transferred, but neither party consciously considers the relationship to be that of mentor/protégé. In many other situations, conversely, employees may aggressively seek out a mentor (also referred to as "patron" or "sponsor") for direction and support. Similarly, some senior managers derive great satisfaction from the mentor role; they continuously search for new subordinates on whom they can "leave their stamp."

Formal mentoring, in contrast, occurs when an organization expressly assigns experienced employees to serve as teachers and role models for subordinates (and, in some cases, for newly arriving peers). Whereas informal mentorships are not managed, structured, or technically recognized by the organization, formal mentor programs are intentionally designed to fulfill specific career management objectives. Some agencies, for example, assign mentors to all junior management personnel, or to anyone newly promoted to a supervisory position, as part of their orientation and socialization efforts. Recently, the practice of assigning senior faculty members to mentor junior faculty has almost become routine in higher education. As the advantages of mentoring programs have become known, formal efforts to foster mentor/protégé relationships have ballooned throughout government.

Historical Background

For something as ubiquitous as mentor relationships, it is not possible to ascertain specific historical stages or momentous events. Mentoring has always "just happened," a reality that is evident in literature and history. Virtually any chronicle of human behavior, from the Bible to Machiavelli's *The Prince*, contains plentiful allusions to mentors and protégés. The term itself is borrowed from the *Odyssey*; Mentor was the wise guardian who was appointed by Odysseus to protect Telemachus as he departed for the Trojan War.

Because mentoring is closely related to affiliation and friendship—differentiated only by the fact that it occurs within an organizational context—it is a pervasive phenomenon that cannot easily be studied. Thus, the management literature has only recently begun to take notice of the inherent significance that mentoring can play in an individual's professional development. Whereas research on mentors was once exceedingly sparse, greatly increased attention has been devoted to the topic during the past 10 to 15 years.

Without question, the primary catalyst for the growing interest in mentoring was the widespread influx of women and minorities into management positions. By the 1970s, researchers were preoccupied with identifying the organizational factors that enhance or impede the career progress of nontraditional managers. The mentor/protégé relationship was soon identified as a potential problem area for two reasons. Since women and minorities are sometimes viewed as interlopers (or, at a minimum, as "different"), they are thought to be less likely to attract the services of mentors. This dilemma is exacerbated by the paucity of women and minorities in high-level positions. With few white male volunteers, and with a shortage of role models who are available to serve in a mentor capacity, women and minorities appear to operate at a decided disadvantage to the white male managers, who typically enjoy plentiful mentor opportunities. Concern over this situation has heightened as research reveals the many advantages that accrue to well-mentored subordinates.

Functions and Benefits of Mentoring

If, as the adage goes, "experience is the best teacher," then mentoring is clearly an effective way to communicate knowledge to new workers. An immediate advantage that appeals to most managers is that a mentor system is virtually cost-free. Because mentoring activities occur on-the-job, there is no "down-time" while a worker is sent elsewhere for job-specific training. Likewise, even a sophisticated mentor program can be established with little outlay of resources. Once mentors and protégés are matched together, the organization's role is largely confined to monitoring progress and (in a highly progressive setting) rewarding employees who prove to be enthusiastic and effective mentors. Otherwise, little proactive effort is required on the organization's part.

The work context in which it takes place also makes mentoring an attractive training technique. The trainer and apprentice may work side-by-side, allowing for instantaneous feedback and reinforcement as complex tasks are learned. One frequently cited example is that of police patrol teams, in which a rookie is paired with an experienced officer. Under this apprentice-like system, job skills are learned while the employee is making a productive contribution to the agency's mission.

For the employee who is lucky enough to have an attentive mentor, the benefits can be profound. According to K. E. Kram (1985), the mentoring process consists of both a "career" function and a "psychosocial" function. The career activities are related to such services as coaching, being shielded from adverse assignments, and receiving access to important networks or work teams. The psychosocial function is reflected in the provision of a nurturing environment in which the mentor provides advice and guidance in a relatively nonjudgmental mode.

The specific benefits of a mentoring relationship have been summarized as follows: (1) acquisition of organizational norms and values, (2) socialization into the organization, (3) coping with structural barriers in the organization, (4) gaining information on career path experience, and

(5) advancement (Hale 1992, p. 89). To this impressive list can be added such related advantages as exposure and visibility, counseling, protection, friendship, and the acquisition of challenging assignments.

A considerable body of research suggests that these benefits of mentoring are real. Individuals who receive personal attention from mentors report significantly higher levels of career success and satisfaction than employees who are not mentored. Extensive mentorship experience also correlates with the absolute number of promotions and with salary growth (Dreher and Ash 1990). These striking advantages of mentorship are thought to be related to the assistance that mentors give their protégés in the area of organizational socialization. They "guide and protect" the subordinate and "convey the necessary knowledge and information concerning organizational history, politics, people, and performance" (Chao et al. 1992, p. 622). Clearly, workers who have access to this type of information concerning their organization's "realpolitik" have a marked advantage over those who do not.

In summarizing much of the research, Mary Hale (1992) concludes that the career enhancement benefits of mentoring are largely attributable to four factors. First, mentored workers are more successful at "coping successfully with organizational barriers" (p. 92), thanks to the advice and counsel of individuals who have already negotiated the bureaucratic maze. Second, because of the access provided by their mentors, they are better able to cultivate linkages with influential decisionmakers and to gain membership on successful teams. Third, they are more likely than unmentored workers to be aware of critical information that assists them in making career choices. Knowledge about career options, salary expectations, and professional development opportunities provides them with a tactical advantage over their competitors. Finally, mentoring relationships have been found to enhance workers' job and career satisfaction. Dee Henderson (1985) found that mentored employees enjoy their jobs more than other workers, are more likely to risk relocating during their careers, and tend to reach executive levels at earlier ages. In sum, the evidence is overwhelming that mentors provide a valuable service to workers striving to climb the organizational ladder.

Although most research attention has focused on the advantages to workers, the mentors themselves also derive certain benefits from the relationships. The psychosocial rewards are mutual in that both the superior and subordinate can enjoy the friendship and comradery that often exist between teacher and protégé. Many individuals are also motivated by the simple satisfaction that is gained from passing on wisdom and developing the next generation of managers (Aldag and Stearns 1987). Their interactions with subordinates, meanwhile, usually intensify the workers' loyalty to the mentor. Thus, managers who are generous with their mentoring talents are usually quite popular among subordinates.

Another important consideration is that one's reputation as a manager, both inside and outside the organization, can be greatly embellished through the mentoring process. Employees who are known for cultivating and nurturing the skills of their subordinates are treasured commodities. They have no difficulty attracting the best assistants to work with them, and they are in great demand by other organizations. One needs only to look at the coaching fraternity to appreciate these realities. The most successful coaches—those who are "household names"—are almost always the best mentors, as evidenced by the number of former assistants who have gone on to productive careers of their own. Interestingly, an identical phenomenon exists in city management, where a few beloved "deans" of the profession are nationally known for developing and refining their former assistants' skills.

Other Research Findings

In general, mentor relationships are most common—and probably most helpful—early in one's career. However, even older managers report significant levels of mentor involvement in many settings. Public executives are more likely than their private-sector counterparts to acquire external mentors, such as college professors or acquaintances in different organizations. Also, the organizational rank of public-sector mentors tends to be higher than those in business and industry. Public managers are much more likely to receive tutoring from a top official—such as an agency director or city manager—than is the typical business worker. Reduced levels of competition, coupled with the public service ethos, have been suggested as possible explanations for this phenomenon.

As mentioned earlier, women reportedly face a particularly difficult challenge in finding effective mentors. Much of the evidence is inconclusive and/or contradictory concerning the severity of this problem. It appears as if women generally have mentors with about the same frequency as men (Hale 1992), or perhaps at even a slightly higher frequency (Henderson 1985).

The primary difference between the two genders is that there is a strong same-sex bias. That is, both men and women prefer to have mentors of their own sex. This preference is partly attributable to sexual tensions between opposite gender pairs. Women are reluctant to initiate mentoring relationships with men because their action may be misconstrued as sexual advances (Ragins and Cotton 1993). Also, same-sex pairings are thought to be more effective because women and men need and expect different types of support from their mentors. Women are in greater need of assistance in such areas as building self-confidence, improving self-awareness of management style, and balancing career and family obligations (Hale 1992, p. 101). Men, in contrast, are more often concerned with tactical considerations and improving task-related skills. The chief consequence of these preferences is that successful women managers are overburdened with requests for mentor assistance from their female subordinates.

Designing Mentor Programs

Managers seeking to maximize the benefits of mentor programs need to consider the differences between the formal and informal approaches. Although having any mentor program is better than not having one at all, mentoring relationships engineered through a formal program are less fruitful than those that arise naturally from personal attraction (Chao et al. 1992). The satisfaction level of workers in informal arrangements is higher, and they report more promotions and salary increases than those in formally sanctioned programs. These differences may be linked to the bad matches that will inevitably result when mentors are assigned and to resentment that is probably generated on both sides of the relationship. The mentor may resent the time and energy demands of the assignment, while the protégé may feel uncomfortable (or even demeaned) by the arrangement. Another potential dilemma is that mentoring may result in a mutual dependency relationship under which the employee loses self-sufficiency and the mentor refuses to "let go" (Vertz 1985). For these reasons, managers who simply assign mentors to new workers are probably following the least effective path.

Short of assigning mentors to all upwardly mobile employees, then, what can management safely do to encourage these relationships? First, most experts agree that managers should target certain groups of workers. One logical application is to the transitional employee who has just been promoted to a managerial position from a technical or professional specialty. Whenever such mentorships are arranged, however, participation should be strictly voluntary for both teacher and protégé. Moreover, the mentorship program should be part of a broader career-planning effort (Phillips-Jones 1983) that also includes peer counseling and structured professional development opportunities.

Another step that managers can take to promote the development of mentor activities is to elevate their visibility within the organization. Perhaps the most effective strategy is to provide potential mentors with training on their roles and responsibilities. This might be supplemented with sessions designed to sensitize managers to the gender-based problems that sometimes surface between opposite-sex pairs.

Some organizations have also discovered that they can foster mentorships by providing increased opportunities for worker interaction. Networking breakfasts and weekend retreats can place workers in situations that encourage informal associations. Often, the truly meaningful mentorships arise from these types of low-pressure contact between superiors and subordinates.

A final step that might be taken to solidify the importance of mentor programs in managers' minds is to include them in the organization's incentive system. If managers receive formal recognition for their mentoring efforts, more are likely to volunteer and to invest the requisite energies in the task. Thus, the inclusion of mentorships in the annual evaluation process, or in salary determinations, is a nonintrusive but highly effective means of encouraging this form of employee development activity.

Bibliography

Aldag, R. J., and T. M. Stearns, 1987. *Management*. Cincinnati, OH: South-Western Publishing, 834–835.

Chao, G., P. Walz, and P. Gardner, 1992. "Formal and Informal Mentorships: A Comparison of the Mentoring Functions and Contrasts with Nonmentored Counterparts." *Personnel Psychology*, vol. 45 (Autumn): 619–636.

Dreher, F., and R. Ash, 1990. "A Comparative Study of Mentoring Among Men and Women in Managerial, Professional, and Technical Positions." *Journal of Applied Psychology*, vol. 75 (Summer): 539–546.

Hale, Mary M., 1992. "Mentoring." In Mary E. Guy, ed., *Women and Men of the States*. Armonk, New York: M. E. Sharpe, 89–108.

Hays, Steve W., and Richard C. Kearney, 1995. "Promotion of Personnel—Career Advancement." In Jack Rabin, Thomas Vocino, W. Bartley Hildreth, and Gerald Miller, eds., *Handbook of Public Personnel Administration*. New York: Marcel Dekker, 499–529.

Henderson, Dee, 1985. "Enlightened Menoring: A Characteristic of Public Management Professionalism." *Public Administration Review*, vol. 45 (November-December): 857–863.

Kram, K. E., 1985. *Mentoring at Work: Developmental Relationships in Organizational Life*. Glenview, IL: Scott, Foresman.

Phillips-Jones, L., 1983. "Establishing a Formalized Mentoring Program." *Training and Development Journal* (February): 38–42.

Ragins, Belle R., and John L. Cotton, 1993. "Wanted: Mentors for Women." *Personnel Journal* (April): 20.

Roche, G., 1979. "Much Ado About Mentors." *Harvard Business Review*, vol. 57 (January–February): 14–28.

Vertz, L., 1985. "Women, Occupational Advancement, and Mentoring: An Analysis of One Public Organization." *Public Administration Review*, vol. 45 (May–June): 415–422.

32

PAY-FOR-PERFORMANCE

Dennis M. Daley,
North Carolina State University, Raleigh

The use of extrinsic monetary incentives to motivate increased or enhanced employee effort and performance (see also **performance appraisal**).

Generally, pay-for-performance is an intricate part of the industrial revolution wherein workers' wages were linked explicitly to the production of specific quantities of a product (piecework). These concerns were reemphasized under Frederick Winslow Taylor's (1856–1915) scientific management movement and the advent of industrial engineering at the end of the nineteenth century (see **Taylor, Frederick W.** and **scientific management**). While Taylor focused on the introduction of productivity-enhancing processes and techniques, later efforts were directed at means of acquiring worker compliance with and motivation in their use.

Very little application of incentive systems was made in the United States to the public sector (outside of the blue-collar, manufacturing functions performed mainly for the military). Since efficiency still had to compete with notions of government as a threat to individual liberty, a highly motivated and effective civil service was not necessarily seen as desirable. Furthermore, market theorists preferred incentive structures that drew the more dynamic individuals to productive business occupations. Insofar as individuals pursuing public employment were concerned, public interest purposes and patriotism were the preferred motivators rather than pecuniary gain.

Even so, merit pay was introduced as part of the positivistic administrative management reforms introduced with the Classification Act of

1923. Exceptional performance was to be rewarded through merit step increases and grade promotion. However, restrictions to prevent favoritism and abuse limited their use. Merit pay soon devolved into a system of automatic annual increases rewarding longevity/loyalty and a means of providing an inflationary cost of living adjustment (COLA).

Pay-for-performance is an application of expectancy theory (see **expectancy theory**). Employee motivation is deemed to be extrinsic and follow the outlines of B. F. Skinner's (1904–1990) operant conditioning models. Expectancy theory posits that employees will be motivated to the extent to which their calculation of the desirability of rewards, the effort required to perform a task, and the probability of successful performance (and of the organization paying off) are viewed favorably. Pay-for-performance schemes concentrate on providing or determining the right balance between extrinsic reward (pay and required effort—performance).

A wide array of extrinsic pay-for-performance schemes exist. The modern pay-for-performance scheme builds upon a base pay system. The salary or wage put "at risk" is such to encourage or motivate the worker without jeopardizing his or her basic financial security. One can address overall individual performance or specific instances; focus can be on group performance at the organizational or team level. Individual systems based on merit pay step increases, annuities, bonuses, and suggestion awards as well as skill-or competency-based approaches abound. In addition group or organization rewards are the focus of gain or goal sharing programs. Performance appraisal systems are the trigger instrument for operationalizing pay-for-performance. The individual performance rating is used to determine which employees are eligible for individual and group awards as well as the amount of reward an individual is entitled to. Management by objectives systems (see **management by objectives**) may also serve as the measurement instrument for a pay-for-performance system (appraisal by objectives formally incorporates MBO into the performance appraisal process).

Merit Pay

Merit step increases, even in systems that are primarily across-the-board longevity awards, are today often modified by the requirement that an employee obtain a minimum (average or fully satisfactory) performance rating in order to be eligible. Mild as such requirements are (less than 5 percent of covered employees are likely to be ineligible), they serve as an incentive encouraging poor performers to improve or to seek opportunities elsewhere.

Merit pay annuities reward the individual's overall performance by an addition to base salary (hence, the term annuity). Because the increased base salary pays dividends throughout the employee's future years, the amount of the pay-for-performance award need be only half that associated with lump-sum bonuses. Currently, a minimum figure of 2.5 percent is suggested (although 5 percent was widely advocated only a few years ago). However, there is little in the way of empirical evidence supporting these figures; they remain, for the most part, the guesses of compensation and benefits experts. What is essential is that the amount be substantial enough from the employee's perspective to serve as a motivating factor. This is likely to depend on both the economic situation and on the individual's relevant equity comparisons. Merit pay annuities may be applied as a set percentage (or dollar) increase added to all who achieve a specified performance rating. On the other hand, different performance rating levels may trigger different percentage (or dollar) increases.

Bonus

The bonus (like the single event suggestion award) is a lump-sum payment. Its advantage is that it recognizes exceptional performance occurring during the year without entailing a commitment to continuous future payments. Because they are one-time rewards, bonuses need to be more substantial than merit pay annuities. A minimum figure of 5 percent is currently suggested; however, results are more likely if bonuses are more on the order of 10 percent or one month's salary at a minimum. Bonuses, like merit pay annuities, can also be prorated to correspond with differing performance rating levels.

While merit annuities and bonuses award overall behavior and results, suggestion systems are attached to specific items. Awards tend to be in the order of 10 percent of the first year's savings or productivity gain. Suggestion programs may also entail various intrinsic rewards (e.g., recognition in newsletters or official meetings in addition to symbolic mementos and trophies). Suggestion systems are designed to unleash the innovative and creative talents of the everyday employee. Successful suggestion systems need to demonstrate that they seriously consider all the suggestions submitted. This may entail offering rewards for meritorious, workable ideas that upper management chooses not to implement.

Suggestion systems often limit awards to 10 percent or a maximum of $10,000. While most ideas are not affected by such limits, it sets a discouraging tone to the whole suggestion program. Mega-awards for extraordinary ideas are analogous to the lottery "big winner." They serve as a very visible public relations advertisement for the success of the suggestion program and encourage others to try their "luck."

Skill-Based Pay

Skill- and competency-based pay rewards employees more for organizational potential than for actual performance. In a way it is an expanded variation of "on-call" pay. Employees are paid extra for possessing the ability to step in and use their acquired skill or competency. In fact, they are paid even if they are never called upon to use their additional skills and competencies. As personnel technicians have narrowly defined "skills," the broader term "competency" has been introduced to represent desired capabilities. The organizational advantage is that needed talent is on call in case of emergency or special circumstances. It allows the organization the ability to temporarily (or permanently) transfer individuals to more needed tasks. In addition to the extra pay, individuals benefit from the intrinsic motivation and revitalization inherent in the learning process and job rotation. They also are able to explore career options without having to abandon their current jobs. Skill- and competency-based pay is also associated with the broadbanding of jobs. An organization's management determines what extra skills or competencies the organization wants or needs. It then pays employees extra who have acquired those skills or competencies; the organization is also very likely to assist employees in acquiring the designated skills or competencies. To continue receiving the extra pay, employees are required periodically to demonstrate proficiency in their skill or competency; the list of needed skills and competencies is also periodically reevaluated by the organization.

One serious problem faced by most pay-for-performance schemes in the public sector is the tendency to cap awards. Locked into older notions of classification pay grades, those who have obtained the maximum pay allowed within their official pay grade may be deemed ineligible for merit annuities or bonuses. Since these awards are touted as being earned through meritorious performance, their denial greatly undermines perceptions not only of the program's efficacy but of organizational fairness as well.

Gain Sharing

Most pay-for-performance systems focus primarily on the individual; however, growing concern for the group or team aspects of the work process is directing attention to group incentives. Total Quality Management (TQM) movements have brought these concerns to the forefront in recent years (see **performance appraisal** for discussion of TQM). While W. Edwards Deming (1900–1993) insisted that the only rewards necessary for TQM were intrinsic, other advocates also embrace the use of extrinsic group rewards.

Gain sharing or goal sharing is the primary group or team incentive system employed to measure and reward organizational performance. It is an outgrowth or refinement of the profit-sharing plans (such as Scanlon, Rucker, or Improshare). Profit sharing focuses on the entire organization and rewards individuals on the basis of its overall performance. Since individual employees materially share in the organization's success, this is expected to motivate their performance.

However, for large or diversified organizations, individuals often do not see how their individual efforts could influence the overall results. Individuals in internal services or staff units also have difficulty in relating their efforts to the overall organization's purpose. Gain sharing addresses those concerns by focusing on organizational subunits instead of the overall organization. Using the organization's budget process and performance management system, savings or productivity gains (in addition to profits) can be used as the basis for group rewards. This enables rewards to be dispensed for staff and service units that reduce costs as well as for units that have made improvements in productivity even if they are still technically losing money.

Gain sharing is quite appealing to public sector organizations. It capitalizes on both the public sector's lack of a profit system and its greater reliance on group processes. As such, gain sharing complements Total Quality Management efforts by providing a mechanism for extrinsic rewards.

A recent refinement to gain sharing has been the notion of goal sharing. Instead of rewards based on documented budget savings, they are tied to the achievement of specified group or team goals. Goals derived from TQM (or strategic planning or MBO) programs are thereby linked to extrinsic rewards for the individual. This serves to assure the individual's attention and motivation.

For gain sharing or goal sharing to be effective, the goals or savings gains must be based on measurable factors under control of employees in the unit. Individual employees must understand what the goals are and feel that they are indeed obtainable through their group's combined teamwork. Employee participation in the selection of the goals is an added means for ensuring understanding and sense of stakeholder status.

Related to this is the requirement that payout pools for gain sharing or goal sharing rewards also be readily understood. Complex formulas or the manipulation of payout formulas undermine confidence in the system's efficacy. Upward adjustments or the ratcheting of expected performance rates or goals also undermine employee confidence.

Payout pools should link together an identifiable "community of interest." Employees must see the people in their pool as being part of a team. The distribution of gain sharing or goal sharing rewards can be across the board (in terms of actual dollars or percentages). It can be linked to individual performance appraisals as an eligibility factor or as a prorating device. It can even be left for the employees themselves to decide.

Variations

The application of pay-for-performance is, at best, erratic if not somewhat faddish. While at any one time many governmental jurisdictions claim to employ one or another of the pay-for-performance schemes, most efforts are limited to short one- to two-year experiments. Comparatively few long-term examples exist. Merit pay systems which are the most often cited examples are seldom more than annual longevity awards or across-the-board pay increases (little distinguished from cost of living adjustments).

The market-oriented, pay-for-performance concept has its strongest appeal in the United States. Other nations currently showing an interest in this concept tend to rely upon U.S. examples. In many other countries the public service already represents one of the more highly prestigious and paid occupations, often a generalist administrative elite drawn predominantly from their society's upper and educated classes. Without recruitment and retention problems extrinsic pay-for-performance systems are not as necessary. With greater emphasis placed upon public or community interests, intrinsic rewards and honors serve as more substantial motivators. These intrinsic factors are reinforced by the somewhat elitist or "aristocratic" aspect of these societies. In nations such as France and

Japan, for example, extrinsic awards in the form of highly paid "early retirement" job placements exist. Group rewards and bonuses, albeit relatively small in size, are found in some nations such as Japan.

Bibliography

Graham-Moore, Brian, and Timothy L. Ross, 1990. *Gainsharing: Plans for Improving Performance*. Washington, DC: BNA Books.

Greiner, John M., Harry P. Hatry, Margo P. Koss, Annie P. Millar, and Jane P. Woodward, 1981. *Productivity and Motivation: A Review of State and Local Government Initiatives*. Washington, DC: Urban Institute.

Lawler III, Edward E., 1990. *Strategic Pay: Aligning Organizational Strategies and Pay Systems*. San Francisco, CA: Jossey-Bass.

Milkovich, George T., and Alexandra K. Wigdor, eds., with Ranae F. Broderick and Anne S. Mavor, 1991. *Pay for Performance: Evaluating Performance Appraisal and Merit Pay*. Washington, DC: National Academy Press.

33

WORKFORCE DIVERSITY

Donald E. Klingner,
Florida International University

The fundamental change in the composition of an organization's workforce that is now occurring in the United States and other developed countries as their cultures and populations become increasingly diverse. This demographic diversity is accompanied by economic pressures, as technological change and globalization of the economy increase public and private employers' demands for a highly trained workforce. And political pressures by women, minorities, older workers, immigrants, and persons with disabilities have resulted in legal changes in the employment rights of groups formerly excluded by law or custom from desirable professional and technical jobs (see **discrimination, age; discrimination, disability; discrimination, gender; discrimination, racial**). As a result of these changes, organizations need to design and implement workforce diversification programs. These involve subtle but sweeping changes in how they do business: changes in organizational mission, culture, policy, and practice.

Because workforce diversity is caused by the impact of societal changes on organizations, the organizational changes it causes are not isolated. Rather, they are related to other emergent trends in public personnel management such as targeted recruitment, employee development, total quality management, and nonadversarial dispute resolution. But they also conflict with other emergent human resource management trends caused by the same pressures: alternative methods of service delivery, temporary employment, and job simplification.

The changes caused by workforce diversification generate changed role expectations for all groups in public agencies: appointed and elected officials, managers and supervisors, employees, and public personnel managers. Because the objectives and underlying assumptions of diversification programs conflict with those of other prevalent management trends, workforce diversification programs generate conflicts that make effective performance by each group more difficult and demanding.

There are many examples of successful and unsuccessful workforce diversification programs in a range of public- and private-sector organizations. And successful programs generally share common characteristics, as do unsuccessful ones. This entry will

1. define workforce diversity and workforce diversification;
2. discuss its origin and history;
3. distinguish workforce diversification from equal employment opportunity and affirmative action;
4. examine its impact on organizational mission, culture, and five areas of personnel management policy and practice: recruitment and retention, job design, education and training, benefits and rewards, and performance measurement and improvement;
5. show its connection to some contemporary public management trends such as employee involvement and participation, employee development, total quality management, and nonadversarial dispute resolution; and its conflicts with other trends such as temporary employment, cost containment, and job simplification;
6. explore how workforce diversification changes role expectations and causes role conflict for elected officials and public administrators (managers, supervisors, employees, human resource managers, and affirmative action compliance specialists);
7. present successful and unsuccessful examples of workforce diversification programs; and based on these examples, describe the characteristics of successful programs, and unsuccessful ones.

Definitions: Workforce Diversity and Workforce Diversification

Workforce diversity is a term that describes the range of employee characteristics that are increasingly present in the contemporary workforce of the United States and other developed countries. Although disagreement does exist over the specific definition of diversity, for our purposes it includes differences in employee and applicant characteristics (race, gender, ethnicity, national origin, language, religion, age, education, intelligence, and disabilities) that constitute the range of variation among human beings in the workforce.

Workforce diversification is a set of changes in organizational mission, culture, policies, and programs designed to enhance an organization's effectiveness by shifting its focus from tolerating diversity to embracing diversity. In public agencies, a diversification program includes a range of personnel functions: job design, recruitment and retention, pay and benefits, orientation and training, and performance evaluation and improvement.

Origin and History of Workforce Diversity

Workforce diversity has its origins in complex and interactive social, economic, political, and legal changes that are taking place in Europe, the United States, and other developed nations today.

The workforce in modern industrialized nations is becoming socially more diverse. In the United States, it is comprised increasingly of immigrants whose primary language is not English and whose primary norms are not those of "mainstream" American culture. And in the United States, for example, only 15 percent of the increase in the work force between 1985 and 2000 will be white, non-Hispanic males; 64 percent of the growth will be women; and the remaining 31 percent will comprise non-white males (native-born and immigrant) (Jamieson and O'Mara 1991). It will be older. And new and current workers will require technical and professional skills increasingly in short supply because of growing deficiencies in our educational system (Johnston and Packer 1987).

Workforce diversity is not an isolated social change. It results from increasing economic pressures for organizations to remain competitive in the new global economy. Organizations strive for diversity because an organization that effectively manages diversity is more effective at producing goods or services suitable for a diverse market. And a diverse organization is more effective at selling them, because consumers from diverse groups are attracted to the products or services of an organization that is attuned to their culture, language, and values.

Workforce diversity is also based on increased political power and legal protection of diverse groups, as these groups evolve through several stages of empowerment and protection. First, members of diverse groups are almost automatically excluded from the workforce, except for unskilled positions, because they are outside the "mainstream" culture. This exclusion may be based in law as well as custom. Second, as economic development and labor shortages increase, these groups are admitted into the labor market, although they face continued economic and legal discrimination and are excluded from consideration for desirable professional and technical positions. Third, as economic development and labor shortages continue, and as their political power continues to increase, group members are accepted for a range of positions, and their employment rights are protected by laws guaranteeing equal employment access (equal employment opportunity). Fourth, as these groups become increasingly powerful politically, efforts to reduce the considerable informal discrimination that continues in recruitment, promotion, pay, and benefits lead to establishment of workplace policies such as salary equality and employment proportionate with their representation in the labor market. Achievement of these goals is encouraged by voluntary affirmative action programs. If voluntary achievement efforts are unsuccessful, conformance may be mandated by affirmative action compliance agencies or court orders. Fifth, continued social and political changes lead to the welcoming of diversity as a desirable political and social condition, and continued economic pressures lead to the development of workforce diversification programs for organizations that desire to remain competitive.

These stages in the evolution of political power and legal protection for diverse groups in the workforce are shown in Table 33.1.

Difference Between Diversification, Equal Employment Opportunity, and Affirmative Action

Because the workforce diversification programs found in the contemporary workplace are the current stage of an evolutionary process defined by increased social participation, political power, and legal protection for minorities, it is understandable that some people consider workforce diversification programs to be simple "old wine in new bottles"—a contemporary variant on the equal employment opportunity or affirmative

TABLE 33.1 Political Power and Legal Protection for Diverse Groups in the Workforce

Stage	*Employment Status*	*Legal Protections*
1	excluded from the workforce	none
2	admitted to the workforce, but excluded from desirable jobs	none
3	accepted into the workforce	equal employment opportunity laws and programs
4	recruited into the workforce	affirmative action laws
5	welcomed into the workforce	diversification programs

action programs that have characterized personnel management in the United States for the past 30 years. However, workforce diversification differs from equal employment opportunity or affirmative action programs in five important respects.

First, their purposes are different. Equal employment opportunity programs are based on organizational efforts to avoid violating employees' or applicants' legal or constitutional rights. And affirmative programs are based on organizational efforts to achieve proportional representation of selected groups. But workforce diversification programs originate from managers' objectives of increasing organizational productivity and effectiveness.

Second, diversification programs include all employees, not just employees in specified groups. Affirmative action laws protect only the employment rights of designated categories of persons (in the United States such groups as Blacks, Hispanics, Native Americans, Asian Americans, workers over 40, women, and Americans with disabilities). But workforce diversification programs are based on recognition not only of these protected groups, but also of the entire spectrum of characteristics (knowledge, skills, and abilities) that managers and personnel directors need to recognize and factor into personnel decisions in order to acquire and develop a productive workforce.

Third, workforce diversification programs affect a broader range of organizational activities. Affirmative action programs emphasize recruitment, selection, and sometimes promotion because those are the personnel functions most closely tied to proportional representation of protected groups (see **representative bureaucracy**). But workforce diversification programs include all personnel functions related to organizational effectiveness (including recruitment, promotion and retention, job design, pay and benefits, education and training, and performance measurement and improvement).

Fourth, workforce diversification programs have a different locus of control. Affirmative action and equal employment opportunity programs are based on managerial responses to outside compliance agencies' requirements. However, workforce diversification programs originate as internal organizational responses to managerial demands for enhanced productivity and effectiveness (although this response is itself a reaction to demographic changes in overall population).

Fifth, because of all of the above factors, the entire effect of diversification programs is different. Affirmative action programs tend to be viewed negatively by managers and employees, because they are based on a negative premise (What changes must we make in recruitment and selection procedures to demonstrate a "good faith effort" to achieve a representative workforce and thereby avoid sanctions by affirmative action compliance agencies or courts?). In contrast, those workforce diversification programs that are most successful tend to be viewed as positive by managers and employees, because they are based on a different question (What changes can we make in our organization's mission, culture, policies, and programs in order to become more effective and more competitive?).

Impact on Organizational Mission, Culture, Policy, and Practice

Workforce diversification has an impact on organizations that is both sweeping and subtle. It affects their mission, culture, policy, and practice in ways that are obvious and unexpected, cumulative and dramatic.

Impact on Organizational Mission

Workforce diversification encourages changes in the organization's mission, or purpose. It starts from a recognition among managers and personnel professionals that human resources are increasingly vital to organizational survival and effectiveness and that diversification programs are the best way to foster the effective use of human resources (National Performance Review 1993).

Impact on Organizational Culture

Workforce diversification requires changes in organizational culture—the values, assumptions, and communication patterns that characterize interaction among employees. These patterns are invented, discovered, or developed by members of the organization as responses to problems; they become part of the culture as they are taught to new members as the correct way to perceive, think, and feel in relation to these problems (Schein 1981). Viewed from this perspective, diversification is a change in the way organizations do business rather than just an adaptation of existing personnel policies and programs to meet the specialized needs of minorities and women. It is an effort to describe and understand the range of knowledge, skills, and abilities (KSAs) that members of diverse cultures or diverse groups can bring to the workplace. It is an effort to consciously utilize these KSAs as a key to making organizations successful and productive.

Impact on Human Resource Management Policy and Practice

An organization's decision to use workforce diversity to increase effectiveness causes changes in its human resource management policy and practice (see **human resources management**). Policy and practice are the rules and procedures that implement organizational objectives. With respect to workforce diversity, these policies and practices are management's strategic plan for accomplishing its mission through workforce diversification. And they are a message to employees, managers, and political leaders about the value the agency places on diversity in particular and on human resources in general. In an agency with effective human resource management and effective workforce diversification policies and programs, this message is explicit and positive.

Workforce diversification programs affect five specific areas of human resource management policy and practice: recruitment and retention, job design, education and training, benefits and rewards, and performance measurement and improvement (see **recruitment, job design, training and development**, and **performance appraisal**).

Recruitment and Retention. Policies and programs include strategies already commonplace in affirmative action programs: increasing the applicant pool of underrepresented groups, increasing their selection rate by developing valid alternatives for tests that have a disparate impact, and evaluating performance evaluation and mentoring systems so as to encourage retention. Yet, they differ because of the ways workforce diversification differs from affirmative action. Their purpose is productivity enhancement through a diverse workforce rather than legal compliance through recruitment or selection quotas (see **goals and quotas**); they apply to a broader spectrum of applicant and employee characteristics; they include a broader range of personnel activities; their locus of control is internal rather than external, and their tone is positive rather than negative.

Job Design. Also affected in workforce diversification efforts, job design usually leads managers to consider changes in where and how employees do work (Morgan and Tucker 1991). To attract and retain women with child- and elder-care responsibilities into the workforce, options that offer flexibility of work locations and schedules need to be considered. To attract and retain persons with disabilities, reasonable accommodation must be offered to make the workplace physically accessible and to make jobs available to persons who are otherwise qualified to perform the primary duties of the position (ADA 1990).

Education and Training. Programs influenced in two ways by diversification programs. First, employer concerns with the educational preparation of future workers have led to greater employer involvement in areas that used to be considered the domain of public school systems. Workforce training programs now include basic skills unrelated to specific job tasks (such as literacy and English as a second language). And there is increasing interest in strengthening federal and state sponsored job training programs and in sponsoring joint business-government policy initiatives such as tax incentives for costs associated with business training programs. Second, employers now routinely develop and present managerial and supervisory training courses on multicultural awareness and sensitivity.

Pay and Benefit. These policies often become more flexible and innovative as diversification progresses. Because women are the traditional family caregivers, an employer's ability to attract a diverse workforce depends upon providing flexible benefits; benefits for part-time as well as full-time positions, parental leave, child- and elder-care support programs, and phased retirement policies for older workers (see **family leave and flexitime**).

Performance Measurement and Productivity Improvement. These programs often change focus because of the assumptions underlying workforce diversification programs. Managers and supervisors now need to consider the differing values and motivational perspectives of a diverse workforce (Rubaii-Barrett and Beck 1993). Workforce diversity has also brought about changing definitions of productivity based on the need for variation in managerial styles and resultant dramatic increases in organizational effectiveness (Loden and Rosener 1991). And as work teams themselves become more diverse, group evaluation techniques that recognize the importance of individual contributions to work teams also need to be encouraged.

The common threads linking these five areas of personnel policy and practice are their common objective of increased organizational effectiveness and their cumulative impact on organizational culture. Organizations that wish to attract and keep a diversified workforce must change the culture of the organization to create a climate in which persons from diverse groups feel accepted, comfortable, and productive. And this is why the tone of workforce diversification programs differs from their affirmative compliance program predecessors—affirming diversity is different from tolerating or accepting it.

Workforce Diversification and Other Management Trends

Public policy and administration is a river of theory and practice comprising many currents, some conflicting with each other. Thus, it is to be expected that workforce diversification programs are consistent with some contemporary management trends in that they share common assumptions and objectives. And these programs are inconsistent with other trends that derive from opposing assumptions and objectives.

Consistent Management Trends

Workforce diversification programs are consistent with trends such as employee involvement and participation, employee development, total quality management, and nonadversarial dispute resolution.

Employee Involvement and Participation. Considered essential for maintaining high productivity (at least among employees in key professional and technical positions). Even in the absence of significant financial rewards, employees tend to work happily and effectively when they have the necessary skills, see their work as meaningful, feel personally responsible for productivity, and have firsthand knowledge of the actual results of their labor. These psychological states are most likely to result from work designed to incorporate characteristics such as variety, significance, self-control, and feedback. They are the objective of workplace innovations such as delegation, flexible work locations and schedules, job sharing, management by objectives (MBO), and total quality management (TQM).

Employee Development. Related to diversification, at least for key professional and technical employees, because it (1) focuses planning and budget analysis on human resources, (2) facilitates cost-benefit analysis of current training and development activities, and (3) facilitates communication and commitment of organizational goals through employee participation and involvement (Rosow and Zager 1988; and Bernhard and Ingols 1988). This includes training for diversity (Solomon 1993).

Total Quality Management (TQM). An organizational change process that involves a combination of top-down and bottom-up activities: assessment of problems, identification of solutions, and designation of responsibilities for resolving them. It focuses on the connection between the quality of the work environment and the quality of individual, team, and organizational performance (Deming 1988). It is similar to team building and organizational development (French and Bell 1990). And it is congruent with workforce diversification efforts because, like diversification, it focuses on a transformation of organizational culture, policies, and programs so as to enhance productivity.

Nonadversarial Dispute Resolution. A philosophy and practice that has become more common because the challenge of channeling diversity into productivity is complicated by the breadth of expectations members of diverse cultures bring to their work, both as individuals and as members of those cultures. Without a method of settling disputes that models the organization's commitment to tolerance and respect, differences lead only to divisiveness that consumes organizational resources without positive results (Thomas 1990). And there is general recognition that traditional adversarial dispute resolution techniques are not particularly effective at resolving organizational conflicts: They build acrimony, harden bargaining positions, and delay the resolution of the original conflict. Therefore, innovative conflict resolution techniques such as "win-win" negotiation and group problem solving have become more popular. These "nonadversarial" techniques are often more effective, and they have the additional advantage of modeling the organization's commitment to respect, tolerance, and dignity.

Opposing Management Trends

Workforce diversification also conflicts with other current trends in human resource management that are caused by some of the same economic pressures: temporary employment, cost containment, and job simplification.

Temporary and Part-Time Employment

An increasingly common phenomenon in the public and private workplace because it offers managers and personnel managers overwhelming advantages—flexibility, cost control, and circumvention of personnel ceilings or civil service rules. But it does have disadvantages for applicants and some employees in that it has also meant the creation of two segmented labor markets (Doeringer and Piore 1975): a primary market for skilled managerial, professional, and technical positions characterized by high pay, high status, and job security; and a secondary market for less-skilled laborer and service positions characterized by low pay, low status, and employment insecurity. While employers will increasingly utilize minorities and women because of changing workforce demographics and a labor shortage, most new jobs will be created in the service sector and filled through the secondary labor market (Hudson Institute 1988), and most employment opportunities for minorities and women will be in these new jobs rather than in more desirable professional and technical positions filled through primary labor markets. Jobs filled (coincidentally mainly by white males) through the primary labor market have relatively high qualifications, and this marked difference in qualifications creates a "glass ceiling" that hinders development or promotion of employees (particularly minorities and women) from jobs filled through the secondary market (see **glass ceiling**).

Cost Containment

Due to economic pressure, cost containment also runs counter to the pay and benefit innovations fostered by workforce diversification programs in that they lead to reduced pay and benefits for all employees. Professional and technical employees will continue to receive comparatively liberal health benefits to help ensure retention and loyalty. But their pension benefits will continue to be eroded by longer vesting periods, higher retirement ages, and a shift to defined-contribution programs. Their health care benefits will continue to be reduced through increased premiums, longer waiting periods, and benefit limitations. But it will be worse for temporary or part-time employees, who often receive no pension, health care, vacation, or sick leave benefits of any kind.

Job Simplification. Also a logical outcome of the increased use of temporary and part-time employees: Employers are forced to lower skill demands or training costs by "simplifying" rather than by "enriching" jobs. That is, employers invest little, if anything, in training temporary employees. And wherever possible, jobs filled through the secondary labor market are redesigned to minimize knowledge and skill requirements so that even untrained and unmotivated employees can perform them satisfactorily. This means designing jobs with simple and repetitive tasks, rather than giving employees control over a complete job. It makes making quality control a supervisory responsibility (as in traditional, hierarchical organizations) rather than empowering individuals or work teams to perform this function themselves. And for these temporary employees, the relationship between employees and employer is unlikely to be more than an economic transaction (pay for work). The assumptions underlying management of "permanent" professional and technical employees (such as involvement, participation, employee development, and careers) will not apply to temporary employees.

Implications for Elected Officials and Public Administrators

Workforce diversity implies changing role expectations and role conflict for elected officials, managers and supervisors, employees, personnel professionals, and affirmative action compliance specialists charged with developing or implementing personnel management policies in public agencies.

Elected Officials

For elected officials, it means making difficult choices among policy options that often conflict. These include pressures for "reinventing" government that take the form of continued pressure on public agencies to measure outputs, increase efficiency, and enhance political accountability. In public personnel administration, it means the relative ascendancy of political responsiveness and efficiency as values and the need for personnel administrators to work with other systems (besides traditional civil service and collective bargaining) to enable agencies to reach objectives and control costs (Klingner and Nalbandian 1998). And providing public services outside of traditional civil service systems controls the apparent size of the public "bureaucracy" while enhancing opportunities for contracting out. Consequently, much government growth has been through secondary labor market mechanisms and through alternative vehicles for delivering public services: purchase of service contracting, franchise agreements, subsidy arrangements, vouchers, volunteers, self-help, regulatory and tax incentives (International City Management Association 1989). Although it is possible to influence the personnel practices of contractors through minority business programs and "set-asides" (contracting quotas), the use of alternative methods of service delivery reduces the ability of the public sector to directly shape agency mission, culture, policies, and procedures so as to achieve workforce diversity.

Managers and Supervisors

Managers and supervisors are faced with the need to maintain productive organizations in the face of two contradictory truths: It is usually easier to make decisions and resolve conflicts in a homogeneous organization, at least in the short run, and organizations must be adaptable to heterogeneous and shifting environments in order to survive in the long run. This means that managers will continue to be evaluated along two criteria—short-term productivity and changes in organizational culture that enable the organization to enhance long-term effectiveness.

Employees

Employees face the need to communicate, interact, form work teams, resolve conflicts, and make decisions with other employees who may be unlike them in many characteristics. And they will do so in a climate of increased workplace tension due to the transformation of labor markets and increased employment opportunity for skilled and unskilled foreign workers. These changes pit workers against each other, and they pit new applicants against current employees.

Human Resource Managers

As always, human resource managers face the need to manage human resource efficiently and effectively. With respect to workforce diversity, this means the need to develop and apply two apparently contradictory human resource strategies: policies for temporary employees designed to control costs and policies for permanent employees designed to ensure loyalty, participation, and asset development as human resources. Yet, because asset development and cost control are both valid objectives, this ambivalence will continue. And because effective human resource management depends upon the communication of clear and consistent messages, public personnel managers find it increasingly difficult when they must send different messages to different employees.

In general, therefore, workforce diversity is consistent with demands on public officials and administrators for more innovation. Human resource managers who recognize the dynamism and conflict inherent in their roles are more likely to maintain an innovative and appropriate balance between conflicting objectives. But cultivating innovation among public managers requires characteristics usually not present in the culture of contemporary organizations—reward systems that reinforce risk taking and do not penalize failure.

Affirmative Action Compliance Specialists

The transition from affirmative action compliance to workforce diversification presents affirmative action compliance specialists with a difficult dilemma. Traditionally, affirmative action specialists have relied upon their authority as interfaces between the organization and external compliance agencies. Given the five critical differences between affirmative action compliance and workforce diversification, these specialists need to redefine their own role and culture in the organization.

Examples of Workforce Diversity Programs in Practice

There are many examples of successful and unsuccessful workforce diversification programs in a range of private- and public-sector organizations. Examples include the following:

- The National Performance Review (1993) recommended a number of changes to move managers from an orientation toward personnel procedures toward creation and maintenance of a quality, diverse workforce.
- Corning Glass Works evaluates managers on their ability to "create a congenial environment" for diverse employees.
- Mobil Corporation created a special committee of executives to identify high-potential female and minority executive job candidates and to place them in line management positions viewed as critical for advancement through the "glass ceiling" (Morgan and Tucker 1991).
- Robert McCabe, President of Miami-Dade Community College, recently won a MacArthur Foundation Award for educational leadership, including a ten-year emphasis on workforce diversity as a key to community involvement and mission achievement.
- AT&T Bell Laboratories focuses its recruitment efforts on acquiring "the best and the brightest, regardless of race, lifestyle, or physical challenges." This has resulted in a comprehensive diversification program.
- Dallas, Texas, developed a diversification program that involved modifications in the delivery of city services and the formation of a development corporation for an underdeveloped minority area of the city.
- San Diego, California, developed a diversification program that involved a shift in organizational culture and consequent changes in policy and practice.

Characteristics of Effective and Ineffective Programs

In almost all cases, the effort to implement workforce diversification programs starts with both top-level support and efforts of a broad-based committee that assesses organizational culture, sets goals, and suggests policy and program alternatives. If the focus of diversification is an organization, the focus of diversification programs is internal climate, policies, and programs. In large organizations, the policy and program alternative stage may involve the work of several related task forces, each focusing on a defined area of personnel practice such as recruitment and retention. If the focus is an entire city or community, the focus may include economic and social development initiatives as well.

Effective Workforce Diversification Programs

Experts have proposed a relatively uniform set of criteria for assessing the effectiveness of workforce diversity policies and programs. These include

- a broad definition of diversity that includes a range of characteristics rather than only those used to define "protected classes" under existing affirmative action programs;
- a systematic assessment of the existing culture to determine how members at all levels view the present organization;
- top-level initiation of, commitment to, and visibility of workforce diversity as an essential organizational policy rather than as a legal compliance issue or staff function;
- establishment of specific objectives;
- integration into the managerial performance evaluation and reward structure;
- coordination with other activities such as employee development, job design, and TQM; and
- continual evaluation and improvement.

Ineffective Workforce Diversification Programs

Insufficient top-level commitment or organizational visibility generally render diversification efforts unsuccessful because the program's long-term impact on organization mission or culture is inadequate (Denison 1990).

Bibliography

ADA (Americans with Disabilities Act), 1990. P.L. 101–336, July 26, 1990.

Bernhard, H., and C. Ingols, 1988. "Six Lessons for the Corporate Classroom." *Harvard Business Review*, vol. 88 (September-October): 40–48.

Deming, W. Edwards, 1988. *Out of the Crisis*. Cambridge: MIT Center for Advanced Engineering Study.

Denison, Daniel, 1990. *Corporate Culture and Organizational Effectiveness*. New York: Wiley.

Doeringer, Peter, and Michael Piore, 1975. "Unemployment and the 'Dual Labor Market.'" *The Public Interest*, vol. 38: 67–79.

French, Wendell, and C. Bell, 1990. *Organizational Development*. 4th ed. Englewood Cliffs, NJ: Prentice-Hall.

Hudson Institute, 1988. *Opportunity 2000: Creating Affirmative Action Strategies for a Changing Workforce*. Indianapolis: Hudson Institute.

International City Management Association, 1989. *Service Delivery in the 90s: Alternative Approaches for Local Governments*. Washington, DC: ICMA.

Jamieson, David, and Julie O'Mara, 1991. *Managing Workforce 2000*. San Francisco, CA: Jossey-Bass.

Johnston, W., and A. Packer, 1987. *Workforce 2000: Work and Workers for the Twenty-First Century*. Indianapolis: Hudson Institute.

Klingner, Donald, and John Nalbandian, 1998. *Public Personnel Management: Contexts and Strategies*. 4th ed. Englewood Cliffs, NJ: Prentice-Hall.

Loden, Marilyn, and Judy Rosener, 1991. *Workforce America! Managing Employee Diversity as a Vital Resource*. Homewood, IL: Business One Irwin.

Morgan, H., and K. Tucker, 1991. *Companies That Care*. New York: Fireside.

National Performance Review, 1993. *Reinventing Human Resource Management*. Washington, DC: National Performance Review, Office of the Vice President.

Rosow, J., and R. Zager, 1988. *Training—The Corporate Edge*. San Francisco, CA: Jossey-Bass.

Rubaii-Barrett, Nadia, and Ann Beck, 1993. "Minorities in the Majority: Implications for Managing Cultural Diversity." *Public Personnel Management*, vol. 22 (Winter): 503–522.

Schein, Edgar, 1981. *Organizational Culture and Leadership*. San Francisco, CA: Jossey-Bass.

Solomon, Charlene, 1993. "Managing Today's Immigrants." *Personnel Journal*, vol. 72 (February): 57–65.

Thomas, R. Roosevelt, 1990. "From Affirmative Action to Affirming Diversity." *Harvard Business Review*, vol. 68: 107–117.

34

Glass Ceiling

Katherine C. Naff,
San Francisco State University

A term used to describe subtle (almost invisible) barriers that women and minorities face as they try to move up the career ladder in organizations. The term was popularized in the 1980s and applied to women. Later, it was acknowledged that minorities also may face elusive barriers in advancement as well. Often it is said that a glass ceiling exists when women and minorities can see the top of a career ladder, but bump their heads against an invisible obstacle when they try to climb it.

Overt discrimination in employment against women and minorities has been unlawful in the United States since the passage of the Civil Rights Act of 1964, and in the past three decades women and minorities have made significant strides in gaining employment in both the private and public sectors (see **discrimination, gender** and **discrimination, racial**). However, these gains have largely been in entry-level positions and nonminority men continue to hold the vast majority of top level jobs. For example, in its report on the Glass Ceiling Initiative released in 1991, the Department of Labor (DOL) noted that in 94 Fortune 1,000–sized companies it reviewed, women held 37 percent and minorities held nearly 16 percent of jobs. However, in these same companies, less than 7 percent of executives were women and less than 3 percent were minorities. In the federal civil service, 47 percent of jobs are held by woman and 27 percent by minorities. But less than 12 percent of senior executives are women and less than 8 percent are minorities. Similar patterns can be found in most state and local governments, where nonminority men are nearly two-thirds of "officials and administrators."

It is the combination of these two factors—the elimination of most forms of overt discrimination and the increased representation of women and minorities in lower-level jobs—that has focused attention on the glass ceiling. If most overt discrimination has been eliminated, but women and minorities do not enjoy the same opportunities for advancement as equally qualified nonminority men, the assumption is that there are more subtle barriers that are standing in their way. These barriers may not take the form of discriminatory practices that can be addressed through litigation, but are a powerful force nonetheless.

Identifying the Barriers

Because, by definition, the glass ceiling is invisible, it is not always easy to identify. However, research has been able to identify some aspects of organizational culture, attitudes, and stereotypes that have the effect of deterring the vertical progress of women and minorities.

For example, in its analysis of the glass ceiling as it affects women in federal employment, the U.S. Merit Systems Protection Board (MSPB) found that there is a common expectation in government agencies that those who are committed to their careers and serious about advancement must be willing and able to work long hours. This informal criteria for advancement works against women in two ways. First, as women still bear primary responsibility for child rearing, those who have children are often unable to work late into the evening. Even those women who are able to work late are presumed to need to leave at a specific time, and so they are often passed over for significant career-enhancing assignments and promotions. Even though women express the same level of commitment to their jobs as men and receive, on average, higher performance appraisals than men, their potential for advancement is frequently underestimated by managers using these traditional kinds of criteria to evaluate advancement potential. This is an example of what comprises a glass ceiling—a promotion requirement that seems to be gender-neutral, but has an adverse impact on women.

Similarly, women and minorities often confront stereotypes that cast doubt on their competence. For example, a task force studying the glass ceiling in the Canadian public service noted that there is a basic belief that women are better suited to support positions than supervisory or management positions. Another common belief is that women work only because they want to and not because they need to support their families. Women are, therefore, not given the same opportunities for developmental assignments that enhance their promotability. DOL found in its private sector review that minorities are also often steered into staff positions such as human resources, research, or administration, where they do not gain the experience necessary to make them competitive for executive positions.

Women and minorities are also disadvantaged by their "token" status in organizations. As Rosabeth Moss Kanter noted in her now classic work *Men and Women of the Corporation* (1977) when women and minorities are proportionally scarce in an organization or at a particular level, they become highly visible and are much more likely to be stereotyped. Any mistakes they make are immediately noticed, and these mistakes often serve as representatives of their category. For example, once a minority does not meet the expectations for a particular job, it is sometimes assumed that no minority will be suitable for that particular job.

Related Structural Metaphors

These are examples of the kinds of dynamics that operate in very subtle ways to thwart the advancement of women and minorities in organizations. Recently, other metaphors have joined the glass ceiling in describing barriers to the full participation of women and minorities in the workplace. "Glass walls" have come to describe occupational segregation, which results in the propensity for women and minorities to be more heavily concentrated in particular kinds of jobs, usually ones that enjoy little power or prestige. The fact that women are often stuck in jobs that are at such a low level that they cannot imagine even bumping into a glass ceiling (e.g., para-professional, administrative support, or service and maintenance jobs), has been called a "sticky floor."

Bibliography

Kanter, Rosabeth Moss, 1977. *Men and Women of the Corporation*. New York: Basic Books.

Task Force on Barriers to Women in the Public Service, 1990. *Beneath the Veneer: The Report of the Task Force on Barriers to Women in the Public Service*. Ottawa: Canadian Government Publishing Centre.

U.S. Department of Labor, 1991. *A Report on the Glass Ceiling Initiative*. Washington, DC: U.S. Department of Labor.

U.S. Merit Systems Protection Board, 1992. *A Question of Equity: Women and the Glass Ceiling in the Federal Government*. Washington, DC: U.S. Merit Systems Protection Board.

Part Ten

Financial Management

35 ——

FINANCIAL ADMINISTRATION

John L. Mikesell,

Indiana University, Bloomington

The management of financial resources, including the analysis of the fiscal impacts of policy options.

Public financial management seeks to create and preserve value in society by helping public decisionmakers and managers (1) to make choices about how large government should be within the capacity of the overall national economy and according to the preferences of the citizenry; (2) to raise resources from private hands so that they may be put to public use, but doing so in a fashion that minimizes social and economic damage; (3) to allocate and control resources carefully when they have been moved to government supervision so that they suffer neither waste nor misappropriation; and (4) to report periodically on the financial and program results to the public, and to legislative and executive bodies, and external observers.

The aggregate resources of society are mostly in the hands of private owners. They are used in the market economy but some resources are transferred to public use by the coercive power of taxation which democratic societies allow the sovereign only under limited circumstances. Public financial management helps to see that these resources are managed at the margin to achieve the maximum benefit to society. Financial administration choices include balancing the private and public use and the alternate use and timing of use of economic resources, the manner in which the revenue system allocates the cost of pụblic operations among sectors of the private economy, the control of public resources to prevent waste and theft, and the creation and operation of systems to provide overall protection of assets in public control.

In many respects, these tasks closely follow those practiced in the financial management of a private business. Managers try to protect and to add to the value of the private firm by judicious allocation and control of that firm's resources. Differences emerge because the nature of goods and services provided in private markets—the domain of private financial management—is fundamentally different from that of the public sector, which causes the terms of the resource constraints faced, the ownership of goods and services, and the objectives of private and public managers to differ. Many tools and skills are, however, substantially transferrable between the sectors. To understand the role and functions of public financial management these differences need to be made explicit.

Public Versus Private

Governments provide services that, although valued by people, will not be provided in socially desirable amounts by private entities, either proprietary or charitable. Government services are not uniquely essential: most governments leave things necessary to life itself—food, clothing, and shelter—largely to the private sector. Indeed, private markets handle most production and consumption choices, but, as articulated in Richard Musgrave's (1959) concept of the multiple roles of the public household, markets cannot be expected (1) to yield optimal results when the actions of one party have external effect for good or evil on others, (2) to alter inequitable income distributions in socially desirable ways, or (3) to correct problems of inflation or general unemployment that contaminate the aggregate market economy. In these respects, a private entity—which can be expected to seek the best rewards for its owners, with casual attention at best to the interests of others—will not act optimally because that entity cannot recoup the external fruits of its actions. Governments legitimately act, even in an economy driven by strong free market principles, when these circumstances create failure in market provision; public financial management helps with the information and control tasks associated with a response to those failures.

Market failure means that true prices cannot be charged for government services, so services will be financed primarily by exercise of the sovereign coercive power of taxation, not voluntary market exchange.

Services may reasonably be publicly provided if their value is greater than the full resource cost of their production; but what are public services worth? Values of services cannot be deduced from what people are willing to pay for them, because private payments reflect only private value, and market failure means that there is external value. People will not willingly pay for a service when those not paying receive the service as well. Therefore, there can be no easy test of profitability (returns minus cost) to measure success or determine viability.

Contingent valuation techniques offer some promise for estimation of values of some public goods, at least in certain circumstances (Hausman 1993), but most program choices will be judgmental and political. Choices will be made by some government process, hopefully a democratic one in which people get a fair chance to have their say. Public financial management can inform these choices, which, having been made, get implemented through other processes of financial management. Therefore, government fiscal choice differs from business finance: governments may tax to enlarge their resources; many entities share a legitimate stake in government decisions; and the return from government services is neither easy to measure nor conveniently collapsible in a single value.

Values of assets and services and rates of exchange between alternatives and across time must, in a market economy, reflect the preferences of the people living in that society, not those of philosopher-bureaucrats, let alone those of public dictators. This makes the task of policymakers and of those carrying out these kinds of policies more difficult, but capturing the interest of a diverse society is what sets democratic society and governments of democracies apart (Buchanan and Tullock 1965). The process of voting and representation adds complications to fiscal decisions. Some in society can gain without compensation given to those who lose; majorities can inflict considerable cost on minorities through transfers, subsidies, taxation, and expenditure programs driven by ballot victories. It is this problem of redistribution, along with major shortages of information, that prevents public financial management from becoming a computerized routine, even if some way to measure the direct value of public services were devised.

In practice, public financial management involves a mix and merger of skills from economics, finance, and accounting to provide information and options to public decisionmakers and managers, giving service to both executive and legislative roles and responsibilities. Over the years, financial administration has evolved from government record-keeping, documentation and control, and theft prevention to an active role in analyzing policy options, tracking likely impacts of policies under consideration, and performing complex forecasting and fiscal impact estimation. This transformation has occurred as public financial management has integrated the analytical modeling of economics and finance with tasks of control and reporting and as data became both more readily available and subject to quick manipulation through computer information management systems.

Electronic information management systems help capture and organize information, regularly monitor operations, handle laborious calculations, and devise complicated "what if " scenarios to sort the implications from options available for choice. But the technology is a tool of financial management, not the skill itself, serving to speed the processes that could be done manually and with careful human logic.

Roles and Tasks

The roles of public financial management include the future (development of spending and revenue plans and forecasts for future fiscal years), the present (delivery of services and administering revenues in the present fiscal year), and the past (audit and evaluation of the record from prior fiscal years).

Several distinct elements of government operations involve financial management. One facet is the preparation of plans for service and of revenues to finance these services. Plans and priorities for both service delivery and revenues are the province of elected officials, not financial managers. Nevertheless, the analysis used to develop these proposals will be done by fiscal analysis units at the instruction of these officials. The work may involve estimation of the finances of maintaining the present fiscal baseline in the next year, estimation of longer-term implications of continuing the current policies, with best estimates of changing workloads and economic conditions, and preparation of fiscal impact statements for proposed policy changes.

Impact statements (or "scoring," in the terminology of the federal budget process) for either spending or revenue programs may encompass (1) static estimates, the effect assuming no public response from the policy change; (2) feedback estimates, the effect from public response to the microeconomics incentives inherent in the new policy; and (3) dynamic estimates, the effect of macroeconomic change produced by the new policy. The first two elements are regularly used in fiscal analysis; the latter is significantly more controversial. Estimation of baseline programs and revenues use the standard techniques of econometric time series analysis; impact statements employ microsimulations of varying degrees of complexity and sophistication.

Another financial management element of government operations is the control and accounting of expenditure programs that have been adopted. Financial management works to ensure that adopted policies are carried out by controlling expenditure flows as they occur during the fiscal year. The concerns are that spending occurs according to the legislatively adopted plan, that spending does not exceed appropriated ceilings, and that reports prepared during the year reflect the actual financial activity during the year.

Control typically employs regular variance reports in which actual and planned activities are compared and corrections are taken on the basis of differences identified there. Much spending at the federal level occurs through the application of entitlement formulae, so control must focus on formula elements, rather than operations against a formal spending plan. The internal control system within spending agencies represents the first line of defense against fraud. These systems, following the principles of the International Organization of Supreme Audit Institutions, function to safeguard assets, check the accuracy and reliability of financial data, promote operating efficiency, and encourage operation according to the standard prescribed by the agency.

Administering revenue systems to obtain funds for government operations is also a financial management task. Governments collect some revenue from sales of goods or services; for instance, when admission is charged for a state recreation area. In these circumstances, collection procedures are no different than for a private business.

But much more revenue comes from taxes. Here, the government raises revenue through its sovereign authority to coerce payment. As Carl Shoup (1969) has pointed out, taxes are administered in several different formats, distinguishable "according to the degree of participation they require of the taxpayer or his agent, and the kind of response they elicit from the taxpayer" (p. 428). Much revenue in the United States comes from taxpayer active taxes, which require considerable taxpayer responsibility and are collected under the principle of voluntary compliance. Such taxes, the federal individual income tax being an example, require considerable effort on the part of the taxpayer to manage records, make progress payments through the year, and file returns on schedule.

The efforts of the government consist of efforts to induce that compliance. For people to make payments of roughly the correct amount of tax, without direct government action, seems to be the most reasonable course of action so that all honest taxpayers are protected. Most collections result without direct government activity, however.

A few taxes, that on real property being a good example, are taxpayer passive: A government agency maintains records, computes the tax base, applies appropriate rates to yield tax liability, and transmits bills, leaving the taxpayer only to protest or pay. Either taxpayer active or taxpayer passive systems can produce equitable collection of revenue; the former involves higher compliance costs relative to administrative costs. The latter involves higher administrative costs relative to compliance costs. Neither has an automatic advantage in terms of lower total collection cost.

Low total collection cost—the sum of administrative and compliance costs—is the desired goal, but only subject to an administration that gives adequate competitive protection to honest taxpayers and inflicts no arbitrary and capricious discrimination against certain types of taxpayers in the collection process.

A fourth facet of financial management is acquiring goods and services for use during the budget period and husbanding those acquired resources against theft, waste, or misuse. Financial managers seek to procure inputs to government production at the best price to taxpayers. They attempt to arrange for external acquisition (contracting) when others can produce the decided-upon level and quality of service on better terms than the government can produce the service itself, to monitor delivery of inputs and services as purchased, and to protect any assets while in public possession. A considerable share of government spending is for human resources, so the financial manager must monitor the arrangements of public pay most carefully so that taxpayer interests can be guarded.

Management of the treasury, including use of short-term idle cash and short-term credit, is another financial management element of government. Collections are regularly quickened by electronic transfer of collections, especially for large payments; disbursements are controlled to ensure accuracy and that prompt payment discounts are taken if they are advantageous, and, while cash is in the treasury between collection and disbursement, something productive is done with it.

The need for treasury management arises because timing of revenue inflows seldom matches that of government outlays. Tax collections in particular lump around periodic due dates, and capital outlays are similarly irregular. During any fiscal year, a government will have periods of net cash inflows and outflows—including periods of high idle cash balance and, often, of negative cash position, even when the government is in surplus for the year as a whole.

Financial managers have to manage the cash position, because those funds are valuable, investable public assets that can earn interest in short-term cash pool investment. But their management must ensure that payments can be made when due. Liquidity and security of principal are the guides for cash management, thus barring from the treasury idle-funds management portfolio long-term instruments, derivative investments, or other media that experience considerable fluctuation in value and, hence, risk to principal when market interest rates change.

A government operation that involves financial management is the management of benefits paid employees, especially investment management of long-term assets in pension systems. Public employee compensation includes a considerable array of fringe benefits. Among the most important are health insurance and retirement programs. In common with all employers, governments have experienced considerable increase in health costs in recent years. The costs have been particularly great because governments, as a rule, provide more generous coverage than do private employers. Public employee retirement programs generally are of the defined benefit type; that is, employees earn defined benefit payments based on employment history. The employer is responsible for financing the promised future benefits; logic of efficiency and equity suggests that the employer meet these payments in the future from funds set aside during the employee's work life (when the liability for the pension was incurred) so that the cohort of citizens receiving the benefits of that work bear the full cost, wage plus promised benefits, of that work. Any benefit payments not available from that accumulated fund will have to be met from taxpayers in the future. When sufficient assets have been set aside to meet those anticipated future liabilities, the pension system is fully funded. Unfortunately, few public employee pension funds are fully funded, but they do contain sizable asset balances.

Politicians often see these funds as "free money," usable as a slush fund for projects that are locally popular but unlikely to be undertaken by a prudent investor. Furthermore, to miss a scheduled pension fund payment is a frequent strategy when a government is experiencing fiscal stress. Failure to meet pension fund contributions is the equivalent of borrowing to support current expenditure and has the same impact on the long-term fiscal condition of the entity.

Management of debt issued for long-term asset acquisition is yet another management task. Governments regularly borrow to finance the purchase of high-price, long-life assets. When the service of the debt is managed across the years in rough match to the useful life of the project being financed, severe fluctuations in local tax rates during infrastructure development will be reduced. Government finances will not be unduly stretched in periods of such development, and taxpayers in the system at the time of project development do not bear excessive burdens in comparison to those receiving services when the project is in full service. Debt managers work to ensure that debt maturity is no longer than the useful life of the project being financed. They try to see to it that debt service guarantees (insurance, bank letters of credit, etc.) are acquired when their premiums are justified by resulting reductions in service costs that buying the guarantee brings, that agents (underwriters, paying agents, financial advisers, etc.) are retained on best terms for the issuer, that bond features (call provisions, serial structures, etc.) are tailored to reduce overall cost, and so on. Strong overall financial management reduces interest cost by improving the ratings on debt as evaluated by the private rating firms that report their estimates of credit worthiness to capital markets.

Government financial management entails the control of risks and use of insurance against potential liability, including the judicious use of self-insurance. Government operations offer abundant opportunities for hazard to people and property. Reducing loss potential can reduce the cost of providing public services. Tasks of risk management involve control of risk by avoiding, preventing, and reducing conditions that can produce loss and then insuring the risk of loss, which cannot be eliminated. The insurance may be either self-provided (with formal reserve funds, or informally by providing no coverage) or purchased from an outside provider. A number of governments have formed insurance pools, essentially establishing combined self-insurance programs as a risk-sharing alternative to private insurance. The risk-management program seeks to protect the citizenry and public resources against loss in a fashion that combines loss reduction with sufficient insurance to cover when loss occurs.

Government financial management operations entail the audit and evaluation of operations at the end of fiscal periods for compliance and accomplishment. Audits seek to establish whether governments have done what they promised when fiscal plans were enacted. Financial and compliance audits examine and verify financial transactions and reports, seeking to establish the fairness of those reports, whether transactions have been properly conducted, and whether the unit has complied with all applicable law. Economy and efficiency audits examine whether the unit has made wise use of resources under its control and seeks uneconomical practices. Program audits consider whether desired results are being accomplished and whether alternatives might achieve the result at lower cost.

Conclusion

Fiscal administration is the practice of balance and control within the guidance of elected representatives. Financial managers are responsible for analysis, control, and reporting, but the resources involved belong to the public. Public financial management, even when operating with broad discretion, advises and implements policies chosen by others. The choices that must be made involve the balancing of opportunity costs, that is, comparing the gain from one action against the gain that could result if that action were not taken. This is the essence of advising the movement of resources from private to public use, of choices between alternative public uses of resources, of deciding between purchasing insurance and using self-insurance, of opting for pay-as-you-use instead of pay-as-you-go finance of capital assets, and so on. The hard part is getting the trade-offs calibrated so that the choices made by elected officials are likely to be made in the public interest.

When a choice has been made, the problem becomes one of delivery and control. Decisions are irrelevant if attention is not paid to whether the decision is carried out according to the adopted plan. Financial administration works to assure accurate reports, timely comparisons of results against intentions, and implementation of corrections if there is variance. Financial administration, by identifying the trades and maintaining control, plays a critical role both in the process of making policy and in the implementation of those adopted policies.

Bibliography

Aronson, J. Richard, and Eli Schwartz, 1987. *Management Policies in Local Government Finance.* Washington, DC: International City Management Association.

Buchanan, James M., and Gordon Tullock, 1965. *The Calculus of Consent:* Ann Arbor, MI: Ann Arbor Paperbacks.

Coe, Charles K., 1989. *Public Financial Management*. Englewood Cliffs, NJ: Prentice-Hall.

Hausman, Jerry A., ed., 1993. *Contingent Valuation: A Critical Assessment*. New York: North Holland.

Internal Control Standards Committee, International Organization of Supreme Audit Institutions, 1992. *Guidelines for Internal Control Standards*. Washington, DC: International Organization of Supreme Audit Institutions.

Mikesell, John L., 1995. *Fiscal Administration, Analysis and Applications for the Public Sector*. Belmont, CA: Wadsworth.

Musgrave, Richard A., 1959. *The Theory of Public Finance*. New York: McGraw-Hill.

Petersen, John E., and Dennis R. Strachota, eds., 1991. *Local Government Finance, Concepts and Practices*. Chicago: Government Finance Officers Association.

Shoup, Carl S., 1969. *Public Finance*. Chicago: Aldine.

Steiss, Alan Walter, 1989. *Financial Management in Public Organizations*. Pacific Grove, CA: Brooks Cole.

36

Congressional Budget Process

Philip G. Joyce,
Syracuse University

The rules and procedures that affect the consideration of the federal budget, from the presentation of budget recommendations by the president to the enactment of laws affecting taxes and spending.

The federal budget process is not actually a single process. Rather, the term broadly refers to all the rules and procedures that affect presidential proposal and congressional consideration of spending and tax legislation. The Constitution does not establish any specific guidelines for a budget process, and budget procedures have been the subject of considerable debate and discussion throughout history. The majority of the major provisions that govern current consideration of the budget were adopted in the last 75 years. They result from two laws—the Budget and Accounting Act of 1921 and the Congressional Budget and Impoundment Control Act of 1974. In addition, the 1980s and 1990s have seen efforts to use the budget process as a tool for deficit reduction.

History of Congressional Budgeting

Congressional budgeting probably got its start in the late eighteenth century with the development of a standing committee system. In the House, a temporary Committee of Ways and Means was first created on July 24, 1789, to advise the House on matters of public finance. The establishment of a standing committee system in the Senate included a Committee on Finance in 1816 that had parallel jurisdiction over money matters. Control over both revenues and expenditures was centralized in a single committee in each chamber. This was the primary reason that the nation's finances could be coherently maintained even without a formal budget process.

The next major change in the budget process involved separating the authorization process from the appropriations process. This separation is neither mandated nor described in the Constitution. The origin of a formal rule mandating the separation of authorizations and appropriations dates to 1835 when the House discussed the increasing delays in enacting appropriations. Including legislative language in appropriation bills created many of these delays. As early as 1837, the Rules of the House were amended to prohibit legislating in appropriation bills. The Senate did not formally adopt a parallel rule until 1850 when it prohibited amendments proposing additional appropriations unless it was for the purpose of carrying out the provisions of an existing law.

This dispersal of appropriations was compounded by a similar lack of coordination in the executive branch. Executive departments submitted their requests for funds directly to the various committees with spending jurisdiction. Although the Treasury did begin compiling the requests of the various departments into a single "Book of Estimates" in 1878, there was no authority for the president to submit a single, coordinated budget proposal, or for Congress to consider one. The president was thus limited in his ability to influence or coordinate the efforts of cabinet members.

The watershed event in the development of an executive budget system was the passage of the Budget and Accounting Act of 1921. This act required the president to submit a single, consolidated budget proposal for congressional consideration each year. The act also established the Bureau of the Budget (predecessor of the current Office of Management and Budget) to provide the president with the resources necessary to produce such a proposal, and the General Accounting Office, to provide Congress with the resources to ensure accountability. The most important changes resulting from that legislation—the requirement for a presidential budget submission, a central budget office, and the General Accounting Office—remain to this day.

The consolidation of presidential budgets did not carry with it a comprehensive approach by the legislative branch. Congress reduced the portion of the budget under the direct control of the Appropriations Committees, instead using "backdoor spending" techniques that bypassed the annual appropriations process. This trend toward backdoor spending continues to this day. In 1974, discretionary spending represented 53 percent of all federal spending; by 1993, the Appropriations Committees controlled less than 39 percent of this spending. Backdoor spending can be created in several forms:

- Borrowing authority, which allows a federal agency to incur obligations and make payments to liquidate those obligations out of borrowed money;
- Contract authority, which allows agencies to enter into obligations in advance of appropriations and compels the Appropriations Committees to provide subsequent funds for the liquidation of the obligation; or
- Entitlements and mandatory appropriations, which establish an obligation for the federal government to make a payment in advance of appropriations. Many entitlements, such as Social Security and interest on the public debt, are provided by permanent appropriations.

Many observers of congressional budgeting became concerned that the failure of Congress to consider the whole budget (promoted by the proliferation of backdoor spending) was leading to irresponsible results. Irresponsible or not, however, members of Congress generally agreed that this piecemeal approach to the budget constrained Congress's ability to make comprehensive policy. At the same time, President Richard Nixon challenged the spending priorities of the Congress by asserting that he had the authority to refuse to spend (or impound) funds appropriated by Congress.

These concerns prompted Congress in 1973 to create the Joint Study Committee on Budget Control. This committee sought to devise new methods to protect congressional budgetary prerogatives. The Joint Study Committee eventually reported two bills to standing committees of the House and Senate (the Joint Committee itself had no legislative jurisdiction). Ultimately, the move toward a congressional budget process culminated in the passage of the Congressional Budget and Impoundment Control Act of 1974. The act attempted to strengthen the congressional role in the making of the budget by beefing up and centralizing its budgetary capacity. It provided for additional committees and staff. The House and Senate Budget Committees were to coordinate congressional consideration of the budget, and the Congressional Budget Office (CBO) was established as a source of nonpartisan analysis and information relating to the budget and the economy. Indeed, perhaps the most important early role for CBO was to provide economic forecasts to Congress independent of those provided by the executive branch.

In trying to impose some order, the act laid out a specific timetable for action on the budget. The instrument created to coordinate various portions of the budget was the concurrent budget resolution, a form of congressional decision that can bind congressional action but does not require a presidential signature. This resolution, which the Budget Committees were to formulate by April 15 and Congress was to pass no later than May 15 each year, was an opportunity for Congress to act on the budget as a unified whole, and provided a general budget blueprint for the authorizing and appropriations committees. Once the resolution was passed, Congress reverted to its old procedures, but the committees were largely forced to live within the parameters set by the resolution.

To curb the president's ability to circumvent Congress's allocative powers, the act also included a procedure for dealing with impoundments. Two forms of presidential cutbacks were permitted—rescissions (removal of budget authority) and deferrals (delay of budget authority). The president could propose both, but to be effective the former needed explicit congressional approval and the latter tacit acquiescence.

There is general agreement that the Congressional Budget Act has led to a reassertion of the congressional role in budgeting, increased the attention of Congress to the whole budget (as well as to its disparate details), and resulted in the control of impoundments. But the attention to budget totals did not, nor was it intended to, result in achieving budgetary balance.

As the budget deficit grew substantially in the wake of the passage of the Reagan economic program in 1981, Congress increasingly became aware that the budget process could not serve as a constraint against these large deficits. Frustration with large deficits and the inability to contain them ultimately led to the passage in 1985 of the Balanced Budget and Emergency Deficit Control Act of 1985, popularly known as Gramm-Rudman-Hollings (GRH) after the sponsors of the legislation: Senators Phil Gramm (R-TX), Warren Rudman (R-NH), and Ernest Hollings (D-SC). GRH attempted to control the deficit through setting gradually declining deficit targets, and was to result in a balanced budget by fiscal year 1991. If the deficit targets were not met, automatic across-the-board spending reductions, or sequestration, took effect.

The passage of GRH represented a fundamental change in the focus of the budget process. For the first time, the budget process was used to specify a result to be achieved, rather than simply the rules to be followed to achieve any number of different budget outcomes. As such, it was a switch from a focus on rules governing decisions, timing, and priority-setting to rules that specify particular budget results, such as levels of spending and the deficit.

The deficit, of course, did not come down as promised by the Gramm-Rudman-Hollings legislation. In fact, the fiscal year 1993 deficit (which would have been zero if the law, as revised in 1987, had met its goal) was actually $255 billion. The act did put a premium on short-term budgeting; under GRH, all that mattered was the single year for which the projections were being made. These annual targets were complied with through short-term fixes and budget gimmickry, including basing the budget on optimistic economic and technical assumptions, selling assets, and shifting costs between fiscal years.

The successor to Gramm-Rudman-Hollings, the Budget Enforcement Act (BEA), was passed in 1990 and was designed to enforce the five-year deficit reduction agreement reached between the president and Congress in that year. The BEA eliminated annual deficit targets, placed limits on the level of discretionary spending through fiscal year 1995, and established the pay-as-you-go (PAYGO) process to ensure that any tax or mandatory spending changes were deficit neutral. Both the discretionary caps and the PAYGO process are enforced through a sequestration of spending in the offending category—discretionary or mandatory—only. The original Budget Enforcement Act would have expired in 1995; the Omnibus Budget Reconciliation Act of 1993 extended both the discretionary caps and PAYGO until 1998.

The importance of the BEA changes was that they shifted the process away from deficit targets to spending controls. By so doing, they focused attention on those actions that Congress and the president could control (spending and revenue actions), rather than those that they could not (primarily, the performance of the economy). As such, it has been described as a "no-fault" budget process. As long as budget rules are followed, the deficit can grow substantially without anyone being held responsible for the increase.

One of the most important developments to emerge from the 1974 Congressional Budget Act has been reconciliation, which developed into an important procedure for implementing the policy decisions and assumptions embraced in the budget resolution in a way that was unforeseen when the Act was written. Under the original design of the Act, reconciliation had a fairly narrow purpose. It was expected to be used in conjunction with a second budget resolution (since deleted) adopted in the fall, and was to apply to a single fiscal year and be directed primarily at spending and revenue legislation acted on between the adoption of the first and second budget resolutions. Congress has subsequently used the procedure to enact far-reaching omnibus budget bills, first in 1980, but most recently in 1990 and 1993.

The Congressional Budget Process Today

As the description of the evolution of the process suggests, the budget process currently in place has become a complex web of rules and enforcement procedures. The budget comes together as a result of myriad actions affecting revenues and expenditures. There is no single action that dictates all budgetary outcomes. Instead the congressional budget process includes consideration of the budget resolution, revenue measures (both temporary and permanent), appropriations bills (13 regular annual appropriations bills as well as any necessary supplemental appropriations bills or continuing resolutions), and authorizations (including entitlement legislation). In addition to these steps, the process periodically may involve other major decisions, such as the consideration of reconciliation legislation or increases in the statutory debt limit.

In practice, the budget process in Congress is normally initiated by presidential submission of the budget proposal each year, as first required by the Budget and Accounting Act of 1921 (31 U.S.C. 1105 requires the president to submit the budget by the first Monday in February). Congress, however, is not bound by any of the president's assumptions or recommendations, and may originate any budgetary legislation it chooses.

The process of developing a congressional budget formally begins when each committee submits its views and estimates to the House or Senate Budget Committee on all budget matters within their jurisdiction (currently required by February 25 each year). This information, as well as other information gathered or produced by the Budget Committees, is used to construct a concurrent resolution on the budget. The Congressional Budget Act provides a deadline of April 15 for adoption of the budget resolution, but final agreement is often not reached until later, often much later. As adopted, this resolution reflects budgetary priorities and assumptions about how the legislative branch expects to achieve its collective budgetary goals.

The Budget Committees also use baseline estimates prepared by CBO to prepare the budget resolution. The CBO baseline projections attempt to project the budget for the future based on current policy. In the case of revenues and mandatory spending, the projections estimate the conditions (economy, caseloads, etc.) that will be present and forecast what revenues and spending would look like if the laws were not changed. In the case of discretionary spending, baseline projections are done by adjusting current service levels for inflation (the exception is that, through 1998, the levels of discretionary spending are prescribed by the BEA). These baseline estimates, along with the CBO economic forecast, are to be presented prior to February 15 each year. They are updated in August or September. The law also requires OMB to do a mid-session review (the president's budget update) by July 16 of each year.

The budget resolution may, but does not have to, recommend changes in programs governing mandatory spending or revenues. Congress is in no way required to make changes in mandatory spending and revenues as a part of the annual budget process. In recent years, reconciliation has become an important procedure used by Congress to make changes in both entitlements and revenues. Reconciliation is triggered when the budget resolution includes instructions directing congressional committees to achieve savings in tax or spending programs under their jurisdiction. Congressional committees comply with these instructions by reporting to the budget committees proposed changes necessary to implement the revenue and spending targets in the budget resolution. The Budget Committees then package these responses into omnibus measures (called Omnibus Budget Reconciliation Acts, or OBRAs) which are then considered in their respective chambers under special procedures described in the Congressional Budget Act. As with the budget resolution, these provisions impose restrictions on both debate and amendments.

In many years, the focus of attention is on the fate of the annual appropriation bills. The passage of these bills is the only budgetary action absolutely required by Congress each year. Both the Senate and the House subdivide appropriations action into 13 separate bills, considered by appropriations subcommittees with jurisdiction over funding for specific portions of the government. After passage by the House, each bill is then referred to a Senate Appropriations subcommittee with jurisdiction parallel to its House counterpart. (By custom, the House considers all appropriation bills first). The overall level of funding in appropriation bills is constrained by the amount allocated to the Appropriations Committee (as well as suballocations and applicable spending cap restrictions imposed by the Budget Enforcement Act) under the budget resolution.

In addition to the budget resolution limits and Appropriations Committee activity, appropriations for individual programs or agencies may also be influenced in various ways by the authorization process. An authorization is legislation establishing a government entity (such as a department or agency), activity, or program. As substantive law, authorizations are permanent unless otherwise specified. By itself, an authorization generally does not permit any funds to be obligated; it only allows appropriations of such funds to be made. In current practice, authorizations establish government programs, agencies, and duties, as well as use statutory language explicitly to authorize the enactment of appropriations, often specifying specific limits or conditions for appropriations. These authorizations of appropriations serve as ceilings on expenditures, rather than floors.

Overarching all of these procedures for enacting budgetary legislation are the procedures for enforcing budgetary discipline. These procedures are currently codified in the Budget Enforcement Act, as enacted in 1990 and revised in 1993. The Act enforces budget discipline through the dual system of discretionary spending caps and the pay-as-you-go process. If Congress appropriates in excess of a spending cap, a sequester order will be issued by the president to reduce budget authority to the required limit. Revenues and mandatory spending are restricted by pay-as-you-go, which would require that the net effect of new mandatory spending and revenue legislation be deficit neutral. Although the level of mandatory spending and revenues can change due to economic or technical factors, Congress is constrained from making changes that would worsen the deficit. If the net effect of congressional actions would increase the deficit, a sequester order would be issued to reduce nonexempt mandatory spending to the level necessary to bring revenues and mandatory spending back into the required balance.

Budget Process Reform Proposals

Despite the numerous reforms described above, there are various other changes to the congressional process that have been proposed in recent years. Some of these proposals are relatively marginal ones, such as those that would allow limited amounts of additional (above the caps) discretionary spending if they were offset by tax increases or reductions in mandatory spending, or those that would tighten the wide latitude that now exists with the emergency designations. (Under this classification, virtually any spending increase or tax cut can be exempted from the discipline of the BEA if the president and the Congress agree to label the action an emergency.) But others involve more fundamental changes to the existing process. The most frequently discussed of these would amend the Constitution to require the federal budget to be balanced or to grant the president item veto authority. A number of other proposals have been considered as well, including capital budgeting and biennial budgeting.

Balanced Budget Amendment

Amending the Constitution to require a balanced budget would create an ultimate constraint against pressures for spending to outpace revenue. Numerous such balanced budget proposals have been introduced in recent sessions of Congress. Both the House and the Senate defeated proposed balanced budget amendments during 1994. In 1995, the House passed a proposed amendment, but the Senate fell one vote shy of the number needed to send the amendment to the states for ratification.

On the one hand, a balanced budget amendment would almost certainly prove a more restrictive limit than Gramm-Rudman-Hollings or the BEA. Such an amendment, however, would have to be implemented through legislation that established the necessary procedures and enforcement mechanisms. There is no particular reason to expect that these processes would not fall prey to the same sorts of gimmicks to which GRH was subject, including short-term fixes and movements to off-budget financing. The fixed deficit targets of the GRH Act have illustrated how such subterfuges can be induced by a rigid standard.

Further, a balanced budget rule could constrain the ability of the federal government to use fiscal policy to manage the economy. The traditional tools of fiscal policy—tax cuts and increases in expenditures—would be much more difficult under a balanced budget constraint and more reliance would be placed on the Federal Reserve to stabilize the economy. Denied the ability to pursue their objectives through spending policies, policymakers may resort to mandates on states, localities, and businesses; expanded regulatory efforts; and tax incentives that distort economic decisions. Such a response could undercut economic efficiency and reduce the visibility and controllability of federal policy.

Line-Item Veto for the President

The line-item veto has been sought by many presidents since Ulysses S. Grant but has never gained much favor in the halls of Congress. At the state level, 43 of the 50 governors currently have such authority to reduce or eliminate specific items in an appropriation bill. The president has only two options—either to sign or veto a bill in its entirety. Proponents argue that the line-item veto would empower the president to reduce low priority spending—so-called "pork-barrel" projects—thus leading to a reduction in the deficit. They argue that the president, as a representative of the general interest, should have the power to strike provisions that focus only on a narrow interest.

The line-item veto, however, could involve a significant shift of power between the branches, since the president could use the threat of such a veto to keep Congress in line with his or her wishes. Research on state experiences with the line-item veto suggest little impact on the level of state spending. Many governors, however, have used the line-item veto for partisan political purposes.

In 1996, the Congress passed, and the president signed, the Line Item Veto Act (P-L-104-130), which is intended as the statutory equivalent of an item veto. This Act faces an uncertain future however, since the U.S. District Court struck it down as unconstitutional in April of 1997.

Capital Budgeting at the National Level

Much of the federal budget consists of expenditures that are long-term in nature. Some people have argued, therefore, for separating the budget into capital and current operation, and removing the capital component from calculation of the deficit. This is the approach taken by most state and local governments. An argument in favor of this change in budgetary treatment of capital spending is that it might promote more spending on capital investment activities. These types of spending may currently be disadvantaged because their costs are front-loaded relative to the benefits that flow from such projects.

Alternatively, the creation of two categories of spending may increase budgetary game playing. There is no clear definition of a capital expenditure. The content of the capital budget, then, depends on subjective assumptions concerning what capital is and how it is to be measured. The tendency may be for proponents to seek protected status for their favorite "investment" activities.

Biennial Budgeting

There have been proposals to go to biennial budgeting, enacting the budget (budget resolution, appropriation bills, and other legislation) every two years, instead of annually. This is a practice currently followed by 19 states. In fact, in 1993, both the vice president's National Performance Review and the Joint Committee on the Organization of Congress recommended that the federal government move to a biennial budget process.

The federal government has experimented in a haphazard way with multiyear budgeting—the 1987 summit agreement represented a two-year budget and the agreements of 1990 and 1993 set budget parameters for five years. A more systematic approach would have two-year budget agreements which could be reached in the first year of each Congress—that is, in odd-numbered years. Proponents have argued that biennial budgeting would free up Congress to concentrate on nonbudgetary issues during the nonbudgetary year. Biennial budgeting, however, might also make agreements more difficult to achieve, since the stakes would be higher. Although some might argue that biennial budgeting would add stability to agency and program planning, uncertainty would increase as well; the ability to forecast budgets for future years is notoriously weak in biennial states. Others have asked whether it is desirable to confront budget decisions less frequently at a time when budget deficits are still at unacceptable proportions.

Conclusion

The creation of a congressional budget process has unquestionably led to a reassertion of the congressional role in budgeting, and has also increased in importance as the federal budget and deficit have moved to center stage. It will probably continue to engender controversy and calls for reform, for two main reasons. First, the many changes that have already been made have made the process much more time-consuming and complicated, and many continue to advocate a simpler set of rules. Second, since the process has been used as a means to attempt to reduce federal deficits and spending, it will continue to be criticized by those who do not approve of budget outcomes.

Bibliography

Doyle, Richard, and Jerry McCaffery. "The Budget Enforcement Act of 1990: The Path to No-Fault Budgeting." *Public Budgeting and Finance*, vol. 11, no. 1:25–40.

Fenno, Richard, 1966. *The Power of the Purse*. Boston: Little Brown.

Fisher, Louis, 1987. *The Politics of Shared Power: Congress and the Executive*. 2nd ed. Washington, D.C.: Congressional Quarterly.

Hanushek, Eric, 1986. "Formula Budgeting: The Economics and Analytics of Fiscal Policy Under Rules." *Journal of Policy Analysis and Management*, vol. 6, no. 1.

Ippolito, Dennis, 1981. *Congressional Spending*. Ithaca: Cornell University Press.

Joyce, Philip G., and Robert D. Reischauer. "Deficit Budgeting: The Federal Budget Process and Budget Reform." *Harvard Journal on Legislation*, vol. 29:429–453.

Lee, Jr., Robert D., and Ronald Johnson, 1989. *Public Budgeting Systems*. Rockville, MD: Aspen Publishers.

LeLoup, Lance, 1980. *The Fiscal Congress*. Westport, CT: Greenwood Press.

Meyers, Roy, 1994. *Strategic Budgeting*. Ann Arbor: University of Michigan Press.

Schick, Allen, 1980. *Congress and Money*. Washington, D.C.: The Urban Institute.

______, 1990. *The Capacity to Budget*. Washington, D.C.: The Urban Institute.

______, 1995. *The Federal Budget: Politics, Policy, Process*. Washington, D.C.: The Brookings Institution.

Stith, Kate, 1988. "Rewriting the Fiscal Constitution: The Case of Gramm-Rudman-Hollings." *California Law Review*, vol. 76, no. 3 (May).

Wildavsky, Aaron, 1988. *The New Politics of the Budgetary Process*. Glenview, Il: Scott Foresman.

37

Target-Based Budgeting

Irene S. Rubin,
Northern Illinois University

A budget reform that requires the budget office to give targets, or maximum amounts to the departments before they draw up their budget requests. The departmental request must be within these targets, or it will be returned to the department for revision.

Overview

In its simplest form, target-based budgeting is a budget reform that rejuggles some of the traditional functions of the budget office and the departments during the process of budget requests. Under traditional, incremental budgeting, budget requests came up from the departments based on few or no prior constraints from the budget office. The totals of the requests would normally exceed the revenue available, forcing the budget office to cut back the departmental requests. Such cutbacks would either be across the board, requiring little knowledge of the department's operations, or be targeted, under the assumption that the budget office was armed to find the fat in department budget proposals.

The traditional model led to a number of widely acknowledged problems. Perhaps the most serious of those problems was an oppositional relationship between the budget office and the departments, and a mood of mutual mistrust and game playing. Department heads often inflated their budget requests because they expected across the board cuts and still had to be able to manage their departments. Budget officers came to look on the departments as duplicitous and their requests as exaggerated. The budget office staff learned to watch out for departmental tricks and sometimes evaluated themselves in terms of their ability to find and catch those tricks.

When the budget office staff tried to find and cut the fat in the departments' budgets, they were often frustrated by their lack of understanding of departmental operations. The results were unpleasant on an interpersonal basis and damaging to management. Unrealistic departmental estimates were often cut back unwisely by the budget office, encouraging even more unrealistic departmental estimates.

Target-based budgets resolve these problems by requiring the budget office to give firm ceilings to the departments for their budget requests at the beginning of the budget process. These ceilings are framed by the budget office's estimates of the total revenue that will be available as well as specific policy guidance from the budget office, mayor, manager, and council. The departments have to keep their requests under this ceiling or target. If they fail to do so, the budget office gives their budget requests back to them for revision. The revisions are accepted only if they come in at or under the ceilings. The decisions of what to cut to get under the ceilings are made by the departments, not by the budget office. Under target-based budgeting, the departmental estimates must be realistic. The game playing and antagonism that characterized incremental budgeting are eliminated. The responsibility for ensuring that budget requests do not exceed revenue lies with the budget office, while the responsibility for making managerially responsible cuts goes to the departments.

History

The earliest reference to target-based budgeting in the budget literature is in Arthur Buck's 1929 text *Public Budgeting*. He describes a system of budgeting in Berkeley, California, in the 1920s that would today be recognized as target-based.

After several years of experimenting with commission government and experiencing the logrolling and high rates of expenditure that came to be associated with that form, a reform group advocating the adoption of the city manager form also argued for budgeting reform and ultimately included requirements for more stringent budgeting in the new Council-Manager Charter effective in 1923. The city had been running deficits in the early 1920s, just prior to the adoption of the city manager form, at least in part because of war-induced inflation and resulting salary increases combined with tax limits and a citizenry unwilling to override the limits.

While the requirement for more stringent budgeting was written into the charter, the new budget system was given life and form by the first city manager, John Edy, and his budget officer, J. H. Jamison. Their goal was to rebalance the budget within the tax limits by controlling the departmental requests while creating a little flexibility in the budget for capital projects and new or expanded services. Many of the conditions that spawned target-based budgeting in the 1920s are similar to conditions today. In 1929, budget reformer Buck (1929) described the system that Edy and Jamison had worked out:

> The manager, with the assistance of his budget officer, J. H. Jamison, makes a careful analysis of the current year's budget in the light of the work program and in this way decides upon the total budget for the forthcoming year, definitely allocating to each spending agency the maximum amount which it may spend during the budget year. Each spending agency is then notified of the maximum amount which it may spend and asked to submit its estimates so as not to exceed this amount. In the event that a spending agency desires to submit requests in excess of the amount allowed by the manager, it must do so on supplementary estimate sheets and arrange the requests in the order of their importance. These additional requests are allowed only in the event and to the extent that revenue is found to be available to meet them at the subsequent date when the budget is formulated. Mr. Edy claims that this method has greatly reduced the work of preparing the city budget, since the estimates require very little revision and practically no redrafting. (p. 307)

Some people think that target-based budgeting is a spinoff of zero-based budgeting, because its prioritization of expenditures is like that of zero-based budgeting, even though in target-based budgeting prioritization occurs only at the margins of the budget. However, the clear existence of target-based budgeting in the 1920s suggests that target-based budgeting existed prior to zero-based budgeting and was not a derivative of it.

Implementing Target-Based Budgeting

In practice, the ceilings, or targets, in target-based budgets are often a percentage of a constant services or maintenance of effort budget. The cost for each department of providing this year's level of services next year is figured by the budget office. The maintenance of effort figure is considered by many budget officers to be the key to keeping the costs of services from growing from year to year. Maintenance of effort is usually calculated by subtracting one-time costs from the present budget, adding in one-time costs for the following year, including specific inflation estimates where appropriate, and sometimes including the estimated increases in labor costs. The targets given to the departments, which provide ceilings for their budget requests, can be more or less than the maintenance of effort figure, but the maintenance of effort figure is normally the starting point.

Departments can be given one target for all expenditures, or two, one for capital and one for operating. The ideal is to use one target, to maximize the kinds of trade-offs that departments can make and encourage department heads to innovate. For example, in meeting a target, a department head might propose to substitute a piece of equipment for several employees, reducing costs. If capital and operating targets are separate, the possibility of such trade-offs is eliminated. However, if it seems likely that a single target would be abused, the dual targets can be substituted. For example, if department heads eliminate all capital items from their requests in order to get under the target in one year, and then argue the next year that they have to have a variety of capital items because they had none the previous year, the greater control of the dual targets may be preferable.

Assuming for a moment a single consolidated target, when a department prepares its request, if its target is less than the constant services or maintenance of effort amount, some of the current year's expenditures have to be squeezed out. If those expenditures are still deemed important, the department head can put the squeezed out items on a second list, sometimes called the unfunded list. Other items can also be placed on the unfunded list, such as service expansions or requests for other items that were not in the current year's budget. Some cities require service expansion requests to be handled on a third form, with a specific justification of need. For each unfunded list, the department rank orders the unfunded items and provides the budget office with an explanation of each item and the managerial and service impacts of not funding it.

Attractions of Target-Based Budgeting

Part of what target-based budgeting is supposed to accomplish is to create some flexibility to accommodate new expenditures or priorities within severely constrained budgets. Department heads are usually given the option of putting new requests into the funded list and taking other, less important items out of the current year's budget to pay for the new items or increases. This creates the possibility of some trade-offs within departmental budgets.

When the unfunded lists are collected from each department, they are merged into a citywide list (or lists) based on citywide priorities. This aggregated list is funded in priority order as far as funding allows. The money to fund the unfunded list comes from the difference between the total of the targets to the departments and the actual amount of expected revenue. In other words, the targets can be set below expected revenue in order to create a pool of funds for both urgent addbacks and new projects. The result may be a small amount of reallocation between departments. In some years, all departments may be forced to cut out their lowest-priority items, while some of them may get their low-priority items back plus other new requests.

Politicians and city managers particularly appreciate the ability of target-based budgeting to create this pool of funds for reallocation or for new policy initiatives within highly constrained budgets. For the city manager, the pool of funds can be used to bolster the capital budget for routine expenses such as street maintenance. Politicians like the ability to fund high-visibility projects such as crime patrols or drug outreach and education.

However, in practice, the reallocation aspect of target-based budgeting may get lost. The system can deteriorate into across-the-board allocations not particularly different in impact from the across-the-board cuts that used to be performed by the budget office in the old incrementalist days. If all departments are given the same target—say 10 percent reduction—and if there are no addbacks, due to constrained revenue, then the target-based budgeting system leads to simple across-the-board reductions. If each department's unfunded priorities list is treated as requiring equal treatment, or as commonly occurs, one department gets a larger share one year balanced by a larger share for another department in another year, the potentials for reallocation are limited.

Another attraction of target-based budgeting for politicians is that it makes it both possible and easy to reduce revenues and to force cuts on departments that the departments have to implement. Some cities that have used target-based budgeting have used it not only when revenues were declining, but when politicians wanted to cut the property tax and get political credit for it. Target-based budgeting makes continual reduction in revenue sources so easy that politicians sometimes find it tempting to continue to cut revenues without much concern for how the departments are coping with effects on management and service delivery. The result can be irrational for the departments because they cannot maintain a constant level of services with continually declining revenues.

Because this temptation is more or less built into target-based budgeting, target-based budgeting is often accompanied by some kind of service-level analysis and a kind of contract between the departments and the council for a certain level of services for a certain level of funding. If the council is willing to have less service for less revenue, the departments have to go along, but the council is bound by the agreement as well as the department and is not supposed to continually reduce resources while expecting the same or higher levels of services. If this kind of agreement is to work, the elected officials have to feel bound by it and have to believe there is not much waste in the departments. These conditions do not always hold.

Bibliography

Buck, A. E., 1929. *Public Budgeting*. New York: Harper.

Lewis, V., 1988. "Reflections on Budget Systems." *Public Budgeting and Finance*, vol. 8, no. 1: 4–19.

Rocca, H., 1935. *Council-Manager Government in Berkeley, California*. Berkeley, CA: James J. Gillick.

Rubin, I. S., 1991. "Budgeting for Our Times: Target-Based Budgeting." *Public Budgeting and Finance*, vol. 11, no. 3: 5–14.

Wenz, T., and A. Nolan, 1982. "Budgeting for the Future: Target Base Budgeting." *Public Budgeting and Finance*, vol. 2, no. 2: 88–91.

Part Eleven

Auditing and Accountability

38 — AUDIT

Ira Sharkansky,
Hebrew University

A systematic examination of accounts or program activities, so as to ascertain their accuracy; a means of verifying the detailed transactions underlying any item in a record.

Dictionary definitions emphasize the auditor's roots in financial control. This is still a central feature of governmental audit. As will be noted below, however, audit has moved beyond financial records to a more general concern with program activities. The auditing that will be at the focus of this entry is *external* or *independent* auditing. This is distinguished from *internal* audit, typically conducted by personnel responsible to the head of an administrative unit. External audit is meant to be independent of the administrative or executive agencies whose activities are reviewed. In many countries, the external auditor is attached to the legislature. In order to bolster its independence, the budget of the audit body may escape the control of the executive budget unit, and its personnel may be outside the general civil service.

External audit has become a significant element in the processes of program evaluation, policy implementation, and political accountability. It has attracted more attention than internal audit from scholars concerned with public policy and administration.

A Long History

The *Book of Kings* reports a financial problem with the construction of Solomon's temple. Solomon had to transfer a number of Galilean towns to Hiram of Tyre in order to settle his debts (1 Kings 9:11). The Israelite kings may not have employed auditors as we know them, but they tolerated shrill criticism by prophets. In periods that are dated from 1000 B.C.E. to 587 B.C.E., Nathan was the critic of King David, Elijah and Micaiah of King Ahab, and Jeremiah of Kings Jehoiakim and Zedekiah.

Chinese auditing occurred as early as the Zhou Dynasty in 1100 B.C.E. A predecessor of the United Kingdom's National Audit Office left a record from the twelfth century C.E. of a sentiment that many auditors still share: "The highest skill at the Exchequer does not lie in calculations, but in judgments of all kinds."

The modern history of the U.S. General Accounting Office (GAO) resembles that of numerous other national auditors. Indeed, the GAO has assumed a leadership position among auditors by propagating its conceptions and techniques in the international associations and journals of governmental auditing. Established in 1921 as an organization responsible to Congress, the GAO assumed functions that had been conducted in the executive branch by a unit of the Treasury Department. The principal work of the early GAO and its predecessor was the auditing of financial records, checking vouchers against items in appropriations bills that authorized outlays for particular purposes. An important point in the history of government auditing was the move to sampling vouchers, rather than the examination of each payment. Later auditors began moving outward from a concern with financial records to a concern with the substance of governmental activities. Until now, however, some national auditors continue with the traditional emphasis of finance, with little or no concern for program issues.

Like other auditors, the GAO has concerned itself with the criticism of problems, or negative findings about programs. Auditors generally let some other body praise those program details that perform well.

A prominent figure in the history of auditing is Elmer Staats, Comptroller General of the United States from 1966 to 1981. He expanded the hiring of auditors with training beyond the fields of accounting and law to graduates of social sciences, natural science, and engineering. During the 1970s Staats popularized the concept of *three E*s as the focus of audit: Efficiency, Economy, and Effectiveness.

The Focus of Auditing

The focus of governmental audit has moved in several directions, some of them controversial. Following the theme of Statts's *three E*s, auditing now deals with issues of equality, equity, the environment, ethics, and electronic technology, as well as evaluation and econometric analyses of program impacts. New trends in government, like privatization and the activities of multinational organizations, have attracted the attention of auditors. The labels *operational auditing, effectiveness auditing, performance auditing, performance review, value for money auditing, system-oriented auditing,* and *program evaluation* appear in audit reports. Though some scholars identify these activities with Staats's concern with effectiveness, economy, or efficiency, others identify nuances that distinguish one audit approach from another. The mix of terminology is apparent in the following sentence taken from a publication of the Swedish National Audit Bureau: "The main task of the Swedish National Audit Bureau's Performance Audit Division is to initiate the examination and promotion of effectiveness and efficiency in Sweden's governmental administration."

It is also possible to distinguish between the audit of accomplishments in the short run (what some call *outputs* or *program results*); and accomplishments in the long run (what some call *outcomes* or *implications*).

Although those who speak for certain audit bodies claim that they review only the administration of policy and not the contents of policy itself, some of their organizations report on major policy options while they are awaiting government decisions. The GAO has employed the term *forward-looking audits* to cover reviews of social and economic problems that, in the view of auditors, have not attracted adequate concern from policymakers.

What all of these approaches have in common is the concern of auditors to go beyond their traditional examinations of financial reports or agency compliance with the law. They emphasize an audit of program accomplishments.

In order to support its extensive inquiries, the GAO offers its staff in-house courses in research methods, statistics, and computer science that resemble the programs of social science faculties at respectable universities. Among the sophisticated audit reports of the GAO are

- a review of education reforms that found indicators for gains in pupil achievement not isolated from the effects of programs to teach testing skills;
- a study of freight trucking that identified some variables useful in predicting high levels of risk from road accidents; and

- a study of fatality rates associated with certain types of passenger vehicles that controlled for numerous variables dealing with traits of drivers, road conditions, and weather.

The Auditor's Structure and Mandate

Numerous audit bodies are headed by a single individual. Others are led by a board or commission, and the German audit body is headed by a body of judges who act like a court in making key decisions about audits. Consistent with principles of independence, head auditor(s) are likely to be appointed for lengthy terms, with extraordinary provisions for removal prior to the expiration of the term. The United States Comptroller General serves for 15 years.

Government auditors typically operate under a law that defines the organizational structure of the audit body, its relationship to the executive and legislative branches, procedures for obtaining funding and personnel, and topics that auditors must examine, may examine, or must not examine. Various audit bodies are explicitly enabled or denied the right to examine the activities of public enterprises and local authorities. Some may examine only those enterprises where the government owns more than one-half of the shares, or has contributed more than one-half of the capital. Some audit bodies are denied the right to examine or assess the goals of government policy. The *three Es* have found their way into a number of laws defining the jurisdictions of state auditors. A typical act enables the auditor to examine the legality of actions undertaken by governmental bodies, as well as the accuracy and completeness of their financial records and the extent to which they have operated in an efficient, economic, and effective manner.

Charting the auditor's jurisdiction is not always simple because laws establishing some bodies may explicitly exclude them from the general statute dealing with the government auditor. Israel's State Comptroller is unusual in having a legal mandate to determine whether audited bodies have operated in a "morally irreproachable manner." This recalls the location of the auditor's head office, only a few kilometers from the place where the prophet Jeremiah directed his shrill criticism against the establishment of his day for its moral shortcomings. The State Comptroller has reprimanded ranking politicians for their patronage activities. It has gone beyond the edges of government, per se, to censure individual citizens who have contributed to more than one political party in violation of what the auditor identifies as appropriate political morals.

In point of fact, the explicit metes and bounds of the auditor's jurisdiction may be less important than the personnel resources at the auditor's disposal and the auditor's decisions as to priorities. Much of what the Israeli State Comptroller has examined under the heading of moral integrity could also have been reached under the headings of legality, economy, efficiency, or effectiveness. Even where audit bodies are denied the right to criticize government policy, they may come so close to that concept (e.g., by examining major program activities that are integrally related to policy goals) as to render the prohibition insignificant.

As auditors have entered issues of special sensitivity, they have become involved in disputes as to "how far should the auditor go?" The Israeli State Comptroller has provoked outbursts from ranking policymakers by reports that expressed opposition to military campaigns. A negative report about weapons research and development reached the Cabinet's table shortly before a vote was scheduled on the continuation of the program. That report may have affected the decision, by a majority of one, to cancel it. The audit produced an outburst against the auditor from the prime minister, who was on the losing side of the vote.

Numerous government auditors tread cautiously in the field of public higher education, perhaps out of respect for the concept of academic freedom and institutional independence. The typical audit in this field concerns issues of institutional administration or equipment acquisition, rather than academic programs. There have been notable exceptions. One report by the UK's National Audit Office (NAO) examined the allocation of resources to specific programs of instruction and research against the criteria of fields said to be important for the national economy. Another report criticized a program to encourage early retirements because it produced staff reductions in those areas (e.g., science and engineering) where the auditor concluded there was a demonstrated need for more teaching. It did not reduce staff numbers in the humanities where, according to the NAO, there were surplus staff and programs. A report of the Swedish National Audit Bureau criticized the suitability of certain courses in programs of architectural education. A report about nine graduate programs at the University of Lund examined the decisions of department heads, the distribution of resources among different categories of students, and outcomes in terms of doctoral dissertations actually completed. The conclusions identified "good" and "bad" departments, recommended restrictions on the number of students in certain programs and the termination of students who prove to be unproductive.

Characteristically, auditors have few if any tangible powers to order that certain activities go forward or desist. The weight of audit reports lies in their prestige and their power to persuade other officials, or the public at large, that officials have erred.

Auditors in some countries have struggled with professional norms concerned with the revelation of wrongdoing against political pressures to support the incumbent regime. The Philippines Commission on Audit produced several incisive criticisms of prominent programs and individuals during the final years of the Marcos regime. Some of these reports were made available for the public at large, while others were provided only to ranking officials. The Commission on Audit also financed research by Filipino scholars, whose papers were delivered at academic conferences. One paper dealt with overt and covert motives for creating government companies and described the tricks used by political insiders to siphon resources from them. Another paper hinted at current problems by describing how a previous generation of Filipino elites had made themselves rich at the state's expense.

The present Comptroller of the United States, Charles A. Bowsher, has argued that there is much work for government auditors that is not on the frontier of their activities. Significant economic and social damage can result from the lack of attention to routine issues of management in established programs. According to Bowsher, the auditor can use the classic principles of public administration to remind key officials about the importance of orderly budgeting, personnel management, program planning, and monitoring.

As auditors have moved into sensitive areas, they have encountered challenges to their activities. One of the individuals criticized by the Israeli State Comptroller for contributing to two political parties appeared on television. He defended his legal and moral rights and questioned the State Comptroller's right to criticize lawful activities that he pursued as a private citizen. He explained that he wanted to assure postelection access for his points of view in an election that seemed likely to be closely contested between the major parties.

A classic book on auditing written by E. Leslie Normanton emphasizes the auditor's role of independence. To the extent that auditors criticize ranking politicians, the goals of government policy, or the failure of policymakers to address social problems, the audit body may lose the capacity to review the activities associated with those politicians or policies in a way that will be seen as objective and above the political fray. Like other key personalities in policymaking and administration, the auditor is well served by political skills and sensitivity. This includes knowing what to examine, how to present the findings, and how to defend audit activities against other participants in policymaking who attack the auditor for reports that are perceived as interfering in politics or policymaking.

Bibliography

Brown, Richard E., Thomas P. Gallagher, and Meredith C. Williams, eds. 1982. *Auditing Performance in Government: Concepts and Cases*. New York: Wiley.

Friedberg, Asher, Benjamin Geist, Nissim Mizrahi, and Ira Sharkansky, eds., 1991. *State Audit and Accountability: A Book of Readings*. Jerusalem: Israeli State Comptroller.

Mosher, Frederick C., 1979. *The GAO: The Quest for Accountability in American Government*. Boulder: Westview Press.

Normanton, E. Leslie, 1966. *The Accountability and Audit of Governments: A Comparative Study*. Manchester, England: Manchester University Press.

Sinclair, Sonja, 1979. *Cordial but Not Cosy: A History of the Office of the Auditor General*. Toronto: Maclelland and Stewart.

39

ACCOUNTABILITY

Barbara S. Romzek,
University of Kansas

Melvin J. Dubnick,
Rutgers, The State University of New Jersey

A relationship in which an individual or agency is held to answer for performance that involves some delegation of authority to act. Accountability mechanisms are the means established for determining whether the delegated tasks have been performed in a satisfactory manner.

Accountability as a relationship involves one individual or agency being held to answer for performance expected by some significant "other." Although our specific concern here is with accountability as it relates to structures of governance and administration, accountability is a generic form of social relationship found in a variety of contexts. Social psychologists and sociologists regard the need of "having to account to others" as a fundamental means through which individuals adjust to social settings.

Accountability relationships in the public sector have distinct and empirically observable phenomena associated with them. In many instances accountability is associated with democratic administration, but in reality it is as relevant to nondemocratic regimes as it is to those tied to popular rule. And although it is often treated as a secondary factor in public administration, accountability plays a crucial role in shaping and directing the day-to-day operations of government.

Governance Problems and Accountability Issues

Accountability relationships focus the attention of public administrators on particular sets of expectations about their performance. To understand accountability both historically and functionally, we can view it as a sequence of problems facing rulers. These include problems related to (1) delegating tasks and establishing expectations; (2) verifying the performance of those tasks; (3) maintaining the responsiveness of accountable agents; (4) assessing blame for accountable actions; (5) sorting out responsibility among many agents; (6) determining the "master;" and (7) managing under conditions of multiple accountability systems.

Problem of Delegating Tasks and Establishing Expectations

Historically, accountability emerged out of necessity as the tasks of the ruling household became too burdensome for the ruler. Such conditions initially lead to the delegation of tasks to others, and eventually to the granting of authority and discretion to act on behalf of the ruler. With those authorizations come explicit and implicit expectations for the performance of those tasks, and it is in this regard that accountability emerges as a governmental function. Thus, accountability does not necessarily imply the existence of democracy; rather it suggests any form of governance conducted through some delegation of authority.

Once the decision is made to delegate some authority or task to another, several questions must be addressed, including: (a) What tasks should be delegated by the rulers to others? (b) To whom should those tasks be delegated? And (c) how much authority and discretion should these others be given? The answers to those questions have varied from society to society over time. The common thread running through all societies is the development of institutionalized accountability relationships that focus on what is expected of the agent who is given assigned tasks and how the agent's actions are overseen. These relationships are found in tribal societies and ancient empires, in Eastern civilizations and in the West, and in modern democratic regimes as well as totalitarian ones.

What are the measures and means for implementing accountability relationships? This general problem itself has two dimensions, one dealing with the need to verify that expectations are being met, and the other with the desire to maintain the responsiveness of the accountable individual or agency.

Problem of Verification

Verification problems in accountability refer to the measures and means for ascertaining whether one's performance expectations have been met. Solutions to the problem of verification are as diverse as the types of accountability that have emerged over the centuries. Record keeping is an ancient mechanism, as are requirements that those records be submitted for review.

Historically, most of this verification effort has been directed at implementing accountability for public finances. Aristotle, for example, wrote of the need for an office "which receives and audits the accounts of other offices" who handle large sums of public money (*Politics*, VI, viii, para. 16). His comments reflect the assumption that such a verifying function was a necessary part of the design of any government that gives a public official discretion involving the expenditure of significant funds. Broader conceptions of the verification function of accountability have emerged with concern about the legality, effectiveness, and efficiency of public sector operations. As a consequence, the tasks of the modern auditor have expanded greatly to include the techniques of evaluation as well as financial accounting.

Problem of Maintaining Responsiveness

Verification that an official is doing what is expected is one thing, but how does one assure the official will remain responsive to the ruler in such situations? This problem represents the more difficult part of the general issue of implementing accountability, for if improperly solved it can defeat the very purposes for which accountability systems are constructed.

As noted previously, accountability relationships are established as means for carrying out the delegation of tasks and communication of expectations. The very effort to establish such a relationship implies that there is no intention of completely surrendering authority over the task. Rather, there is every indication that the ruler intends to retain ultimate control. Thus, in deferring to an accountable agent, the ruler seeks to maintain some control. Excessive control or overcontrol, however, can be stifling. Too lax control or undercontrol can lead to the abuse of authority or drift. The problem is to design and operate an accountability relationship that focuses on the maintenance of responsiveness to the ruler while allowing for the exercise of needed discretion by the accountable agent.

Here we find a wide range of approaches and mechanisms for resolving an accountability problem. Typically the solution has been found in the development of legal requirements and sanctions, as well as mechanisms of institutionalized oversight. The methods used in ancient Athens would not seem too strange to the rulers of modern democracies. Regular reviews of how officials conducted the city-state's business were part of the public agenda, and a general review capped every magistrate's term in office. Accusations brought by auditors and citizens could lead to public trials, with punishments ranging from reprimand and impeachment to imprisonment and death.

Problem of Blame Assessment

Implied in the development of accountability relationships is a dilemma rooted in the possibility that the accountable individual may or may not be causally responsible for any failure in task performance or in meeting established expectations. The dilemma requires that any accountability relationship be capable of dealing with situations wherein causal responsibility for a success or failure is questionable.

The problem of blame assessment is not merely a technical one, for assessing blame is a social action and is therefore sensitive to the cultural context in which it occurs. To better understand the nature of this problem, consider the four types of settings posited in Figure 39.1. The settings are derived by counterposing two factors related to accountability: formal answerability and empirical blameworthiness. Formal answerability refers to whether the accountable actor can be officially called to answer for a failed action. Empirical blameworthiness refers to whether there is an established causal link between the failed action and the official who is being held "to account" for the outcome.

A Type I scenario implies a cultural setting that holds an official accountable only when he or she is found to be both formally answerable and empirically blameworthy. In such a setting the individual being held to account must hold a position where he or she is formally responsible for the action and there is empirical evidence linking the individual to the outcome of interest. In what is perhaps the most famous American example of this, U.S. President Richard Nixon was held accountable for his actions in the Watergate cover-up because he was both formally answerable for the actions of his staff and there was empirical evidence of his involvement in the cover-up. It is likely Nixon would have escaped legal sanction for the actions of his subordinates if the "smoking gun" tape recordings, which established Nixon's empirical blameworthiness, had not been available as evidence.

Under Type II cultural conditions of accountability, it is possible for an official who is not formally answerable to be called "to account" if there is sufficient evidence (which itself may be culturally determined) that he or she helped cause the performance failure. In such a setting, while a supervisor of a governmental unit may not be explicitly answerable for corruption, poor performance, or even misbehavior by his or her subordinates, charges that the individual was lax in performing oversight duties or training subordinates can result in demands for reprimand or resignation. The widespread practice of holding military officers answerable for an event that occurred "on their watch" represents such an accountability culture. While no formal actions may be taken against the officer as a direct consequence of the event or performance evaluation, notations in a personnel file can mean that promotions or future assignments can be adversely adjusted as an indirect consequence.

Type III cultural settings promote the idea of accountability when an official is answerable even though he or she is not empirically blameworthy. A weak form of this type of accountability is found in the symbolic gestures of many American governmental and corporate leaders when they publicly assume responsibility for a failure or problem. Despite the public humiliation that might result from these mea culpa declarations, those same officials often escape major sanctions (e.g., resignation) by noting that they were not really to blame due to ignorance or the malfeasance of some subordinate. Every so often, however, one hears of a major agency head or corporate official in a similar situation submitting his or her resignation as a matter of honor or obligation. Such a story is more likely to come from Japan, where the culture expects such responses from their top managers. Thus, after a serious jetliner crash in 1985, the head of one company submitted his resignation as a matter of honor. Similarly, the head of another major Japanese firm resigned as a means of apologizing for his firm's legal wrongdoing. In neither case was the resigning official directly or indirectly linked to the episodes in question. Rather, it was a reflection of Japanese cultural commitments to both assume responsi-

FIGURE 39.1 Cultural Settings for Accountability

		Formal Answerability	
		Yes	No
Empirical Blameworthiness	Yes	I	II
	No	III	IV

bility for the entire organization and to defend one's honor (*giri*) (Benedict, 1946, especially ch. 7).

Finally, Type IV cultural settings of accountability permit someone or some group to be held accountable despite both blamelessness and the lack of formal answerability. This is an accountability system based on scapegoating strategies: the individual or group held "to account" neither caused the outcome nor had any formal answerability for it. Such a cultural setting can be fertile ground for the kind of demonizing nationalism that leads to genocide and "ethnic cleansing." In less nationalistic soil, it can still emerge in the form of generalized bureaucracy bashing, where the major problems of society and government are laid at the feet of some stereotyped group of civil servants. Organizationally, blame can be assessed on "the workers" or "middle management" or some ambiguous group of outsiders. A fairly common example might be a situation where a local chief of police holds minority community leaders responsible for the police department's inability to lower community crime rates.

There is little doubt that to those nurtured in Western cultures, Type I settings are likely to constitute the ideal among the four alternatives. However, the reality is that at any point in time and place, an accountability relationship will be influenced by its cultural setting. Thus, it would be a mistake to regard the existence of even formal Type I accountability relationship as a bulwark against the inherent biases of these settings. A highly legalistic system of accountability relationships is no guarantee of protection for an innocent person who is "set up" to take the blame for a policy or program failure—especially when the society or organization is ready and willing to accept the accusation.

This was the lesson of the infamous Dreyfus Affair. The sensational events surrounding the arrest, trial, conviction, and sentencing of Captain Alfred Dreyfus in France in 1894 and his retrial in 1899 are well documented. Historians now accept the fact that the French army manufactured evidence that blamed Dreyfus for being a spy. But it is unlikely that a corrupted legal proceeding would have sufficed to convict Dreyfus. The pervasive anti-Semitism that characterized French culture at the end of the nineteenth century was conducive to laying the blame on a Jewish officer to deflect criticism from the army in an effort to bring closure to an otherwise politically sensitive administrative situation. A subsequent bill passed in 1906 restoring Dreyfus to the army and assigning him a promotion and military decorations indicated the official position of the French government that, upon reexamination, there was no evidence of empirical blameworthiness on Dreyfus's part.

Objectively, the problem for the "rulers" is to design accountability relationships so that they can be kept within desired cultural parameters. Such solutions, however, are subject to challenge by others who might find their consequences too narrow or morally reprehensible. An overly legalistic accountability relationship (Type I) might result in allowing some blameworthy individual to escape sanctions, while a Type IV setting (scapegoating) can produce genocidal results, as it did in Hitler's Germany.

Problem of Many-Handed Government

Complicating attempts to deal with the issue of blame assessment is a phenomenon that Dennis Thompson (1987) has termed the problem of "many hands." Modern government is characterized by a proliferation of officials and agencies, and the delegation of authority for particular government policies and programs is often dispersed among several of them. This is especially true in federal systems such as the United States where many social and regulatory programs are implemented through an elaborate array of intergovernmental arrangements. Even if blame assessment is not an issue, accountability relationships must be designed to contend with such situations through mechanisms that were frequently established to deal with simpler forms of authority delegation.

One consequence of this problem is an ongoing effort to reform and reorganize government administration with the intention of making public officials more accountable. Traditional solutions to this problem have involved efforts to consolidate and centralize administrative units dealing with a particular policy or program (e.g., the creation of the U.S. Environmental Protection Agency), while other solutions have involved programmatic budgeting, the use of task forces and similar organizational tools, and the extension of judicial remedies for those who seek redress for specific actions by public officials.

Problem of Multiple Masters

Modernity has also created the problem of multiple masters. The single legitimate source of authority implied in the above prior problems has been replaced by situations where there are multiple claimants on the behavior and actions of public administrators, each with a sufficient degree of legitimacy to warrant attention. Despite attempts by some to posit a single or ultimate master (e.g., the Constitution, the public interest, public opinion, the chief executive, social justice), the real world of accountability reflects the ambiguities and confusion of administrative life in modern democratic states. Pluralist democracies necessarily create a dilemma for those seeking or desiring a unified source of authority. This dilemma is perhaps more familiar to public administrators than any other group involved in democratic governance.

The dilemma posed by this problem has been expressed in a variety of models. The present authors, for example, have posited the existence of at least four accountability systems, each designed to reflect a major—and legitimate—source of expectations for administrative behavior and each reflecting different accountability relationships (see Figure 39.2).

Hierarchical Accountability. Hierarchical accountability relationships are those most readily recognized by administrators and the general public because these relationships conform to popular conceptions of accountability, including close supervision for compliance with directives. Those favoring hierarchical accountability systems ask administrators to give priority to the expectations of supervisors and other top officials within the organization. Under such a system the administrator may be afforded little discretion and is usually expected to comply with supervisory directives, rules, and standard operating procedures. An example of a hierarchical accountability mechanism is the annual or semi-annual individual performance review, wherein a supervisor reviews and evaluates the performance of a subordinate for compliance with expectations concerning the individual's job accomplishments during that period.

FIGURE 39.2 Types of Accountability Relationships in Democratic Systems

		Source of Control	
		Internal	External
Degree of Control	High	Hierarchical	Legal
	Low	Professional	Political

Legal Accountability. Legal accountability relationships emerge from an arena where authorities expect accountable officials to carry out tasks in accordance with constitutional principles, laws, or contractual obligations. The emphasis in this form of accountability is on administrators' obligations in light of the expectations from sources external to the agency or the individual's office. Accountability relationships in this legal category emphasize oversight and monitoring of public officials by individuals external to their office or agency to ascertain whether the obligations have been met. The anticorruption investigations which Italian magistrates conducted throughout the early to mid-1990s into the bribery practices that pervaded the leadership of their government is an example of legal accountability mechanisms at work. Annual financial audits are a more common example of this kind of accountability relationship. In the United States, court review of police arrest procedures is another common example of a legal accountability relationship.

Political Accountability. Political accountability relationships are stressed by those who demand that responsiveness take priority. Under this kind of accountability system, stress is placed on administrators exercising discretion regarding the various expectations they face from external groups or market forces. The relationship of responsiveness to external groups is easiest to observe in the relationship of elected officials to voting constituents. The ballot box represents a straightforward accountability relationship based on responsiveness to citizen voters. Elected officials who are not sufficiently responsive are not reelected.

For administrators, political accountability typically manifests itself in emphases on satisfaction of key stakeholders and clientele-centered management. Popular management reforms of the 1990s, including total quality management and "reinventing government," are examples of management that emphasizes the exercise of discretion with an emphasis on responsiveness to key external groups, with a particular focus on customer satisfaction and citizens as customers. Community-based policing is a law enforcement example of government administration that emphasizes political accountability relationships. Under this form of policing officers shift roles from primarily law enforcers who emphasize arresting suspected criminals to neighborhood public servants who assist citizens in community problem solving. Performance under this responsiveness standard is judged by how satisfied communities are with outcomes, such as the level of crime in their neighborhoods and their perceptions of neighborhood safety, rather than with the number of arrests of criminal suspects.

Professional Accountability. The professional accountability relationships stress the individual responsibility of the administrator above all else as that individual exercises discretion on the job. Administrators operating under professional accountability systems are expected to exercise that discretion in a manner that is consistent with the best professional practices. Underlying this system is the belief that workers granted such discretion will monitor and regulate themselves through adherence to professional norms. The relationship is one of supervisory deference to the expertise of the administrator. An example of professional accountability relationships at work can be seen in the deference granted to engineers in the design of roads and bridges. People without design expertise will defer to engineers' judgment concerning roadbed specifications and load-bearing limits of construction materials. Management practices that emphasize worker participation in decision making exemplify this deference to the discretion of workers based on their specialized knowledge.

The problem with this multiple masters context is that public agencies and public managers find themselves facing more than one set of legitimate accountability expectations simultaneously (Dubnick and Romzek, 1993). While each system by itself might represent a relatively unambiguous set of expectations to guide and assess behavior, their simultaneous application renders accountability one of the great challenges both for government bureaucracies and those who seek to hold them accountable. For managers and agencies in this situation the challenge is deciding how to prioritize and manage these various institutionalized sets of expectations. Their goal is to accommodate as many expectations as possible while avoiding alienation of those actors whose expectations cannot be accommodated sufficiently.

Aggravating this problem for managers and agencies is the shifting nature of the accountability systems and the dynamics among them. Given the complex and frequently contradictory nature of the multiple expectations administrators face, the very process of meeting some expectations may entail failing to meet other expectations. Furthermore, the very act of giving priority to one set of expectations over another is likely to generate other expectations and conflict.

How does one get effective performance from accountable officials subjected to the problem of multiple masters? Put briefly, for those who hold public administrators accountable, the question is how to overcome the actual and potential deterioration of public services that is likely to develop as a result of the multiple masters problem. At this level, the problem once again may be a matter of how the accountability systems are designed and applied. Depending on how this problem is perceived, proposed and actual solutions have run the range from centralization (to focus the attention of administrators on the priorities of a single master) to market-based strategies such as privatization and contracting out (that focus attention on the desires of multiple masters).

Problems of Managing Under Accountability Systems

Accountability relationships are one of the great challenges for both government bureaucracies and those who seek to hold them accountable. There is a tendency to view accountability as one-way relationships, with the focus on the influence of the controller on the controlled administrator's behavior. In fact, public administrators often play active roles in these accountability relationships, influencing the expectations others have for their performance and the choice of mechanisms under which they will be held to account for that performance.

Modern forms of accountability involve highly complex relationships and they are especially significant for those who must deal with their managerial implications. The combination of the problem of multiple masters and the diverse and often conflicting expectations they are likely to generate presents practitioners with an accountability dilemma. The essence of this dilemma is the inability of "accountable" entities to resolve the problem of many masters and manage the government's business under conditions of multiple accountability relationships and systems. This dilemma is an important issue emerging from the current state of public administration. The management problem posed by accountability relationships is both inescapable and ongoing.

For public administrators, management under this dilemma is a challenge that can be approached in a variety of ways. Under conditions set by the accountability dilemma public managers face role choices ranging from doing nothing or preparing for "damage control" to seizing the initiative and shaping the situations and expectations their agencies might face. We can view those alternatives along a continuum and logically identify four orientations managers can assume vis-à-vis the accountability dilemma: passivity, reaction, adaptation, and strategic control (see Figure 39.3).

Passivity—ignoring or maintaining an indifferent stance regarding the dilemma—is by definition the absence of a solution to the management problem. Assuming this position subjects the administrators to the whims of political fortune. While such an orientation might be an unwise choice, some administrators may find they have no other option given circumstances that would punish a more active stance.

Reactive managers, in contrast, are those who focus their attention on dealing with the consequences that the accountability dilemma has for themselves and their agencies. Rather than monitoring or taking anticipatory actions in light of changing expectations, reactive managers choose to wait and see what will result from a given situation and deal with the consequences that result. For example, rather than trying to influence their agency's budget allocation, reactive managers take whatever actions are necessary to deal with the consequences of any budget cuts or increases as they occur.

Adaptive managers are likely to assess emerging situations and take anticipatory steps to minimize costly consequences. For example, looking ahead at how the central budget office or the legislature is likely to respond to alternative actions, adaptive managers will select that option that might satisfy or maximize the most positive outcome from the individual's or agency's perspective.

Strategic managers view their job as dealing with agency task environments in order to help shape and direct—even control—the emerging accountability dilemma that their organizations might encounter and to influence likely consequences. Thus, a manager might find it worthwhile to lobby both the budget office and the legislative body in order to instill in them a sense of what they should expect from the agency.

FIGURE 39.3 Solutions to Managerial Challenge of Multiple Masters Role Choice

	Passive	*Reactive*	*Adaptive*	*Strategic*
Focus Influence on				
Environment	—	—	—	XXX
Situations	—	—	XXX	XXX
Consequences	—	XXX	XXX	XXX

Summary

The reality of administrative dynamics is such that we sometimes lose sight of the fact that accountability involves a number of interrelated and ancient problems. Many of the problems derive from the need for the "ruler" to determine what to delegate and how to hold the authorized agent to account for his or her actions. Others reflect problems derived from the enormous scale and scope of modern governments—problems related to the many hands and many masters that characterize today's political systems.

The fundamental dynamic of accountability remains that of ensuring that public administrators pursue publicly valued goals and satisfy legitimate expectations for performance. As a result of dealing with these problems over time and across different contexts, contemporary accountability relationships are inherently complex, reflecting diverse cultural settings, varied institutional arrangements, and individual role choices. None of those many and various solutions, however, can or should be expected to bring an end to the problems of accountability.

Bibliography

Benedict, Ruth, 1946. *The Chrysanthemum and the Sword: Patterns of Japanese Culture*. Boston, MA: Houghton Mifflin.

Burke, John P., 1986. *Bureaucratic Responsibility*. Baltimore, MD: Johns Hopkins University Press.

Dubnick, Melvin, and Barbara S. Romzek, 1993. "Accountability and the Centrality of Expectations." In James Perry, ed., *Research in Public Administration*. Greenwich, CT: JAI Press, pp. 37–78.

Finer, Herman, 1941. "Administrative Responsibility and Democratic Government." *Public Administration Review*, vol. 1: 335–350.

Friedrich, Carl J., 1940. "Public Policy and the Nature of Administrative Responsibility." In C. J. Friedrich and E. S. Mason, eds., *Public Policy*. Cambridge: Harvard University Press.

Romzek, Barbara S., and Melvin J. Dubnick, 1987. "Accountability in the Public Service: Lessons from the Challenger Tragedy." *Public Administration Review*, vol. 47, no. 3: 227–239.

Romzek, Barbara S., and Melvin J. Dubnick, 1994. "Issues of Accountability in Flexible Personnel Systems." In Patricia W. Ingraham and Barbara S. Romzek, eds., *New Paradigms for Government: Issues for the Changing Public Service*. San Francisco: Jossey-Bass.

Thompson, Dennis F., 1987. *Political Ethics and Public Office*, Cambridge: Harvard University Press.

40

STEWARDSHIP

Douglas F. Morgan,
Portland State University

The disinterested performance of a duty by government and/or its agents on behalf of a superior.

Despite the variety of uses of the term "stewardship" in the literature and practice of public administration, it has retained a surprising consistency of meaning that reflects its etymological roots. Although the term has biblical origins, its use in government arose during the medieval period. It was associated with the work performed on behalf of a lord or, in the case of kingship, on behalf of the crown. Normally, this work involved responsibility for managing the basic financial and household activities of the estate. After the English civil wars in the 1640s, stewardship increasingly became associated with action undertaken on behalf of the "people" or their surrogates. Thus, when the term "stewardship" is found in the literature and practice of contemporary public administration, it still reflects its etymological origins of disinterested performance of householdlike duties by government and/or its agents on behalf of a superior.

There are three characteristics of the term that have been consistently reflected throughout history and are retained in their current usage in the literature and practice of public administration. First, stewardship has always entailed some kind of subordinate role to a superior on whose behalf one acts as a steward. Second, stewardship has always been associated with managing the basic, but critically important, activities of an enterprise that is too large and complicated to be performed by one person. Finally, the activities undertaken by stewards have always required a distinctive competence in managing those rudimentary financial, legal, and housekeeping functions that are critical to the well-being of the larger organizational entity. Each of these characteristics is responsible for creating a distinctive set of questions and, consequently, for the considerable debate and writing about the appropriate stewardship role of career administrators in systems of democratic governance.

1. Upon whose behalf do public administrators act as stewards?
2. What managerial functions and tasks can appropriately be delegated to administrative subordinates?
3. What kind of expertise and competence is necessary for the successful performance of one's stewardship role?

Stewardship: Who Do Career Administrators Serve?

Who do career administrators serve when they perform their stewardship responsibilities? This question is answered quite differently depending on which system of governance one uses as the basis for answering the question. The answer is somewhat clearer in France and England than it is in the United States, where career administrators carry out their work within a separation of powers system in which no one branch of government is sovereign over the other. In England, career administrators operate under a doctrine of "ministerial responsibility," which attaches their stewardship responsibility to the government ministers of the day (Rohr, in Cooper 1994, Chap. 27). In France, however, where the principle of the "general will" is embodied in the doctrine of parliamentary supremacy, career administrators hold stewardship allegiance to Parliament rather than to the individual government ministers themselves. At a practical level, this creates the possibility for career administrators in France to invoke their stewardship responsibility to Parliament as a whole in opposition to the policies or practices of a given minister.

Because of the American constitutional tradition of separation of powers, the locus of stewardship responsibility is much more problematic for career administrators in the United States. To whom do administrators owe allegiance? Is it Congress, that makes the laws? Or is it the president who executes the laws? Or is it the courts who interpret the laws? Or is it the U.S. Constitution as a whole and its encompassing web of offices, processes, and institutions? An increasing number of scholars have argued that career administrators in the United States are stewards of the constitutional enterprise as a whole (Rohr 1986, 1987; Burke 1986; Kass and Catron 1990, Chaps. 2 and 4; Morgan, in Cooper 1994, Chap. 7). In charging administrators with responsibility for the whole, the question arises as to what distinguishes the stewardship responsibility of career administrators from other public officials, such as judges and elected officeholders who also pledge their allegiance to the constitutional enterprise as a whole?

John Rohr, one of the leading advocates of a central stewardship role for career administrators in the American democratic process, answers this question by arguing that the career public service now performs a role originally intended by the founders to be played by both the U.S. House and Senate. Senatorial attributes like duration, expertise, and stability have been eroded by electoral changes. "In a word, today's Senate is not the sort of institution the Federalists wanted and the Anti-Federalists feared. The closest approximation . . . can be found in the career civil service, especially at its higher levels." Rohr also argued that with its merit system and affirmative action policies, the American bureaucracy serves to curb the excessive filtering and refining, which the Anti-Federalists feared would undermine the representative function of the House of Representatives. In short, "the administrative state with its huge career public service, heals and repairs a defect in the Constitution of the United States" (Rohr 1987, p. 142; Rohr 1986).

A variation on Rohr's argument uses the balance wheel metaphor to emphasize the important stewardship role American career administrators play as "keepers of the central questions" that are necessary to hold the American system of constitutional governance on course: balancing concerns for efficiency and effectiveness with the need for responsiveness, balancing the protection of individual rights with majority rule, and balancing the substantive claims of liberty, property, and equality. The justification for career administrators playing this role rests on two considerations: the peculiar competence that career administrators bring to their work and the social and economic transformations that have eroded the capacity of the various social and governance institutions to participate meaningfully in helping to perform this balancing role (Morgan, in Cooper 1994, Chap. 7).

Stewardship and the Limits of Delegation

Stewardship presupposes the delegation of authority by a superior to act on the superior's behalf. This presupposition affects two central domains of administrative practice, one involving internal management systems and the other involving the relationship of administrative entities and their agents to the other institutions of democratic governance. The managerial domain is concerned with creating the most propitious conditions for delegating responsibility downward within an organization in order to achieve effectively the organization's mission. In like manner, the governance domain is concerned with creating the necessary authority for administrators to exercise their stewardship responsibility, regardless of what managerial system is in place.

The managerial side of the delegation issue has been influenced by the same kind of considerations that have dominated private-sector organizations. Much energy has been devoted to designing organizational structures, employee incentive systems, and task management mechanisms that will result in the most productive outcomes and highest levels of employee satisfaction (Likert 1961; McGregor 1967; Deming 1986). The governance side of the delegation issue has focused on various efforts to strike an appropriate balance between controlling the abuses of administrative discretion and structuring its exercise in ways that recognize the distinctive contributions of the administrative function in contrast to the legislative and judicial activities of democratic governance.

The starting point for striking this balance necessarily begins in modern day rule-of-law systems with an affirmative grant of authority by the administrator's legally constituted superior. There is a presumption that career administrators have no authority to act without legal authorization to do so. In practice, this legal authorization is frequently difficult to find, since the vast majority of action undertaken by administrative agents comes from informal action that cannot be tied directly and immediately to any formal legal process such as rulemaking, adjudication, or judicial review. In the case of the United States, where formal administrative rulemaking is more widely practiced than in any other country, one student of the administrative process has estimated that 80 to 90 percent of administrative discretion is exercised without any direct and formal connection to any legal authorization (Davis 1971). Many argue that since the practical realities of administrative life preclude this kind of direct legal authority, in order to preserve "a government of laws and not of men," administrative systems should rely much more extensively on internally initiated organizational processes that confine, structure, and check the exercise of administrative discretion (Davis 1971) and on the passage of laws with clearer administrative standards (Lowi 1979).

Despite Herculean efforts to make administrative stewardship legally safe for democracy, vast amounts of discretion continue to exist without very precise legal guidelines for its exercise. When legal controls have been pushed as far as possible, the debate over administrative discretion shifts away from a focus on the negative merit of controlling its abuse through law to a focus on the positive merit that arises from the distinctive contributions that administrative stewards can make to the democratic governance process. At this point adherence to law as the focal point of administrative stewardship gives way to discussions of administrative competence.

Stewardship and Competence

It goes without saying that one entrusts others with stewardship responsibility only to the extent that they possess the competence to carry out the functions entrusted to them. But what kind of competence do administrators need, especially in modern systems of democratic governance? Three different answers can be found to this question in the literature and writing on public administration. Each answer reflects the kind of peculiar competence that is believed necessary to preserve a healthy system of democratic governance—public accountability, efficient and effective administration of the public's business, and the protection of individual rights.

Ensuring Accountability

When legal accountability proves insufficient to guide the discretionary exercise of stewardship authority, nonlegal forms of accountability increase in importance. There are as many different versions of administrative accountability as there are democratic masters. Are these masters the elected officials? Are they the organized interest groups that attempt to influence the electoral and administrative processes? Or are they the public institutions, their organizational missions, and the collective wisdom that these institutions embody? Answers to these questions give rise to at least three types of nonlegal administrative accountability: policy accountability, facilitative accountability, and institutional accountability. A somewhat different kind of administrative competence is necessary to successfully carry out each of these models of accountability.

The most common model of administrative accountability, made famous by Woodrow Wilson, draws a distinction between policy-level questions that determine "what to do" and administrative-level questions that shape "how to" carry out these directions. Under this model, administrative competence consists of the capacity to apply one's skills in a neutral technical manner, indifferent to the ends being served.

Increasingly, the Wilsonian model of policy accountability has been undermined in the Western industrialized world by the proliferation of a multiplicity of interest groups and the simultaneous difficulty this creates for sustaining a consistent societywide policy consensus. In this kind of hyperpluralistic environment, the model of neutral administrative competence gives way to even-handed facilitation of the contested claims of various constituency interests. In the words of one student of the current administrative process in Great Britain, career administrators increasingly negotiate "the common ground of disputed value territory . . . keep the show on the road, settle disputes and make things happen" (Richards 1992, p. 17). This view is even more pervasive in the United States, where interest groups have long dominated the policy and administrative processes (Lowi 1979).

Closely aligned with the model of facilitative accountability is the role career administrators can play in structuring and facilitating an ongoing dialogue with citizens in what have been characterized as "public encounters" (Goodsell 1981). These encounters provide an opportunity for administrators to educate the citizenry by modeling the conditions for healthy public discourse between the government and its citizens. Many argue that this kind of stewardship activity plays a decisive role in building and maintaining a community of shared meaning (Fox and Miller 1994; Cooper 1991; White, in Kass and Catron 1990, Chap. 5).

A final version of accountability that is emphasized by some scholars focuses on the wisdom and prudence embodied in institutional practices and the unique qualities of the bureaucratic setting, such as the rules of evidence, burdens of proof, and decision rules. Taken together, these arm administrators with a special kind of prudence or practical wisdom that enables them to coalesce considerations of workability, acceptability, and the proper fit of a proposed administrative course of action with the circumstances and capacity of the agency (Morgan, in Kass and Catron 1990, Chap. 2; Terry 1995; Morgan, in Bowman 1991, Chap. 2). This model of institutional accountability emphasizes the importance of being guided by what has proven to be workable in the past in addition to being guided by the policy directives of elected officials and the preferences of constituency interests.

Promoting Efficiency and Effectiveness

The most widely recognized competence associated with administrative stewardship is the promotion of the efficient and effective management of the public's business. In fact, the values of efficiency and effectiveness have served as the driving force, especially in the United States, for the creation of a professional cadre of career public servants (Stever 1988). It is the framework that has guided the classical Weberian model of bureaucracy and the policy-administration dichotomy made famous by Woodrow Wilson. But even in Great Britain and France, where the principle of civil servant autonomy is not as evident, assisting the ministers (as is the case in Great Britain's system of ministerial responsibility) or assisting the Parliament (as is the case in France's system of parliamentary supremacy) is done in the name of, and for the sake of, making governmental policy initiatives more efficient and effective.

Protection of Individual Rights

The stewardship responsibility of career administrators to protect individual rights is especially evident in the United States. Lockean principles of democratic self-government, a strong separation of powers tradition, and a very active Supreme Court have actualized the commitment to individual rights by career administrators in ways that go far beyond the administrative practices found in England and France. This tradition of individual rights is so strong that some scholars have made it the primary moral responsibility of career administrators in the United States (Davis 1971).

In summary, the usage of the term "stewardship" in discussions involving public policy and public administration in modern democratic systems of governance reflect two characteristics that are part of its etymological history. First, administrators are fiduciary agents of their democratic lords and masters. At times, this lord and master is seen as the *vox populi*, but, more often, it is the elected representatives, the laws, and the constitutions that are the mediating expressions of the *vox populi*. Second, career administrators are increasingly viewed as critically important, if not equal partners, in stewarding the healthy functioning of our modern systems of constitutional democracy.

Bibliography

Bowman, James S., 1991. *Ethical Frontiers in Public Management*. San Francisco, CA: Jossey-Bass.

Burke, John P., 1986. *Bureaucratic Responsibility*. Baltimore, MD: Johns Hopkins University Press.

Cooper, Terry, 1994. *Handbook of Public Administrative Ethics*. New York: Marcel Dekker.

______, 1991. *An Ethic of Citizenship for Public Administration*. Englewood Cliffs, NJ: Prentice-Hall.

Davis, Kenneth Culp., 1971. *Discretionary Justice: A Preliminary Inquiry*. Urbana: University of Illinois Press.

Deming, W. Edwards, 1986. *Out of the Crisis*. Cambridge, MA: MIT Press.

Fox, Charles, and Hugh T. Miller, 1994. *Postmodern Public Administration: Toward Discourse*. Newbury Park, CA: Sage.

Goodsell, Charles T., ed., 1981. *The Public Encounter: Where State and Citizen Meet*. Bloomington: Indiana University Press.

Kass, Henry D., and Catron, Bayard, 1990. *Images and Identities in Public Administration*. Newbury Park, CA: Sage.

Likert, Rensis, 1961. *New Patterns of Management*. New York: McGraw-Hill.

Lowi, Theodore, 1979. *The End of Liberalism: The Second Republic of the U.S.* 2d ed. New York: W. W. Norton.

McGregor, Douglas M., 1967. *The Professional Manager*. New York: McGraw-Hill.

Richards, Sue, 1992. "Changing Patterns of Legitimation in Public Management." *Public Policy and Administration*, vol. 7 (Winter): 15–28.

Rohr, John A., 1986. *To Run a Constitution: The Legitimacy of the Administrative State*. Lawrence: University of Kansas.

______1987. *Ethics for Bureaucrats: An Essay on Law and Values*. Rev. New York: Marcel Dekker.

Stever, James A., 1988. *The End of Public Administration: Problems of the Profession in the Post-Progressive Era*. New York: Transnational Publishers.

Terry, Larry, 1995. *The Administrator As Conservator: The Leadership of Public Bureaucracies*. Newbury Park, CA: Sage.

Part Twelve

Ethics

41

Administrative Morality

Willa Marie Bruce,

University of Illinois, Springfield

Recognizing that one is a fiduciary of the public trust and responsibly serving the public interest with honesty, fairness, and integrity while overseeing the operations of government.

Administrative morality in public administration is a difficult concept to define. "Administrative" refers to those persons who occupy positions of authority within government. They perform the duties identified by Gulick in his 1937 report for the Brownlow Commission as POSDCORB: planning, organizing, staffing, directing, coordinating, reporting, and budgeting. They may perform these functions at the executive, managerial, or supervisory levels. They may be political appointees, career civil servants, or simply persons who earn their living in federal, state, or local governments and in not-for-profit organizations. Administrators are those who carry on the business of government by ensuring that equitable and legitimate services are delivered efficiently and fairly. They are often called bureaucrats because they work in a bureaucracy.

"Morality" refers to both character and behavior. It is a term that captures who one is, as well as what one does. Moral administrators are honest and honorable. They can tell right from wrong. They serve the public interest with integrity and justice. They put the interest of the government and citizens above their own personal interest. They have an inner core of strength which enables them to make difficult decisions, and they live their commitment to uphold the law of their land.

John Rohr, an American scholar, says that administrative morality is a function of the regime, that is, of the fundamental political order of a country. In his book *Ethics for Bureaucrats* (1989), Rohr argues that unless an administrator believes in the value and morality of the underlying political order of his or her country, issues of administrative morality are impossible to address. One cannot retain personal morality while enforcing laws or implementing programs of a fundamentally immoral regime.

The concept of administrative morality implies that private virtue extends to public virtue. Dennis Thompson, in his discussion of "Integrity in the Public Service" (1992), explains, "Personal ethics originates in face to face relations among individuals, and it aims to make people morally better. Political ethics arises from the need to set standards for impersonal relations among people who may never meet, and it seeks only to make public policy better by making public officials more accountable." In other words, administrative morality requires both good character and just behavior. It is the opposite of administrative corruption, which is the abuse of one's governmental role to promote one's private advantage.

Origin and Subsequent History

Administrative morality has been a topic of discussion for more than twenty centuries. This brief description of its history is not meant to be comprehensive, but illustrative. In China, Confucius (c. 500 B.C.E.) taught that those who enter public service must have high moral virtue, seek after knowledge, and have a propensity toward action which maintains justice and peace. In the Judaic-Christian tradition, humankind is asked to love mercy, do justice, and walk humbly with their deity. The fourth century (B.C.E.) philosopher Aristotle provided a framework for understanding morality that continues to influence thinking about administrative morality today.

Aristotle's vision of morality is described by Glenn Tinder in *Political Thinking: The Perennial Questions* (1991): "living well is not doing just as one pleases but depends on understanding and adhering to a pattern of life that is valid for all human beings; discovery of this pattern requires unusual insight as well as the gradual development of tradition; most people, therefore, need society to provide moral illumination and structure for their lives; government is the principal agent of society and thus is properly involved in the fulfillment of society's moral responsibilities" (p. 176).

How, then does the moral administrator act in his or her role as "principal agent"? Tinder explains, "Moreover the moral responsibilities of government should be carried out less through coercion than through example, through education, and through the respect, rather than fear, inspired by the laws" (p. 176).

Justice is an important theme through the centuries of discussion about administrative morality, although, historically, scholars have not agreed on what is meant by justice. For Aristotle in the fourth century justice meant distribution in accordance with merit. For Marxist philosophers, justice means distribution in accordance with need.

In her book *Six Theories of Justice* Lebacqz (1986) captures the complexity when she raises these questions: "Does justice require maximizing utility, benefiting the least advantaged, accepting the consequences of choice, honoring human dignity, treating equally, or liberating the poor and oppressed?" These questions remain critical as one explores the definition of administrative morality, for, indeed, the moral administrator must "do justice and act with benevolence and integrity" (Denhardt, 1991).

The founders of the United States were convinced that humankind are creatures of self-interest, and determined that the only way that administrative morality could be ensured was thorough a constitutional system of checks and balances. James Madison, who has been called the philosopher of the U.S. Constitution, explained in *Federalist* No. 51, "If men were angels, no government would be necessary. . . . In framing a government which is to be administered by men over men, the great difficulty lies in this: you must first enable the government to control the governed; and in the next place oblige it to control itself."

Professional and scholarly discussion of administrative morality in the field of public administration began in the United States in the late nineteenth century. In a reaction to populist government the earliest scholars, namely Eaton (1880) and Wilson (1887), cast administrative morality in terms of efficiency and productivity. Terry Cooper, in his introductory chapter to the *Handbook of Administrative Ethics* (1994), explains, "Although the Progressives were concerned about the unfairness of unequal treatment of the citizenry based on willingness to lend support to a political machine, they were even more disturbed by the inefficiency of these informal governments. . . . One comes away with the impression that the more serious defect in machine government was thought to be its inefficiency rather than its lack of justice or liberty. Ethical conduct (administrative morality) for the Progressives was efficient action" (p. 4).

Thus, the origin and history of a concern with administrative morality stretches through the centuries. Although neither serious scholars nor practicing administrators have come to a firm agreement on what is meant by the term, they do agree that it is necessary for good government. They also agree that it somehow entails an element of justice, and that it is both a part of the fiber of the administrator and the results of administrative actions. What they're not as certain about is how to ensure administrative morality.

Underlying Theoretical Framework

In this latter part of the twentieth century, there is not yet an underlying theoretical framework of administrative morality. Rather there is a conglomerate group of scholars, each investigating and theorizing about some small part of what it means to be a moral administrator, or how a government or a citizenry encourages administrative morality, or how administrative morality can be taught, encouraged, or enforced. Today's scholarly divergence is rooted in what has come to be known as the "Friedrich-Finer debate."

Begun in the late 1930s, the debate was summarized by Finer (1941) as follows: "My chief difference with Professor Friedrich was and is my insistence upon distinguishing responsibility as an arrangement of correction and punishment even up to dismissal both of politicians and officials, while he believed and believes in reliance upon responsibility as a sense of responsibility, largely unsanctioned, except by deference or loyalty to professional standards."

This debate has continued in one form or another through the years. In 1995, it has become a part of two large frameworks which Brent Wall (1991) calls the "bureaucratic ethos" and the "democratic ethos." Within the bureaucratic ethos paradigm, the public administrator is viewed as a technocrat who is employed to follow directions, and who requires control mechanisms to ensure responsible moral conduct. Administrative morality here is couched in terms of technical expertise and efficient government service. Within this paradigm, public administrators are viewed as functionaries, not critically responsible humans. Their authority is predicated upon Weber's *zwerkrationale*: legal rational authority. In this set of assumptions, administrative morality emerges from a system of legitimation rather than a system of values. Here the moral dilemma is how to enforce the rules—what is known as how to get administrators to "do the thing right."

The democratic ethos, on the other hand, places administrative morality in a societal framework, where the moral administrator is described in relation to regime values, citizenship, serving the public interest, and commitment to social equity. The democratic ethos calls for responsive and responsible decisionmakers who are able to define the ethical dimensions of a problem, and to identify and respond to an ethic of public service. Those who argue for a democratic ethos in administrative ethics suggest that no public servant is insulated from politics, and that simply following the rules may be an inadequate moral response. Within the philosophy of a democratic ethos lies the recognition that a public administrator may be required to choose between two equally legal possibilities, and must, therefore determine "to do the right thing."

The horns of the dilemma can be captured in the current concerns worldwide about controlling corruption in government. The bureaucratic functionary carrying out carefully prescribed technical responsibilities will have little opportunity to act corruptly, to counter, or even to report corruption of political officials. Bureaucracy is predicated upon control by laws and sanctions. The bureaucrat whose behavior must be controlled is seen as a technocrat, not a moral actor. As the nineteenth century philosopher de Tocqueville pointed out, it takes moral effort to probe for personal insight. An emphasis on following the rules diminishes the ability to make moral judgments.

On the other hand, the public administrator who is a responsible citizen first is not so easily controllable. This administrator exercises discretion, rather than blind obedience. For an administrator seeking to "do the right thing," John Rohr (1988) suggests that the moral problem is "how to exercise his discretionary powers in a responsible manner even though he is not formally accountable to the electorate" (p. 170). Here, administrative morality requires integrity, which has been characterized by Dobel (1990) as "regime accountability, personal responsibility, and prudence." Such integrity may mean that the public employee is less controllable, but more responsible.

The ideological difference between controlled behavior and socially responsible behavior is captured in what's known as the ethical "low" and "high" roads. The "low road" is reactive and negative. It emphasizes compliance, and can result in adherence to the letter of the law while the intent of the law goes unaddressed. The "low road" focuses on prohibiting wrongdoing and requires elaborate rules with strict enforcement procedures. Here administrative morality can be described as obedience and compliance.

The "high road" is an affirmative strategy that expects administrative discretion, encourages ethical behavior, and deters, rather than merely detects, problems. The "high road" is proactive and affirming. It is the road of people with high standards. Here administrative morality can be described as responsible, responsive behavior at its best.

What kinds of administrators are able to take the high road? They were first described by Stephen Bailey in a 1964 article in *Public Administration Review*. Bailey identified three mental attitudes and three moral qualities necessary for administrative morality. Public servants, he said, must have the qualities of optimism, courage, and fairness tempered by charity. These qualities will interact to enable the administrator to overcome the inadequate information, ambiguity, and indecision that are inherent in the government workplace. Bailey's description of administrative morality is the foundation upon which the current discussion of virtue and ethics are based.

Clearly there is disagreement about how to describe administrative morality and how to ensure it. As Jos (1990) noted, "Public administration's attempts to develop an account of the morally responsible administrator now span 50 years, and while the effort has been worthwhile, the results have been disappointing."

Current Practice in the United States

According to John Rohr (1989) in his study of administrative ethics in four countries:

> Ethics in American public administration falls conveniently into two major categories—the legally enforceable and the aspirational. The first deals almost exclusively with financial irregularities in such matters as bribery, conflict of interest, and financial disclosure. For the most part, these questions are governed more by statutory construction than by constitutional principle. The second category goes beyond legal obligation and looks for practical ways in which civil servants might operationalize their oath to uphold the constitution of the United States (p. 505).

Current practice in the United States can be illustrated by the results of recent surveys. Patrick Dobel's (1990) survey of U.S. government employees indicates that 22.4 percent of the respondents believe that public organizations follow the "low road," with "a reactive, legalistic, blame-punishment approach that focuses on discouraging and detecting unethical behavior among public employees." The "high road" was much less evident in this survey, with only 7 percent of the respondents reporting that their organizations utilize "proactive, human-development, problem-solving approaches that focus on encouraging ethical behavior and deterring unethical behavior." Notably, 63.9 percent of the respondents believed that "most organizations have no consistent approach."

A survey of members of the American Society for Public Administration (Bowman, 1990) yielded similar results, with 7 percent of the respondents reporting that their organizations utilize a "high road" to ethics, while nearly one-fourth report a "low road" approach (p. 347).

The most comprehensive collection of empirical research on current practices in regard to administrative morality in the Unites States is contained in Frederickson (1993), *Ethics and Public Administration*. Cooper's (1994) *Handbook of Administrative Ethics* provides extensive discussions about administrative morality by the most distinguished scholars in the field.

Variations of Practice

Variations occur in how persons in different countries name their concern with administrative morality. In the United States, most scholars refer to "administrative ethics," while in many other countries the emphasis is on "controlling corruption." Ethics and corruption are, of course, opposites of one another. Ethical people act rightly. Corrupt people deviate from norms of good and appropriate behavior. The difference in terminology, however, reflects a profound difference in underlying assumptions about the nature of humankind. Those who seek to control corruption most surely expect malpractice, and strive to prevent it. Those who reflect upon *administrative morality* expect responsible behavior, and endeavor to encourage it.

What is called administrative morality may also vary according to culture and regime values. Cooper's (1994) *Handbook of Administrative Ethics* contains a section called "Administrative Ethics in Other Cultures," which describes the different practices in China, Canada, France, the United Kingdom, the United States, Zimbabwe, and Australia.

In a survey of municipal clerks in Australia, Canada, Cyprus, Great Britain, Israel, Malaysia, Netherlands, New Zealand, Switzerland, South Africa, and the United States, Bruce (1994) found few statistically significant differences between the responses of persons in the United States and persons in the other countries. In cities where respondents reported that "most people employed in my city are ethical," certain conditions exist. These include government-provided education and guidelines about what is legal and what is not, organizational sanctions which define punishment for corrupt behavior, a municipal code which clearly defines expected standards, and citizens who would be outraged if those standards were violated in their government.

This survey indicates that administrative morality is more likely to occur in a climate where government employees have high personal standards, where supervisors encourage truth, and where employees regularly come together to discuss ethical problems. These are statistically interrelated activities that represent ethical "high road" conditions. These activities emerge from assumptions that public employees exhibit responsible behavior when encouraged to do so. They support Dobel's (1990) argument in his "Integrity in the Public Service" that no one approach to encouraging administrative morality is sufficient.

Bibliography

Bailey, Stephen, 1964. "Ethics and the Public Service." *Public Administration Review*, vol. 24: 234–243.

Bowman, James, 1990. "Ethics in Government: A National Survey of Public Administrators." *Public Administration Review*, vol. 50, no. 3: 345–353.

Bruce, Willa, 1994. "Controlling Corruption in Municipal Governments Around the Globe." In Urie Berlinsky, A. Friedberg, B. Wemer, eds., *Corruption in a Changing World: Comparisons, Theories, and Controlling Strategies*. Jerusalem: Israel Chen Press (Moshe).

Cooper, Terry, 1994. *Handbook of Administrative Ethics*. New York: Marcel Dekker.

Denhardt, K., 1991. "Unearthing the Moral Foundations of Public Administration: Honor, Benevolence, and Justice." In James S. Bowman, ed., *Ethical Frontiers in Public Management*. San Francisco: Jossey-Bass.

Dobel, J. Patrick, 1990. "Integrity in the Public Service." *Public Administration Review* (May/June): 354–366.

Eaton, Dorman B., 1880. *Civil Service in Great Britain*. New York: Harper Bros.

Finer, Herman, 1941. "Administrative Responsibility in Democratic Government," *Public Administration Review*, vol. 1 (Autumn).

Frederickson, H. George, 1993. *Ethics and Public Administration*. Armonk, NY: M. E. Sharpe.

Friedrich, Carl, 1940. "Public Policy and the Nature of Administrative Responsibility." In E. S. Mason and C. T. Friedrich, eds., *Public Policy*. Cambridge: Harvard University Press.

Gulick, Luther, and Lyndoll Urwick, eds., 1937. *Papers on the Service of Public Administration*. New York: Institute of Public Administration.

Jos, Philip H. 1990. "Administrative Responsibility Revisited: Moral Consensus and Moral Autonomy." *Administration and Society*, vol. 22, no. 2 (August): 228–248.

Lebacqz, Karen, 1986. *Perspectives from Philosophical and Theological Ethics*. Minneapolis: Augsburg Publishing House.

Pugh, Darrell, 1991. "The Origins of Ethical Framework in Public Administration." In James S. Bowman, ed., *Ethical Frontiers in Public Management*. San Francisco: Jossey-Bass, pp. 9–33.

Rohr, John, 1988. "Bureaucratic Morality in the United States." *International Political Science Review*, vol. 9, no. 3: 167–178.

______, 1989. *Ethics for Bureaucrats*. 2d ed. New York: Marcel Dekker.

Thompson, Dennis F., 1992. "Three Paradoxes in Government Ethics." *The Public Manager* (Summer): 57–60.

Tinder, Glenn, 1991. *Political Thinking: The Perennial Questions*. 5th ed. New York: HarperCollins.

Wall, Brent, 1991. "Assessing Ethics Theories from a Democratic Viewpoint." In James Bowman, ed., *Ethical Frontiers in Public Management*. San Francisco: Jossey-Bass, pp. 135–157.

Wilson, Woodrow, 1887. "The Study of Administration." *Political Science Quarterly*, vol. 2 (June).

42

Standards of Conduct

April Hejka-Ekins,
California State University, Stanislaus

Ethical guidelines for behavior that prescribe how someone ought to act. A "standard" is most commonly thought of as a rule, value, or principle, sanctioned by an authority, that is used as a basis in making a judgement. In this case, the term "standard of conduct" has an ethical connotation because it offers a moral imperative as to how one should act in relationship to others. The Ten Commandments in Judeo-Christian belief or the Eight-fold Path in Buddhism reflect examples of religious standards of conduct, but the term has relevance in a variety of other contexts as well.

From the viewpoint of public administration, a standard of conduct presumes a public manager behaves according to a defined role with an accompanying set of responsibilities. Standards of conduct provide the basis for how an administrator should act in fulfilling these responsibilities. Often standards are put in the form of moral principles, such as the five outlined in the Code of Ethics for the American Society for Public Administration (1994): (1) serve the public interest, (2) respect the Constitution and the law, (3) demonstrate personal integrity, (4) promote ethical organizations, and (5) strive for professional excellence. In other instances, they may be put in the form of exhortations or prohibitions. For example, the 1980 Code of Ethics for Government Service in the United States admonishes public employees to adhere to nine standards of conduct, such as, "Put loyalty to the highest moral principles and to country above loyalty to persons, party, or Government department" and "Make no private promises of any kind binding upon duties of office, since a government employee has no private word which can be binding on public duty."

Sometimes values, principles, and rules are combined into one specific standard of conduct, such as one taken from the International City Managers' Association Code of Ethics: "Professional Respect. Members seeking a management position should show professional respect for persons formally holding the position or for others who might be applying for the same position. Professional respect does not preclude honest differences of opinion; it does preclude attacking a person's motives or integrity in order to be appointed to a position."

In this case, the principle of "professional respect" is emphasized with an ethical rule that provides a guideline for conduct. Embedded within the standard are a cluster of implied values such as respect, honesty, and freedom of opinion. Taken altogether, this standard of conduct clearly delineates the boundaries of appropriate conduct as it applies to a specific aspect of professionalism.

Standards of conduct emanating from the administrative role reflect two kinds of responsibility. One type of responsibility could be thought of as "objective" in that expectations for behavior are imposed from external authorities such as one's organization, the law that one is obliged to implement, one's profession, and the citizenry. Objective responsibilities obligate the public official to complete certain tasks and be accountable to external authorities for the way in which they are accomplished. Standards of conduct prescribe ethical guidelines for how one is to behave in fulfilling these objective responsibilities. For instance, a federal agency may require its public employees to respect and protect privileged information by upholding confidentiality within the organization, or a professional association may promote the principle of respect for the law by exhorting its members to prevent all forms of mismanagement of public funds by establishing and maintaining strong fiscal and management controls and by supporting audits and investigative activities. In each case, an external authority is determining what constitutes acceptable ethical behavior.

However, a second kind of responsibility affecting administrative standards of conduct could be termed "subjective" because it reveals an individual manager's idealized value system, the core of which springs from one's feelings and beliefs based on personal experience and professional development. In other words, one's idealized value system becomes the foundation for internal standards of conduct. In this regard, public administrators become their own authority for establishing a set of standards by which to conduct themselves. For instance, if public servants believe in fairness, this may lead them to act with impartiality and consistency in their provision of service to all citizens, or if commitment is a strong personal value, the public servant may strive to administer the public's business in the most competent manner possible. The emphasis here is on the formation of the standard from within the personal framework of the administrator.

Thus, the role of a public official is informed by both objective and subjective responsibilities that give rise to a plethora of standards. Sometimes internal standards of conduct are congruent with external standards of conduct. As an illustration, from a personal and professional perspective a city manager may consider honesty to be a core value. This would resonate with numerous standards of conduct found in the International City Management Association Code of Ethics (1987) such as its guideline regarding credentials: "An application for employment should be complete and accurate as to all pertinent details of education, and personal history. Members should recognize that both omissions and inaccuracies must be avoided." In this case, both objective and subjective responsibilities lead the public administrator to uphold mutually compatible standards of conduct.

However, the variety of authorities that the public manager must serve in fulfilling both kinds of responsibilities can lead to ethical dilemmas involving contending standards of conduct. As a case in point, the fourth principle of the Code of Ethics for the American Society for Public Administration encourages its members to "promote ethical organizations." Among a number of guidelines, one advocates that public officials "subordinate institutional loyalties to the public good." This may clash with the organizational expectation that public employees comply with the directives of their superiors. In this instance, dissension exists between a professional and an organizational standard of conduct.

This example highlights the major strength and weakness of standards of conduct. On the one hand, their primary benefit is that they provide ethical rules of thumb by which the public administrator can discern the boundaries of appropriate behavior. On the other hand, their major liability is that they are limited in instructing managers as to what specific courses of action should be taken in particular situations. In short, adhering to standards of conduct does not ensure that a public official will act ethically, but they can provide useful parameters for responsible administrative action by public servants.

Bibliography

American Society for Public Administration, 1994. "Code of Ethics." Washington, DC: American Society for Public Administration.

"Code of Ethics for Government Service," 1980. Public Law 96-303, Washington, DC: United States Congress.

Cooper, Terry L., 1990. *The Responsible Administrator: An Approach to Ethics for the Administrative Role*. 3d ed. San Francisco, CA: Jossey-Bass.

International City Management Association, 1987. "Code of Ethics with Guidelines." Washington, DC: ICMA.

Mertins, Herman, Jr., Frances Burke, Robert W. Kweit, and Gerald M. Pops, 1994. "Applying Professional Standards and Ethics in the Nineties: A Workbook and Study Guide with Cases for Public Administrators." Washington, DC: American Society for Public Administration.

Richter, William L., Frances Burke, and Jameson W. Doig, eds., 1990. *Combating Corruption/Encouraging Ethics: A Sourcebook for Public Service Ethics*. Washington, DC: American Society for Public Administration.

43

REGIME VALUES

John A. Rohr,
Virginia Polytechnic Institute and State University

An expression used frequently in public administration literature to denote the fundamental principles of a polity which, ordinarily, should guide administrative behavior. Although the term applies in principle to any polity, de facto it appears almost exclusively in literature focused on the United States. The expression entered the public administration literature in the first edition of this author's *Ethics for Bureaucrats: An Essay on Law and Values.*

When the Watergate scandal turned professional attention to questions of ethics in the mid-1970s, professors of public administration puzzled over how to go about teaching ethics to their students. At least four possible approaches emerged: legal, philosophical, psychological, and socially equitable.

Each approach brought certain problems in its wake. The legal approach was too narrow and too negative. Neither students nor their professors seemed willing to rest content in compliance with conflict-of-interest statutes and financial disclosure regulations. Philosophy was found wanting because few public administration students could be reasonably expected to have the specialized background required to grasp and apply the subtle complexities of philosophical argument. Humanistic psychology held considerable appeal, but proved inadequate because of its failure to address the demands of "role morality" that inevitably arise in the field of professional ethics. That is, professional ethics necessarily deals with the standards suitable for a particular calling—for example, lawyers must not suborn perjury, physicians must get informed consent, and so forth. Psychology quite properly focuses on the well-being of the human person as such and, consequently, raises questions far broader than the relatively narrow concerns of any profession, including public administration.

The "social equity" movement associated with the "New Public Administration" had an enormous impact on the field, but its egalitarian and redistributive thrust was too controversial to serve as a broad-based ethical standard for the entire field of public administration.

The "regime values" method attempted to fill the gap in the ethics literature by arguing that since public servants were often required to take an oath to uphold the Constitution as a condition of employment, that oath should serve as a starting point for their ethical formation. Since American civil servants could be assumed to support the Constitution of the United States, this document could serve as a foundation for a community of moral discourse on just what the Constitution and its traditions might mean concretely for contemporary public administrators. Students were encouraged to examine the richness of the constitutional tradition in order to stimulate their moral imagination. The breadth of this tradition, with its conflicts and contradictions, would safeguard against the collapse of the regime values method into a narrow orthodoxy. Supreme Court decisions with their multiple opinions—opinions of the Court, plurality, concurring and dissenting opinions—were proposed as particularly effective pedagogical devices to encourage informed argument about fundamental principles. To focus the discussions in classrooms and training centers, equality, freedom, and property were designated as examples of salient fundamental values that helped to shape and define the American regime established in 1789. Hence, these values were called "regime values"—regime being considered the most suitable translation of Aristotle's *politeia*. Those who used the expression "regime values" were advised to make clear the Aristotelian origin of the term in order to avoid confusion with the journalistic use of the word, as in "the Clinton regime," "the Bush regime," and so forth.

44

Lying with Statistics

Claire Felbinger,
The American University

The misuse in communication of data in print or presentation, either intentionally or unintentionally, the result of which misleads those to whom the communication is directed.

A classic example of associating statistics with lying is attributed to British Prime Minister Disraeli, who declared, "There are three kinds of lies: lies, damned lies, and statistics." More contemporary and book length efforts to explore lying and statistics include Darrel Huff's (1954) *How to Lie with Statistics* and Robert Hooke's (1983) *How to Tell the Liars from the Statisticians.* Neither of these books were intended to be primers for lying but, rather, light-hearted guides for nonstatisticians in how to distinguish between complete statistical disclosure and good statistical reasoning on the one hand and misleading or malicious reporting of data on the other.

Increasingly, we rely on statistics to determine trends, to judge public opinion, and even to learn which toothpaste reduces cavity production. Hooke (1983) distinguishes between statistics in the plural and in the singular. Most people think of statistics as plural—as sets of numbers and figures and data. Statisticians think of it as singular—a subject matter that allows one to understand chance, cause and effect, correlation, and the scientific method. People who gather data (statistics plural) are not necessarily statisticians. If these "data pushers," as Hooke refers to them, use the data in an incomplete or uninformed manner, then their manipulation, intended or not intended, is considered lying.

When someone is lying with statistics, they are unaware of or purposely ignoring statistical assumptions or rules and then make incorrect interpretations about what the data infer. An oftentimes cited example of violating statistical assumptions resulting in an incorrect result was the 1936 *Literary Digest* magazine presidential preference poll that predicted Alf Landon would defeat Franklin Roosevelt in a landslide. Roosevelt won the election. So, what went wrong?

The pollsters at the *Literary Digest* used a biased sample. According to statistics, one can only make predictions from a random sample of the population, in this case, of all eligible voters. In random sampling, each person in the population must have an equal and nonzero chance of being included in the sample. Potential respondents to the *Literary Digest* poll were readers of the magazine and people who had telephones. The poll was taken during the Great Depression when most poor people did not have phones. The sample was biased against poor people. In addition, the poll was biased in favor of people with higher educations; they read the literary magazine. Wealthy people and those better educated tended to be Republicans, Landon's party. The "data" indicated Landon would win; the data, and those reporting them, lied.

Closely related to biased samples are those "lies" which are generated by using a small number of cases, or the "small N" problem. Consumers presented with a statement of the type "Seventy-five percent of citizens are satisfied with local services" should also be given information about the number of cases in the sample and whether the sample was drawn randomly. If a city manager can pick the citizens he or she wants to ask about the quality of services (biased sampling) and there are only four citizens in the sample (small N), then the assumptions of statistics cannot be used to make inferences about citizens' evaluation of services. Probability theory allows statisticians to make inferences from random samples to populations only if the number of cases is large enough. There are mathematical equations to determine how large the number should be to be confident about the findings. In studies involving citizens and public administration, a sample of four is never large enough.

Pollsters should also report the margin of error of their findings. For example, let us say a school district is interested in finding out if voters would support a levy (tax increase) to secure funding for extracurricular activities. A responsible survey researcher finds that the randomly selected sample of 1,500 voters indicated that 55 percent of the voters supported the levy. Without a report of the margin for error, the "lie" might be that there is good support for the levy, and the school district officials should be comfortable with the campaign. However, if the margin for error is plus or minus 7 percent, the support may be as high as 62 percent but as low as 48 percent (losing). Probability theory allows statisticians to determine how confident the researcher is that the sample reflects the population and the margin for error around the statistic—in this case, percent of support. Therefore, consumers of this information should be given information about the randomness of the sample, the number of cases included in the sample, the confidence level, and the margin of error in the statistic in order to evaluate the "truth" of the statistics. Hooke (1983) implies that failure to report these figures should be interpreted as hiding them or lying with them.

Another problem concerns the reporting of the averages. Take the following statement, for example, "The average citizen consumes 38 pounds of rice a year." A savvy statistical consumer would want to know what kind of average is being reported. The median is the point at which 50 percent of the cases are below it and 50 percent of the cases are above it. The arithmetic mean is affected by extreme scores either low or high. When the cases are normally distributed, the median and mean are similar. However, when there are outliers, the mean is pulled in the direction of the extreme scores. In the example above, if the unit of analysis is a city that has a small section inhabited predominantly by ethnic groups whose diets revolve around rice and their average consumption is 100 pounds a year, then the mean for all citizens could be 38 while the median might be 10 pounds. In cases where the distribution may be affected by extreme scores, the median is usually the best measure of the "average." In any case, the particular statistic used should be reported.

When statistics are reported, the consumer should be concerned with how the data compare with other statistics. Comparison is a fundamental enterprise in science. Therefore, when data are reported, they should be explained in comparison to something else. That something else may be a temporal trend, another group of cases, or some baseline so that the consumer can evaluate the worth of the statistic.

However, just comparison is not enough. Probability theory allows us to determine whether differences seen in data are true differences. This is what is meant by something being "statistically significantly" different from something else. Tests of statistical significance can tell whether a group's having an average income of $30,000 is significantly different than a group's having one of $29,500. To avoid the appearance of lying, data should be reported revealing whether the differences are statistically significant.

Comparisons are also made between variables in studies. The statistics often used to estimate the strength of relationships between variables are called correlations. A positive 1.0 correlation indicates a perfect positive relationship; as one variable takes on a higher value, the other one also takes on a higher value. A negative 1.0 is a perfect negative relationship; as one variable increases in value, the other one decreases in value. No relationship results in a 0.0 correlation. One way one could lie with a correlation statistic is to report a correlation that is statistically insignificant. When correlations do not achieve significance, it means that there is no real relationship at all.

However, when the number of cases increases, almost any correlation can be statistically significant—it is an artifact of the mathematics involved. Therefore, the strength of the association becomes even more significant than statistical significance. The correlation coefficient itself is the measure of the strength of the association.

One of the lies made by using correlations is the assumption that all things that are correlated are causally related. Correlation does not equal causation. This is true especially in light of large numbers of cases and their effect on statistical significance. Correlation is a necessary, though not sufficient, condition for inferring causation. The others are temporal sequencing (one variable occurs before the other), the association makes theoretical sense, and all other variables have been ruled out as causal agents (the relationship is not "spurious").

A widely used example makes this point. There is a strong, statistically significant association between the number of storks migrating to Sweden in the fall and the birth rate of children in the country during that season. If one assumes correlation is the same as causation, then the inference can be made that storks "cause" babies in Sweden. Obviously this is not the case.

Another method to lie with statistics is to distort tabular presentations. With the widespread use of computer-generated tables and figures, this is an important lie about which a statistics consumer should be skeptical. One example is changing the units of measure on a trend line by changing the scale on the abscissa or ordinate (*X*- or *Y*-axis) in order to accentuate a trend or to smooth one out. Another is cutting out the middle of charts for no apparent reason than to accentuate an apparent increase or decrease of interest. Either way, this represents altering a scale to comport with one's desired visual findings.

Increasingly, popular media have been using one-dimensional pictures to graphically display statistics. For example, one subgroup of a population makes a certain income, displayed by a money bag. If another subpopulation makes double that amount, then their money bag is pictured twice as high. This makes intuitive sense. However, while increasing the height, the width is also increased, making it twice as wide. In actuality, the second figure is actually occupying four times as much area as the first. This distortion can leave a big, though untrue, impression regarding the status of the first group relative to the second.

There are many and varied methods one can use to "lie" with statistics. However, most public administrators are not that unethical and would not knowingly distort findings for citizens. Huff (1954) suggests that consumers of statistics should be active participants in the data-relaying process; they should ask questions and challenge the reporter to verify the statistics presented. He suggests that consumers should "look a phoney statistic in the eye and face it down" but also "recognize sound and usable data in the wilderness of fraud," which may be out there (p. 122). He proposes five simple questions consumers may pose when confronting the veracity of statistics:

1. *Who says so?* Who generated the statistics and do they stand behind them? Or are the implications from the statistics subject to a reporter's interpretation of them?
2. *How does he or she know?* Was the sample biased? Is the N large enough to permit a reliable conclusion? Is the statistical significance reported?
3. *What's missing?* Is the number of cases reported? What about the standard error? Which average is being reported? Are expected comparisons or baselines missing?
4. *Did somebody change the subject?* Did the incidence of a condition increase over time or are the data gathered more carefully now? Did crime rate go up or are newspapers competing by reporting more crime in print? Have definitions of a condition changed over time?
5. *Does it make sense?* Are impressively precise figures reported that contradict common sense? Are extrapolations from the statistics reasonable given what is known about the culture?

The best defense against those accused of lying with statistics is caveat emptor—let the informed consumer beware.

Bibliography

Hooke, Robert, 1983. *How to Tell the Liars from the Statisticians*. New York: Marcel Dekker.

Huff, Darrell, 1954. *How to Lie with Statistics*. New York: W. W. Norton.

45

WHISTLEBLOWER

Deborah D. Goldman,
National Association of Schools of Public Affairs and Administration

David H. Rosenbloom,
The American University

"The disclosure by organizational members (former or current) of illegal, immoral, or illegitimate practices under the control of their employers, to persons or organizations that may be able to effect action" (Miceli and Near 1992). But several definitional issues remain: (1) Should the definition be expanded to include individuals who are not organizational members per se, but who are in an indirect employment relationship with the wrongdoer, such as employees of a firm doing contract work for a government agency who expose abuse within that agency? (2) Should the definition include action by individuals whose job requires that they report wrongdoing, such as auditors and inspectors general? (3) Must the disclosure be external to qualify as whistleblowing? (4) Should the term be limited to activity that is illegal or against public policy, or should it extend to breaches of codes of ethics and to behavior that is merely wasteful or otherwise incorrect? (5) Are individuals who directly benefit from exposing wrongdoing within working relationships accurately called "whistleblowers," or should the term be reserved for those who act out of altruism? In practice, these definitional matters are addressed in the wide variety of federal and state statutes that seek to protect whistleblowing. However defined in technical terms, the fact that public policy seeks to protect whistleblowing at all is a relatively recent and remarkable development. Although much contemporary law considers whistleblowing to be a public virtue and seeks to encourage it, typical organizational cultures treat it as the sin of insubordination and attempt to stifle it. The tension between these two views is often manifested in statutes that seek to protect whistleblowers from reprisals but do not offer strong incentives to engage in whistleblowing. There are several categories of law pertaining to whistleblowers.

Federal Law Regarding Federal Employees

The federal Civil Service Reform Act of 1978 specifically sought to protect whistleblowing, which it defines substantively as disclosure of a violation of law, rule or regulation, mismanagement, gross waste of funds, abuse of authority, or substantial and specific danger to public health or safety. Since a very broad array of personnel activity is covered by law or administrative regulation, the scope of whistleblowing extends to illegal discrimination based on race, sex, national origin, age, handicap, marital status, or political affiliation; actions violating merit principles; coercion of political activity; nepotism; reprisals for appealing adverse actions; and other activity. The act placed enforcement powers in an Office of the Special Counsel (OSC), which was located within the Merit Systems Protection Board. The Whistleblower Protection Act of 1989 strengthened enforcement by making the OSC independent. Disclosure by federal employees may be internal and/or external to their organizations. External disclosure to the OSC triggers an investigation by that unit. These statutes seek to protect employees from reprisals if they reasonably believe their allegations of wrongdoing are true. In other words, an employee cannot legally be disciplined for making incorrect charges as long as he or she did not make them unreasonably, that is, with knowledge that they were false or indifference to their truth or falsity.

The Civil Service Reform Act and the Whistleblower Protection Act are based on the assumption that protection against reprisals is a key ingredient in making whistleblowing feasible. Employees who believe they have been subject to reprisals for whistleblowing can file complaints with the OSC, which can seek corrective action before the Merit Systems Protection Board (MSPB). At the OSC's initiative, federal officials can be disciplined for violations of the whistleblower protection law. If the OSC does not take the action to the MSPB, then the employee can pursue the matter in federal district court. Remedies for the employee include appropriate corrective action, costs, and attorneys' fees. Sanctions for the employer include dismissal or lesser discipline, up to five years debarment from federal employment, and fines of up to $1,000.

Other measures also seek to protect and facilitate whistleblowing by federal employees. The General Accounting Office has operated a fraud, waste, and abuse hotline, where employees and others can report misconduct. Federal inspectors general and their staffs have a specific legal duty to report wrongdoing within agencies to Congress.

Federal Contractors Under the False Claims Act

The False Claims Act of 1863, as revised in 1986, is intended to encourage whistleblowing by individuals who have knowledge of fraud or cheating against the government by federal contractors. The act seeks to protect whistleblowers from retaliation. However, unlike the acts covering federal employees, it also provides a financial incentive to disclose wrongdoing. The False Claims Act authorizes individuals to file *qui tam* actions and potentially to collect substantial sums from the company involved. *Qui tam* suites are actions brought by private individuals on behalf of the government as well. If the Department of Justice joins the action, the individual can collect up to 25 percent of the judgment; otherwise the individual is eligible for up to 30 percent. Suits can be filed within ten years of the alleged fraud and triple damages are potentially available. According to Terry Dworkin (1992), who relies on studies by the Justice Department, as much as 10 percent of the federal budget, or US$100 billion, is lost through fraud annually. Thus far, Dworkin noted the revised act seems to be working as the number of suits filed "increased twenty-fold" between 1986 and 1989 (p. 247).

Other Federal Statutes

A number of federal laws specifically afford protection to individuals who report violations of their statutory provisions. Among these are laws pertaining to the environment, mining, labor relations, and equal employment opportunity. The whistleblower protections vary widely with regard to process, remedy for the employee, and sanction on the employer. For instance, violations of the Fair Labor Standards Act can potentially be punished by fines for up to US $10,000 and six months imprisonment, whereas violations of the Clean Air Act and the National Labor Relations Act require corrective action only.

State Laws

At least 34 states offer legal protection to some category of whistleblowers (Dworkin 1992, pp. 260–273). Every statute covers public employees; some cover employees working for government contractors; and others cover all employees. In terms of the substance of whistleblower allegations, all the statutes cover violations of law, but not necessarily every law. Thus, Louisiana's whistleblower protection extends only to those disclosing violations of federal, state, or local environmental laws or regulations. New York's protection for private employees pertains only to violations that involve substantial and specific dangers to the public's health or safety. In addition to violations of law, most public-sector substantive coverage extends to some form of maladministration—generally including mismanagement, gross waste or misuse of public funds, or abuse of authority. Colorado broadly protects disclosure by public employees of activities that are not in the "public interest" (Dworkin 1992, p. 261). By contrast, California, Delaware, Hawaii, Kansas, Michigan, Minnesota, New Hampshire, New Jersey, Rhode Island, and Texas protect public employees' whistleblowing only when it reports violations of law. Pennsylvania appears to be the only state that specifically extends whistleblower protection to disclosed breaches of ethical codes.

The substance of a whistleblower's charges is only one element that determines whether the disclosure is protected. The quality of the individual's belief in their truth or falsity is also important. Claims that are known by the whistleblower to be false are not protected. However, false charges are likely to be protected if they are made in good faith or with a reasonable belief that they are true. Pennsylvania, West Virginia, and Wisconsin may withhold protection from those seeking to gain personally by whistleblowing. From a practical perspective, of course, whistleblowers should make a reasonable effort to ascertain the truth of their charges; failure to do so will typically preclude protection under the various statutes.

The state statutes create an array of procedures for whistleblowers to follow in making their disclosures. Several require that the first effort to expose the wrongdoing be made internally within the employee's organization. Others allow disclosure directly to an external state agency, such as a personnel board, an auditor's office, or a law enforcement authority.

Remedies for protected employees who are harmed by their whistleblowing also vary among the states. Public employees will generally be eligible for reinstatement with backpay, benefits, and seniority as well as attorney's fees. In some states, they may receive punitive damages as well (Kentucky, Montana, New Jersey, Texas). South Carolina allows protected whistleblowers to keep 25 percent of the savings gained by disclosure, up to US$2,000 for one year (Dworkin 1992, p. 271).

Finally, the states differ with regard to the sanctions imposed on employers for actions they may take against whistleblowers, including efforts to prevent disclosure or public inquiry. Alaska allows fines of up to $10,000; Colorado notes the violation on the offender's personnel record. Other states provide for lesser fines and more severe personnel actions, including dismissal and, in Missouri, debarment from public employment for up to two years. Public employees who violate Oregon's whistleblower protection law potentially face a year in prison and debarment from the public service for five years.

Constitutional Protection

Public employees who engage in whistleblowing have also had clear constitutional protection since the U.S. Supreme Court's decision in *Pickering v. Board of Education* (1968). Under the current standard, "the determination of whether a public employer has properly discharged an employee for engaging in speech requires "a balance between the interests of the [employee] as a citizen, in commenting upon matters of public concern and the interests of the State, as an employer, in promoting the efficiency of the public services it performs through its employees" (*Rankin v. McPherson* 1986, p. 384). The Court has defined "public concern" so broadly as to include even expression of hope that if an assassination attempt is made on the president, it is successful. In *Waters v. Churchill* (1994), the Court held that the required balancing could be applied to what the public employer reasonably thought the employee remarked rather than only to what the employee actually said.

In practice, this constitutional standard gives public employees considerable protection in disclosing violations of law and specific and immediate dangers to the public's health or safety. However, unless of considerable interest to the community at large, disruptive speech or complaints about mismanagement and inefficiency may be overridden by the public employer's interest in maintaining efficiency (*Connick v. Meyers* 1983). The character of the employee's position also has a bearing on whether his or her remarks on matters of public concern are protected. Employees whose positions do not involve policymaking, confidential relationships, or public contact are likely to have wider latitude in expressing themselves.

There are several remedies for violations of public employees' constitutional right to speak out on matters of public concern. Most generally, in nonfederal jurisdictions, suits may be brought for money damages under the Civil Rights Act of 1871, now codified as 42 US Code §1983, against state employees in their personal capacities, local governments, and local employees. Remedies may also be available under state civil service regulation and whistleblower laws (as discussed above). Federal remedies generally require actions before the MSPB.

Who Are the Whistleblowers and Why Do They Blow the Whistle?

Whistleblowing is an uncomfortable act that may expose an individual to ill treatment, emotional distress, physical threats, and substantial expenses. Despite the protective laws, whistleblowers are frequently viewed as "snitches." They often face ostracism by their employers and coworkers, dismissal, attacks on their credibility, probes of their personal lives, and dead-ended careers. Employers may be very reluctant to hire persons known to have blown the whistle elsewhere. Given the high personal price often paid for whistleblowing, who is inclined to do it and why?

After reviewing the limited number of studies available, Marcia Miceli and Janet Near (1992) reached the following tentative conclusions regarding the personality traits of whistleblowers. Whistleblowers are better able to recognize wrongdoing than others and have a higher level of moral judgment. They are also action oriented. There is reason, but not evidence, to suggest that whistleblowers also have higher levels of self-confidence or self-esteem than do others in their organizations. Approval is less important to them than to other employees. In terms of social characteristics, whistleblowers tend to be male, older, more senior, and better educated than other employees of the organization. Jobwise, whistleblowers do not appear to be disgruntled employees. They tend to be higher performers, better paid, and more satisfied than others. Socially, whistleblowers enjoy support from their families and friends.

Miceli and Near also offer some tentative findings regarding the situational factors that promote whistleblowing. These include clear and direct evidence of wrongdoing, illegal as opposed to otherwise objectionable behavior, the ability to report through external channels, employment in a field office, organizational responsiveness to whistleblowing, and participatory organizational cultures. By contrast, whistleblowing is less likely where wrongdoing is widely observed or when it threatens the organization's survival. It is not known whether providing cash incentives encourages whistleblowing. Surprisingly, threat of reprisal apparently has no general impact on whistleblowing.

Miceli and Near were unable to explain organizational responses to whistleblowing. Clearly, these vary dramatically, but it is not currently known why.

Conclusion

Whistleblowing and whistleblowers have become standard features of contemporary administrative life. Public policy protects and encourages whistleblowing, especially in the public sector and when it reveals illegality, mismanagement, gross waste, fraud, abuse, and/or specific dangers to the public's health or safety. There is naturally opposition to whistleblowers by those exposed in wrongdoing and by those who must respond to frivolous or potentially damaging false charges. Nevertheless, in developed and highly mechanized nations like the United States, ordinary individuals are not always or easily able to judge the safety of the transportation, food, water, and other vital services and goods they use. Liability law may deter wrongdoing, but there are incomparable advantages to being forewarned that, say, a particular make of automobile is likely to explode on impact, an elevator dangerously malfunctions, or that a type of airplane is unsafe in cold weather. School yard culture notwithstanding, there is every reason to expect that whistleblowers will increasingly be viewed as heroes.

Bibliography

Dworkin, Terry Morehead, 1992. "Legal Approaches to Whistle-Blowing." In Marcia Miceli and Janet Near, *Blowing the Whistle*. New York: Lexington Books, pp. 232–279 .

Miceli, Marcia, and Janet Near, 1992. *Blowing the Whistle: The Organizational and Legal Implications for Companies and Employees*. New York: Lexington Books.

Legal Cases:
Connick v. Meyers, 1983. 461 U.S. 138.
Pickering v. Board of Education, 1968. 391 U.S. 563.
Rankin v. McPherson, 1987. 483 U.S. 378.
Waters v. Churchill, 1994. 62 Law Week 4397.

APPENDIX

A Complete List of the Articles in The International Encyclopedia of Public Policy and Administration

ability to pay
absenteeism
absolute immunity
accountability
accountability
accounting
Acquired Immunodeficiency Syndrome (AIDS) policy
acronym
action learning
action research
action theory
active listening
adjudication
administocracy
administration
administrative conservatorship
administrative corporatism
administrative discretion
administrative disinvestment
administrative fiction
administrative law
administrative law judge
administrative modernization in African developing countries
administrative morality
administrative natural justice
administrative policies
administrative praxis
administrative procedure acts
administrative searches and seizures
administrative state
adversary system
adverse impact
advocacy
advocacy organizations
affirmative action
affirmative action plan
AFL-CIO (American Federation of Labor–Congress of Industrial Organizations)
African administrative tradition
agency
agency budget success
agency mission
agency theory
agency theory
alcoholism
Al-Farabi, Abu Al-Nassar Mohammed (872–950)
Al-Ghazali, Abu Hamed Mohammed Ahmad (1058–1111)
alienation
Al-Marwardi, Abu Al-Hassan Ali Bin Habeeb Al-Basri (957–1058)
alternative dispute resolution
alternative fund
American administrative tradition
American Association of Fund-Raising Counsel, Inc. (AAFRC)
annexation
annual campaign
antitrust
applied behavioral science (ABS)
apprentice
appropriate technology

civil service commission
civil service examinations
civil service reform
class action
client orientation
code word
codes of conduct
codes of ethics
cognitive dissonance
collective bargaining
collective responsibility
colonial liberalism
combined operations
command
commercialization
commitment, employee
Common Foreign and Security Policy (CFSP)
communitarianism
community control
community foundations
community policing
community power
comparable worth
comparative public administration
comparative public budgeting
compensation policy
competence
competition policy
competitive tendering
comprehensive planning
conflict management
conflict management, organizational
conflict of interest
conflict resolution
Congressional Budget Office
congressional budget process
congressional government
consolidation (agency level)
Constitution of the United States
constitutional framework
constitutional law
constitutional reform
constitutionalism
constructivism
consultants
Consumer Price Index (CPI)
contingency planning
contract administration
contract failure
contractarianism
contracting out
contractorization
control (internal controls)
Coombs Commission
co-optation
coproduction
corporate foundations
corporate funders
corporate management
corporate planning
corporatization
corrections administration
corruption
cost accounting
cost effectiveness
Cost of Living Adjustments (COLAs)
cost overruns
cost-effectiveness analysis
costing-out
Council of Economic Advisers (CEA)
Council of Europe
Council on Foundations
county
county supremacy movement
Court of Justice of the European Communities
court order
covenant or restrictive covenant
credit ratings
credit reform
credit reform implementation
crime control policy
crisis intervention
criteria/alternatives matrix
critical theory (of public organizations)
crosswalk
crowding out
crowd-out
cultural bias
cultural imperialism
cutback management

damages
data protection
de facto (and de jure)
debt, national
decentralization
decision
decision theory
decisionmaking in the European Union
defaults, municipal

deference principle
deferred giving
deficit
deinstitutionalization
delegation doctrine
Delphi technique
deregulation
deterrence
development
development administration
development governance
development officer
devolution
Dimock, Marshall Edward (1903–1991)
diplomacy
diplomatic privileges and immunities
directive
discipline
discourse
discrimination, age
discrimination, disabilities
discrimination, gender
discrimination, pregnancy
discrimination, racial
discrimination, sexual orientation
dismissal
division of labor
doctrine of exhaustion
domestic partnership benefits
donations
donor
downsizing
Dror, Yehezkel (1928–)
drug testing
dual-career couples
due process
duty of fair representation

earmarked revenue
Ecole Nationale d'Administration (ENA)
economic rationalism
economic warfare
economies of scale
education aid
education policy
effectiveness
efficiency
emergency management
eminent domain
employee assistance program (EAP)
employment at will
employment policy
enabling act
endowment
energy policy
enterprise zones
entitlement
entrepreneurial public administration
environmental justice
environmental policy, domestic
environmental policy, international
equal employment opportunity
equal protection
equitable delivery of services
estoppel
ethics in nonprofit organizations
Euratom
European Bank for Reconstruction and Development (EBRD)
European capital budgeting
European Coal and Steel Community
European Economic Area (EEA)
European Free Trade Association (EFTA)
European Institute of Public Administration (EIPA)
European Parliament
evaluation
ex post facto laws
executive agency policy
executive agreement
executive budget
executive director
executive order
executive privilege
exit interview
expectancy theory
expenditure forecasting

Fabian Society, the
family allowances
family leave
family policy
Fayol, Henri (1841–1925)
Federal Reserve System
federalism
federated fund-raising
feminist theory of public administration
field theory
Filer Commission
financial administration
financial emergency
financial indicators

injunction
innovation
inspector general
Institute of Public Administration (IPA) of Saudi Arabia
intelligence agency
intelligence policy
intercultural communication
interest groups
intergovernmental management (IGM)
intergovernmental relations
internal security protection
International Association of Schools and Institutes of Administration (IASIA)
International City/County Management Association
International Institute of Administrative Sciences
international intelligence
interorganizational collaboration
interorganizational collaboration in the nonprofit sector
interpersonal communication
interstate compact
interviewing
Islamic administrative tradition

Japanese administrative culture
job action
job analysis and evaluation
job design
job satisfaction
job sharing
job tenure
judicial activism/restraint
judicial administration
judicial review
jurisdiction

Kaufman, Herbert (1922–)

labor law
labor movement
labor organization
labor organizer
labor relations
laboratory training and T (training)-groups
labor-management cooperation
Lambert Commission
Latin American administrative tradition
layoffs
leadership
leadership, agential
leave policy
legal services
level playing field
Lewin, Kurt (1890–1947)
Lindblom, Charles E. (1917–)
line and staff conflict
line-item budget
line-item veto
loan guarantees
lobbying
local government budgeting
local government leadership
local governments
logistics
lotteries
Luhmannian perspectives on public administration and policy
lying with statistics

Machiavelli, Niccolo di Bernado dei (1469–1527)
machinery of government
machinery of government, Australia
Malaysian administrative tradition
management accounting
management audit
management by fear
management by objectives (MBO)
management control
management information system (MIS)
management science
management, contingency
management, principles of
managerialism
mandates
Manhattan Project, the
market socialism
market testing
markup
martial law
Maslow, Abraham H. (1908–1970)
Master of Public Administration (MPA)
masters of nonprofit management
matrix organization
McGregor, Douglas M. (1906–1964)
mediating institutions
mentoring
merit system
metaphor, organizational

metropolitan organization
Mexican administrative tradition
microeconomic reform
micromanagement
middle management
Miles's Law
military-industrial complex
ministerial advisers
ministerial responsibility
minority set-aside
mission statement
mixed economy
Monash, Sir John (1865–1931)
monetary policy
Monnet, Jean (1888–1979)
morale
Moses, Robert (1888–1981)
motivation-hygiene theory (MHT)
muckrakers
muddling through
multicommunity partnerships
multiculturalism
multiculturalism policy
municipal bonds
municipal bonds: policy and strategy
municipal bonds: security
municipal housekeeping
municipal research bureaus
mutual benefit organization

National Charities Information Bureau (NCIB)
national interest
national security
National Society for Fund Raising Executives (NSFRE)
nationalization
natural law
natural resource policy
needs assessment
neighborhood-based organizations (NBOs)
neocorporatism
nepotism
new public management
new urbanism
New Zealand model
noblesse oblige
nondistribution constraint
nonfeasance
nongovernmental organization
nonprofit entrepreneurship
nonprofit organization
Nonprofit Sector Research Fund
Northcote-Trevelyan Report

objective setting
occupational safety and health
off-budget
official immunity
offsetting collections
Omar ibn-al-Khattab (also Umar oo'mär) (581–644)
ombudsman
opportunity cost
optimizing principles
organization development
Organization for Economic Cooperation and Development (OECD)
organization theory
organizational architecture
organizational behavior
organizational change
organizational culture
organizational learning
organizational psychodynamics
organizational renewal
organizational trust
original intent
outsourcing

Parkinson's Law
parliamentary appropriation
parliamentary procedure
parliamentary scrutiny
parliamentary system
parole
participation management
patronage
pay-for-performance
performance appraisal
performance audit
performance budget
performance indicator
performance management
performance measurement
permanent secretary
Persian/Iranian administrative tradition
personal integrity
PERT
Peter Principle
Philanthropic Advisory Service (PAS)
philanthropy

philanthropy, historical and philosophical foundations
picketing
pillarization
planning, programming, budgeting system (PPBS)
Plowden Report
pluralism
police administration
police review board
policy
policy advice
policy analysis
policy leadership
policy monitoring
policy network
policy studies
political commissar
political economy
political machine
political neutrality
politics-administration dichotomy
position classification
positivism
post-Communist budgeting
postmodern organization
poverty
practice of public administration
pragmatism
prices and incomes policy
primary jurisdiction
Prime Minister's Office (PMO)
private foundation
privatization
Privy Council
Privy Council Office (PCO)
procurement
productivity
productivity politics
productivity savings
profession
professionalism
program budgeting
progressive movement
project control
project management
property tax
prostitution policy
province
public administration
Public Administration Committee (PAC)
public administration education
public administration journals
public administration, new
public affairs
public assistance
public authorities
public broadcasting
public choice
public enterprise
public goods
public hearing
public management
public pensions (retirement)
public personnel administration
public policy analysis
public policy entrepreneur
public sector administrative reforms
public sector engineering
public service
public trust
public welfare

qualified immunity
quality awards in Europe
quality circles
quality control
quality improvement
quality of work life (QWL)
QUANGOs (Quasi-autonomous, non-governmental organizations)
quasi-governmental
quasi-judicial power
quiet expenditures

rainy day fund
rationality in public administration
recommendation
reconciliation
recruitment
red tape
reduction in force (RIF)
reengineering
regime values
region
regional development
regionalism
regulation
regulation (EC)
reinventing government
religious organizations
reorganization

representative bureaucracy
reproductive rights policy
republicanism
resource dependence theory
respondeat superior
retirement
revenue budgeting
revenue diversification
revenue forecasting
revenue sharing
reverse discrimination
reviewability
revolving fund
Riggs, Fred W. (1917–)
right to die
right to privacy
right-to-work law
ripeness principle
risk assessment
Roosevelt, Franklin Delano (1882–1945)
royal commissions
rule
rule of law
rule of three, the
rulemaking
rural governance

salary equity
sales and consumption taxes
scenario development planning
Schengen Agreement
Schuman, Robert (1886–1963)
science, technology, and public policy
scientific management
scope of review
Section 1983
senior executive service
seniority
separation of powers
settlement houses
sexual harassment
shared services
Simon, Herbert Alexander (1916–)
Single European Act (or European Act)
Smith, Adam (1723–1790)
social design
social equity
social indicator
social responsibility of business
social security systems (U.S.)
social services
social welfare organization
social-political governance
solicitation of gifts
solid waste administration
sovereign immunity
space policy
special districts
special relationship
speed-ups and slow-downs
spoils system
Staats, Elmer B. (1914–)
staffing
stakeholder
standards of conduct
standing
state government
state reinvention
state-local relations
statistics, history of
statutory corporation
Stein, Freiherr Heinrich Fredrich Karl vom und zum (1757–1831)
Stein, Lorenz von (1815–1890)
stewardship
Stone, Donald Crawford (1903–1995)
strategic budgeting
strategic leadership
strategic planning
strategic supply management
strategy
street-level bureaucrats
stress
strike
structure (organizational)
subsidiarity
suggestion systems
sunset laws
sunshine laws
supply-side economics
supranational organization
survey method
systems analysis
systems theory

tactics
target-based budgeting
tax administration
tax amnesty
tax expenditure
tax incidence
tax revolt

taxes
tax-exempt organization
Taylor, Frederick Winslow (1856–1915)
technology transfer
telecommunications policy
terrorism
Thatcherism
third party government
time and motion studies
time management
tool tropism
Tort Claims Act
tort liability (in government)
total quality management (TQM)
trade blocks
tragedy of the commons, the
training and development
transactional analysis (TA)
transportation policy
Treaty on European Union
trinitarian change: alpha, beta, and gamma
trust fund
turnover
twin-headed executive in France

unemployment insurance
unfair labor practice
unified budget
union
union security provision
United Way
unrelated business income tax
up-or-out systems
user fees and charges
U.S. Office of Management and Budget

values assessment
verwaltungsmanagement
veterans' preference
Vickers, Sir Geoffrey (1894–1982)
virtual organization
voluntarism
voluntary action
voluntary sector
voluntary social service agencies
volunteer administration
voucher system

wage and price controls
Waldo, Dwight (1913–)
war cabinet
war on poverty
Watergate
Webb, James Edwin (1906–1992)
Weber, Max (1864–1920)
wellness programs
whistleblower
White, Leonard D. (1891–1958)
Whitehall
Wildavsky, Aaron (1930–1993)
Wilson, Woodrow (1856–1924)
wise use movement
work/family policies
workers' compensation
workforce diversity
workload measures

zero-based budgeting
zoning

INDEX